T0238224

Lecture Notes in Artificial Intelligence 590

Subseries of Lecture Notes in Computer Science
Edited by J. Siekmann

Lecture Notes in Computer Science

Edited by G. Goos and J. Hartmanis

B. Fronhöfer G. Wrightson (Eds.)

Parallelization
in Inference Systems

International Workshop
Dagstuhl Castle, Germany, December 17-18, 1990
Proceedings

Springer-Verlag

Berlin Heidelberg New York
London Paris Tokyo
Hong Kong Barcelona
Budapest

Series Editor

Jörg Siekmann
University of Saarland
German Research Center for Artificial Intelligence (DFKI)
Stuhlsatzenhausweg 3, W-6600 Saarbrücken 11, FRG

Volume Editors

Bertram Fronhöfer
TU München, Institut für Informatik
Postfach 20 24 20, W-8000 München 2

Graham Wrightson
University Newcastle, Dept. Computer Science
Newcastle NSW, Australia

CR Subject Classification (1991): I.2.3, D.1.6, C.1.2

ISBN 3-540-55425-4 Springer-Verlag Berlin Heidelberg New York
ISBN 0-387-55425-4 Springer-Verlag New York Berlin Heidelberg

Typesetting: Camera ready by author
Printing and binding: Druckhaus Beltz, Hemsbach/Bergstr.
45/3140-543210 - Printed on acid-free paper

Preface

Interest in parallel computing is growing rapidly. With an ever greater prospect of inexpensive hardware the opportunities for applications seem endless. So there is increased research activity, both within industry as well as in academia, to press forward into many areas with this new approach to computing. Naturally, there are investigations of how to apply parallelism in all the traditional areas of computer science and artificial intelligence. Since logic is one of the main formalisms used in these fields it is not surprising that inference systems[1] form a major focal point for applications of parallel computation.

As a consequence we made an attempt to bring together researchers working in the field of parallelism in inference systems. At a three-day workshop held at Schloß Dagstuhl near Saarbrücken, Germany[2] a number of researchers presented talks outlining some of their recent ideas and results. These have been collected together in hardcopy form for this volume. Unfortunately many of those we would like to have had at the conference were unable to attend and contribute. So we invited these people to submit a paper nevertheless, and some of them have taken this opportunity. Of course, we also wanted to provide a general overview for those who do not want to delve deeply into technicalities.

As a result survey papers were solicited for this still rather young research domain of parallelism in inference systems. These form the first part of this volume. Franz Kurfeß' paper expounds the general potential for parallelism which is inherent in the structure of logical reasoning. Johann Schumann follows with a closer view of parallel reasoning systems for classical theorem proving. Fadi Sibai then discusses the unification process and surveys the work performed towards its parallelisation. A radically different approach to the parallelisation of reasoning, namely through the exploitation of the massive parallelism provided by neural networks, is set out in the overview paper written by Hans Werner Güsgen and Steffen Hölldobler.

The second part of the book comprises articles on specific issues in current research. This forms the main body of the book. Claude Kirchner and Patrick Viry describe the implementation of a parallel rewriting system as efficient concurrent rewriting so that it can be given a semantics and also run on ex-

---

[1] Although there is a lot of research taking place into parallel logic programming we felt that it is already receiving enough exposure elsewhere. As a consequence there are not so many contributions on that topic in this volume.

[2] This workshop was sponsored by SFB 342, "Tools and Methods for the Application of Parallel Architectures", DAAD Procope Cooperation Project between Technical University Munich and LERI Nîmes on "Reasoning and Neural Models", IBFI (Schloß Dagstuhl).

isting loosely-coupled parallel machines. Ewing Lusk and William McCune briefly describe the idea of their parallel deduction system, ROO, and look at its performance for a number of example runs. Mounira Belmesk, Zineb Habbas and Philippe Jorrand present a semantics for a process algebra over the Herbrand universe. This is aimed at designing a tool for describing parallelism, particularly in term rewriting and deduction systems.

Hakan Millroth provides a technique for parallel logic programming based on an approach of Tärnlund. Wolfgang Ertel offers an innovative technique, called random competition, which lends itself to parallel execution in inference systems with nondeterministic choices. David Powers attempts the development of a Prolog-style language in which there is little explicit control whilst at the same time exploiting the immense parallelism of the connection graph theorem proving method. In another paper Walter Hower presents a parallel approach to global constraint satisfaction.

Christian Suttner describes the Partheo theorem prover for first-order logic, in particular the architecture and the distribution of work among the processors. Jiwei Wang, Andy Marsh and Simon Lavington look at two computational models of parallelism, namely the replacing of a WAM by associative memory and the separation of unification from inference in logic programming.

Data flow machines are also considered. Wolfgang Schreiner describes the design and implementation of his Adam machine, whilst Roman Blasko considers an asynchronous data-flow model for the parallelisation of logic programs.

The current enthusiasm for neural networks has also flowed over to logic systems, as mentioned in the survey paper. So it is not surprising to find two papers here dealing with specifics. Claude Touzet and N. Giambiasi investigate the usefulness of connectionism for rule-based systems, and Steffen Hölldobler and Franz Kurfeß describe a connectionist inference system for Horn logic.

In addition, we were also keen to learn how many systems were actually being constructed in this field. The response to our e-mailed requests for brief project summaries, whilst short and possibly neither exhaustive nor representative, nevertheless gives some idea of the research activity. These summaries form the third part of this volume.

Munich
Newcastle, NSW
February 1992

B. Fronhöfer
G. Wrightson

Table of Contents

PART I

OVERVIEW SECTION

POTENTIALITY OF PARALLELISM IN LOGIC

Franz Kurfeß
International Computer Science Institute,
1947 Center Street,
Berkeley, CA 94704, U.S.A.

The processing of knowledge is becoming a major area of applications for computer systems. In contrast to data processing, the current stronghold of computer use, where well-structured data are manipulated through well-defined algorithms, the treatment of knowledge requires more intricate representation schemes as well as refined methods to manipulate the represented information. Among the many candidates proposed for representing and processing knowledge, logic has a number of important advantages, although it also suffers from some drawbacks. One of the advantages is the availability of a strong formal background with a large assortment of techniques for dealing with the representation and processing of knowledge. A considerable disadvantage so far is the amount and complexity of computation required to perform even simple tasks in the area of logic. One promising approach to overcome this problem is the use of parallel processing techniques, enabling an ensemble of processing elements to cooperate in the solution of a problem. The goal of this paper is to investigate the combination of parallelism and logic.

1 Parallelism in Inference Systems

The best-known instance of an inference mechanism in computer science is the use of PROLOG as logic programming language. As a consequence, most approaches to combine parallelism and inference systems are based on PROLOG or a derivative thereof as language, and evaluation mechanisms based on the resolution calculus. Among these approaches, OR-parallelism and AND-parallelism are almost exclusively used, either isolated or a combination of both. In the following, we will show that there is quite a variety of other categories of parallelism, sometimes with distinct advantages over AND-/OR-parallelism. Our investigation will concentrate on Horn clause logic and first order predicate logic, and not include extensions or specializations like temporal logic, modal logic, higer order logic, fuzzy logic, probabilistic reasoning, etc.

For most of our investigations, we will also assume that a general-purpose parallel architecture will be used as execution vehicle. Such an architecure may provide inadequate support for certain basic operations in the evaluation of logic programs (selection of clause heads, unification), but experience with dedicated machines leads to the conclusion that the gain in performance in general-purpose architectures is overwhelming compared to special-purpose ones. We will not restrict ourselves, however, to a certain processing mode, architecture or topology; in particular, we want to overcome the severe implications imposed by the inherently sequential execution mode of a stack-based Warren Abstract Machine WAM [Warren, 1983] and resolution as underlying calculus. This will give us the freedom to investigate different computational models, especially with respect to their suitability for parallel evaluation.

2   Categories of Parallelism

This section gives an overview of various categories of parallelism which can be identified in inference systems. From a conceptual point of view, parallelism can be introduced by two ways: first by identifying independent parts in the program to be evaluated, and executing these parts separately. It is also possible, however, to view the program to be evaluated as data, which are transformed by certain operations according to a particular inference mechanism, and apply some of these operations in parallel to the whole, or parts of the original program.

Table 1 shows an overview of the categories of parallelism, arranged according to the granularity and the components of a logic program. It identifies the particular data structures and operations applied in a category.

The notation used in Table 1 is based on viewing a logic program as a collection of clauses, possibly organized into modules (or objects). The clauses consist of literals, arranged as head and tail. A literal is identified through a predicate, and may have arbitrarily complex terms composed from functions, constants, and variables. Further notational details depending on the particular category of parallelism will be given at the appropriate place.

Symbol	Meaning
P	logical program or formula
$\{\mathcal{P}_1, \ldots, \mathcal{P}_m\}$	distinct programs
$\mathcal{P} = \{\mathcal{M}_1, \ldots, \mathcal{M}_m\}$	program composed of modules
$\mathcal{P} = \{\mathcal{SPS}_1, \ldots, \mathcal{SPS}_s\}$	spanning sets in a program
$\tilde{\mathrm{P}}$	modified program
C	clause
L	literal
$\{\mathcal{R}_1, \ldots, \mathcal{R}_r\}$	routes in a program
$t = \{st_1, \ldots, st_s\},$	term, composed of subterms
(t, t')	pair of terms to be unified
$\{f^1, f^2, f^3, \ldots\}$	occurrences of one function
$f(t_1, \ldots, t_m),$	function with arbitrary terms as arguments
$(g_1, \ldots, g_m),$	ground terms
$\{\mathrm{INF}_1, \ldots, \mathrm{INF}_n\}$	different inference mechanisms
$\widetilde{\mathrm{INF}}$	modified inference mechanism
$\{\mathrm{RED}_1, \ldots, \mathrm{RED}_r\}$	reduction transformations
$\{\mathrm{UNIF}_1, \ldots, \mathrm{UNIF}_r\}$	unification mechanisms

Multitasking

Independent programs can be evaluated at the same time. This concept is well-known from traditional operating systems and does not involve major problems, at least from our point of view. Difficulties which may arise are only on the operating system level, e.g. through the utilization of shared resources, load balancing, built-in predicates, and should be solved on that level without intervention from the inference mechanism or the user. Multitasking may be of interest for the evaluation of logic programs from different users on a shared, large multiprocessor machine.3

Competition

The evaluation of a logic program can be done in a number of different ways, usually described in the form of a calculus. The idea of competition is to apply different evaluation mechanisms to one and the same program. Whereas in principle this results in redundant computation, different calculi are well suited for different classes of programs [Ertel, 1990, Ertel, 1991] (see also the contribution of W. Ertel in this volume). Often it is not even necessary to use

Level	Data Structures	Operations	Category
Formula	$\{\mathcal{P}_1, \ldots, \mathcal{P}_m\}$	INF	*Multitasking*
	$\mathcal{P}$	$\{\text{INF}_1, \ldots, \text{INF}_n\}$	*Competition*
	$\mathcal{P}$	$\{\text{INF}_1, \ldots, \text{INF}_n\}$	*Cooperation*
	$\mathcal{P}$	$\{\text{INF}_{Pr_1}, \ldots, \text{INF}_{Pr_n}\}$	*Precision*
	$\mathcal{P} = \{\mathcal{M}_1, \ldots, \mathcal{M}_m\}$	INF	*Modularity*
	$\mathcal{P}$	$\{\text{RED}_1, \ldots, \text{RED}_r\}$	*Reductions*
	$\tilde{\mathrm{P}}$	$\widetilde{\text{INF}}$	*Recursion*
	$\mathcal{P} = \{\mathcal{SPS}_1, \ldots, \mathcal{SPS}_s\}$	INF$_{ConnectionMethod}$	*Spanning Sets*
Clause	$\{\mathcal{L}, \mathcal{C}_1, \ldots, \mathcal{C}_s\}$	INF$_{Resolution}$	*OR-Parallelism*
Literal	$\{\mathcal{R}_1, \ldots, \mathcal{R}_r\}$	UNIF	*Routes*
	$\{\mathcal{L}_1, \ldots, \mathcal{L}_n; \mathcal{C}_1, \ldots, \mathcal{C}_n\}$	Resolution Steps	*AND-Parallelism*
	$\{\mathcal{L}_1, \ldots, \mathcal{L}_n; \mathcal{C}_1, \ldots, \mathcal{C}_n\}$	Pipelined Resolution Steps	*Pipelining-Parallelism*
Term	$\{(t_1, t'_1), \ldots, (t_n, t'_n)\}$	UNIF	*Term Parallelism*
	(t_1, t'_1)	$\{\text{UNIF}_1, \ldots, \text{UNIF}_r\}$	*Unification Competition*
	(t_1, t'_1)	$\{\text{UNIF}_1, \ldots, \text{UNIF}_r\}$	*Unification Cooperation*
	(t_1, t'_1)	Cycles	*Occur Check*
	$t = \{st_1, \ldots, st_s\},$ $t' = \{st'_1, \ldots, st'_s\}$	Unification	*Separability*
	$\{f^1, f^2, f^3, \ldots\}$	Function Evaluation	*Function Call*
	$f(t_1, \ldots, t_m),$ $f(t'_1, \ldots, t'_m)$	Decomposition of Unification	*Forwarding*
	$(g_1, \ldots, g_m), (g'_1, \ldots, g'_m)$	Composition of Unification	*Bottom Up*
Atom	arrays	SIMD Operation	*Data Parallelism*
	lists	Incremental Evaluation	*Streams*
	e.g. feature maps	e.g. Search for Global Minimum	*Subsymbolic Representation*

Table 1: Categories of parallelism in logic

different calculi: changing the strategy to traverse the search space can make a tremendous difference and is often the source of claims to superlinear speedup in the parallel evaluation of logic programs. To illustrate this point, consider the way PROLOG builds the proof tree for a program, with its depth-first, left-to-right strategy. In the worst case, it gets stuck in an infinite branch in the left part of the proof tree, whereas a solution would be found easily on the other side of the tree. Changing the search strategy, either from depth-first to breadth-first or from left-to-right to right-to-left, would lead to a rapid detection of the solution. On the other hand, PROLOG programs written by experienced PROLOG programmers usually rely on knowledge about the underlying execution mechanism, and changing it may have disastrous results. The use of competition is better suited for areas like automated theorem proving where the formulation of a program is derived from the specification of the problem to be solved and not so much through the description of the solution process with logical means.

Cooperation

The cooperation category is based on the exchange of useful information between different inference mechanisms working on the same program, and thus can be viewed as a counterpart to the previously described competition approach [Fronhöfer and Kurfeß, 1987]. Useful information can consist of intermediate results, e.g. in the form of lemmata, or a partitioning of the search space into sections treated by the different mechanisms, or meta-level information, e.g. the (estimated) probability that a proof can be found in a certain part of the search space. There is certainly a large potential of useful information to be exchanged, but also a tradeoff between the amount of data to be transferred as well as the overhead to determine which information is worth while transferring, and the gain that arises from the avaliability of these data.

Precision

Whereas in the competition approach different inference mechanisms are employed, precision relies on the use of basically the same inference mechanism, but with various degrees of precision through changes in the unification procedure. The range of precision is from the propositional "skeleton" of the formula (no unification) over weak unification (substitutions are only computed locally) and unification without occur check (cyclic substitutions can occur) to predicate logic with full unification. Inference mechanisms with different precision operate fully in parallel or in a pipelined fashion, where the ones with low precision proceed faster, thus eliminating dead branches earlier and reducing the remaining search space for the more precise mechanisms.

Modularity

A widely accepted methodology for the development of large software systems is to structure the overall system into largely independent subsystems with clearly defined interfaces. This approach obviously is also relevant for inference systems and logic programs, and emerges in three variants. First, it is possible not to impose any additional syntactical structuring on large programs, but to rely on the inherent structuring as result of the particular problem together with the style of the particular programmer. The resulting program is analysed, and independent parts are identified. The second approach is to explicitly characterize modules in the source code, which eliminates the potentially costly analysis of the program. A further step is to integrate object-oriented concepts into the logic programming paradigm.

The common theme for these approaches is to group the program into parts which have few interactions among each other, and thus can be evaluated more or less independently. Restrictions in the parallel evaluation, however, can still be imposed through time or data dependencies.

Reductions

An analysis of the program to be evaluated is also a central point for reductions. The goal here, however, is to eliminate redundant or unnecessary code, thus restricting the search space to be traversed. The application of reductions must maintain important properties of the program, and they are usually grouped into equivalence-preserving and satisfiability-preserving transformations. Some reductions operate locally on parts of the program (single clauses, pairs or sets of clauses), whereas others require information about the program as a whole. While reductions may change the text of the program, they can be applied in parallel since the transformations do not change the important properties of the program.

Recursion

The use of recursion on one hand can be used to write simpler programs, but on the other hand is difficult for parallelization because the unrolling of recursive clauses typically is done dynamically at execution time. This is due to the fact that the number of iterations can only be determined from the actual goal together with the program. Once that goal is available, however, simple calculations often can be made to determine or estimate the number of iterations. Then in some cases it is possible to apply conventional parallelization techniques to transform the sequence of operations in the loop into operations executed in parallel [Millroth, 1991]. The potential gain from this technique is especially large if it can be used to predetermine the structure of the AND/OR-tree, and thus reduce the complexity of managing of the binding environments.

Spanning Sets

One important advantage of the spanning set concept as well is to make the run-time management of bindings simpler. This is based on a statical analysis of the program with the goal of identifying parts of the program (spanning sets of connections) which represent alternative solutions [Bibel, 1987, Wang, 1989, Ibañez, 1988, Ibañez, 1989, Kurfeß, 1990] (see also the contribution of Wang, Marsh and Lavington in this volume). These solutions then can be computed completely independent of each other, without the necessity of maintaining complex run-time environments for variable bindings. The limitation of this concept lies in the treatment of recursive parts, because these cannot in general be expanded statically. A combination of spanning sets with the techniques for unrolling recursion looks quite promising at least for certain simple kinds of recursion.

OR-Parallelism

Spanning sets and OR-parallelism exploit the same feature, namely the computation of alternative solutions, but with different techniques. Whereas spanning sets use statical analysis, OR-parallelism usually invokes new threads of computation dynamically whenever there are multiple clauses for resolving a subgoal. This technique is a straightforward extension of the resolution mechanism and can be incorporated into existing PROLOG implementations without major problems. The disadvantage, however, is the management of the variable bindings for different threads of computation, which must be open to backtracking in the case that a candidate for a solution turns out to be invalid.

Routes

The routes concept again relies on a statical analysis of the program, identifying sequences of connections (or resolution steps) which will have to be followed through in the evaluation, and which contain OR-parallel connections only at the end points [Ibañez, 1988, Ibañez, 1989, Kurfeß, 1990]. The crucial point with respect to parallelism is that these routes do not necessarily have to be treated in a sequential way; they may as well be combined pairwise with logarithmic execution time instead of linear. The problem here is the same as with the spanning sets: the appearance of recursive parts requires dynamical treatment, but again a combination with the unrolling of recursion can improve the situation.

AND-Parallelism

This category is widely used in parallel logic programming, and relies on a concurrent evaluation of the literals in the clause body (subgoals). Problems occur if variables are shared between literals, since they must assume identical values [DeGroot, 1984, DeGroot, 1988]. On the other hand, shared variables are a convenient way to express synchronization between different threads of computation, which makes languages based on AND-parallelism also well suited for low-level tasks such as systems programming. Especially when OR- and AND-parallelism are combined in one execution model, the management of variable bindings can get very complicated, so that sometimes the parallel evaluation is restricted to independent subgoals, i.e. subgoals which do not share variables.

Pipelining-Parallelism

Instead of evaluating the subgoals in a clause fully in parallel, they can be processed in a pipelined fashion [Beer and Giloi, 1987, Beer, 1989]. The advantage is the full compatibility with the standard PROLOG evaluation mechanism, which proceeds from left to right in the body of a clause. The performance gain achieved through this scheme (which relies on dedicated hardware), however, is very limited, and is easily outperformed by the performance progress in general-purpose architectures.

Term Parallelism

The task of evaluating a logic program can conceptually be devided into two parts: one is to navigate through the search space as indicated by the relations between the predicates in the program, the other to guarantee that the variable bindings made during the traversal are consistent. The second is based on unification as underlying operation for determining the variable bindings in order to make two terms equal. In analogy to the simultaneous application of inference operations to distinct logic programs, unification can be performed simultaneously on different term pairs (or, more generally, sets of terms). Parallelism on the term level underlies two important restrictions: first, the task of unification can be inherently sequential in the worst case [Yasuura, 1984, Dwork et al., 1988]; second, the grain size for unification tasks tends to be rather small with a PROLOG-based evaluation model. The first restriction is of a fundamental nature, but depends to a large degree on the formulation and representation of the problem to be solved. The second restriction can be overcome by choosing a different evaluation mechanism [Bibel, 1987, Wang, 1989, Ibañez, 1988, Ibañez, 1989, Kurfeß, 1990].

Unification Competition

Conceptually similar to competition in the inference mechanism, competition can be used for unification by applying different unification mechanisms to one and the same term pair. It is questionable, however, if this kind of parallelism is very useful since the variety of unification mechanisms is not too large, and performance differences largely can be attributed to the term size, and not so much to the internal structure of the terms [Corbin and Bidoit, 1983].

Unification Cooperation

The use of cooperation during unification has a close affinity to unification competition described above: it seems feasible, but with current techniques probably does not result in substantial advantages.

Occur Check

The task of the occur check is to identify situations where a term is substituted by a subterm of itself, resulting in cyclic substitutions [Plaisted, 1984]. Whereas it is possible to define a semantics which allows the occurrence of infinite substitutions [Colmerauer, 1982], or in many situations to just neglect potential problems and omit an occur check (as in many PROLOG implementations), there are cases where cyclic substitutions should not be accepted. The occur check is basically a search of a graph for cycles, an operation which can be implemented independent of unification per se. It is not possible to perform these two operations completely in parallel since the structure of the terms involved is changed during unification, and cyclic substitutions may be introduced through unification. At best unification and occur check can be performed in a pipelined fashion, where the occur check is performed incrementally on the section of the terms already unified [Hager and Moser, 1989].

Separability

This category corresponds to modularity on the program level by identifying sections in the terms to be unified which are more or less independent. It is probably only useful to exploit this kind of parallelism if there is already a partitioning induced by the structure of the program or its representation, since the cost of performing such an analysis is not much smaller than actually performing unification.

Function Call

A considerable amount of work during the unification process can consist of evaluating functions; this work may be done independent of the rest of unification, possibly even at compile time. The basic idea is the to try to evaluate all or some of the function calls in parallel to the rest of unification, replacing the calls by the computed results. To some degree this parallelism is speculative since work may be done which actually is not needed; the advantage, however, is that it can be used to occupy idling processing elements, for example in the initial phase of unification when only a few processing elements are working close to the roots of the terms.

Forwarding

The process of unifying tow terms can be viewed as assignment or comparison for atomic components (variable or constant symbols), and propagating the task of unification to the corresponding subterms. Forwarding denotes the propagation of unification to subterms in parallel. A problem arises for multiple occurrences of one and the same symbol (or whole subterm), which must have the same value. It can be solved by a suitable representation, for example as dags (directed acyclic graph), where multiple occurrences of substructures are represented only once, but with severla incoming pointers.

Bottom Up

In this case, activation starts from the constants and instantiated variables in order to reduce the complexity of the terms to be unified by replacing function calls with their results and instantiating variables where possible. This is again a case of speculative parallelism since the correlation between substructures from the left and right term can only be determined in a top-down way.

Data Parallelism

Data structures in logic programs are usually characterized through terms, which may have a highly irregular internal structure. In many practical cases, however, regular data structures are used, the prototype being an array of elements of some type. Such regular data structures open the door to another category of parallelism, usually referred to as data parallelism [Hillis and Steele, 1986]. Here, one and the same operation is applied to all or a subset of the single elements in a SIMD (Single Instruction Multiple Data) way. Whereas typical logic programs may not contain many data structures where data parallelism can be applied, there certainly are many applications with highly regular data structures which can profit from this combination, such as deductive data bases, image processing, or scientific computations [Fagin, 1991, Succi and Marino, 1991].

Streams

The concept of streams is based on an incremental evaluation of large data structures, e.g. lists which change dynamically [Ito et al., 1987, Takeuchi et al., 1987]. Usually operations involving the whole data structure, like comparing two lists, are only applicable if and when the whole data structures are available. In some cases, operations can be applied while these data structures still evolve, like appending elements to the end of the list. This category may be on the borderline of parallelism, but eases some synchronization constraints in the parallel evaluation of programs.

Subsymbolic Representations

All the categories described so far implicitly rely on a symbolic representation, where an atomic part of the program has a direct correspondence to the internal representation in the execution vehicle, typically one or more memory cells. The most important operations here are assignment, where the value of a symbol is set to the result of an operation, and pointer manipulation, where references between symbols are established or changed. An important aspect of this representation scheme is that applied to symbols, or at least to substantial parts of symbols. It is conceivable – and considerable interest has been devoted to this recently – to construct inference mechanisms based on subsymbolic representations, where there is no direct correlation between symbols and machine-internal representations [Touretzky and Hinton, 1985, Touretzky and Hinton, 1988, Ballard, 1986, Smolensky, 1987, Lange and Dyer, 1989, Shastri, 1988, Shastri and Ajjanagadde, 1989, Pinkas, 1990]. One approach is to represent symbols and programs as patterns of activation and interconnection distributed a network of simple units, which are connected through weighted links [Hölldobler, 1990a, Hölldobler and Kurfeß, 1991][1]. The computation then is performed by a spreading activation scheme which settles into a stable state when a solution is found. This category opens up a whole new dimension of parallel evaluation due to its different representation and computation paradigm.

3 Exploitation of Parallelism

The identification of sources for parallelism in inference systems is an interexting topic for itself, but in order to be practically applicable must be accompanied by an investigation of which kinds of parallelism are worth while to be exploited. This becomes rather complicated, especially when one tries to combine different categories of parallelism in one evaluation mechanism.

3.1 Analysis of Parallelism

An inportant method for the exploitation of parallelism in logic is the analysis of programs, for example by determining the potential parallel factor [Harland and Jaffar, 1987] or more complex measures. This can be done in a general investigation, analysing many logic programs with the aim of identifying common, useful ways to exploit parallelism for (classes of) logic programs [Onai and et al., 1984, Delcher and Kasif, 1989, Debray, 1989, Debray et al., 1990]. The same can be done for individual programs through a static analysis at compile time, or through symbolic evaluation to capture also some dynamic aspects of the program execution. To go even further, one can perform sample executions of a program with a set of typical goals, thus gaining information for the dynamic behavior of the program in real use.

3.2 Control of Parallelism

The analysis of programs before the actual execution can provide important information about the expected dynamic behavior, but will in many cases not be sufficient to completely

---

[1]see also this volume

determine the actual execution pattern. The control of parallelism at run-time can be achieved on three different levels: through specifications provided by the user in the program itself, through strategies determined by the compiler, and through measures of the operating system. A problem here is to find a balance between two conflicting goals: high performance, and easy program development. Highest performance can be achieved by giving the user direct access to operating system features, e.g. for communication, synchronization, load balancing, I/O, etc. The price to be paid is that in this case the user needs an intimate knowledge of the execution mechanism, the operating system, and the underlying hardware architecture. The other extrem is to relieve the user form all these low-level tasks, only requiring a formal problem specification based on logic. This, however, may result in disappointingly poor performance, at least as long as the development in terms of automated analysis and control mechanisms is not developped very far.

A partial solution to this dilemma might lie in the use of *control abstraction*, which follows a strategy similar to data abstraction [Crowl and LeBlanc, 1991]. The basic idea is to provide a safe way to introduce explicit, user-definable control constructs for parallelism. The introduction of these constructs is separated into two parts: one describes the desired properties in a formal definition, the other provides the actual implementation, based both on the formal definition as well as on features of the machine used for execution. Whereas this method still requires some effort from the user's side in order to achieve high performance, it allows the definition of problem-specific control constructs based on efficiently implemented control primitives provided by the operating system. Another advantage is better partability, since the architecture-dependent features are concentrated in one place, namely the particular implementation of the construct.

This method fits nicely into the logic framework e.g. through modules (or objects) and meta-evaluation, but requires some higher-order logic features.

3.3 Restrictions

While the abstract potential of parallelism in logic is quite high, its practical exploitation is subject to a number of restrictions. Some of these are under a limited control from the user, like the problem structure, specification and representation, as well as the actual encoding in the form of a program. Others are implied through the underlying evaluation mechanism, the runtime environment (shared binding environments), operating sytem, and hardware architecture.

4 Conclusions

The goal of this paper has been to illuminate the potentiality of parallelism in logic programming and inference systems. For this purpose, we investigated different categories of parallelism derived from the evaluation of predicate logic program, without having a particular calculus, abstract machine, or underlying hardware in mind. The outcome is a variety of different categories, far beyond the AND-/OR-parallelism usually found in attempts to parallelize PROLOG. Admittedly some of these categories are not very relevant in combination with present technology. Others, however, in particular the ones based on static program analysis in combination with programming methodologies aiming at easier program development while maintaining the possibility to finetuning for high performance, have a very good potential for the exploitation of parallelism in inference systems.

References

[Ajjanagadde, 1990] Ajjanagadde, V. (1990). Reasoning with function symbols in a connectionist system. Technical report, Department of Computer and Information Science, University of Pennsylvania.

[Ajjanagadde and Shastri, 1991] Ajjanagadde, V. and Shastri, L. (1991). Rules and variables in neural nets. *Neural Computation*, 3:121–134.

[Ali, 1987] Ali, K. (1987). OR-parallel execution of Prolog on a multi-sequential machine. *Parallel Programming*, 15(3).

[Amthor, 1989] Amthor, R. (1989). Simulation eines Beweisers auf einer Multi-Prozessor Architektur. Master's thesis, Institut für Informatik, Technische Universität München.

[Aso and Onai, 1983] Aso, M. and Onai, R. (1983). XP's: An Extended OR-Parallel Prolog System. Technical Report TR 023, Institute for New Generation Computer Technology (ICOT).

[Auburn, 1989] Auburn (1989). Parallel logic programming architectures: Final report. Technical report, Department of Computer Science and Engineering, Auburn University, Auburn, AL.

[Bachinger, 1987] Bachinger, J. (1987). Implementierung eines parallelen Theorembeweisers und Simulation der Ausführung auf einer Mehrprozessormaschine. Master's thesis, Institut für Informatik, Technische Universität München.

[Ballard, 1986] Ballard, D. (1986). Parallel Logical Inference and Energy Minimization. Technical Report TR 142, Computer Science Department, University of Rochester.

[Bansal and Potter, 1990] Bansal, A. and Potter, J. (1990). A data-parallel model for efficient execution of logic programs on associative supercomputers. In *North American Conference on Logic Programming*.

[Barnden, 1988] Barnden, J. (1988). Simulations of Conposit, a Supra-Connectionist Architecture for Commonsense Reasoning. In *2nd Symposium on the Frontiers of Massively Parallel Computation, Fairfax, VA., Las Cruces*.

[Baron et al., 1988] Baron, U., Chassin, J., and Syre, J. (1988). The Parallel ECRC Prolog System PEPSys: An overview and evaluation results. In *FGCS '88*.

[Baron et al., 1987] Baron, U., Ing, B., Ratcliffe, M., and Robert, P. (1987). A Distributed Architecture for the PEPSys Parallel Logic Programming System. Technical report, ECRC Computer Architecture Group, München.

[Beer, 1989] Beer, J. (1989). *Concepts, Design, and Performance Analysis of a Parallel Prolog Machine*, volume 404 of *Lecture Notes in Computer Science*. Springer.

[Beer and Giloi, 1987] Beer, J. and Giloi, W. K. (1987). POPE - A Parallel-Operating Prolog Engine. *Future Generations Computer Systems*, pages 83–92.

[Ben-Ari, 1984] Ben-Ari, M. (1984). *Principles of Concurrent Programming*. Prentice Hall.

[Bibel, 1987] Bibel, W. (1987). *Automated Theorem Proving*. Vieweg, Braunschweig, Wiesbaden, second edition.

[Bibel and Aspetsberger, 1985] Bibel, W. and Aspetsberger, K. (1985). A Bibliography on Parallel Inference Machines. *Symbolic Computation*, 1(1):115–118.

[Bibel and Buchberger, 1984] Bibel, W. and Buchberger, B. (1984). Towards a Connection Machine for Logic Inference. *Future Generation Computer Systems*, 1(3):177–188.

[Bibel and Jorrand, 1986] Bibel, W. and Jorrand, P., editors (1986). *Fundamentals of Artificial Intelligence*, volume 232 of *Lecture Notes in Computer Science*, Berlin. Springer.

[Bibel et al., 1987] Bibel, W., Kurfeß, F., Aspetsberger, K., Hintenaus, P., and Schumann, J. (1987). Parallel inference machines. In [Treleaven and Vanneschi, 1987], pages 185–226.

[Bic, 1984] Bic, L. (1984). A Data-Driven Model for Parallel Interpretation of Logic Programs. In *Proceedings of the International Conference on Fifth Generation Computer Systems 1984*, pages 517–523. Institute for New Generation Computer Technology (ICOT).

[Bitar and Chen, 1990] Bitar, P. and Chen, C. (1990). The OR+AND Modeling Framework for Parallel Prolog Models. UCB/CSD 90/604, Computer Science Division, University of California, Berkeley, CA 94720.

[Blelloch, 1989] Blelloch, G. (1989). Scans as primitive parallel operations. *IEEE Transactions on Computers*, 38(11):1526–1538.

[Blelloch and Sabot, 1990] Blelloch, G. and Sabot, G. (1990). Compiling collection-oriented languages onto massively parallel computers. *Parallel and Distributed Computing*, 8(2):119–134.

[Böck, 1989] Böck, K.-H. (1989). Studying an application for a parallel logic programming system. Master's thesis, Institut für Informatik, Technische Universität München.

[Bode, 1991] Bode, A., editor (1991). *Distributed Memory Computing. 2nd European Conference, EDMCC2*, number 487 in Lecture Notes in Computer Science, Munich, FRG. Apringer.

[Borgwardt, 1984] Borgwardt, P. (1984). Parallel Prolog Using Stack Segments on Shared Memory Multiprocessors. In *International Symposium On Logic Programming*, Atlantic City, NJ.

[Bose et al., 1989] Bose, S., Clarke, E. M., Long, D. E., and Spiro, M. (1989). Parthenon. Technical report, LICS.

[Brogi and Gorrieri, 1989] Brogi, A. and Gorrieri, R. (1989). A Distributed, Net Oriented Semantics for Delta Prolog. In *TAPSOFT '89*, pages 162–177.

[Caferra and Jorrand, 1985] Caferra, R. and Jorrand, P. (1985). Unification with Refined Linearity Check as a Network of Parallell Processes. Technical report, LIFIA, Laboratoire d'Informatique Fondamentale et d'Intelligence Artificielle IMAG, Grenoble, France.

[Chandy and Misra, 1988] Chandy, K. M. and Misra, J. (1988). *Parallel Program Design*. Addison-Wesley, Reading, MA.

[Chassin de Kergommeaux et al., 1988] Chassin de Kergommeaux, J., Baron, U., Rapp, W., and Ratcliffe, M. (1988). Performance Analysis of Parallel Prolog: A Correlated Approach. Technical report, ECRC Munich.

[Chassin de Kergommeaux et al., 1989] Chassin de Kergommeaux, J., Codognet, P., Robert, P., and Syre, J.-C. (1989). Une programmation logique parallele: premiere partie: Langages gardes. *Technique et Science Informatiques*, 8:205–224.

[Cheese, 1991] Cheese, A. (1991). Implementing committed-choice logic programming languages on distributed memory computers. In [Bode, 1991].

[Chen et al., 1988] Chen, C., Singhal, A., and Patt, Y. N. (1988). PUP: An Architecture to Exploit Parallel Unification in Prolog. Technical Report UCB/CSD 88/414, University of California, Computer Science Department), Berkeley, CA 94720.

[Chengzheng and Yungui, 1990] Chengzheng, S. and Yungui, C. (1990). The OR-forest-based parallel execution model of logic programs. *Future Generation Computer Systems*, 6(1):25–34.

[Chu and Itano, 1984] Chu, Y. and Itano, K. (1984). Organisation of a Parallel PROLOG Machine. *Proc. Intern. Workshop on HLCA*.

[Ciepielewski and Haridi, 1984a] Ciepielewski, A. and Haridi, S. (1984a). Control of Activities in the OR-parallel Token Machine. Technical report, Department Of Telecommunications and Comping Systems, Royal Institute of Technology, Stockholm.

[Ciepielewski and Haridi, 1984b] Ciepielewski, A. and Haridi, S. (1984b). Execution of Bagof on the OR-parallel Token Machine. In *International Conference on Fifth Generation Computer Systems*, pages 551–562, Tokyo.

[Citrin, 1988] Citrin, W. (1988). Parallel Unification Scheduling in Prolog. Technical Report UCB/CSD 88/415, Department of Electrical Engineering and Computer Science, University of California, Berkeley, CA.

[Clark and Gregory, 1981] Clark, K. and Gregory, S. (1981). A Relational Language for Parallel Programming. In *ACM Conference on Functional Programming Languages and Computer Architecture*, pages 171–178.

[Clark and Gregory, 1984] Clark, K. and Gregory, S. (1984). Notes on Systems Programming in Parlog. *Proc. Of the International Conference On Fifth Generation Computer Systems*, pages 299–306.

[Clark and Gregory, 1986] Clark, K. and Gregory, S. (1986). PARLOG: Parallel Programming in Logic. *ACM Transactions on Programming Languages and Systems*, 1986(8):1–49.

[Clark, 1988] Clark, K. L. (1988). Parlog and Its Applications. *IEEE Transactions on Software Engineering*, 14:1792–1804.

[Colmerauer, 1982] Colmerauer, A. (1982). Prolog and Infinite Trees. *Logic Programming*, pages 231–251.

[Conery, 1983] Conery, J. S. (1983). *The AND/OR Process Model for Parallel Execution of Logic Programs*. PhD thesis, University of California, Irvine. Technical report 204, Department of Information and Computer Science.

[Corbin and Bidoit, 1983] Corbin, J. and Bidoit, M. (1983). A Rehabilitation of Robinson's Unification Algorithm. *Information Processing '83*, pages 909–914.

[Corsini et al., 1989a] Corsini, P., Frosini, G., and Rizzo, L. (1989a). Implementing a Parallel PROLOG Interpreter by Using OCCAM and Transputers. *Microprocessors and Microsystems*, 13(4):271–279.

[Corsini et al., 1989b] Corsini, P., Frosini, G., and Speranza, G. (1989b). The Parallel Interpretation of Logic Programs in Distributed Architectures. *Computer Journal*, 32:29–35.

[Crammond, 1985] Crammond, J. (1985). A Comparative Study of Unification Algorithms for OR-Parallel Execution of Logic Languages. *IEEE*, pages 131–138.

[Crammond, 1986] Crammond, J. A. (1986). An Execution Model for Committed-Choice Nondeterministic Languages. In *Symposium on Logic Programming '86*, pages 148–158.

[Crowl and LeBlanc, 1991] Crowl, L. A. and LeBlanc, T. J. (1991). Architectural adaptability in parallle programming via control abstraction. Technical Report 359, Department of Computer Science, University of Rochester, Rochester, NY 14627.

[Cunha et al., 1989] Cunha, J. C., Ferreira, M. C., and Moniz Pereira, L. (1989). Programming in Delta Prolog. In *Logic Programming Conference '89*.

[Darlington and Reeve, 1983] Darlington, J. and Reeve, M. (1983). ALICE and the Parallel Evaluation of Logic Programs. *10th Annual International Symposium on Computer Architecture*.

[Davison, 1989] Davison (1989). Polka: A parlog object oriented language. Technical report, Dept. of Computing, Imperial College, London, UK.

[de Boer and Palamidessi, 1990a] de Boer, F. S. and Palamidessi, C. (1990a). Concurrent logic programming: Asynchronism and language comparison. Technical Report TR - 6/90, University of Pisa, Department of Computer Science, 56100 Pisa, Italy.

[de Boer and Palamidessi, 1990b] de Boer, F. S. and Palamidessi, C. (1990b). A fully abstract model for concurrent logic languages. Technical Report CS-R9046, Centre for Mathematics and Computer Science, Amsterdam, The Netherlands.

[De Nicola and Ferrari, 1990] De Nicola, R. and Ferrari, G. (1990). Observational logics and concurrency models. Technical Report TR - 10/90, University of Pisa, Department of Computer Science, 56100 Pisa, Italy.

[Debray, 1989] Debray, S. K. (1989). Static inference of modes and data dependencies in logic programs. *ACM Transactions on Programming Languages and Systems*, 11(3):419–450.

[Debray et al., 1990] Debray, S. K., Lin, N.-W., and Hermenegildo, M. (1990). Task granularity analysis in logic programs. Technical Report TR 90-16, Department of Computer Science, University of Arizona, Tucson, AZ 85721.

[DeGroot, 1984] DeGroot, D. (1984). Restricted AND-Parallelism. In *International Conference on Fifth Generation Computer Systems*, pages 471–478. Institute for New Generation Computer Technology (ICOT).

[DeGroot, 1988] DeGroot, D. (1988). A Technique for Compiling Execution Graph Expressions for Restricted And-Parallelism in Logic Programs. *Journal of Parallel and Distributed Computing*, (5):494–516.

[DeGroot, 1990] DeGroot, D. (1990). On the inherently speculative nature of parallel logic programming. In *North American Conference on Logic Programming*.

[Delcher and Kasif, 1989] Delcher, A. and Kasif, S. (1989). Some results in the complexity of exploiting data dependency in parallel logic programs. *Logic Programming*, 6:229–241.

[Delcher and Kasif, 1988] Delcher, A. L. and Kasif, S. (1988). Efficient Parallel Term Matching. Technical report, Computer Science Department, Johns Hopkins University, Baltimore, MD 21218.

[Delgado-Rannauro et al., 1991] Delgado-Rannauro, S. A., Dorochevsky, M., Scherman, K., Véron, A., and Xu, J. (1991). A shared environment parallel logic programming system on distributed memory architectures. In [Bode, 1991].

[Despain et al., 1986] Despain, A., Patt, Y., Dobry, T., Chang, J., and Citrin, W. (1986). High Performance Prolog: The Multiplicative Effect of Several Levels of Implementation. In *COMPCON 86*, Berkeley.

[Despain and Patt, 1985] Despain, A. M. and Patt, Y. N. (1985). Aquarius - A High Performance Computing System for Symbolic and Numeric Applications. In *COMPCON '85*, Berkeley, CA.

[Diel et al., 1986] Diel, H., Lenz, N., and Welsch, H. M. (1986). System Structure for Parallel Logic Programming. *Future Generation Computer Systems*, 2:225–231.

[Dixon and deKleer, 1988] Dixon, M. and deKleer, J. (1988). Massively parallel assumption-based truth maintenance. In Smith, R. G. and Mitchell, T. M., editors, *Seventh National Conference on Artificial Intelligence*, volume 1/2, pages 199–204, St. Paul, MN. American Association for Artificial Intelligence, Morgan Kaufman.

[Dwork et al., 1986] Dwork, C., Kanellakis, P., and Stockmeyer, L. (1986). Parallel Algorithms for Term Matching. In *CADE '86*, pages 416–430, Berlin. Springer.

[Dwork et al., 1988] Dwork, C., Kanellakis, P. C., and Stockmeyer, L. (1988). Parallel algorithms for term matching. *SIAM Journal of Computing*, 17(4):711–731.

[Dyer, 1989] Dyer, M. G. (1989). Symbolic processing techniques in connectionist networks and their application to high-level cognitive tasks. In Brauer, W. and Freksa, C., editors, *International GI Congress on Knowledge Based Systems*, Informatik Fachberichte, Munich. Springer.

[Eckmiller et al., 1990] Eckmiller, R., Hartmann, G., and Hauske, G., editors (1990). *Parallel Processing in Neural Systems and Computers*. Elsevier.

[Eisenstadt and Brayshaw, 1988] Eisenstadt, M. and Brayshaw, M. (1988). The Transparent Prolog Machine (TPM): An Execution Model and Graphical Debugger for Logic Programming. *Logic Programming*, pages 277–342.

[Eliens, 1991a] Eliens, A. (1991a). Distributed logic programming for artificial intelligence. *AI Communications*, 4(1):11–21.

[Eliens, 1991b] Eliens, A. (1991b). *DLP - A Language for Distributed Logic Programming*. PhD thesis, Centre for Mathematics and Computer Science, Amsterdam, Netherlands.

[Engels, 1988] Engels, J. (1988). A Model for Or-parallel Execution of (Full) Prolog and its Proposed Implementation. Technical report, Institut für Informatik III, Universität Bonn, Bonn.

[Ertel, 1990] Ertel, W. (1990). Random competition: A simple, but efficient method for parallelizing inference systems. Technical Report FKI 143-90, Institut für Informatik, Technische Universität München.

[Ertel, 1991] Ertel, W. (1991). Performance of competitive or-parallelism. ICLP Workshop on Parallel Inferencing.

[Ertel et al., 1989] Ertel, W., Kurfeß, F., Letz, R., Pandolfi, X., and Schumann, J. (1989). PARTHEO: A Parallel Inference Machine. In *PARLE '89*.

[Fagin, 1990] Fagin, B. (1990). Data-parallel logic programming. In *North American Conference on Logic Programming*.

[Fagin, 1991] Fagin, B. (1991). Data-parallel logic programming systems. Technical report, Thayer School of Engineering, Dartmouth College, Hanover, NH 03755.

[Fagin and Despain, 1987] Fagin, B. and Despain, A. M. (1987). Performance Studies of a Parallel Prolog Architecture. Technical report, Computer Science Division, University of California, Berkeley, CA. preprint from ISCA, June '87.

[Fagin and Despain, 1990] Fagin, B. S. and Despain, A. M. (1990). The performance of parallel Prolog programs. *IEEE Transactions on Computers*, 39(12):1434–1445.

[Fahlman and Hinton, 1987] Fahlman, S. and Hinton, G. (1987). Connectionist Architectures for Artificial Intelligence. *Computer*, 20:100–118.

[Feldman, 1990] Feldman, J. A. (1990). Conventional and connectionist parallel computation. GMD-Spiegel.

[Foster, 1990] Foster, I. (1990). *Systems Programming in Parallel Logic Languages*. Prentice Hall.

[Foster and Taylor, 1987] Foster, I. and Taylor, S. (1987). Flat Parlog: A Basis for Comparison. *Parallel Programming*, 16:87–125.

[Foster and Taylor, 1989] Foster, I. and Taylor, S. (1989). *STRAND: New Concepts in Parallel Programming*. Prentice Hall.

[Fronhöfer and Kurfeß, 1987] Fronhöfer, B. and Kurfeß, F. (1987). Cooperative Competition: A modest proposal concerning the use of multi-processor systems for automated reasoning. Technical report, Institut für Informatik, Technische Universität München.

[Futo, 1988] Futo, I. (1988). Parallele Programmierung in CS-Prolog. *Artificial Intelligence Newsletter*, 9, 10:13–15, 16–19.

[Futo and Kacsuk, 1989] Futo, I. and Kacsuk, P. (1989). CS-Prolog on multitransputer systems. *Microprocessors and Microsystems*, 13:103–112.

[Georgescu, 1986] Georgescu, I. (1986). An Inference Processor based on reactive memory. Technical report, Institute for Computers and Informatics, Department of Robotics and Artificial Intelligence, Bucharest.

[Giambiasi et al., 1989] Giambiasi, N., Lbath, R., and Touzet, C. (1989). Une approche connexionniste pour calculer l'implication floue dans les systemes a base de regles. Technical report, Universite de Nimes.

[Gonzalez-Rubio et al., 1987] Gonzalez-Rubio, R., Bradier, A., and Rohmer, J. (1987). DDC Delta Driven Computer - a Parallel Machine for Symbolic Processing. In [Treleaven and Vanneschi, 1987].

[Goto et al., 1983] Goto, A., Aida, H., Maruyama, T., Yuhara, M., Tanaka, H., and Moto-OKA, T. (1983). A Highly Parallel Inference Engine: PIE. In *Logic Programming Conference*. Institute for New Generation Computer Technology (ICOT).

[Goto et al., 1988] Goto, A., Sato, M., Nakajima, K., Taki, K., and Matsumoto, A. (1988). Overview of the Parallel Inference Machine Architecture (PIM). In *International Conference on Fifth Generation Computer Systems*, pages 209–229, Tokyo. Institute for New Generation Computer Technology (ICOT).

[Goto et al., 1984] Goto, A., Tanaka, H., and Moto-Oka, T. (1984). Highly Parallel Inference Engine: PIE. Goal Rewriting Model and Machine Architecture. *New Generation Computing*.

[Goto and Uchida, 1985] Goto, A. and Uchida, S. (1985). Current Research Status of PIM: Parallel Inference Machine. In *Third Japanese-Swedish Workshop*, number TM - 140. Institute for New Generation Computer Technology (ICOT).

[Goto and Uchida, 1986] Goto, A. and Uchida, S. (1986). Toward a High Performance Parallel Inference Machine – The Intermediate State Plan of PIM –. Technical report, Institute for New Generation Computer Technology (ICOT).

[Goto and Uchida, 1987] Goto, A. and Uchida, S. (1987). Towards a High Performance Parallel Inference Machine - The Intermediate Stage Plan for PIM. In [Treleaven and Vanneschi, 1987].

[Gregory, 1984] Gregory, S. (1984). Implementing PARLOG on the ALICE Machine. Technical report, Imperial College, London.

[Gregory, 1987] Gregory, S. (1987). *Parallel Logic Programming with PARLOG: The Language and its Implementation*. Addison Wesley.

[Gregory et al., 1989] Gregory, S., Foster, I. T., Burt, A. D., and Ringwood, G. A. (1989). An Abstract Machine for the Implementation of PARLOG on Uniprocessors. *New Generation Computing*, (6):389–420.

[Güntzer et al., 1986] Güntzer, U., Kiessling, W., and Bayer, R. (1986). Evaluation Paradigms for Deductive Databases: from Systolic to As-You-Please. Technical Report TUM-I-86-05, Institut für Informatik, Technische Universität München.

[Hager and Moser, 1989] Hager, J. and Moser, M. (1989). An Approach to Parallel Unification Using Transputers. In *GWAI '89*, pages 83–91. Springer.

[Hailperin and Westphal, 1986] Hailperin, M. and Westphal, H. (1986). A Computational Model for PEPSys. Technical Report CA-16, ECRC.

[Halim, 1986] Halim, Z. (1986). A Data-Driven Machine for Or-Parallel Evaluation of Logic Programs. *New Generation Computing*, Vol.4, No.1:5–33.

[Harland and Jaffar, 1987] Harland, J. and Jaffar, J. (1987). On Parallel Unification for Prolog. *New Generation Computing*, 5:259–279.

[Hattori et al., 1989] Hattori, A., Shinogoi, T., Kumon, K., and Goto, A. (1989). PIM-p: A Hierarchical Parallel Inference Machine. Technical Report TR-514, Institute for New Generation Computer Technology (ICOT), Tokyo, Japan.

[Hellerstein and Shapiro, 1986] Hellerstein, L. and Shapiro, E. (1986). Implementing Parallel Allgorithms in Concurrent Prolog: The Maxflow Experience. *Logic Programming*, 2:157–184.

[Hermenegildo, 1986] Hermenegildo, M. (1986). An Abstract Machine for Restricted AND-Parallel Execution of Logic Programs. In *Third International Conference On Logic Programming 86*, pages 25–39.

[Hermenegildo and Nasr, 1986] Hermenegildo, M. and Nasr, R. (1986). Efficient Management of Backtracking in AND-Parallelism. In *Third International Conference On Logic Programming 86*, pages 40–54.

[Hermenegildo and Rossi, 1989] Hermenegildo, M. and Rossi, F. (1989). On the Correctness and Efficiency of Independent AND-Parallelism in Logic Programs. In *North American Conference on Logic Programming*, pages 369–389. MIT Press.

[Hertzberger and van de Riet, 1984] Hertzberger, L. and van de Riet, R. (1984). Progress in the Fith Generation Inference Architectures. *Future Generations Computer Systems*, 1(2):93–102.

[Hillis, 1985] Hillis, D. W. (1985). *The Connection Machine*. MIT Press, Cambridge, MA.

[Hillis and Steele, 1986] Hillis, W. and Steele, G. (1986). Data Parallel Algorithms. *Communications of the ACM*, 29:1170–1183.

[Hillyer and Shaw, 1983] Hillyer, B. and Shaw, D. (1983). Rapid Execution of AI Production Systems on the NON-VON Supercomputer. Technical report, Department of Computer Science, Columbia University, New York.

[Hölldobler, 1990a] Hölldobler, S. (1990a). CHCL – a connectionist inference system for horn logic based on the connection method. Technical Report TR-90-042, International Computer Science Institute, Berkeley, CA 94704.

[Hölldobler, 1990b] Hölldobler, S. (1990b). A structured connectionist unification algorithm. In *AAAI '90*, pages 587–593. A long version appeared as Technical Report TR-90-012, International Computer Science Institute, Berkeley, CA.

[Hölldobler, 1990c] Hölldobler, S. (1990c). Towards a connectionist inference system. In *Proceedings of the International Symposium on Computational Intelligence*.

[Hölldobler and Kurfeß, 1991] Hölldobler, S. and Kurfeß, F. (1991). CHCL – A Connectionist Inference System. International Computer Science Institute.

[Houri and Shapiro, 1986] Houri, A. and Shapiro, E. (1986). A Sequential Abstract Machine for Flat concurrent Prolog. Technical Report CS86-20, Weizmann Institute of Science, Rehovot, Israel.

[Hwang and Briggs, 1984] Hwang, K. and Briggs, F. (1984). *Computer Architecture and Parallel Processing*. Mc Graw-Hill, New York.

[Hwang et al., 1987] Hwang, K., Ghosh, J., and R.Chokwanyun (1987). Computer Architectures for Artificial Intelligence Processing. *Computer*, 20:19–30.

[Ibañez, 1988] Ibañez, M. B. (1988). Parallel inferencing in first-order logic based on the connection method. In *Artificial Intelligence: Methodology, Systems, Applications '88*. Varna, North-Holland.

[Ibañez, 1989] Ibañez, M. B. (1989). *Inférence parallèle et processus communicants pour les clauses de Horn. Extension au premier ordre par la méthode de connexion*. PhD thesis, I.N.P. de Grenoble, France.

[ICLP91, 1991] ICLP91 (1991). *ICLP 91 Workshop on Parallel Execution of Logic Programs*, Paris, France.

[Ino and Koelbl, 1988] Ino, E. and Koelbl, D. (1988). Sequentielle und parallele Architekturansätze für logische Programmiersprachen. *Informatik Forschung und Entwicklung*, 3:182–194.

[Ito et al., 1987] Ito, N., Kuno, E., and Oohara, T. (1987). Efficient Stream Processing in GHC and Its Evaluation on a Parallel Inference Machine. *Journal of Information Processing*, 10:237–244.

[Ito et al., 1983a] Ito, N., Masuda, K., and Shimizu, H. (August 1983a). Parallel Prolog Machine. Technical report, Institute for New Generation Computer Technology (ICOT), Tokyo.

[Ito and Masuda, 1983] Ito, N. and Masuda, Y. (1983). Parallel Inference Machine Based on the Data Flow Model. Technical Report TR-033, Institute for New Generation Computer Technology (ICOT).

[Ito et al., 1983b] Ito, N., Onai, R., Masuda, K., and Shimizu, H. (1983b). Parallel Prolog Machine Based on Data Flow Mechanism. In *Logic Programming Conference '83*. Institute for New Generation Computer Technology (ICOT).

[Jorrand, 1986] Jorrand, P. (1986). Term Rewriting as a Basis for the Design of a Functional and Parallel Programming Language. A case study: the Language FP2. In [Bibel and Jorrand, 1986], pages 221–276.

[Jorrand, 1987] Jorrand, P. (1987). Design and Implementation of a Parallel Inference Machine for First-Order Logic: An Overview. In *PARLE 87*, volume 258 of *Lecture Notes in Computer Science*, Berlin. Springer.

[Kacsuk, 1991] Kacsuk, P. (1991). A Parallel PROLOG Abstract Machine and its Multi-Transputer Implementation. *Computer*, 34(1):52–63.

[Kacsuk and Bale, 1987] Kacsuk, P. and Bale, A. (1987). DAP Prolog: A Set-oriented Approach to Prolog. *Computer*, 30(5):393–403.

[Kahn, 1986] Kahn, K. e. a. (1986). Objects in concurrent logic languages. In *OOPSLA 86*, pages 242–257.

[Kalé, 1988] Kalé, L. (1988). A Tree Representation for Parallel Problem Solving. In *AAAI '88*, pages 677–681.

[Kalé, 1985] Kalé, L. V. (1985). *Parallel Architectures for Problem Solving*. PhD thesis, State University of New York, Stony Brook.

[Kalé, 1987] Kalé, L. V. (1987). Completeness and full parallelism of parallel logic programming schemes. In *IEEE Symposium on Logic Programming*, pages 125–133, San Francisco, CA. IEEE.

[Kalé, 1989] Kalé, L. V. (1989). The REDUCE OR Process Model for Parallel Execution of Logic Programs. *Journal of Logic Programming*.

[Kalé and Ramkumar, 1990] Kalé, L. V. and Ramkumar, B. (1990). Joining AND Parallel Solutions in AND/OR Parallel Systems: Part I - Static Analysis. In *ICLP '90*.

[Kalé et al., 1988] Kalé, L. V., Ramkumar, B., and Shu, W. (1988). A Memory Organisation Independent Binding Environment for AND and OR Parallel Execution of Logic Programs. In *ICLP '88*, volume 2, University of Illinois at Urbana-Champaign.

[Kalé and Saletore, 1988] Kalé, L. V. and Saletore, V. (1988). Obtaining first solution faster in parallel problem solving. Technical Report UIUCDCS-R-88-1481, Department of Computer Science, University of Illinois at Urbana-Champaign, Urbana, IL.

[Kaplan, 1988] Kaplan, S. (1988). Algorithmic complexity of logic programs. In *International Conference and Symposium on Logic Programming*, pages 780–793, Seattle, WA.

[Karam, 1988] Karam (1988). Prototyping Concurrent Systems with Multilog. Technical report, Department of Systems and Computer Engineering, Carleton University.

[Kasif et al., 1983] Kasif, S., Kohli, M., and Minker, J. (1983). PRISM: A Parallel Inference System for Problem Solving. In *Logic Programming Workshop '83*, pages 123–152, Lisboa, Portugal. Universidade Nova de Lisboa.

[Kasif and Minker,] Kasif, S. and Minker, J. The Intelligent Channel: A Scheme for Result Sharing in Logic Programs. Technical report, University of Maryland.

[Kasif et al., 1987] Kasif, S., Reif, J. H., and Sherlekar, D. D. (1987). Formula Dissection: A Parallel Algorithm for Constraint Satisfaction. In *IJCAI '87*.

[Kibler and Conery,] Kibler, D. and Conery, J. Parallelism in AI Programs. Technical report, Irvine Computational Intelligence Project, Information and Computer Science Department, University of California, Irvine.

[Kimura and Chikayama, 1987] Kimura, Y. and Chikayama, T. (1987). An Abstract KL1 Machine and its Instruction Set. Technical Report TR-246, Institute for New Generation Computer Technology (ICOT), Tokyo, Japan.

[Kliger et al., 1988] Kliger, S., Yardeni, E., Kahn, K., and Shapiro, E. (1988). The Language FCP(:,?). In *FGCS '88*, pages 763–783, Tokyo. Institute for New Generation Computer Technology (ICOT).

[Knight, 1989] Knight, K. (1989). Unification: A multidisciplinary survey. *ACM Computing Surveys*, 21(1):93–124.

[Kober, 1988] Kober, R., editor (1988). *Parallelrechner-Architekturen*. Springer, Berlin.

[Kumar et al., 1988] Kumar, V., Ramesh, K., and Rao, V. (1988). Parallel Best-First Search of State-Space Graphs: A Summary of Results. In *AAAI '88*, volume 1, pages 122–127.

[Kumon et al., 1986] Kumon, K., Masuzawa, H., Itashiki, A., Satoh, K., and Sohma, Y. (1986). Kabu-Wake: A New Parallel Inference Method and its Evaluation. *IEEE*, pages 168–172.

[Kung, 1985] Kung, C.-H. (1985). High Parallelism and a Proof Procedure. *Decision Support Systems*, 1:323–331.

[Kurfeß, 1988] Kurfeß, F. (1988). Logic and reasoning with neural models (extended abstract). *Neural Networks*, 1, Suppl. 1 (Abstracts of INNS 88):192.

[Kurfeß, 1990] Kurfeß, F. (1990). *Parallelism in Logic — Its Potential for Performance and Program Development*. PhD thesis, Institut für Informatik, Technische Universität München. published as book by Vieweg Verlag, Wiesbaden (1991).

[Kurfeß, 1991] Kurfeß, F. (1991). Massive parallelism in inference systems. IJCAI '91 Workshop on Parallel Processing for Artificial Intelligence.

[Kurfeß et al., 1989] Kurfeß, F., Pandolfi, X., Belmesk, Z., Ertel, W., Letz, R., and Schumann, J. (1989). PARTHEO and FP2: Design of a parallel inference machine. In [Treleaven, 1989], chapter 9.

[Kurfeß and Reich, 1989] Kurfeß, F. and Reich, M. (1989). Logic and reasoning with neural models. In *Connectionism in Perspective*, pages 365–376, Amsterdam. Elsevier.

[Kurozumi, 1989] Kurozumi, T. (1989). Outline of the fifth generation computer systems project and ICOT activities. Technical Report TR-523, Institute for New Generation Computer Technology (ICOT), Tokyo, Japan.

[Lake, 1988] Lake, T. (1988). Languages for Parallel Processing (Sprachen für die parallele Datenverarbeitung). *Informationstechnik it*, 30(2).

[Lange and Dyer, 1989] Lange, T. E. and Dyer, M. G. (1989). High-level inferencing in a connectionist network. *Connection Science*, 1:181–217.

[Levi, 1986] Levi, G. (1986). Concurrency Issues in Logic Languages. In [Treleaven and Vanneschi, 1987].

[Levi and Palamidessi, 1988] Levi, G. and Palamidessi, C. (1988). Contributions to the Semantics of Logic Perpetual Processes. *Acta Informatica*, 25:691–711.

[Levy, 1986a] Levy, J. (1986a). CFL-A Concurrent Functional Language Embedded in a Concurrent Logic Programming Environment. Technical report, Weizmann Institute of Science, Rehovot, Israel.

[Levy, 1986b] Levy, J. (1986b). Shared Memory Execution of Committed-Choice Languages. In *Conference On Logic Programming 86*, pages 299–312.

[Levy and Friedmann, 1986] Levy, J. and Friedmann, N. (1986). Concurrent Prolog Implementations - Two New Schemes. Technical report, Weizmann Institute of Science, Rehovot, Israel.

[Li and Wah, 1985] Li, G. and Wah, B. (1985). MANIP-2: A Multicomputer Architecture for Evaluating Logic Programs. *IEEE*, pages 123–130.

[Lichtenwalder, 1988] Lichtenwalder, K. (1988). Spezifikation einer parallelen Inferenzmaschine in Hinblick auf ein Transputersystem. Master's thesis, Institut für Informatik, Technische Universität München.

[Lin and Kumar, 1988] Lin, Y.-J. and Kumar, V. (1988). An Execution Model for Exploiting AND-Parallelism in Logic Programs. *New Generation Computing*, 5:393–425.

[Lusk et al., 1988] Lusk, E., Butler, R., Disz, T., Olson, R., Overbeek, R., Stevens, R., Warren, D. H. D., Calderwood, A., Szeredi, P., Haridi, S., Brand, P., Carlsson, M., Ciepielewski, A., and Haussmann, B. (1988). The AURORA OR-Parallel PROLOG System. In *International Conference on Fifth Generation Computer Systems*, pages 819–830.

[Lütke-Holz, 1989] Lütke-Holz, B. (1989). Simulation eines parallelen Hornklauselinterpreters nach dem Prinzip der Cooperative Competition. Master's thesis, Institut für Informatik, Technische Universität München.

[Mariyama and et al., 1983] Mariyama, T. and et al. (1983). A Highly Parallel Inference Engine PIE. In *Electronic Computer Society of IEEE of Japan*, volume EC 83-39, Japan.

[Matsuda and Kokata, 1985] Matsuda, H. and Kokata, M. e. a. (1985). Parallel Prolog Machine PARK: Its Hardware Structure and Prolog System. In *Conference on Logic Programming '85*, pages 148–158.

[Matsumoto, 1985] Matsumoto, H. (1985). A Static Analysis of Prolog Programs. *SIGPLAN Notices*, 20(10):48–59.

[Mayr and Reich, 1988] Mayr, K. and Reich, M. (1988). Hochparallele Algorithmen für das Erfüllbarkeitsproblem in der Aussagenlogik – implementiert auf einem Simulator für neuronale Netze. Technical report, Institut für Informatik, Technische Universität München.

[McCorduck, 1983] McCorduck, P. (1983). Introduction to the Fifth Generation. *Communications of the ACM*, 6(9):629–645.

[Meseguer, 1990a] Meseguer, J. (1990a). Conditional rewriting logic: Deduction, models and concurrency. Technical Report SRI-CSL-90-14, SRI International, Menlo Park, CA 94025.

[Meseguer, 1990b] Meseguer, J. (1990b). A logical theory of concurrent objects. Technical Report SRI-CSL-90-07, SRI International, Menlo Park, CA 94025.

[Millroth, 1991] Millroth, H. (1991). Reforming compilation of logic programs. In *ILPS 91*.

[Mills, 1989] Mills, J. W. (1989). A pipelined architecture for logic programming with a complex but single-cycle instruction set. Technical Report TR 284, Computer Science Department, Indiana University, Bloomington, IN 47405.

[Mills, 1990] Mills, J. W. (1990). Connectionist logic programming. Technical Report TR 315, Computer Science Department, Indiana University, Bloomington IN 47405.

[Mills et al., 1990] Mills, J. W., Beavers, M. G., and Daffinger, C. A. (1990). Lukasiewicz logic arrays. Technical Report TR 296, Computer Science Department, Indiana University, Bloomington, IN 47405.

[Mills and Daffinger, 1990a] Mills, J. W. and Daffinger, C. A. (1990a). An Analog VLSI Array Processor for Classical and Connectionist AI. Technical Report TR 313, Computer Science Department, Indiana University, Bloomington, IN 47405.

[Mills and Daffinger, 1990b] Mills, J. W. and Daffinger, C. A. (1990b). CMOS VLSI Lukasiewicz Logic Arrays. Technical Report TR 312, Computer Science Department, Indiana University, Bloomington, IN 47405.

[Minsky, 1990] Minsky, M. (1990). Logical vs. analogical or symbolic vs. connectionist or neat vs. scruffy. In *Frontiers of Artificial Intelligence*, chapter 9, pages 218–243. MIT Press.

[Moniz Pereira et al., 1988] Moniz Pereira, L., Monteiro, L., and Cunha, Jose C.and Aparicio, J. (1988). Concurrency and Communication in Delta Prolog. In *IEEE International Specialists Seminar on The Design and Applications of Parallel Digital Processors*, pages 94–104, Lisbon.

[Moto-Oka and Fuchi, 1983] Moto-Oka, T. and Fuchi, K. (1983). The architectures in the fifth generation computer. *Information Processing*.

[Moto-Oka et al., 1984] Moto-Oka, T., Tanaka, H., Aida, H., Hirata, K., and Maruyama, T. (1984). The Architecture of a Parallel Inference Engine PIE. In *Conference on Fifth Generation Computer Systems*, pages 479–488. Institute for New Generation Computer Technology (ICOT).

[Muller, 1984] Muller, J.-P. (1984). Paralog: A Parallel Logic Programming System. In *ECAI '86*, pages 115–119. Elsevier.

[Munsch, 1989] Munsch, F. (1989). Ausnutzung von Parallelität bei Theorembeweisern durch Kooperation. Master's thesis, Institut für Informatik, Technische Universität München.

[Murakami et al., 1984] Murakami, K., Kakuta, T., and Onai, R. (1984). Architectures and hardware systems: Parallel inference machine and knowledge base machine. *Fifth Generation Computer Systems*, pages 18–35.

[Nilsson and Tanaka, 1988] Nilsson, M. and Tanaka, H. (1988). Massively Parallel Implementation of Flat GHC on the Connection Machine. In *International Conference on Fifth Generation Computer Systems*, pages 1031–1040.

[NSF / ICOT, 1990] NSF / ICOT (1990). *NSF / ICOT Joint Workshop on Parallel Logic Programming and Knowledge Representation*, Tokyo, Japan.

[Ohki et al., 1987] Ohki, M., Takeuchi, A., and Furukawa, K. (1987). An Object-oriented Language Based on the Parallel Logic Programming Language KL1. In *Conference on Logic Programming '87*, pages 894–909. MIT Press.

[Onai et al., 1984] Onai, R., Asou, M., and Takeuchi, A. (1984). An approach to a parallel inference machine based on control- driven and data-driven mechanisms. Technical Report TR-042, Institute for New Generation Computer Technology (ICOT).

[Onai and et al., 1984] Onai, R. and et al. (May 1984). Analysis of Sequential Prolog Programs. Technical Report 48, Tokyo.

[Onai et al.,] Onai, R., Shimizu, H., Masuda, K., Matsumoto, A., and Aso, M. Architecture and evaluation of a reduction-based parallel inference machine: Pim-r. Technical report, Institute for New Generation Computer Technology (ICOT), Tokyo.

[Park et al., 1988] Park, C.-I., Park, K. H., and Kim, M. (1988). Efficient Backward Execution in AND/OR Process Model. *Information Processing Letters*, 29:191-198.

[Percebois et al., 1991] Percebois, C., Signès, N., and Agnoletto, P. (1991). A compiler for a distributed inference model. In [Bode, 1991].

[Pereira and Nasr, 1984] Pereira, L. and Nasr, R. (1984). Delta-Prolog: A Distributed Logic Programming Language. In *International Conference On Fifth Generation Computer Systems*, pages 283-291. Institute for New Generation Computer Technology (ICOT).

[Peterson and Stickel, 1982] Peterson, G. and Stickel, M. (1982). Complete Systems of Reductions Using Associative AND/OR Commutative Unifications. Technical report, SRI International, Menlo Park, CA.

[Pinkas, 1990] Pinkas, G. (1990). Connectionist energy minimization and logic satisfiability. Technical report, Center for Intelligent Computing Systems, Department of Computer Science, Washington University.

[Pinkas, 1991] Pinkas, G. (1991). Symmetric neural networks and propositional logic satisfiability. *Neural Computation*, 3(2):282-291.

[Plaisted, 1984] Plaisted, D. (1984). The Occur-Check Problem in Prolog. *New Generation Computing*, 2:309-322.

[Pollack, 1990] Pollack, J. B. (1990). Recursive distributed representations. *Artificial Intelligence*, 46:77-105.

[Ponder and Patt, 1984] Ponder, C. and Patt, Y. (1984). Alternative Proposals for Implementing Prolog Concurrently and Implications Regarding their Respective Microarchitectures. In *17th Annual Microprogramming Workshop*.

[Potter, 1985] Potter, J. (1985). *The Massively Parallel Processor*. MIT Press.

[Powers, 1990a] Powers, D. M. W. (1990a). Compartmentalized Connection Graphs for Logic Programming I: Compartmentalization, Transformation and Examples. SEKI - Report SR-90-16, Fachbereich Informatik, Universität Kaiserslautern, D-6750 Kaiserslautern, Germany.

[Powers, 1990b] Powers, D. M. W. (1990b). Compartmentalized Connection Graphs for Logic Programming II: Parallelism, Indexing and Unification. SEKI - Report SR-90-17, Fachbereich Informatik, Universität Kaiserslautern, D-6750 Kaiserslautern, Germany.

[Ramesh and Ramakrishnan, 1990] Ramesh, R. and Ramakrishnan, I. (1990). Parallel tree pattern matching. *Symbolic Computation*, 9(4):704-716.

[Ramesh et al., 1989] Ramesh, R., Verma, R., Krishnaprasad, T., and Ramakrishnan, I. (1989). Term matching on parallel computers. *Logic Programming*, pages 213-228.

[Ramkumar and Kalé, 1989a] Ramkumar, B. and Kalé, L. V. (1989a). Compiled Execution of the REDUCE-OR Process Model on Multiprocessors. In *NACLP '89*, pages 313-331.

[Ramkumar and Kalé, 1989b] Ramkumar, B. and Kalé, L. V. (1989b). On the Compilation of Parallel Prolog for Shared and Nonshared Memory Machines. Technical report, Department of Computer Science, University of Illinois at Urbana-Champaign, Urbana, IL.

[Ramkumar and Kalé, 1990] Ramkumar, B. and Kalé, L. V. (1990). A Chare Kernel Implementation of a Parallel Prolog Compiler. In *Second Conference on Principles and Practice of Parallel Programming*, Seattle.

[Rapp, 1988] Rapp, W. (1988). PEPSys Sequential Module on the MX-500 Users Manual. Technical Report PEPSys-26, European Computer Research Center (ECRC), München, München.

[Ratcliffe and Robert, 1986] Ratcliffe, M. and Robert, P. (1986). PEPSys: A Prolog for Parallel Processing. Technical Report CA-17, European Computer Research Center (ECRC), München, München.

[Ratcliffe and Syre, 1987] Ratcliffe, M. and Syre, J.-C. (1987). Virtual Machines for Parallel Architectures. Technical report, European Computer Research Center (ECRC), München, München.

[Ringwood, 1988] Ringwood, G. (1988). Parlog86 and the Dining Logicians. *Communications of the ACM*, 31:10–25.

[Rohmer et al., 1986] Rohmer, J., Gonzalez-Rubio, R., and Bradier, A. (1986). Delta driven computer: A parallel machine for symbolic processing. In [Treleaven and Vanneschi, 1987].

[Safra, 1986] Safra, S. (1986). Partial Evaluation of Concurrent Prolog and its Implication. Technical Report CS86-24, Weizmann Institute of Science.

[Saletore and Kalé, 1990] Saletore, V. A. and Kalé, L. V. (1990). Consistent Linear Speedups to a First Solution in Parallel State-Space Search. Technical report, Department of Computer Science, University of Illinois at Urbana-Champaign.

[Saletore et al., 1990] Saletore, V. A., Ramkumar, B., and Kalé, L. V. (1990). Consistent First Solution Speedups in OR-Parallel Execution of Logic Programs. Technical Report UIUCDCS-R-90-1586, Department of Computer Science, University of Illinois at Urbana-Champaign, Urbana, IL.

[Saraswat, 1986] Saraswat, V. (1986). Problems with Concurrent Prolog. Technical Report CME-CS-86-100, Carnegie-Mellon University.

[Schmid, 1988] Schmid, E. (1988). Implementierung eines parallelen Theroembeweisers auf einem Multiprozessor-Simulator. Fortgeschrittenenpraktikum für informatiker, Institut für Informatik, Technische Universität München, München.

[Schumann, 1991] Schumann, J. (1991). *Efficient Theorem Provers based on an Abstract Machine*. PhD thesis, Institut für Informatik, Technische Universität München.

[Schumann and Letz, 1990] Schumann, J. and Letz, R. (1990). PARTHEO: A High Performance Parallel Theorem Prover. In Stickel, M., editor, *CADE '90*, volume 449 of *Lecture Notes in Computer Science*, pages 40 – 56, Kaiserslautern. Springer.

[Schumann et al., 1990] Schumann, J., Letz, R., and Kurfeß, F. (1990). Tutorial on high-performance theorem provers: Efficient implementation and parallelization. In [Stickel, 1990].

[Schwaab and Tusera, 1988] Schwaab, F. and Tusera, D. (1988). Un Algorithme Distribue pour l'Execution Parallele de Prolog. Technical report, INRIA, Le Chesnay.

[Shapiro, 1983] Shapiro, E. (1983). A Systolic Concurrent PROLOG Machine – Lecture notes on the Bagel. Technical Report TR-035, Institute for New Generation Computer Technology (ICOT), Tokyo.

[Shapiro, 1984] Shapiro, E. (1984). Systolic Programming: A Paradigm of Parallel Processing. *International Conference on Fifth Generation Computer Systems*, pages 458–470.

[Shapiro, 1986] Shapiro, E. (1986). Concurrent prolog: A progress report. *Computer*, 1986(8):44–58. also in [Bibel and Jorrand, 1986].

[Shapiro, 1988] Shapiro, E. (1988). *Concurrent Prolog*. MIT Press.

[Shapiro, 1989a] Shapiro, E. (1989a). The family of concurrent logic programming languages. *ACM Computing Surveys*, 21(3):413–510.

[Shapiro, 1989b] Shapiro, E. (1989b). Or-Parallel PROLOG in Flat Concurrent PROLOG. *Logic Programming*, (6):243–267.

[Shapiro and Takeuchi, 1983] Shapiro, E. and Takeuchi, A. (1983). Object-Oriented Programming in Concurrent Prolog. *New Generation Computing*, (1):25–48.

[Shastri, 1988] Shastri, L. (1988). A connectionist approach to knowledge representation and limited inference. *Cognitive Science*, 12:331–392.

[Shastri and Ajjanagadde, 1989] Shastri, L. and Ajjanagadde, V. (1989). A connectionist system for rule based reasoning with multi-place predicates and variables. Technical report, University of Pennsylvania, Computer and Information Science Department, Philadelphia.

[Shastri and Ajjanagadde, 1990] Shastri, L. and Ajjanagadde, V. (1990). From simple associations to systematic reasoning: A connectionist representation of rules, variables and dynamic bindings. Technical Report MS-CIS-90-05, Computer And Information Science Department, University of Pennsylvania, Philadelphia, PA 19104.

[Shastri and Feldman, 1985] Shastri, L. and Feldman, J. A. (1985). Evidential Reasoning in Semantic Networks: A Formal Theory. In *IJCAI '85*, pages 465–474.

[Shaw, 1981] Shaw, D. (1981). NON-VON: A Parallel Machine Architecture for Knowledge Based Information Processing. In *IJCAI '81*, pages 961–963, Vancouver.

[Shaw, 1987] Shaw, D. (1987). On the range of applicability of an artificial intelligence machine. *Artificial Intelligence*, 32:252–172.

[Shen and Warren, 1987] Shen, K. and Warren, D. (1987). A simulation study of the Argonne model for OR-parallel execution of Prolog. In *Symposium on Logic Programming '87*, pages 54–86.

[Shrobe et al., 1988] Shrobe, H., Aspinall, J., and Mayle, N. (1988). Towards A Virtual Parallel Inference Engine. In *AAAI '88*, pages 654–659.

[Singhal, 1990] Singhal, A. (1990). *Exploiting Fine Grain Parallelism in Prolog*. PhD thesis, University of California, Berkeley. TR CSD 90/588.

[Smolensky, 1987] Smolensky, P. (1987). On variable binding and the representation of symbolic structures in connectionist systems. CU-CS 355-87, Department of Computer Science and Institute of Cognitive Science, University of Colorado.

[Sohma et al., 1985] Sohma, Y., Satoh, K., Kumon, K., Masuzawa, H., and Itashiki, A. (1985). A new parallel inference mechanism based on sequential processing. In *IFIP TC-10 Working Conference on Fifth Generation Computer Architecture*, UMIST, Manchester.

[Stanfill, 1988] Stanfill, C. (1988). Parallel computing for information retrieval. Technical Report DR88-1, Thinking Machines Corporation, Cambridge, MA.

[Stanfill and Waltz, 1986] Stanfill, C. and Waltz, D. (1986). Toward Memory-Based Reasoning. *Communications of the ACM*, 29:1213–1228.

[Stanfill and Waltz, 1988a] Stanfill, C. and Waltz, D. (1988a). Artificial intelligence on the connection machine: A snapshot. Technical Report G88-1, Thinking Machines Corporation, Cambridge, MA.

[Stanfill and Waltz, 1988b] Stanfill, C. and Waltz, D. (1988b). The memory-based reasoning paradigm. In *Case-Based Reasoning Workshop*, pages 414–424, Clearwater Beach, FL.

[Stender, 1987] Stender, J. (1987). Parallele Prolog-Implementierung auf Transputern. *Hard and Soft*, Juli/August 87:17–23.

[Stern, 1988] Stern, A. (1988). *Matrix Logic*. North Holland, Amsterdam.

[Stickel, 1989] Stickel, M., editor (1989). *1989 AAAI Spring Symposium on Representation and Compilation in High Performance Theorem Proving*. SRI International.

[Stickel, 1990] Stickel, M., editor (1990). *CADE '90: 10th International Conference on Automated Deduction*, volume 449 of *Lecture Notes in Artificial Intelligence*, Kaiserslautern. Springer.

[Stolcke, 1989] Stolcke, A. (1989). Unification as constraint satisfaction in structured connectionist networks. *Neural Computation*, (1):559–567.

[Stolcke and Wu, 1991] Stolcke, A. and Wu, D. (1991). Tree matching with recursive distributed representations. International Computer Science Institute.

[Stolfo, 1983] Stolfo, S. (1983). The DADO Parallel Computer. Technical report, Department of Computer Science, Columbia University, New York.

[Stolfo, 1987a] Stolfo, S. (1987a). Initial Performance of the DADO-2 Prototype. *Computer*, 20:75–85.

[Stolfo, 1987b] Stolfo, S. (1987b). On the Limitations of Massively Parallel (SIMD) Architectures for Logic Programming. In *US-Japan AI Symposium*.

[Stolfo et al., 1983] Stolfo, S., Miranker, D., and Shaw, D. (1983). Architecture and applications of DADO: A large-scale parallel computer for artificial intelligence. In *IJCAI '83*, pages 850–854, Karlsruhe, BRD.

[Succi and Marino, 1991] Succi, G. and Marino, G. (1991). Data Parallelism in Logic Programming. In [ICLP91, 1991].

[Syre, 1985] Syre, J.-C. (1985). A Review of Computer Architectures for Functional and Logic Programming Systems. Technical report, European Computer Research Center (ECRC), München.

[Syre and Westphal, 1985] Syre, J.-C. and Westphal, H. (1985). A Review of Parallel Models for Logic Programming Languages. Technical report, European Computer Research Center (ECRC), München.

[Szeredi, 1989] Szeredi, P. (1989). Performance Analysis of the Aurora OR-parallel Prolog System. In *North American Conference on Logic Programming*.

[Takeuchi and Furukawa, 1985] Takeuchi, A. and Furukawa, K. (1985). Interprocess Communication in Concurrent Prolog. Technical report, Institute for New Generation Computer Technology (ICOT), Tokyo.

[Takeuchi and Furukawa, 1986] Takeuchi, A. and Furukawa, K. (1986). Parallel Logic Programming Languages. In *Third International Conference On Logic Programming '86*, pages 242–254.

[Takeuchi et al., 1987] Takeuchi, A., Takahashi, K., and Shimizu, H. (1987). A Description Language with AND/OR Parallelism for Concurrent Systems and Its Stream-Based realization. Technical report, Institute for New Generation Computer Technology, Tokyo.

[Tamaki, 1985] Tamaki, H. (1985). A Distributed Unification Scheme for Systolic Logic Programs. pages 552–559. IEEE.

[Tamura and Kanada, 1984] Tamura, N. and Kanada, Y. (1984). Implementing Parallel Prolog on a Multiprocessor Machine. In *International Symposium On Logic Programming '84*, Atlantic City, NJ.

[Tanaka, 1988] Tanaka, J. (1988). Meta-interpreters and Reflective Operations in GHC. In *Future Generation Computer Systems*, pages 775–783, Tokyo. Institute for New Generation Computer Technology (ICOT).

[Taylor, 1989] Taylor, S. (1989). *Parallel Logic Programming Techniques*. Prentice Hall.

[Taylor et al., 1983] Taylor, S., Maio, C., Stolfo, S., and Shaw, D. (1983). Prolog on the DADO Machine: A Parallel System for High-speed Logic Programming. Technical report, Department of Computer Science, Columbia University, New York.

[Tick, 1988] Tick, E. (1988). Compile-time granularity analysis for parallel logic programming languages. In *International Conference on Fifth Generation Computer Systems*, pages 994–1000, Tokyo, Japan.

[Tick and Warren, 1984] Tick, E. and Warren, D. (1984). Towards a Pipelined Prolog Processor. *New Generation Computing*, 2:323–345.

[Touretzky and Hinton, 1985] Touretzky, D. and Hinton, G. (1985). Symbols Among the Neurons: Details of a Connectionist Inference Architecture. In *IJCAI '85*, pages 238–243, Pittsburgh.

[Touretzky and Hinton, 1988] Touretzky, D. S. and Hinton, G. E. (1988). A distributed connectionist production system. *Cognitive Science*, 12:423–466.

[Treleaven, 1989] Treleaven, P. C., editor (1989). *Parallel Computers: Object-Oriented, Functional and Logic*. Wiley, Chichester.

[Treleaven and Refenes, 1985] Treleaven, P. C. and Refenes, A. N. (1985). Fifth Generation and VLSI Architectures. *Future Generation Computer Systems*, 1(6):387–396.

[Treleaven et al., 1987] Treleaven, P. C., Refenes, A. N., Lees, K., and McCabe, S. (1987). Computer Architectures for Artificial Intelligence. In [Treleaven and Vanneschi, 1987].

[Treleaven et al., 1986] Treleaven, P. C., Refenes, A. N., Lees, K. J., and Mccabe, S. C. (1986). Computer Architectures for Artificial Intelligence. Technical report, University College, London; Ferranti Computer Systems, Bracknell; THORN-EMI Central Research Labs., Hayes.

[Treleaven and Vanneschi, 1987] Treleaven, P. C. and Vanneschi, M., editors (1987). *Future Parallel Computers*, volume 272 of *Lecture Notes in Computer Science*, Berlin. Springer.

[Uchida, 1983] Uchida (1983). Inference Machine: From Sequential to Parallel. In *10th Annual International Symposium On Computer Architecture*, Schweden.

[Uchida,] Uchida, S. Inference Machines in FCGS Project. Technical Report TR-278, Institute for New Generation Computer Technology, Tokyo.

[Uchida, 1987] Uchida, S. (1987). Parallel Inference Machines at ICOT. *Future Generation Computer Systems*, (3):245–252.

[Uchida et al., 1986] Uchida, S., K, T., Goto, A., Nakajima, K., Nakashima, H., Yokota, M., Nishikawa, H., Yamamoto, A., and Mitsui, M. (1986). Logic Computers and Japan's FGCS Project. In [Treleaven and Vanneschi, 1987].

[Uchida et al., 1988] Uchida, S., Taki, K., Nakajima, K., Goto, A., and Chikayama, T. (1988). Research and Development of the Parallel Inference System in the Intermediate Stage of the FGCS Project. In *International Conference on Fifth Generation Computer Systems*, pages 17–36, Tokyo. Institute for New Generation Computer Technology (ICOT).

[Ueda, 1985] Ueda, K. (1985). Guarded Horn Clauses. Technical Report TR-103, Institute for New Generation Computer Technology (ICOT).

[Ueda, 1986] Ueda, K. (1986). Guarded Horn Clauses: A Parallel Logic Programming Language with the Concept of a Guard. Technical Report TR-208, Institute for New Generation Computer Technology (ICOT), Tokyo, Japan.

[Ueda, 1989] Ueda, K. (1989). Parallelism in logic programming. Technical Report TR-495, Institute for New Generation Computer Technology (ICOT), Tokyo, Japan.

[Ultsch et al., 1990] Ultsch, A., Hannuschka, R., Hartmann, U., and Weber, V. (1990). Learning of control knowledge for symbolic proofs with backpropagation networks. In [Eckmiller et al., 1990], pages 499-502.

[Vitter and Simons, 1986] Vitter, J. and Simons, R. (1986). New classes for parallel complexity:. *IEEE Transactions on Computers*, 35(5):403-418.

[Wah, 1987] Wah, B. (1987). New Computers for Artificial Intelligence Processing. *Computer*, 20:10-19.

[Waltz, 1990] Waltz, D. L. (1990). Massively Parallel AI. In *Ninth National Conference on Artificial Intelligence*, Boston, MA. American Association for Artificial Intelligence.

[Waltz and Stanfill, 1988a] Waltz, D. L. and Stanfill, C. (1988a). Artificial Intelligence Related Research on the Connection Machine. In *International Conference on Fifth Generation Computer Systems*, pages 1010-1024, Tokyo. Institute for New Generation Computer Technology (ICOT).

[Waltz and Stanfill, 1988b] Waltz, D. L. and Stanfill, C. (1988b). Artificial Intelligence Related Research on the Connection Machine. In *International Conference on Fifth Generation Computer Systems*, pages 1010-1024, Tokyo. Institute for New Generation Computer Technology (ICOT).

[Wang, 1989] Wang, J. (1989). Towards a New Computational Model for Logic Languages. Technical report, Department of Computer Science, University of Essex, Colchester.

[Wang et al., 1990] Wang, J., Marsh, A., and Lavington, S. (1990). Non-WAM Models of Logic Programming and their Support by Novel Parallel Hardware. International Workshop on Massively Parallel Inference Systems.

[Warren, 1987] Warren, D. (1987). The SRI model for OR-parallel execution of Prolog. In *Symposium on Logic Programming '87*, pages 92-102.

[Warren, 1983] Warren, D. H. (1983). An Abstract Prolog Instruction Set. Technical Report 309, SRI International, Artificial Intelligence Center, Menlo Park, California.

[Watzlawik, 1991] Watzlawik, G. (1991). European Declarative System (EDS): Architecture and Interprocess Communication. In [Bode, 1991], pages 485-494.

[Weinbaum and Shapiro, 1986] Weinbaum, D. and Shapiro, E. (1986). Hardware Description and Simulation Using Concurrent Prolog. Technical Report CS86-25, Weizmann Institute of Science, Rehovot, Israel.

[Westphal, 1986] Westphal, H. (1986). Eine Beurteilung paralleler Modelle für Prolog. In *GI-Jahrestagung '86*, pages 227-240, Berlin. Springer.

[Westphal et al., 1987] Westphal, H., Robert, P., Chassin, J., and Syre, J. (1987). The PEPSys model: Combining Backtracking, AND- and OR-parallelism. In *Symposium on Logic Programming '87*, pages 436-448.

[Yamaguchi et al.,] Yamaguchi, T., Tezuka, Y., and Kakusho, O. Parallel Processing of Resolution. Technical report, Osaka University.

[Yang, 1987] Yang, R. (1987). *P-Prolog – A Parallel Logic Programming Language*. World Scientific, Singapore.

[Yasuura, 1984] Yasuura, H. (1984). On Parallel Computational Complexity of Unification. In *International Conference on Fifth Generation Computer Systems*, pages 235-243. Institute for New Generation Computer Technology (ICOT).

[Zhiyi and Shouren, 1990] Zhiyi, H. and Shouren, H. (1990). A compiling approach for exploiting AND-parallelism in logic programs. *Future Generation Computer Systems*, 1(1):35-42.

Parallel Theorem Provers
— An Overview —

Johann M. Ph. Schumann
Institut für Informatik, Technische Universität München
Augustenstr. 46, D-8000 München 2
Tel: +49–89–52 10 98
e-mail: schumann@lan.informatik.tu-muenchen.de
Germany

1 Introduction

In the last few years, one special kind of inference systems has gained a wide popularity: the *execution of logic*. A large variety of theorem provers, most of them suited to process formulae of first order predicate logic has been developed. The success of the execution of logic is also due to the wide-spread use of PROLOG, being both a programming language and a language for inferencing at the same time. High efficiency could be obtained, although at the cost of soundness, completeness, and a clean denotational semantics. Theorem provers also aim at high performance and efficiency, but have to implement a sound and complete proof calculus.

Both kinds of inference systems have a characteristic: they are *searching* for a solution. The problems often span a large search space which has to be explored. Accordingly, these systems are of very high (if not exponential) complexity, if the calculus is decideable at all. This leads to very long execution times which is in contrast to the wishes of the user for a short answer time.

Therefore, these kinds of systems seem to be ideal candidates for *parallelisation*. With the use of a parallel hardware and execution model, the performance can be increased tremendously. Furthermore, they are very interesting with respect to their parallelisation, since a large variety of different possibilities for exploiting parallelism exists. This could be shown impressingly by F. Kurfeßin [Kur90] (see also Figure 1 and the paper by F. Kurfeßin this volume).

In this paper, we will have a look at some well known parallel theorem provers. Many sequential theorem provers use technologies which have been developed in the area of PROLOG (e.g. compiling techniques, abstract machines (WAM)). Examples for these sequential theorem provers are PTTP [Sti88] or SETHEO [LSBB90]. Techniques for the parallel execution of PROLOG have also influenced many of the parallel theorem provers.

Therefore, we include major parallel PROLOG systems in the list of *parallel inference systems*[1] to be described here.

---

[1] In the following, we use the notion *inference system* for a PROLOG system or a theorem prover.

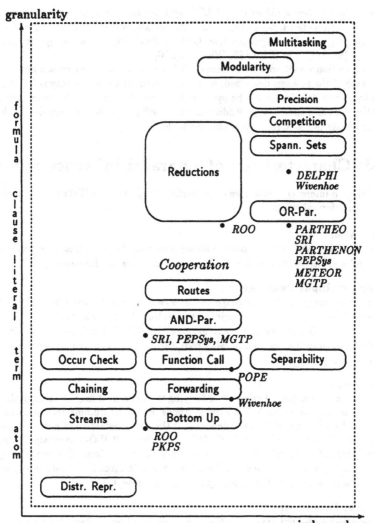

Figure 1: The space of parallelism in logic (from [Kur90])

Unfortunately, the number of different PROLOG systems and languages has grown so large that we cannot give a complete survey in this area. We will also not cover systems for the execution of parallel logic programming languages, like GHC or PARLOG. Good surveys on this topic can be found e.g. in [Sha89], or in [BKA⁺86, Wis86, Kur90].

In the following section we set up a list of items which are suited to *characterise* a parallel inference system. For each of the systems described, we set up a table of these characteristics. These tables allow us to focus the description of the systems to a few characteristic features, and to clearly recognise differences and similarities. Additionally, we will give a short description of the systems and show the results of measurements where available.

2 Basic Characteristics of a parallel Inference System

When describing an inference system, we characterise the system by a llist of the following criteria (presented in an informal way):

Application Area

The systems surveyed in this paper are *theorem provers* (i.e. *searching* for a proof) or *parallel PROLOG systems* which are used for *logic programming* and inferencing.

Programming or Input Language

The input or programming language of the systems ranges from standard mathematical notation of first order predicate logic with quantors, logic in clausal normal form or Horn clauses to PROLOG and language extensions of PROLOG. Furthermore, it is important to note if the language has *explicit* parallel constructs. Otherwise, the system exploits *implicit* parallelism only.

Logical Calculus

This point covers the logical calculus underlying the system. It may be an analytical calculus (e.g. the Connection Method, Tableaux methods, or Model Elimination) or a *synthetic* calculus (e.g. Resolution). It is also interesting if the implementation of a calculus is *complete* and *sound*. For example, most PROLOGs with the "PROLOG unification" and the unbounded depth-first search are neither sound nor complete. Some theorem proving systems have also implemented certain extensions, e.g. to handle equality or to do theory unification. Also methods for pruning the search space may be present.

Exploitation of Parallelism

A major criterion for our systems is their exploitation of parallelism. We locate each system in the space of parallelism (independence vs. granularity) as set up by F. Kurfeß. In Figure 1, each system is denoted by a "•". The granularity is defined as the size of the syntactical parts of a formula which are handled by one process. The independence of the parts indirectly reflects the amount of communication which is necessary for the parallel execution.

Model of Computation

The model of computation describes what is done where and how. On each processor of the parallel system, an *inference component* is located, a program (or hardware) which realizes parts of the calculus. The *inference component* may be multiple, i.e. a complete inference machine exists for each process or processor. Alternatively, there is a number of specialized units which together make up the inference component as a whole. The *memory model* describes how the necessary data-structures are stored and accessed by the different processes. Here, the type of memory (shared vs. local memory) is also important. The *process model* gives in a tabular form the most important features of the parallel model of computation (a similar table can be found in [Sha89]).

process How is a process defined in that particular model?

network of processes Is there any structure when looking at all processes at once. For example, the network of processes could describe the search space (OR-parallelism) or two terms to be unified.

instruction for process action Which kind of "code" one process has to execute, depending on data the process has at hand? E.g., this can be solving a subgoal, or comparison of two constants.

communication medium This can be seen on two different levels: on the level of implementation this concerns the question, whether two (or more) processes communicate via a message channel or share a common memory. On an abstract level, communication may for example take place along logical connections of the formula.

communication principle How do two or more processes communicate with each other? (message passing, shared variables, unification, etc.)

synchronization How is synchronization accomplished? For example, by semaphoores, by unification (delay until terms are unifiable), or synchronous communication.

control How is the exploitation of parallelism controlled? For example by language constructs or by dynamic rules.

scheduling Are scheduling algorithms used to exploit/control the parallelism? (e.g. an algorithm for finding work "nearest" to an idle processor)

Implementation

This point deals with the implementation issues of the system. Is there an implementation on a real parallel hardware, or are there only simulations on a single processor? What kind of hardware and how many processors have been used? What are the communication primitives of the underlying operating system and the implementation language.

Beside this list of criteria, presented as a table for each system, we will give a short description of the system, some performance measurements and references. Most of the common benchmarks could be found in the Wilson and Minker Study [WM76] and in [Sti88]. In the following section, we start our overview with systems exhibiting large grain-size and large independence (upper right corner of Figure 1), and proceed "downwards", ending with systems with a fine grain-size (lower left corner).

3 The Systems

3.1 The DelPhi Model

Name	DelPhi Model	
Application Area	PROLOG system	
Input language	PROLOG, TABLOG	
Calculus	SLD-resolution (PROLOG)	
Parallelism	OR-parallelism, spanning-set parallelism	
Inference Component	one control processor to generate oracles, path processors are complete inference components without backtracking (deterministic proof executors)	
Model of Computation	*process*	path in the proof tree
	process network	entire search tree to a certain number of inferences
	instruction for process action	clauses
	comm. medium	message passing of oracles (bit strings)
	comm. principle	transfer of computation state via message passing
	synchronization	path-processor (PP): busy/idle, control-processor: poll the PP's for success, fail or incompleteness result
	control	implicit: strategies to extend oracles
	scheduling	—
Implementation	parallel implementation on a network of workstations	

Table 1: Characteristics of the DelPhi Model

The DelPhi Parallel Inference Machine [Clo87, AM88] is an OR-parallel execution model for the execution of PROLOG (and TABLOG). To overcome the problem of sharing data structures and variable bindings over processors, the DelPhi model was developed in a way that no copying of computation states of processors is necessary. The state of a processor is encoded by the *path* from the root node to the current node in the search tree. As the program is transformed in such a way that the resulting proof tree is a *binary tree*, a path can be represented by a bit string, called an *oracle*[2] (0 = go left, 1 = go right).

A DelPhi machine consists of a number of *path processors* and one *control processor* which generates the oracles. These processors have local memory each (see Figure 2) and are connected via an interconnection network. Each path processor gets an oracle from the control processor and executes it, i.e. it executes a deterministic proof of that path. Success or failure are reported as well as the situation that a path of the proof tree is not yet complete, i.e. there are still unsolved subgoals. In this case, the control processor extends the oracle and sends the newly generated ones

---

[2]The DelPhi machine is called after the legendary Delphic Oracle.

to idle path processors. This implies that some *recomputation* by the path processor is necessary, but the overhead is acceptable. The extension is done according to a *control strategy*.

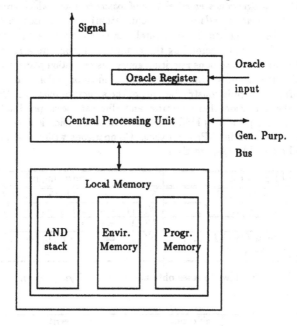

Figure 2: A DelPhi path processor (from [Clo87])

The encoding of work in oracles is similar to the coding of tasks done in PARTHEO (see 3.5). In the DelPhi model, however, no control is done to minimize the amount of recomputation. Also in the DelPhi model there is only very little feedback from the path processors (doing unifications, essentially) and the control processors (compare the Wivenhoe-model in 3.2).

Several simulations have been done on a single processor machine and implementations on a network of workstations connected via a LAN (DEC VAXes).

3.2 The Wivenhoe Model

Name	Wivenhoe Model
Application Area	Theorem Prover
Input language	Horn Clauses
Calculus	Prawitz Matrix Method
Parallelism	Unification parallelism, (partial) OR-parallelism
Inference Component	unification unit(s), plan generator, control generator
Model of Computation	see Table 3
Implementation	implementation on the Intelligent File Store (IFS) [Lav88] is planned

Table 2: Characteristics of the Wivenhoe Model

The *Wivenhoe Model* [Wan89] is a computational model for pure Horn clause logic languages. The underlying calculus is the Prawitz Matrix Method [Pra70] which is an analytical calculus. In the Wivenhoe Model, a logic program is seen consisting of *logical relations* which are used to construct *refutation plans* and the *structure relations* (the unification) which is used to check the validity of a refutation plan. The logical and the structural relations are separated. Structural relations are extracted from the formula by compiling the connection graph into a rewriting system (see Figure 3) and simplifying it. Continuous rewriting generates refutation plans, which are unified in one step (Large grain, large quantity unification). The unification is done (in parallel) on a DAG (Directed Acyclic Graph) which is constructed out of the structure relations. Unification failures have a feedback to the refutation-plan generator and eliminate some possibilities there (*failure patterns*). Also, some (very primitive) kind of recognition of recursion is done.

A test-simulation implemented in C-Prolog exists. Comparisons with the delphi-model [AM88, Clo87] and the DAG model [Amt89] are given.

Type of logical rule	logical rule	rewriting rule	
query	$? - L_1, \ldots, L_n.$	$S \implies N(L_1) * \ldots * N(L_n)$	
rule	$L_1 :- L_2, \ldots, L_n.$	$N(L_1) \implies N(L_2) * \ldots * N(L_n)$	
unit clause	$L.$	$N(L) \implies \epsilon$	
OR-branch between literal L and $L_1, \ldots, L_r$ with connections $t_i, 1 \leq i \leq r$	$N(L) \implies t_1 * N(L_1) + \ldots + t_r * N(L_r)$		

Figure 3: Rewrite rules obtained from the logic program

	unification	rewriting
process	node in labeled dag	refutation plan
process network	structure relation of formula	OR-search space
instruction for process action	chaining, comparison	rewriting
communication medium	arcs in the dag	from unification
communication principle	message passing	message passing
synchronization	data flow	w.r.t. unification
control	by refutation plan	by unification (fail patterns)
scheduling	one unification	one refutation plan

Table 3: The Model of Computation of the Wivenhoe Model

3.3 The SRI Model

Name	SRI-Model
Application Area	PROLOG system
Input language	PROLOG
Calculus	SLD-resolution (PROLOG)
Parallelism	OR-parallelism, additionally AND-parallelism (the *Andorra Model*)
Inference Component	PROLOG inference machine per node (ANL-WAM)
Model of Computation	see Table 5
Implementation	parallel implementation on a Balance NS32032 with 8 nodes, and a Symmetry 386 with up to 30 nodes

Table 4: Characteristics of the SRI Model

	OR-parallelism	AND-parallelism (Andorra model)
process	goal with more than on connection (OR-branch)	(sub-) goal
process network	OR-search space	set of subgoals
instruction for process action	clause	clause(s)
comm. medium	binding arrays for shared variables in common memory	shared logical variables
comm. principle	shared data structures (e.g. binding arrays)	streams on logical variables
synchronization	memory access	instantiation of logical variables as we have stream-dependent AND-parallelism. Parallel execution can take place as soon as variables become instantiated.
control	public and private nodes (=choice-points) to control granularity of tasks (private nodes must be executed sequentially)	implicit via instantiation of subgoals
scheduling	procedure *find_work()*: find nearest piece of work in the tree. procedure *release_work()*: find nearest idle worker	

Table 5: The Model of Computation of the SRI and Andorra Model

The SRI-model [War87] for parallel execution of PROLOG has been developed within the *Gigalips* project, a project carried through in Manchester, Argonne, and Stockholm. Its aims are the exploitation of *implicit* parallelism on architectures with *shared memory*. The SRI model is an *OR-parallel* model based on the Warren Abstract Machine WAM [War83]. It uses *binding arrays* to keep track of the values to which the logical variables are bound to. The implementation bases on the so-called *cactus stacks* (the stacks of the WAM: control stack, environment stack, trail, and heap) which are kept in the shared memory and are accessible for all processors. The binding arrays itself are kept in the local memory of each processor. This memory model allows that almost all operations (dereferencing, binding, etc.) remain *constant time* operations (except task switching). To gain high efficiency the implementation is kept close to sequential techniques, and the granularity of tasks can be controlled by keeping choice-points *private*, i.e. the search below this choice-point is done by one processor only. By applying a scheduling algorithm which tries to find work "nearest" to the current node, the locality (w.r.t. shared memory) can be optimized and the task switching overhead can be kept low.

An implementation on an 8-node Balance 32032 showed a performance of about 23 Klips; a performance of 600 Klips is to be reached with a 30-node Symmetry 386's.

The *Andorra Model* adds *stream dependent AND-parallelism* to the OR-parallel SRI model. Its basic idea is that goals can be executed in parallel (AND-parallelism) as soon as they become determinate. This is in contrast to other parallel PROLOG languages (cf. [Sha89]) where goals must be delayed until certain additional conditions are met.

3.4 Parthenon

Name	Parthenon	
Application Area	Theorem Prover	
Input language	First order logic in clausal normal form	
Calculus	Model Elimination	
Parallelism	OR-parallelism	
Inference Component	full inference node on each processor	
Model of Computation	*process*	a Model Elimination tableau
	process network	entire search tree
	instruction for process action	clauses
	comm. medium	shared memory, binding of variables
	comm. principle	extracting work from choice-points
	synchronization	memory access, locking of choice-points
	control	implicit: task-stealing
	scheduling	Idle processors look for work in the nodes *nearest* to their current node
Implementation	parallel implementation on an Encore MultiMax (16 Nodes) in C with C-threads under the Mach operating system.	

Table 6: Characteristics of Parthenon

Parthenon (PARallel THEorem prover for NON-horn clauses) is an *OR-parallel* theorem prover for first order logic based on Model Elimination [BCLM89]. It uses a modification of the SRI-model for OR-parallelism. This means that the independent parts of the OR search tree may be executed by different processors. When a processor becomes idle, i.e. it has searched the entire subtree it has to search work on other processors. If an unexplored subtree could be found on a processor it is stolen from that processor (*task stealing*). Each choice-point is marked *shared* if work is available at this choice point for other processors.

With a different binding scheme for variables than in the SRI model, the dereferencing of variables could be made much faster. So, a speed-up of 20-50% over the version of Parthenon using the SRI model could be reached.

Parthenon is implemented on a parallel machine, the Encore Multimax with 16 processors with shared memory. It is written in C, using threads and interlocks for synchronization. The underlying operating system is *Mach*.

Parthenon has been tested with a large number of benchmark examples from [Sti88]. Table 7 shows execution times and speed-up values for some problems, running on a Encore Multimax (This table is taken from [BCLM89]). Values are given for $T(1), T(5)$, and $T(15)$. A value of $s(N)$ denotes a speed-up on N processors. When comparing these figures to the speed-up values obtained by PARTHEO (see Table 8. we find a similar behavior (e.g. a very high speed-up for the example WOS4). $T(1)$, however, differs very much from the results of SETHEO. This is due to a different implementation of the Model Elimiation calculus.

Execution times in seconds and speed-up values for Parthenon					
Problem	$T(1)$	$T(5)$	$s(5)$	$T(15)$	$s(15)$
apabhp	875.9	213.8	4.1	93.3	9.4
LS36	1735.3	268.7	6.5	143.4	12.1
Wos4	8692.1	237.4	36.6	155.4	55.9
Wos10	129.3	33.1	3.9	8.2	15.8

Table 7: Execution times (in seconds) and speed-up values for Parthenon on the Encore Multimax with 1, 5, and 15 processors

3.5 PARTHEO

Name	PARTHEO
Application Area	Theorem Proving and Logic Programming
Input language	First order predicate logic (transformed into Clausal Normal Form), Logic Programming Language MPLOP
Calculus	Model Elimination
Parallelism	OR-parallelism
Inference Component	one complete inference machine per node (SAM)
Model of Computation	*process* — a Model Elimination tableau
	process network — entire search tree
	instruction for process action — compiled clauses
	comm. medium — message passing of (coded) tasks
	comm. principle — message passing of requests for tasks and stolen tasks
	synchronization — task-stealing
	control — parameters for task generation and task-stealing
	scheduling — idle processors ask neighbors for tasks
Implementation	parallel implementation on a Transputer System (16+1) and on an intel Hypercube ipsc/2 (32 Processors) with MMK [BBLT90]. Several simulations [BEKS87, JJ91]

Table 8: Characteristics of PARTHEO

Problem	$T(1)$ [sec] (SETHEO)	$T(16)$ [sec] (PARTHEO)	s speed-up	$s/16$ rel. speed-up
Wos4	3413.0	1.84	1.85×10^3	1.16×10^2
Wos9	64.0	2.16	29.70	1.860
Wos10	262.6	135.60	1.94	.121
Wos16	36490.0	5.89	6.19×10^3	3.87×10^2
Wos25	575.3	114.20	5.03	.314
LS36	1666.0	352.00	4.73	.296
LS108	136.6	15.04	9.08	.568
LS121	44.2	10.25	4.32	.270
Queens8	16.9	1.84	9.20	.575
Queens9	83.6	9.21	9.06	.566
Queens10	370.5	24.68	15.01	.983

Table 9: Execution Times and Speed-up values s for PARTHEO on 16 T800

PARTHEO (PARallel THEOrem prover) is an OR-parallel theoorem prover for full first order logic based on the Model Elimination Calculus [Lov78]. Model Elimination can be seen as a specialisation of the Connection Method [Bib87]. It has been implemented on a network of (currently) 16 inmos transputers T800 and an intel Hypercube ipsc/II with 32 processors, both architectures featuring distributed memory and message passing.

PARTHEO has been built on top of the sequential theorem prover SETHEO [LSBB90] which uses abstract machine technology, semi-compilation, and which has several powerful built-in methods for pruning the search space. Such an abstract machine is running on each processor node of PARTHEO. OR-parallelism can be exploited by distributing the OR-search tree which is spanned by the formula, among the processors.

Each node of the search tree and one of its possible continuations (within the Model Elimination Calculus) comprise a *task*, the basic piece of data which is exchanged between the processors via message passing. Each processor executes such tasks and tries to *extend* them by applying Model Elimination extension or reduction steps. If a new node in the OR-tree is encountered, i.e. there is more than one possibility to proceed, new tasks are generated. They are kept in the local memory, the *Task Store*, and are transmitted on *request* only.

This *task stealing model* works without a global control unit and allows for a good load balance and a fast distribution of the work-load. To reduce the amount of data to be transmitted over the network, the tasks are *encoded* (to less than 300 Bytes in most cases), and the state of the abstract machine is reconstructed by recalculation at the receiving processor. Table 9 shows results of measurements made on the transputer system with 16+1 T800 processors.

3.6 METEOR

METEOR [AL91] is an OR-parallel theorem prover for first order predicate logic. Its underlying calculus is Model Elimination. It has been developed on a Butterfly GP1000 with shared memory. A further implementation on a network of sun SPARC workstations exists. Like in PARTHEO (see 3.5), the information about a task is transferred between the processors by *coding* the tasks and recomputing the stacks of the WAM on the receiving processor. The distribution of work is done with the help of a *global pool* (SASS-Pool: Simultaneous Access of Selectively Shared objects) into which a choice-point from each processor's run-time stack is put. From there it is publicly available.

A number of different completeness modes (depth bound, inference bound, weighted depth, Rollbacks) with iterative deepening ensures the completeness of METEOR. Several pruning methods have been implemented to reduce the size of the search space. Table 11 shows the results of several measurements obtained on a Butterfly GP1000 with 30 processors.

Name	METEOR		
Application Area	Theorem Prover		
Input language	First order predicate logic in Clausal Normal Form		
Calculus	Model Elimination		
Parallelism	OR-parallelism		
Inference Component	one inference machine per node (WAM)		
Model of Computation	*process*	a Model Elimination tableau	
	process network	entire search tree	
	instruction for process action	compiled clauses	
	comm. medium	shared memory or distributed memory	
	comm. principle	transfer of coded tasks,tasks in global pool SASS	
	synchronization	access to common pool SASS. Locks via CREW	
	control	public choice-points in the common pool	
	scheduling	—	
Implementation	Butterfly GP1000 (30 Nodes), LAN of sun SPARC 1+		

Table 10: Characteristics of METEOR

problem	T(1)[s]	T(30) [s]	speed-up
apabhp	22	1.986	11.07
ls36	41	1.820	22.53
wos1	318	10.3	30.87
wos4	10.3	1.1	9.36
wos10	227	6.6	34.40
wos21	6373	274	23.26

Table 11: Execution times in seconds and speed-up values of METEOR on a Butterfly GP1000 with 30 nodes

3.7 MGTP

Name	parallel MGTP		
Application Area	parallel theorem prover		
Input language	first order predicate logic in Clausal Normal Form		
Calculus	Model Generation		
Parallelism	OR-parallelism (AND-parallelism)		
Inference Component	Model generator and satisfiability test		
Model of Computation	*process*	a KL1 process, the check for satisfiability with a model candidate, and the extension of the model candidate	
	process network	all model candidates for the given formula	
	instruction for process action	the model candidates and the compiled clause to which the Model Generation rule is applied	
	comm. medium	distributed memory of the Multi-PSI, shared variables in KL1	
	comm. principle	KL1 execution	
	synchronization	KL1 execution (suspension of subgoals)	
	control	"simple allocation" [FH90] and "bounded OR-parallelism"	
	scheduling	KL1 execution	
Implementation	parallel implementation on a Multi-PSI (16 Nodes see [FH90])		

Table 12: Characteristics of the parallel MGTP

MGTP [FH90, HFF90] is a Model Generation based Theorem Prover for first order predicate logic. It is implemented in KL1 [Sus89]. The model generation method has first been used in SATCHMO [MB88]. MGTP shows a high efficiency for *range-restricted*[3] non-Horn formulae [MB88].

MGTP starts proving with an empty set as a model candidate and tries to construct a model for the given set of clauses by extending the model candidates and checking their satisfiability with respect to the given clauses.

The input clauses are compiled into KL1 clauses and executed on the parallel inference machine Multi-PSI [NII+89]. In order to increase the efficiency of MGTP, several improvements have been made, e.g. the "Ramified Stack Algorithm".

The current version of MGTP exploits OR-parallelism, ie. the handling of multiple model candidates and the exploitation of multiple clauses to which the model generation rules can be applied, are done in parallel. In order to avoid excessive creation of new processes in a system with limited resources, "bounded OR-parallelism" is used. Tasks are distributed only, if the number of clause candidates is smaller than the number of processors.

Table 13 shows results of measurements with MGTP on a Multi-PSI (Table from [FH90]). The

---

[3]A clause is called *range-restricted*, if every variable in the clause has at least one occurrence in its antecedent.

n-queens problem which has been used to obtain the results is formalized with $n + 1$ clauses (see [FH90], pg. 13). This is in contrast to the standard PROLOG queens benchmark which uses lists as data-structures. The times are given for obtaining all solutions.

	Number of Processors				
$n =$	1	2	4	8	16
4	40ms(1.00)	40ms(1.00)	39ms(1.02)	44ms(0.90)	44ms(0.90)
8	12538ms(1.00)	6425ms(1.95)	3336ms(3.76)	1815ms(6.91)	1005ms(12.50)
10	315498ms(1.00)	159881ms(1.97)	79921ms(3.94)	40852ms(7.72)	21820ms(14.50)

Table 13: Performance of MGTP on Multi-PSI for the n queens examples: execution times in milli-seconds and speed-up values

3.8 PEPSys

Name	PEPSys
Application Area	parallel PROLOG system
Input language	PEPSys Language based on PROLOG with explicit parallel constructs
Calculus	SLD-resolution (PROLOG)
Parallelism	OR-parallelism, independent AND-parallelism
Inference Component	PEPSys Abstract Machine (extension of WAM) on each processor
Model of Computation	see Table 15
Implementation	parallel implementation on a Siemens MX500. Simulation of the cluster architecture

Table 14: Characteristics of PEPSys

PEPSys (Parallel ECRC Prolog System) [BKH+88, BIRR88] is a parallel PROLOG system featuring *independent AND-* and *OR-parallelism*. PEPSys has been developed at the ECRC, Munich. To *explicitly* control parallelism, the PEPSys language has been designed. It provides *modularity*, the control of AND-parallelism via the "#" operator, and the control of OR-parallelism by gathering predicates by a *property declaration*. With the latter construct, the programmer can specify, whether *all* solutions have to be searched, or only *one*. Modularity is used as an easy and clean way to separate sequential and parallel parts of the program. In a sequential module, the programmer has a sequential PROLOG environment (including "dirty" predicates). The following example of the programming language is a part of the *queens problem* found in [BKH+88]:

```
?-export(get_solutions/2).              % export entry point
...
-properties([solutions(one),clauses(ordered),execution(lazy)]).
                                        % control of OR-parallelism
  safe(X,Y,□).
  safe(X,Y,[square(I,J)|L]) :-
    not(threatened(I,J,X,Y)) # safe(X,Y,L). % AND-parallel (#) construct
```

The computational model supports the AND- and OR-parallelism, together with shallow (in PROLOG stacks) and deep variable bindings using an *explicit time-stamp mechanism*. During the execution of an OR-parallel predicate, a *branch point* (choice-point) is created, controlling sequential

	AND-parallelism	OR-parallelism
process	goal	a group of predicates gathered by property definitions
process network	subgoals separated by #	OR-part of the search space
instruction for process action	clause	clause(s)
comm. medium	shared memory - join cells	shared memory - choice points
comm. principle	data-flow: gathering all solutions in solution lists	
synchronization	joining	choice-points
control	explicit (# operator)	explicit (properties)
scheduling	RHS goals may be taken by idle processors	looking in choice-points for work; in clusters: look first in local work pool before getting work from a remote processor

Table 15: The Model of Computation of PEPSys

backtracking and which work may be taken by idle processors. The creation of AND-parallel processes is similar to that of OR-processes. The left-hand solutions and the right-hand solutions of two subgoals solved in parallel are gathered in *solution lists* and *joined* in the fashion of "eager evaluation".

A PEPSys Abstract Machine (an extension of the WAM) has been designed to run on each processor. PEPSys has been implemented on a Sequent Balance 8000 (Siemens MX500) with 8 processors. Also, an emulation has been implemented, grouping the processing elements into clusters which are connected by a communication network. Each cluster has a special *cluster processor*, containing a local *work pool* which holds work for that cluster. Inter-cluster distribution of work is done in a demand-driven manner.

Both, the implementation and the simulation show good speed-up results up to about 6.9 on 8 processors using the queens problem [BKH+88] with little overhead w.r.t. a sequential implementation.

3.9 ROO

ROO (Radically Optimized OTTER) is parallel theorem prover for first order predicate logic based on resolution. Most of its software is taken from its sequential predecessor, OTTER, also developed at the Argonne Natl. Labs [McC88]. This algorithm tries to compute the *logical closure* of a given formula. In ROO, this is done in parallel with two kinds of processes of type A and B (see Figure 4). A number of tasks of the type A take a formula out of the formula data base and performs all possible resolution steps with it, resulting in new literals $L_1, \ldots, L_n$. These may be put into the formula data base. To avoid the size of the data base to explode, however, *subsumption* must be performed between the literals $L_1, \ldots, L_n$ and the data base (forward and backward subsumption). To keep the formula data base consistent and to avoid a write access to the data base by many processors, this subsumption is done in two steps as shown in Figure 4.

Name	ROO
Application Area	Theorem Prover
Input language	first order predicate logic in Clausal Normal Form
Calculus	several types of resolution
Parallelism	generation of new literals (kind of OR-parallelism), subsumption(Reductions)
Inference Component	generator and partial subsumption module
Model of Computation	*process*	A: generate new literals, B: Subsumption and update of the database
	process network	A: generation of a part of the logical closure
	instruction for process action	(global) index in data base
	comm. medium	shared memory: data base (read only for A), list K
	comm. principle	data-flow control between A's and B via list K.
	synchronization	Monitor operations on K [BBD+87]
	control	parameters and set of support in process A
	scheduling	Process B is started only, if there are enough literals in list K. B runs until K is exhausted.
Implementation	parallel implementation on a Sequent Symmetry (24 procs)

Table 16: Characteristics of ROO

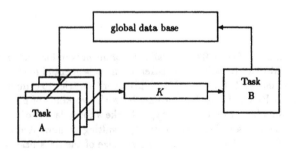

Figure 4: Process structure in ROO

Tasks of the type A only perform a *partial* subsumption, i.e. they locally try to perform subsumption, using the data base in a read only way. No update of the data base is allowed. Henceforth, this subsumption is only partial. The remaining new literals L_i are put in a small global list K. If a certain amount of literals in K is reached, *one* process of type B takes the literals from K and performs *full* forward and backward subsumption. All remaining literals are added to the data base.

This model takes into account that, after a first phase for stabilisation, the number of newly generated literals which are put into K after the partial subsumption is very small, and consequently the amount of additional work which has to be performed by task B (second subsumption) is neglegible. Experimental results are quite impressing, speed-ups of up to 21.9 on 24 processors (and 13.4 with 16 processors) could be obtained, using a formula of implicational calculus (imp4) [LM90].

3.10 POPE

Name	POPE	
Application Area	PROLOG system	
Input language	PROLOG	
Calculus	SLD-resolution (PROLOG)	
Parallelism	pipelining	
Inference Component	μ-programmable unification processor	
Model of Computation	*process*	unification, creation of control information (choice-point, environment), passing of arguments and entry points
	process network	execution of the PROLOG program
	instruction for process action	compiled PROLOG program (modified WAM instructions)
	comm. medium	pipeline buffers controlled by semaphores
	comm. principle	transfer of goal arguments and control information via the pipeline buffers
	synchronization	pipeline buffers: hardware semaphores controlling the availability of arguments. shared memory: explicit control via control registers
	control	implicit control via the availability of data (data-flow). No explicit control.
	scheduling	is done implicitly by the flow of data
Implementation	no implementation, simulation with up to 8 processors	

Table 17: Characteristics of POPE

POPE (Parallel Operating Prolog Engine) [BG87] is an architecture for the parallel execution of sequential PROLOG. Although it shows quite a different architecture as the other systems shown in this article, it features an interesting application of a WAM in a parallel environment. It consists of a pipeline of *unification processors* each of them connected to its *right* neighbor by a *pipeline buffer*. Additionally, the first and the last processor are connected to yield a circular arrangement. Each of the unification processors executes a PROLOG instruction set, similar to that of the WAM [War83]. Each processor has access to a *shared memory*, containing the stack (local stack), heap (global stack), and the trail. Additionally, each processor has its own local memory to store the code of the program. The pipeline buffers are ring buffers, controlled by hardware semaphores, and contain the *arguments* of the subgoal to solve, and some *control registers*.

A processor may fetch such a buffer block from its left neighbor. According to the code of the program, it tries to unify the parameters of the goal with those in the head of a clause. At the same time it sends the entry address of new subgoals to its right neighbor. As soon as the arguments of this subgoal become available, they will be sent to the right neighbor, which can start to solve the new subgoal. A short example from [BG87] illustrates this. Consider the following PROLOG program to be executed by a pipeline of three processors P_1, P_2, P_3:

```
?- h(X,a,Y,b).              % C1
h(c,Z,e,b) :- g(Z,U),...    % C2
g(a,a).                     % C3
```

Assume P_1 starts the execution of C1. It sends the entry address of C2 to P_2. After that, it transfers the parameters of C1 to P_2 (via the pipeline buffer). P_2 fetches the data from the pipeline buffer and starts executing the unification. At the same time, it already sends the entry point of C3 to $P3$. As soon as P_2 managed to unify a with Z, Z (actually a pointer to it) will be sent to P_3, which, consequentl, can start with the execution of C3 in the same way as described above.

The synchronization of the access of the parameters and control information is obtained by using *hardware semaphores*. Access to the shared memory is synchronized explicitly via the availability of the control registers pointing into these areas (e.g. stack pointer). Compilation techniques support these control.

Simulation results with up to 8 unification processors yielded good results (up to more than 1000 KLIPS for classical benchmarks), even if these programs show no "classical" form of parallelism. Simulations also showed that a line of three pipelining processors are sufficient in most cases, and that with increasing their number no better results could be obtained.

3.11 PKPS – A Parallel Knowledge Processing System

The PKPS (Parallel Knowledge Processing System) [Geo86c, Geo86d, Geo86a] is a theorem prover built around the *Reactive Memory* (RM) [Geo86b], an associative memory.

The reactive memory is a uniform array of cells, each of fixed length. Each row of cells is attached to a cell processor which is able to perform basic operations on the memory cells. A number of buses connect the rows. Figure 5 (from [Geo86b]) shows the basic structure of a reactive memory cell. Each memory field (MF) is attached to a field processing element (FPE) which can perform individual operations on each MF, like *clear, load, store*, and *compare*. The FPE's are controlled by a cell processing element which is in charge of performing operations on the entire cell, like *select, deselect*, and *read* the status register.

Name	PKPS
Application Area	Knowledge Processing, Inferencing
Input language	first order predicate logic in Clausal Normal Form, many sorted logic
Calculus	Resolution with Set of Support
Parallelism	selection of parent clauses, selection of resolution candidates, unification
Inference Component	R-PIP (Resolution Parallel Inference Processor)
Model of Computation	*process* — part of term (cell of RM)
	process network — all terms (= RM)
	instruction for process action — comparisons
	comm. medium — internal buses of the RM
	comm. principle — selection and common control of FPE's
	synchronization — synchronous operation (Φ_{RM})
	control — via Cell Processing Elements
	scheduling — —
Implementation	unknown

Table 18: Characteristics of the PKPS

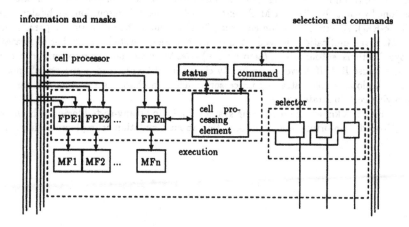

Figure 5: Basic structure of a reactive memory cell

With the help of the selection lines, certain memory cells may be activated according to prior executed operations (e.g. compare). This allows to access the Reactive Memory in an associative way.

The PKPS consists of a number of R-PIP's (Reactive Parallel Inference Processors) connected by buses. As shown in Figure 6 (from [Geo86a]), the Reactive Memory is used to store clauses and terms during the resolution procedure. Due to the fixed length of the memory cells, the literals

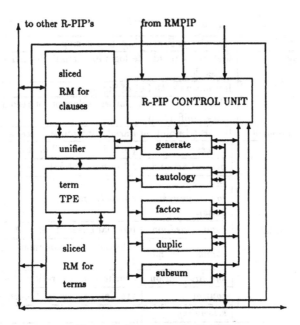

Figure 6: Structure of a R-PIP

and terms are distributed in a appropriate way over several cells.

The R-PIP control unit selects parent clauses according to.the employed *level saturation* strategy. This is done by using the Clause-RM. A next step selects possible resolution candidates (again from the Clause-RM). A term processing element (TPE) attempts the unification in parallel, using the Term-RM. If the unification succeeds, the resolvents are generated. A number of strategies (e.g. tautology deletions, subsumption, factorization) tries to delete the new resolvent prior to entering it into the clause-RM. If, however, an empty clause could be resolved, a success is reported. The RMPIP is a global control strategy processor which is in charge of selecting the parent clauses and applying certain strategies.

Using the PKPS, a knowledge processing system employing many-sorted logic has been developed as well [Geo86d]. Unfortunately, no information about simulation or implementation is available.

4 Conclusions

This paper has tried to give an overview of existing parallel theorem provers and some well-known parallel PROLOG systems. Due to the rapidly growing number of existing systems, however, the selection of systems has to be incomplete. Furthermore, the field of parallel logic programming languages (e.g. GHC,PARLOG), and parallel implementations thereof (e.g. [Sus89] and other work done at ICOT), is not covered. We have set up a list of characteristic items which are interesting for a comparison and classification of parallel theorem provers and PROLOG systems. Within such a framework, common characteristics and differences of the systems can be expressed more clearly.

We have had a closer look at 11 systems, 7 of them theorem provers. They revealed some interesting common features:

- The input language of most of the parallel systems is the same as that of their sequential counter-parts. This means that there are no explicit parallel constructs in the language. This approach seems to be promising, since it frees the user from writing down his formula or program in a (complicated) parallel language. The structure of PROLOG (or of logic in general) seems to be suited for an automatic parallelisation. A similar approach has been used quite successfully with vectorising Fortran Compilers in the area of supercomputing.

- Most systems propose a rather *coarse* grain parallelism (often OR-parallelism) with a comparatively small number of processes. This may be due to the structure and architecture of the hardware available which has a comparatively small number of processors.

- Most parallel theorem provers employ some kind of OR-parallelism. This kind of parallelism seems to be appropriate to cut down the large search space which is to be explored in theorem proving.

- AND-parallelism is exploited in very few systems only. It is interesting especially in the area of logic programs (solving subgoals in parallel). Its complicated structure and large amount of communication (caused by "shared variables"), however, restricts its usefulness in many of today's systems.

- Many theorem provers, especially those which are based on Model Elimination use technology developed in the area of PROLOG systems (e.g. the WAM, compilation technique, parallelisation).

This survey of parallel theorem provers has shown that much area in the "map" of potential parallelism — the coordinate system spanned by "independence" and "granularity" (Figure 1) is still "white" and unexpored.

Future work will show, in how far these kinds of parallelism produce good speed-up results. Requirements for new parallel architectures will also evolve from such work. Furthermore, systems should be developed which can explore more than one kind of parallelism. Such systems could even cooperate (see e.g. [Kur90, FK87]) and thus exhibit synergetic effects which may result in extremely good performance for inferencing.

References

[AL91]   O. L. Astrachan and D. W. Loveland. METEORs: High performance theorem provers using model elimination. Technical Report CS-1991-08, Dept. of CS, Duke University, Durham, North Carolina, 1991.

[AM88]   H. Alshawi and D. B. Moran. The Delphi Model and some preliminary experiments. In *Proc. of 5th Int. Conf. and Symposium*, pages 1578–1589. MIT-Press, 1988.

[Amt89] Robert Amthor. Simulation eines Beweisers auf einer Multi – Prozessorarchitektur. Master's thesis, Technische Universitä München, 1989.

[BBD+87] J. Boyle, R. Butler, T. Disz, B. Glickfled, E. Lusk, and et.al. *Portable Programs for Parallel Processors*. Holt, Rinehart, Winston, New York, 1987.

[BBLT90] Th. Bemmerl, A. Bode, Th. Ludwig, and S. Tritscher. MMK - Multiprocessor Multitasking Kernel (User's Guide and User's Reference Manual). SFB Bericht Nr. 342/26/90A, Technische Universität München, 1990.

[BCLM89] Soumitra Bose, Edmund M. Clarke, David E. Long, and Spiro Michaylov. Parthenon: A Parallel Theorem Prover for Non-Horn Clauses. *Journal of Automated Reasoning*, 1989.

[BEKS87] S. Bayerl, W. Ertel, F. Kurfeß, and J. Schumann. PARTHEO/3: Experimentation with PARallel Automated THEOrem Prover Based on the Connection Method for Horn Clause Logic. ESPRIT 415F Deliverable D12, 1987.

[BG87]   J. Beer and W. K. Giloi. POPE — a Parallel–Operating Prolog Engine. *Future Comp. Systems*, 3:83–92, 1987.

[Bib87] W. Bibel. *Automated Theorem Proving*. Vieweg Verlag, Braunschweig, second edition, 1987.

[BIRR88] Uri Baron, Bounthara Ing, Michael Ratcliffe, and Philippe Robert. A distributed architecture for the PEPSys parallel logic programming system. In *Int. Conference on Parallel Processing*, Chicago, 1988.

[BKA+86] W. Bibel, F. Kurfeß, K. Aspetsberger, P. Hintenaus, and J. Schumann. Parallel inference machines. In *Future Parallel Computers*, pages 185–226. Springer Verlag, 1986.

[BKH+88] U. Baron, J. C. de Kergommeaux, M. Hailperin, M. Ratcliffe, M. Robert, J.-Cl. Syre, and H. Westphal. The parallel ECRC Prolog System PEPSys: An Overview and Evaluation Results. In *Future Generation Computing Systems*, 1988.

[Clo87] W. F. Clocksin. Principles of the DelPhi Parallel Inference Machine. *Comp. Journal*, 30(5):386–392, 1987.

[FH90]   H. Fujita and R. Hasegawa. A model generation theorem prover in KL1 using a ramified-stack algorithm. Technical Report TR-606, ICOT, Tokyo, Japan, 1990.

[FK87]   Bertram Fronhöfer and Franz Kurfeß. Cooperative competition: A modest proposal concerning the use of multi-processor systems for automated reasoning. Technical report, Technische Universität München, 1987.

[Geo86a] Joan Georgescu. Implicit parallelism in reactive memory based inference processors. Technical report, Inst. for Computers and Informatics, Dept. of Robotics and AI, Bucharest, Romania, 1986.

[Geo86b] Joan Georgescu. An inference processor based on reactive memory. TR AI–FD063, Inst. for Computers and Informatics, Dept. of Robotics and AI, Bucharest, Romania, 1986.

[Geo86c] Joan Georgescu. PKPS – a parallel knowledge processing system. Technical report, Inst. for Computers and Informatics, Dept. of Robotics and AI, Bucharest, Romania, 1986.

[Geo86d] Joan Georgescu. PKPS – a parallel knowledge processing system for reasoning with knowlegde and belief. Technical report, Inst. for Computers and Informatics, Dept. of Robotics and AI, Bucharest, Romania, 1986.

[HFF90] R. Hasegawa, H. Fujita, and M. Fujita. A parallel theorem prover in KL1 and its application to program synthesis. Technical Report TR-588, ICOT, Tokyo, Japan, 1990.

[JJ91] M. R. Jobmann and Schumann J. Modelling and performance analysis of a parallel theorem prover. In A. Lehmann and F. Lehmann, editors, *Messung,Modellierung und Bewertung von Rechensystemen*, volume 286 of *Informatik Fachberichte*, pages 228–243, Neubiberg, Sep 1991. 6. GI/ITG-Fachtagung, Springer.

[Kur90] F. Kurfeß. *Parallelism in Logic — Its Potential for Performance and Program Development.* PhD thesis, Technische Universität München, 1990.

[Lav88] S. H. Lavington. Technical overview of the Intelligent File Store. Technical report, Department of Computer Science, University of Essex, Colchester, UK, 1988.

[LM90] Ewing Lusk and William McCune. Tutorial on high- performance automated theorem proving. In *CADE 10*, page 681. Springer Verlag, 1990.

[Lov78] D. W. Loveland. *Automated Theorem Proving: a Logical Basis.* North–Holland, 1978.

[LSBB90] R. Letz, J. Schumann, S. Bayerl, and W. Bibel. SETHEO: A High-Performance Theorem Prover. Technical report, Technische Universität München, 1990. To appear in Journal of Automated Reasoning.

[MB88] R. Manthey and F. Bry. SATCHMO: a theorem prover implemented in Prolog. In *Conference on Automated Deduction (CADE)*, 1988.

[McC88] W. McCune. OTTER users' guide. Technical report, Mathematics and Computer Sci. Division, Argonne National Laboratory, Argonne, Ill., USA, 1988.

[NII+89] K. Nakajima, Y. Inamura, N. Ichyoshi, K. Rokusawa, and T. Chikayama. Distributed implementation of KL1 on the Multi-PSI/V2. In *Proc. of 6th Intern. Conf. on Logic Programming (ICLP)*, 1989.

[Pra70] D. Prawitz. A Proof Procedure with Matrix Reduction. In *Symposium on Automatic Demonstration, Lecture Notes in Mathematics 125*, pages 207–214. Springer, 1970.

[Sha89]   E. Shapiro. The family of concurrent logic programming languages. *acm computing surveys*, 21(3):412–510, 1989.

[Sti88]   M. E. Stickel. A Prolog Technology Theorem Prover: Implementation by an Extended Prolog Compiler. *Journal of Automated Reasoning*, 4:353–380, 1988.

[Sus89]   Kasumi Susaki. KL1 Programming. Technical Report TM-949, ICOT, Tokyo, Japan, 1989.

[Wan89]   Jiwei Wang. Towards a new computational model for logic languages. Tech-rept CSM-128, Dept. of CS, University of Essex, 1989.

[War83]   D. H. D. Warren. An Abstract PROLOG Instruction Set. Technical report, SRI, Menlo Park, Ca, USA, 1983.

[War87]   D. H. D Warren. The SRI model for OR–parallel execution of Prolog — abstract design and implementation issues. In *International Symposion on Logic Programming*, pages 92–102, 1987.

[Wis86]   Michael J. Wise. *Prolog Multiprocessors*. Prentice Hall, 1986.

[WM76]   G. A. Wilson and J. Minker. Resolution, Refinements, and Search Strategies: a Comparative Study. *IEEE Transactions on Computers*, C–25:782–801, 1976.

Parallel Unification: Theory and Implementations

Fadi N. Sibai

Department of Electrical Engineering
University of Akron
Akron, Ohio 44325-3904
U.S.A.

Abstract

This Chapter deals with parallel unification architectures and algorithms. We show how parallel unification can be exploited and we review a parallel unification algorithm. Static scheduling, binding environment, and memory representation of terms are also discussed. Finally, we review some of the parallel unification projects.

1 Introduction

Unification is widely considered to be the bread and butter operation of Prolog interpreters and theorem provers. Unification is the Prolog operation for assigning values to variables, for passing parameters in procedure calls, and for equality tests. In some applications, it has been measured that the unification operation consumes more than 50% of Prolog programs' total execution time. The other portion is mainly attributed to binding environment maintenance and backtracking. Thus, from Amdahl's law, and assuming that the unification operation consumes exactly 50% of Prolog programs and that the speedup of parallel unification over serial unification is S_u, the total Prolog speedup due to parallelizing unification is $2 / (1 + 1 / S_u)$. Thus parallelizing unification has a great potential to speed up (by a factor of 2 based on the above assumptions) the execution of Prolog-based programs.

Unification is known to be serial (in time) in the worst case. Dwork et al. [1] and Yasuura [2] showed that unification cannot probably (and if possible, hardly can) be executable in parallel in polylog time. However, Citrin [3] showed that although some pairs of terms cannot be unified quickly on a parallel unifier hardware, there exist many pairs of terms which can. In fact, the worst case serial execution of unification is rare to encounter, and based on simulations of common Prolog benchmarks, a great number of terms can benefit from parallelizing the unification operation.

In this Chapter, we review serial and parallel computer architectures and algorithms for unification. In the next section, we define the unification operation. In section 3, we discuss serial unification algorithms and serial unification hardware. In section 4, we focus on parallel unification algorithms, and techniques used in parallel implementations of unification including static data dependence analysis, static scheduling, binding environment and memory representation of terms. Section 4 is concluded by a brief description of parallel unification projects.

2 Unification

First-order unification, a bidirectional, commutative and monotonic pattern matching operation, was originally developed by J. A. Robinson [4]. This operation which was designed to be used in the Resolution inference rule, can be briefly summarized as follows. Starting with two logic terms constructed with symbols, constants, and variables, find and return, if possible, a most general substitution of terms for each variable in the terms such that the two terms are equal. Robinson's algorithm accepts two lists of terms to be unified, and returns a substitution called the most general unifier (MGU), containing the variable bindings, or Fail, in case of unification failure. Robinson's algorithm was terribly inefficient. In fact it had an exponential time and space complexity.

In general, a term can be one of constant, variable, list, or function (structure). Constants will be denoted by lower-case letters such as a. Variables will be denoted by capital letters such as X. Structures are composed of a head called the functor which is a symbol such as f or g, and an integer, called the arity, representing the number of arguments in the structure, as well as one or more arguments which are terms. An example of a structure is $f(X,d, g(Y))$. The unification algorithm can be described as follows. Given T1 and T2, two lists of n terms to be unified, return a substitution S (MGU) in case of success or Fail in case of failure. For that purpose, do the following for the i th member of T1 and T2, $1 \leq i \leq n$:

i. If either term is a variable V occurring in the second term, return Fail and stop, else if either term is a variable not occurring in the second term, then the binding "V / other term " is appended to S, the list of bindings (MGU) to be returned at the end of the unification operation in case of unification success; (This single step in commonly known as the "occur check" step which prevents infinite bindings such as $X / f(X)$ from triggering a non-ending loop during the process of updating the binding reference of X. See Knight [5] for an explanation of why the occur check is commonly left out in Prolog-based systems).

ii. If one term is a constant and the other is a structure then return Fail and stop;

iii. If both terms are structures with different functors then return Fail and stop;

iv. If both terms are structures with equal functors then the arguments of the first structure are appended to list T1, while the arguments of the second structure are appended to T2;

v. Repeat the above operations for all members of T1 and T2. Stop when Fail is returned or when all the members of T1 and T2 have been successfully unified. In the latter case, return S as the result of unification.

Binding a variable as in step (i.) is efficiently done by updating pointers to the terms bound. An alternative is to copy the binding term in its entirety in the variable slot. An efficient representation of compound terms, i.e. lists and structures, in memory is called structure sharing.

In structure sharing, a structure is represented by a graph instead of a tree, allowing for subterms to be shared and resulting in savings in memory and avoiding copying of long structures [5]. In Fig. 1, the structure f(Y, a, Y) is represented by a tree (Fig. 1.a) and by a graph (Fig 1.b) where the variable Y is shared and not duplicated. Usually, the larger the shared subterm, the more the savings.

3 Serial Unification
A Serial Unification Algorithms

The best sequential unification algorithm is attributed to Paterson and Wegman [6]. This algorithm has a linear time complexity and uses directed acyclic graphs (dags) for data structure. De Champeaux [7] later corrected this algorithm and analyzed the performance of Paterson and Wegman's algorithm. He attributed the bad performance of Robinson's algorithm to its inability to recognize structure sharing and to its exponential generation of large structures due to the left-right processing convention. He attributed the better performance of the Paterson and Wegman's algorithm to their use of a horizontal pointer between the graphs of the structures to be unified, and to the policy of matching a pair of nodes in the two graphs only after all their ancestor nodes have been matched.

Martelli and Montanari [8] proposed an algorithm based on two functions: COMMON and FRONTIER. Applying COMMON to a list of terms returns the common part of that list which is the term common to all terms in the lists. For instance, the common term of the list $\{ f(X), f(h(Y)), f(h(a)) \}$ is $f(X)$. FRONTIER associates with each variable in the list all the possible bindings, e.g., the FRONTIER of the above list is $\{ X= \{h(Y), h(a)\}, Y=a \}$, and is referred to as a multiequation. Martelli and Montanari's algorithm also relies on multiequation reduction and compactification to manipulate the multiequations, merge them, and break them down into variable bindings. Martelli and Montanari compared their algorithm with Paterson and Wegman's linear algorithm and concluded that Paterson and Wegman's algorithm is better than theirs for terms with very high probability of unification success or cycles. However, they believe that their algorithm is superior for terms with very high probability of unification failure.

Martelli and Rossi [9] proposed a slower algorithm with time complexity $O(\,n\,\alpha(n))$, where $\alpha(n)$ is the inverse of Ackerman's function, and allowing for the unification of infinite terms.

B Serial Unification Hardware

Citrin [3] identified three approaches taken in serial unification implementations:
i. library routines: for instance in SPUR Prolog [10];

ii. microcoded unification: for instance in WAM-based machines [11], a KL0-based machine [12], and a Lisp-based machine [13], and the PLM machine [14]; and

iii. hardware support: for instance in the AT&T hardware unification unit (HUU) [15,16] and other hardware units described below.

- UNIF: In 1981, S. Chang [17] pioneered attempts to implement unification in hardware at the California Institute of Technology. Chang's machine, the UNIF chip, was designed to execute Robinson's unification algorithm. It generates the variable bindings during the unification operation and stores these bindings temporarily on-chip. At the end of unification, UNIF transfers these bindings off-chip to an external RAM when the operation succeeds, else it indicates the failure of the operation. No implementation or performance evaluation of UNIF are available.

- SUM: At Syracuse University, the SUM unification co-processor [18] equipped with a content-addressable memory (CAM) was designed to support an LMI Lambda Lisp machine. The host Lambda machine, whenever encountering a unification task, assigns it to the SUM co-processor. The SUM co-processor conducts unification assisted by the CAM for fast access of binding agents. This co-processor is divided into: 1) a communication agent with the task of coordinating the communication with the host Lambda machine; 2) an analysis agent responsible for issuing binding tasks when the two terms to be unified can bind successfully, based on the analysis of the term tags; 3) a binding agent acting as storage for the variable bindings; and 4) a binding controller responsible for controlling the binding agent.

- HUU: The AT&T hardware unification unit (HUU) consisting of a hardware processing unit and a variable stack, was developed by Woo [15,16]. It was shown to improve the performance of unification considerably. The unify function implemented in hardware is composed of eight routines, each dealing with one data type. The microprogrammed HUU has 16 bits wide microinstructions and a microprogram which is 130 words long. This unification unit sets a flip-flop whenever unification succeeds. If nested terms are encountered, the unit invokes itself recursively for each nesting. Woo measured HUU's performance to be 14-15 times faster than the UNSW interpreter's unify function (on a VAX 11/780) that it was designed to replace, assuming a microcycle time of 150ns, an internal memory access time of 300 ns, and an external memory access time of 600 ns.

- UNIFIC: UNIFIC, a 54-pin unification co-processor chip with 32-bit data words, was designed by Gollakota [19] at Texas A&M University. At the start of the unification operation, the host processor supplies UNIFIC with the starting address of the two lists of terms to be unified and the arity denoting the number of terms in the lists. UNIFIC, like the SUM, is equipped with a content-addressable binding memory to reduce the search time of variables. Gollakota claims that UNIFIC performs 6%-37% faster than the HUU based on simulations. This is mainly due to UNIFIC's CAM. After the terms are read by UNIFIC, they are decoded, and depending on their types, one out of nine routines is executed. For instance, if both terms are structures, the arities of the two functions are checked for equality, and if equal, several registers are pushed on an on-chip stack and UNIFIC enters a new state. UNIFIC invokes itself recursively if nested functions are encountered. This co-processor is designed to operate with a microcycle period of 50 ns. Memory accesses take four cycles. UNIFIC can address up to 16K words in memory. The organization of UNIFIC is shown in Fig. 2.

It is essentially a one-bus processor with a binding memory which is half CAM half RAM used to hold variable bindings, a stack used to hold the contents of saved registers during recursive invocations, two memory address registers, MAR1 and MAR2, used to hold the addresses of the two lists in memory, three data registers, DIN, DR1, and DR2, a register used to hold the arity and another (TEMP) used to hold initially the arity and addresses of the two terms to be unified. The last-in first-out (LIFO) stack is 32 words deep and restricts the level of nesting in nested functions to a maximum of 10 nestings. Memory pointers in the binding memory are 13 bits wide, restricting the memory space for variable bindings to 8Kwords. Parikh [20] designed the microcontroller of UNIFIC and modified the organization of UNIFIC to include two buses.

4 Parallel Unification
A Introduction

Dwork et al. [1] showed that unification is log-space complete for P, the set of functions that are computed in deterministic polynomial time on a sequential processor. Consequently, it is highly improbable that unification can be computed in time $O(log^k n)$ using a polynomial number of processors. In fact, unification has a component which is inherently sequential and which cannot be parallelized. Unification is composed of two major steps: argument matching and consistency check. For example the unification of $f(X, Y, Y)$ and $f(b, X, a)$ is conducted as follows: the functors of the two terms match successfully, and the arguments of the two structures are matched (unified) by pairs yielding the bindings: X / b, Y / X, and Y / a. The three bindings are then checked for consistency to insure that no variable bindings are inconsistent with each other, based on the binding rule that a free (unbound) variable can only be bound to one single ground term. The consistency check step in the above example fails since X is bound to b while Y is bound to a, clearly a conflict with X / Y. The consistency check step is believed to be the sequential component of unification because it is possible to unify two variable bindings during the consistency check step itself (e.g. during checking the consistency of the bindings: X / a, $Y / f(X)$, and $Z / f(b)$), a step which is not highly parallelizable. Dwork et al. also showed that the match algorithm, a special case of the unification algorithm , and responsible for term matching, can be computed in $O(log^2 n)$ time if the input is in dag form, on a parallel RAM with $n^{O(1)}$ processors. Maluszynski and Komorowski [21] discouraged by Dwork's results discussed a form of logic programming that uses the match algorithm instead of unification. Ramesh et al. [22] presented a parallel algorithm for term matching on $O(n^{1-e})$ processors which takes $O(n^e log n)$ time on the exclusive-read exclusive-write (EREW) PRAM model, n being the length of the input terms, e is a constant such that $0 \le e \le 1$, and takes $O(log n)$ time on the concurrent-read concurrent-write (CRCW) PRAM model with n processors.

Yasuura [2] also studied the complexity of unification. His results agree with Dwork's. He also presented a parallel algorithm in time $O(log^2 n)$ on a combinational logic circuit of depth $O(log^2 n + m log m)$, where n is the number of terms to be unified, and m is the number of variables in the terms. Vitter and Simons [23] showed that unification is parallelizable with running time $O(E + V)$ on a sequential RAM and $O(E / P + V log P)$ on an exclusive-read exclusive-write (EREW) RAM with P processors, V being the number of vertices, and E being the number of edges in the graph. Thus Vitter and Simons algorithm seemed to prove that although unification may not be the most highly parallelizable algorithm, yet it is parallelizable. Harland and Jaffar [24] compared a parallel version of Jaffar's algorithm with Yasuura's and Vitter and Simons' algorithms.

B Parallel Unification Algorithms

As Dwork et al.'s results suggest, unification is composed of a step which is highly parallelizable,namely the match step, and of a step which is more serial in nature than parallelizable, namely the consistency check step. In this section, we will describe how unification can be parallelized and study a parallel unification algorithm.

Unification parallelism is a branch of Prolog parallelism (including AND-parallelism, OR-parallelsism, stream parallelsism, ...) at the finest grain and at the lowest level. In unification parallelism, the arguments of two compound terms are unified concurrently. Perhaps, the best description of how unification can be parallelized is due to the one who created unification in the first place, J. A. Robinson. Robinson [25] described a parallel unification procedure using directed acyclic graphs (dags) as data structures. That is the two terms to be unified are represented by two dags. This data structures exploits indirect addressing (pointers) and subterm sharing as explained in section 2. We will illustrate a unification example using Robinson's procedure.

In the dag, a non-leaf node with n out-arcs, labeled 1, ..., n, represents a list with n arguments (starting with argument 1 and ending with argument n). Leaf nodes (leaves) represent either atoms or variables. For instance, Fig. 3 shows a dag representation of the structure $g(a, X, f(X,Y))$. Note how a special node is at the root of a structure representation, and how its first (leftmost in general) child is the functor node, a symbol, and its last (rightmost in general) child is the structure's last argument. Now, we shall illustrate the unification of the two term lists { $g(X,a)$ $f(Y,d,Z)$ Z } and { U $f(U,V,W)$ c } using Robinson's procedure. The dags representing these two term lists are shown in Fig. 4. The first step in the procedure is to equate (unify) the two roots (nodes 1 and 2) of the dags by merging nodes 1 and 2 together as shown in Fig. 5. Now, every node N_a and N_b in the dags reached by two arcs labeled by the same number and originating from a common node are equated $N_a = N_b$. This step can be parallelized by concurrently equating every such N_a and N_b nodes in the dags. The result of these steps in our example yields the dag of Fig. 6. Note how nodes 3 and 13, 4 and 5, and 12 and 16, have been equated and merged into common nodes.

The previous step is again repeated (essentially on merged node 4, 5) thereby equating nodes (3, 13) and 10; 11 and 14; and (12, 16) and 15. The final dag is illustrated in Fig. 7. Since there are no more nodes that can be merged, the procedure ends with the following variable binding list as a result: { $Y=U=g(X,a)$, $V=d$, $Z=W=c$ }. Note how the equating of the nodes proceeds from ancestor nodes to child nodes (top to bottom) and how several nodes are equated at each level of the graph in parallel.

Perhaps the greatest speedup that can be obtained from parallel unification over serial unification is in the following example. In this example, two very long structures with many arguments, with equal functors and arities, are unified. The matchings of all the pairs of arguments except the last pair do not fail. Only the matching of the last pair of arguments fails at the match level. Such an example is illustrated in Fig. 8. Since in parallel unification all the pairs of arguments can be matched simultaneously, the failure of the match of the last pair can be quickly detected near the beginning of the unification operation resulting in a fast result: Fail. On the other hand, when the unification of these two structures is conducted serially, the failure of the last pair of arguments' matching is only detected after the unification of all the other pairs of arguments and after checking their consistencies. This is due to the serial unification convention of unifying the leftmost arguments first, and the rightmost arguments last, as in the Prolog convention. Furthermore, in serial unification, as soon as a pair of arguments are matched, the generated bindings are checked for consistency with the previous variable bindings before the next pair of arguments are matched. This contributes to the very long unification time of all the pair of arguments before the last pair. Therefore, the result of serial unification is available after a much longer time than the time required by parallel unification to provide the result of the operation.

A parallel unification algorithm that detects early unification failure at the match level and conducts the matchings of the structure arguments simultaneously while pipelining the argument match steps with the consistency check steps of the variable bindings was presented by Sibai [26-28]. The parallel algorithm is given in Fig. 9. It is designed to execute on the parallel unification machine [26-28] shown in Fig. 10.

This machine architecture allows for full match parallelism to take place by providing for the terms' arguments to be read and matched concurrently. Each match processor, MPi, initially reads a word holding the addresses and the number of pair of arguments to match from memory module MMi, then reads a pair of arguments, matches them by checking their data types for compatibility or equality if of the same type, and generates a variable binding packet if either argument is a variable and provided that the other is not the same variable, decrements the number of pair of arguments to match, reads the next pair of arguments... The same cycle is repeated in each MPi until all pairs of arguments are matched by that MPi. Note that the structure's arguments in a memory module are stored in consecutive memory locations so that the address of only the first argument in the module is needed at the beginning, and the next arguments are accessed by incrementing that address. The occur-check which is the operation of checking whether a variable occurs in another term is not adopted for efficiency purposes and thus infinite terms are allowed. The variable binding packet consisting of a variable word followed by its binding is sent to the VBS, a variable binding stack, where it is stored, and simultaneously to the consistency check processor (CCP) where the new variable's binding is compared for consistency with any binding that the variable previously had. The CCP processor maintains the variable binding information in a content-addressable memory with parallel write and search capabilities, and the bindings in an internal binding RAM.

The four MPs and the CCP are interconnected by a common variable binding bus, VBB, arbitrated by the control unit (CU). This means that only one MP can transfer its variable binding packet to the CCP, and if other MPs have generated variable bindings ready to be sent to the CCP to be checked, they have to wait until the CCP is done checking the consistency of the current binding. The variable bindings when sent to the CCP are simultaneously pushed onto the VBS and thus no extra time is spent on storing the bindings at the end of unification, as is often needed in other unification architectures [37,39]. The CU in addition to arbitrating the VBB bus (it grants a request of a variable binding packet transfer to the first MP from left), is in charge of communicating with the host processor and informing it of the result of the operation.

The unification algorithm implemented in the parallel unification machine (PUM), and which is given in Fig. 9, proceeds as follows. At the start of unification, each MPi reads the address word from memory module MMi. This 32-bit word holds the addresses of the first pair of arguments to unify in MMi and the number of such arguments in MMi. The MATCH algorithm is executed by the array of MPs while the CONSISTENCY_CHECK algorithm is executed by the CCP. In procedure UNIFY, the function "arity(x)" returns the arity of structure x. Essentially, the MATCH procedure accepts two arguments X and Y and generates the binding X/Y if the match operation succeeds, else it sets the FAIL flag. In the MATCH and CONSISTENCY_CHECK procedures, f and g represent structures or functors, X, Y, Z, and U variables, and a and b

constants. Also, CON, VAR, and FUN refer respectively to the constant, variable, and structure types. Note that lists are a special case of structures and can be handled by the FUN type (where both functors are nil).

The CONSISTENCY_CHECK procedure accepts the binding X/Y where X is always a variable and Y is of any type. If variable X is not bound by previous substitutions then the binding X/Y is recorded. If variable X was previously bound, the new and old bindings are checked for consistency. This procedure is recursively invoked in the CCP in the case where the variable in the variable binding packet read by the CCP is previously bound to a structure, and the binding in the variable binding packet is either a structure or a variable previously bound to a structure. This makes the CCP almost as powerful as a serial unification processor and is only used as a serial unification processor when two variables previously bound to structures are input to it or when a variable previously bound to a structure and a structure are input to it. In these cases, the CCP reads from its internal binding memory the structure to which the variable in the variable binding packet was previously bound to (and similarly reads the structure to which the variable in the binding part of the variable binding packet was previously bound to if it is the case) and unifies the i th argument of the first structure to the i th argument of the second structure, for all i. In all other cases (when the two inputs are not both structures), the CCP checks the consistency of the new binding to any previous bindings the variable had. At the end of unification, the MGU is in the VBS and in the internal memory of the CCP. The algorithm ends and the machine stops operation when 1) the CU detects any failing match operation in the MPs or any failing consistency check operation in the CCP, by checking the status of the FAIL flag; or 2) all MP and CCP processors end operation with success, in which case unification succeeds; this situation occurs when the SUCCEED flag is set. This scheme is a source of high speedup over machines which conduct unification serially due to concurrent match operations which are pipelined with consistency check operations, as well as a capability of early match failure detection.

C Binding Environment and Memory Formats

Binding environment has been well addressed in the literature. Most implementations are based on structure sharing and efficient variable binding information representation. Kale et al. [30] described a binding environment and representations of logic terms in memory. They use structure sharing and distinguish between ground and nonground (i.e. which have unbound variables) terms. To facilitate term referencing and binding, structures with ground arguments and with no reference to tuples are labeled as closed terms, whereas ground terms with tuple references are represented by molecules, which are pointers to terms and tuples. They also described a two-phase unification algorithm. In the first phase, the variable bindings are generated, while in the second phase, the binding management is conducted using a *close* operation.

Whereas some of the binding environments are centralized in some implementations, others are distributed. For instance, in PUM [26-28], the variable bindings are stored in a special store, the VBS. In PUM, four data types and 32-bit words are used. These are variable, function (structure), list, and constant. An encoding similar to the PLM [14] and UNIFIC [19] is adopted. Essentially, a two-bit tag distinguishes between the four types. Constants can be one of: integer, floating point, nil, and symbol. A symbol word can hold up to three characters, and if the symbol contains more than three characters, the remaining characters are stored in the following words in groups of three per word. A variable word has a binding status field indicating whether the variable is not bound (free), temporarily bound (i.e. bound to another free unbound variable), bound to a constant, or bound to a structure. A 20-bit pointer field in the variable word points to the variable symbol in memory. Fig. 11 shows the memory representation of the structure $f(a, h(X),Z,d,g(b,Y))$ and the distribution of its arguments among the memory modules of PUM.

The use of of a content-addressable memory (CAM) to maintain the binding information has proven its success in the SUM [18], UNIFIC [19], and other inference processors. CAMs have not only been used to hold the binding information of variables in Prolog systems, but also to hold clause heads of complete Prolog programs thus implementing OR-parallelism. For instance, Ian Robinson [31] proposed a pattern addressable memory where Prolog clause heads are stored and are matched concurrently (OR-parallelism) against an input goal.

In unification, the use of a content-addressable memory (CAM) can best be examplified by the content-addressable binding memory in the CCP processor of the PUM machine. It is used for holding the variable information in the CCP and allows for parallel search of the variable identifier in the CAM entries and fast retrieval of the binding information of the variable entry that matches the variable identifier. The binding memory in the CCP is composed of a short size CAM holding the variable binding information (BI), the variable identifier and a pointer to the variable's binding in the binding RAM if the variable is bound, and of a binding RAM holding the actual variable bindings. The binding information (BI) is interpreted as follows. The first bit indicates that the variable is temporarily bound to another variable if it is cleared, otherwise it indicates that the variable is bound. When the variable is temporarily bound, the second BI bit is a don't care. When the variable is bound, the second BI bit reflects the type of the binding, for if set, it states that the binding is a structure, otherwise it is a constant.

Fig. 12 illustrates how the variable information and the variable's binding are stored in the binding memory of PUM. It is assumed that the machine is reset and the binding memory cleared initially. Then, as the MPs read and match the pair of arguments and transfer the variable binding packets to the CCP one at a time, the CCP reads these packets and updates the contents of its binding memory according to the variable's binding and the variable's old binding status. In Fig. 12-a, the variable binding $X / g(a)$ is read by the CCP. The variable X is searched in the variables' CAM to match any variable identifier. But no match is found since the CAM is empty. A CAM word for X is created with BI = 11 since X is bound to a structure. The next available entry in the RAM is used to store the binding $g(a)$, and a pointer to that entry is stored in the CAM word's pointer field. In Fig. 12-b, the binding X / Y is received by the CCP, X is searched in the CAM and found to be bound. Y in turn is searched and found to be previously unbound since no entry for Y exists in the CAM. Next, an entry for Y is created in the CAM in which Y is bound to X's binding with the same binding status as X. The binding packet Z / b is then read by the CCP which updates its binding memory as shown in Fig. 12-c. A new CAM word is created for Z with BI= 10 since it is bound to a constant. The pointer field contains the binding RAM's address at which Z's binding "b" is stored. Finally, in Fig. 12-d, the binding packet $X / g(U)$ is read, X is searched in the CAM and found to match its first entry. X's new binding "$g(U)$" is then unified with its old binding "$g(a)$" to check it for consistency. This results in the unification of U with a and the binding U / a is stored in the binding memory by creating a new CAM entry for U and pointing it to the location of a in the RAM.

D Static Scheduling and Data Dependence Analysis

Citrin [3] identified three models for unification parallelism. In the first model, the pair of terms to be simultaneously unified are dynamically selected during run time. The scheduling algorithm is complex since it must guarantee that the pairs of terms to be concurrently unified have no data dependency so that two independent unifications do not bind a common shared variable to two different values. In the second model, all the pairs of terms are unified in parallel, and the generated bindings are checked for consistency. After the consistency check, the bindings are grouped together into one coherent group of variable bindings. PUM [26-28] for instance follows this second model by concurrently unifying (matching) the pairs of arguments of the two structures. This operation results in a number of variable bindings generated. A second operation, which is pipelined and overlapped in time with the match operation, checks the consistency of the bindings. If inconsistent, unification is declared to have failed. The third model of unification parallelism, a data analysis conducted prior to run time determines which terms contain shared variables, i.e. which ones have data dependency. Only those terms which have been identified to be free of data dependencies are allowed to be unified in parallel. The results of these unifications can be safely written in their final destination, memory, and not in temporary storage, because they are guaranteed by the compile-time data analysis to be free of inconsistencies. Thus in the third model, no consistency check is required.

Citrin [3] based his scheduling algorithm on the third model because it does not require consistency checks following matchings and because it avoids the lengthy runtime overheads of the dynamic scheduling of the first model. Thus, the matchings of the pairs of arguments of terms like $f(X,Y,Z) / f(a,b,c)$ are allowed to be processed in parallel due to lack of variable sharing among the arguments of these terms, whereas the matchings of the pairs of arguments in terms like $f(X,Y,X)$ / $f(a,b,c)$ are prevented from being processed in parallel due to the existence of variable sharing among the arguments (in this example, the first and third arguments of the second term share the variable X). In the latter case, the matchings of the pairs of arguments must be done serially. The static data dependency analysis on which Citrin based his static scheduling algorithm is due to Chang [32].

The selection of a static scheduling over dynamic scheduling by Citrin was justified by Delcher and Kasif's [33] argument of the decreased efficiency of dynamically scheduled AND-parallelism with regard to statically scheduled AND-parallelism. This decrease in efficiency was attributed to the NP-completeness of the dynamic scheduling. Since unification parallelism is a special case of AND-parallelism, the same argument applies to unification parallelism. Citrin also stated the disadvantages of dynamic scheduling which, beside resulting in slower execution (due to scheduling overhead), results in a redundant schedule recomputations of several calls to the same entry mode.

Citrin incorporated a procedure splitting technique in Chang's static data dependence analysis scheme. Procedure splitting is used to facilitate the static scheduling of parallel unification of clause heads that are called with goals with different argument dependencies. For instance, one copy of the procedure can handle goals with arguments with no data dependencies and thus the arguments of the clause head and the goal can be unified in parallel. The other copy would handle calls from goals with data dependencies and thus the unification of the arguments of the clause head with those of the goal would have to be processed serially. Citrin also explored ways to control infinite procedure splitting in recursive calls of increasing complexity.

E Parallel Unification Hardware

In this section, we briefly summarize and discuss the architecture and performance of some parallel unifiers that have been proposed and/or implemented.

-PUM: PUM was described in section B. Two versions exist. One with shared memory [26-27] and the other with distributed memory [28]. With a machine cycle time of 50 ns, the PUM with shared memory exhibited a speedup of 1.5-2.5 for terms of average size over the serial unification co-processor UNIFIC [19]. However, for more complex terms with larger arities (larger than 3) speedups of larger than 2.5 were possible. On the average, PUM with shared memory conducts unification roughly 3-6 times faster than the HUU unit [26-27]. PUM with distributed memory distributes the arguments of terms to be unified over a number of independent memory modules equal to the number of match processors (MPs) used. PUM with distributed memory exhibited a speedup of 2-3 for average sized terms over UNIFIC. For complex terms with large arities, large speedups were recorded. In the extreme cases conforming to the example in Fig. 8, speedups larger than 21 were recorded [28]. For average sized terms, and with a shared memory, only 3 MPs were necessary to reach top performance, and the speedup curve started to saturate after 3 MPs. These results agree with Citrin's recommendation of using 2 to 3 unification processors, and with Singhal and Patt's [34-35] results, as well as Inagawa's [36].This is attributed to the average number of arguments per compound term which was measured to be around 3.

Sibai [29] compared the performance of PUM with shared memory (PUM-SM) to the version with distributed memory (PUM-DM). For average sized terms, PUM-DM only offerred a mediocre speedup over PUM-SM in the range 1.03-1.32 with 2 MPs, and 1.05-1.40 with 3 MPs. In general, for successful unifications, mediocre speedup of PUM-DM over PUM-SM were recorded. However when failing complex unifications with large arities were simulated, speedups larger than 4 were obtained. This was attributed to the early failure detection at the match level of PUM. The failure detection capability was further enhanced by the distribution of the arguments over independent memory modules. Again, the result that larger unification parallelism speedups can be recorded for more complex terms with large arities agrees with Citrin's [3].

-PMV-2: Shobatake and Aiso [37] at Keio University designed a uniform cellular hardware structure to perform unification. This cellular systolic array is VLSI-implementable and is composed of a number of processing cells. Each processing cell contains two registers. The first is capable of storing a symbol with its arity and the second register is capable of holding a symbol without its arity. Each cell has a left channel and a right channel connecting the cell with its left and right neighbors, and hardware for comparing the symbols in the registers. Also, each cell is connected to a common bus. This systolic array performs unification by shifting the two terms to be unified, the first from right to left and the other from left to right until they meet in a cell in the middle of the array where the symbols are compared. The machine follows a structure copy scheme and utilizes shifting mechanisms to replace variables by their bindings. This architecture offers a simple implementation of the occur check. However, the critical characteristic of this design is that for n symbols in the input terms, the required number of cells which represents the length of the array is very large and is on the order of $O(n^{2n})$.

Shobatake and Aiso [38] later presented a parallel Prolog architecture, PMV-2, that is based on the cellular unifiers described above [37] and with processing speed estimated at 450 KLIPS. Several cellular unifiers operate in parallel, and are connected by a tree-like goal mapper/collector packet-switching network to the goal reducer, a unit which maintains binding information and supplies the cellular unifiers with goal terms to be unified. Essentially, a kind of OR-parallelism takes place in the unifiers where the goal terms sent by the goal reducer are unified in parallel with their own program clause head. The cellular unifier whose unification succeeds sends the bindings back to the goal reducer. The length of the cell array is determined by the length of the program clauses and the lengths of the terms in them. In the simulation studies, Shobatake and Aiso assumed a cellular array unifier length of 128 cells, and a depth of the tree network of 16 levels and an array length of the reduce goal buffer of 512 cells. They also assume a memory access time of 25 ns. Their results show that the speed of the machine is enhanced by reducing the mean packet length. Also, the longer the list length, the faster the execution. They recorded a machine speed of 466 KLIPS for a list length of 15 for the *member* procedure.

- Overlapping Unification Array: Chen an Hsieh [39] proposed an overlapping algorithm originating from Robinson's algorithm and a one-dimensional systolic array that executes this algorithm. This systolic array with overlapped matching and substitution phases consists of one matching unit (MU) and a number of substitution units (SU) connected by two buses: the U-bus and the D-bus. The architecture of this machine is given in Fig. 13. In Robinson's original unification algorithm, the substitution generated by the unification of the terms' first arguments is applied to all the remaining arguments before the terms' second arguments are unified. In other words, Robinson's algorithm executes the matching phase and the substitution phase sequentially. In Chen and Hsieh's unification algorithm and machine, the matching and substitution phases are overlapped and executed sequentially. This can be seen in the unification of $f(X,b,h(X,Y))$ and $f(a,Y,h(X,Z))$ as illustrated below.

1. Matching the term heads, f and f, succeeds.
2. Unifying the first arguments generates the first substitution X/a.
3. The first substitution X/a is applied to the second arguments without changing them.
4. The first substitution X/a is applied to the third arguments updating the two terms to $f(X,b,h(a,Y))$ and $f(a,Y,h(a,Z))$ while, simultaneously, the second arguments are unified to yield the second substitution Y/b.
5. The second substitution Y/b is applied to the third arguments updating the two terms to $f(a,b,h(a,b))$ and $f(a,b,h(a,Z))$.
6. Unifying the third arguments yields the substitution Z/b.
7. The MGU consisting of the three substitutions { X/a, Y/b, Z/b } is generated.

The overlapped matching and substitution phases are clearly seen in step 4. More overlapped matching and substitution phases take place in terms of larger arity. The following is a step-by-step description of Chen and Hsieh's unification array unifying the above two terms.

1. Initially, the two terms are stored in SU1 (see Fig. 13).
2. SU1 sends { f, f } to MU via the D-bus.
3. SU1 sends { X, a } to MU via the D-bus.
4. MU generates the substitution X/a and sends it back to SU1 via the U-bus.

5. SU1 applies the substitution X/a on the second arguments $\{ b, Y \}$ and sends $\{ b, Y \}$ to be matched in MU via the D-bus.

6. MU generates the second substitution b/Y and sends it over the U-bus to SU2, while SU1 applies the first substitution on the third arguments $h(X,Y)$ and $h(X,Z)$ and then sends the result $\{ h(a,Y), h(a,Z) \}$ to SU2.

7. SU2 applies b/Y to $\{ h(a,Y),h(a,Z) \}$ and sends $\{h(a,b),h(a,Z) \}$ to MU over the D-bus.

8. MU generates b/Z and sends it to SU3 via the U-bus.

Obviously, this simple one-dimensional array generates the substitutions in linear time. However, the number of substitution units needed must be exactly equal to the number of substitutions in the terms being unified. Since the number of substitutions in the terms depends on the terms themselves and more specifically on the argument types themselves, the worst case scenario should be assumed in determining the number of SUs needed. For instance, the number of SUs needed to unify two terms such that all arguments of one term are different variables, and all arguments of the second term are ground, is the number of variables in the first term which is the arity of the term. This, as is the case in Shobatake and Aiso's cellular array, makes the design very costly.

Another problem with the overlapping unification array is the low utilization rate of the SUs. Assuming that the worst case scenario is adopted, a large number of SUs will be incorporated in the array, and since on the average, Prolog terms have only three arguments, a large number of these SUs will be idle. Furthermore, reading the two terms to be unified in their entirety at the beginning of the unification operation as indicated by step 1 of the previous example is a serious source of inefficiency of this design. This is because reading the two terms in their entirety is wasted when an early failure of unification exists. For example, this systolic machine cannot detect the early unification failure in the terms $f(a,g(X,h(U),b,c),h(X),h(Y),d)$ and $f(b,g(X,h(U),b,c),h(V),Z,d)$. In fact, reading these two terms before detecting the early failure makes the machine considerably slower than other unification machines (e.g. PUM) which read the heads of these terms and then the arguments one by one (and not the entire two terms at once) and match the arguments as they are read.

-PUP/PLUM: Singhal [40] designed a parallel unification processor (PUP) that consists of several unification units (simulation specifies this number to be three), a node table, a control unit, and a prefetch unit. The architecture of PUP is given in Fig. 14. Since it is based on the WAM model, it can process any of the *get*, *put*, or *unify* WAM instructions that are fetched by the prefetch unit to one of the unification units.To synchronize the unifications that take place in the unification units, write-once registers are used, that is the registers in their first access are always written, and later on accesses to these registers are reads. Simulation of the PUP reveals speedups between 1.4-2.44 over PLM [14].

Singhal and Patt [34-35] then proposed the PLUM processor, a Prolog processor exploiting fine grain parallelism and into which the PUP is integrated. PLUM with three unification units has been shown to achieve an average speedup of 3.2 over VLSI-PLM [34]. The Prolog processing in PLUM is enhanced by overlapping choicepoint maintenance and backtracking operations with unification operations. It consists of several caches, an environment unit, a choicepoint unit, a trail unit, a fetch unit, an arithmetic unit, as well as several unification units. Two write buses connect the unification units with the trail unit, arithmetic unit, and the prefetch unit. Although an instruction may be scheduled to a functional unit, the unit idles until its operands are available. Each functional unit has eight register sets with eight argument registers and eight special registers. The consistency of the contents of the registers is ensured by forcing the updates of registers to use one of the two write buses. Access to the heap pointer is synchronized, unification operations that bind variables stall until the previous procedure completes, and unifications of pairs of arguments of a clause head which share one or more variable are synchronized so that all bindings are consistent. They identify the following problems with Citrin's static scheduling scheme: i) the execution time of each set of unifications is directly determined by the time of the longest unification in the set; and ii) after a variable shared by more than one term is bound, the unification of the terms cannot be overlapped. For that purpose, they use an improved version of Citrin's static scheduling in which they distinguish between shared variables assigned to registers (type 1) and those which are unbound in memory and whose reference is shared by more than one argument (type 2). Type 2 variables, although rare to occur as their simulations of common Prolog benchmarks reveal, require synchronization to avoid inconsistencies. A static analysis is used to recognize the type 2 variables, and the unifications of arguments that share these variables are serialized by PLUM's prefetch unit which is designed to assign/fetch these unifications to the same unification unit. Simulation of PLUM reveals that PLUM with 4 unification units can execute unification on the average 1.7 times faster than PLUM with a single unification unit can. This speedup limit is attributed to the limited unification parallelism that Prolog benchmarks can provide. (This is also true for other parallel unification machines such as PUM).

- Other projects: Shih and Irani [41] proposed a two-dimensional mesh of hardware unifiers exploiting AND-parallelism. This mesh of unifiers was designed to be used as a co-processor and to be invoked mainly when the number of terms (subgoals) in a clause body and the size of the program (i.e. number of clauses) are both large. Shih and Irani also proposed four binding algorithms responsible for determining the destination columns of tokens in the mesh and studied their performance on their proposed architecture. This two-dimensional array of unifiers is composed of unification units each enclosing a CPU with comparison capability, and two buffer memories to hold the tokens, and an arbiter-multiplexer to direct tokens to one of five possible destinations encompassing the four neighboring unification units and one buffer memory inside the unit.

Inagawa et al. [36] developed a shared-memory PROLOG multiprocessor with four 16-bit processors with each 8Kbytes of local memory, and 512 Kbytes of shared memory. The multiprocessor performs parallel unification and achieves a 55 KLIPS performance with a machine cycle time of 550 nanoseconds. This machine uses a compiler-interpreter combination based on DEC 10 PROLOG. The interpreter executes the PROLOG machine instructions into which the source program is translated, while the compiler decomposes compound terms, allocates processes to the processors, places the object code into memory and allocates variables to processors. If the unification of a pair of arguments fails in one processor, the processor requests backtracking, all four processors terminate their execution, and the variables, registers, and stacks are reset. If unification succeeds, the processors write the bindings to the shared memory. Inagawa et al.'s multiprocessor conducts the consistency check on the generated bindings as follows. Variables requiring consistency checks, that is the variables shared by a structure's arguments, are stored in the shared memory. Before updating the values of the variables in memory, the old values are read by the processor and checked for consistency with the new binding, and if both bindings are consistent, the new binding is written in the shared memory. In order to parallelize unification, structures are decomposed into functors and arguments and a compile-time clustering scheme is used whereby some consistency checks on some variables may be eliminated by allocating the same variables to an assigned processor.

Tanabe and Aiso [42] proposed a four-stage pipelined unification processor. The terms are expressed as sequences of symbols with their arities as in [37]. The occur check is handled by the pipeline. They perform the creation of the disagreement set [4] of the terms and the consistency check in a pipelined fashion. They as in [26-27] note that the consistency check and the term matchings can be performed independently by different processors. Although this pipelined processor can detect early unification failure of structures with distinct functors, it does not perform the term matchings in different processors as PUM [26-28] does, and thus does not possess PUM's early detection capability of other unification failures at the match level. They claim that the hardware cost of the pipelined processor has a quadratic complexity order and that its computation complexity is of linear order after reordering the terms to be unified.

Ito et al. [43] proposed a data flow model that incorporates parallel unification. Incorporated are capabilities for term unification, consistency checks, substitutions, and structure decomposition.

Beer and Giloi [44] proposed a ring of unification units. The units idle until their arguments are available. The units have their own local memory and access a shared memory holding the local stack, trail stack, and global stack. These resources have no contention problems due to the passing of the pointers to these resources around the ring. Specifically, the unification units relinquish access to those resources by passing the pointers to another unit in the ring, after being finished with accessing these resources. The trail pointer is also made a shared resource capability that is passed around the ring to avoid binding inconsistencies.

Kogge et al. [45] discussed the use of CAMs in unification, clause filtering, backtracking and dereferencing. As in several hardware unifiers, the use of CAM in unification avoids the need for a trail after unification backtracking, following a unification failure. They also pointed out the suitability of CAMs to hold multiple copies of variable bindings in Parallel Prolog systems. Finally, Ng et al. [46] proposed a content-addressable table for unification processing with four cycles: two search cycles, one tag manipulation cycle, and one read/write cycle.

5 Conclusion

We have described techniques for parallel unification, reviewed the theory behind it, and reviewed parallel unification algorithms, as well as parallel architectures for unification. Among these summarized architectures for unification are systolic arrays, pipelined machines, and multiprocessors. An effort was made to identify the advantages and disadvantages of each design.

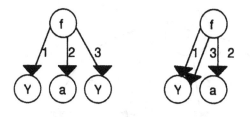

a. Tree Representation   b. Graph Representation with Sharing

Fig. 1   Compound Term Representations

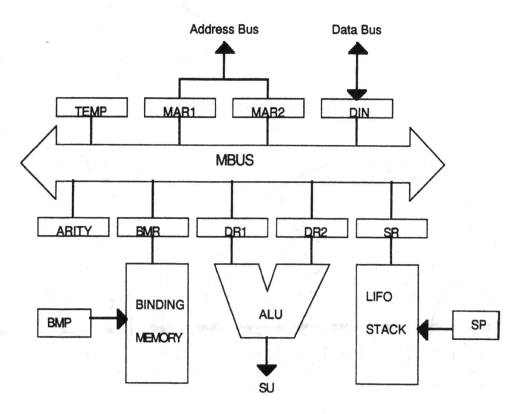

Fig. 2   Organization of UNIFIC

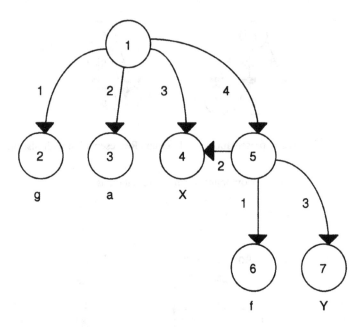

Fig. 3   Dag Representation of *g(a, X, f(X, Y))*

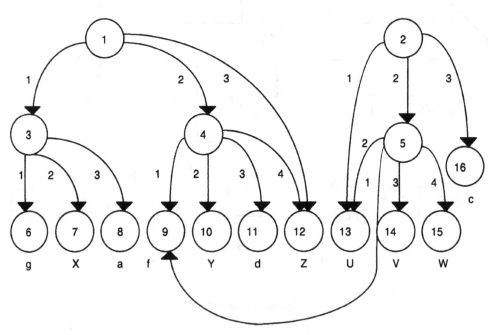

Fig. 4   Dags for [*g(X, a) f(Y, d, Z) Z*] and [*U f(U, V, W) c*]

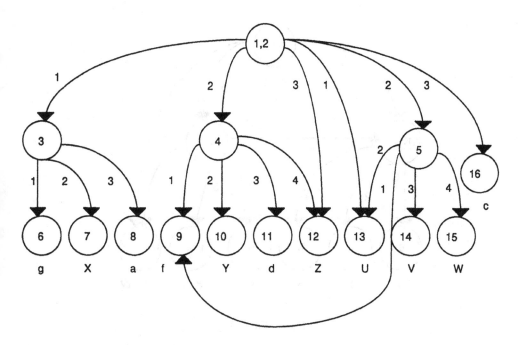

Fig. 5 Combined Dag After Merging Nodes 1 and 2

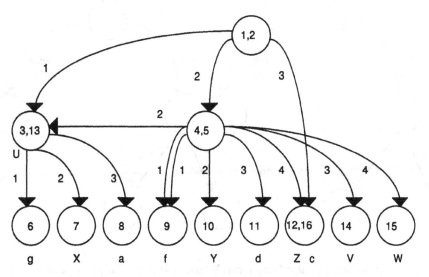

Fig. 6 Dag After the Merger of Nodes 3 and 13, and 4 and 5

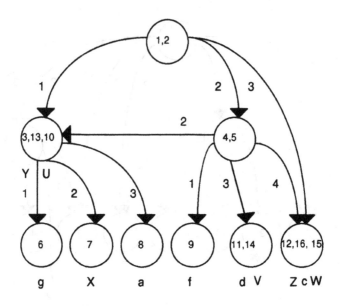

Fig. 7   Final Dag

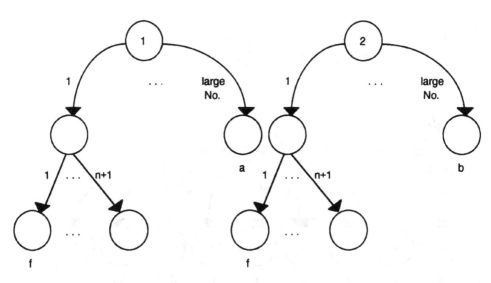

Fig. 8   Dags for Two Non-unifiable Long Terms Whose Unification Fails in the Last Arguments

PROCEDURE UNIFY: PARALLEL_BEGIN_UNIFY

> **PARFOR** i:=1 to 4 **DO**
>> **BEGIN_PARFOR**
>>> Read address word from memory module MMi and
>>> Load number of pair of arguments to match into ARCNTi
>>> **WHILE** ARCNTi not zero **DO**
>>>> **BEGIN_WHILE**
>>>>> Read arguments (x, y)
>>>>> MATCH(x,y) and **IF** both x and y are functors
>>>>> **THEN** ARCNTi = ARCNTi + arity(x)
>>>>> **IF** match fails **THEN** set FAIL flag and **STOP**
>>>>> **ELSE IF** a binding x/y is generated
>>>>>> **THEN** request transfer of binding to CCP and VBS
>>>>> ARCNTi = ARCNTi - 1 and wait until binding is transferred
>>>> **END_WHILE**
>> **END_PARFOR**

> **LOOP FOREVER**
>> **IF** there is a granted transfer request **THEN** transfer the
>> variable binding x/y to CCP and to VBS from the requesting MP
>> CONSISTENCY_CHECK(x, y)
>> **IF** check fails **THEN** set FAIL flag and **STOP**
>>> **ELSE IF** last binding **THEN** set SUCCEED flag and **STOP**
> **END_LOOP**

PARALLEL_END_UNIFY

PROCEDURE MATCH(x, y) : BEGIN_MATCH

> **CASE** x, y **OF**
>> both CON: **IF** x ≠ y **THEN** set FAIL flag
>> both VAR: temporarily bind x/y
>> VAR/CON or CON/VAR: bind VAR to CON
>> FUN/VAR or VAR/FUN: bind VAR to FUN [note: no occur check]
>> FUN/CON or CON/FUN: set FAIL flag
>> FUN/FUN: **IF** x≠y **THEN** set FAIL flag

END_MATCH

Fig. 9 Parallel Unification Algorithm

PROCEDURE CONSISTENCY_CHECK(X,Y): BEGIN_CONSISTENCY_CHECK

CASE Y OF

CON a: CASE X OF
X not bound: record X/a
X bound to b: IF a≠b **THEN** set FAIL flag
X bound to f: set FAIL flag
X temp. bound to Y: record X,Y/a

VAR Y: CASE X, Y OF
both not bound: temporarily bind X/Y
X/a, Y/f or X/f, Y/a: set FAIL flag
X/a, Y/b: IF a≠b **THEN** set FAIL flag
X/a or f, Y not bound: record Y/a or f
X not bound, Y/a or f: record X/a or f
X/Z, Y/U: temporarily bind X/Y/Z/U
X/Z, Y not bound: record X/Y/Z
X not bound, Y/Z: record X/Y/Z
X/Z, Y/a or f: record X/Z/a or f
X/a or f, Y/Z: record Y/Z/a or f
X/g, Y/f: IF functor(g)≠functor(f)
THEN set FAIL flag
ELSE FOR i=1 **TO** arity(f) **DO**   [assume arity(f)=arity(g)]
CONSISTENCY_CHECK(ith argument of g, ith argument of f)

FUN f: CASE X OF
X not bound: record X/f
X temp. bound to Z: record X/Z/f
X bound to a: set FAIL flag
X bound to g: IF functor(g)≠functor(f)
THEN set FAIL flag
ELSE FOR i=1 **TO** arity(f) **DO**   [assume arity(f)=arity(g)]
CONSISTENCY_CHECK(ith argument of g, ith argument of f)

END_CONSISTENCY_CHECK

Fig. 9 Parallel Unification Algorithm (Continued)

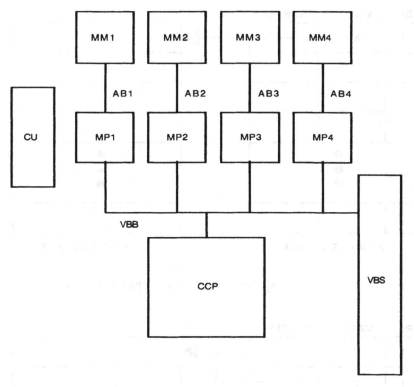

Fig. 10 Architecture of the Parallel Unification Machine with Distributed Memory

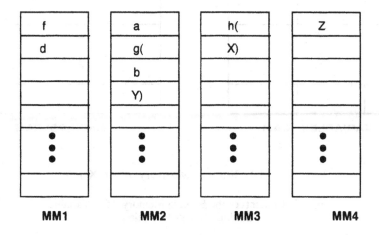

Fig. 11   Distribution of the Arguments of the Structure $f(a, h(X),Z,d,g(b,Y))$ in Memory

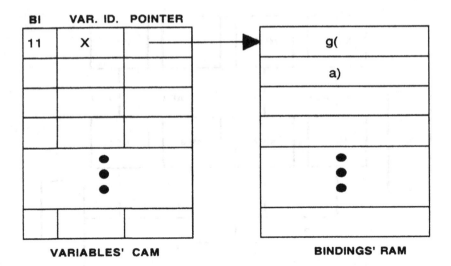

a) Binding Memory after X / g(a)

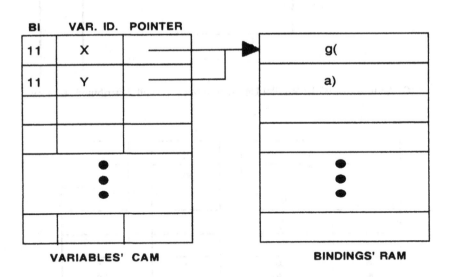

b) Binding Memory after X / Y

Fig. 12 Contents of the Binding Memory After Variable
Binding Packets Reception

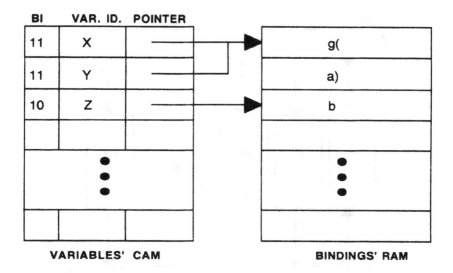

c) Binding Memory after Z / b

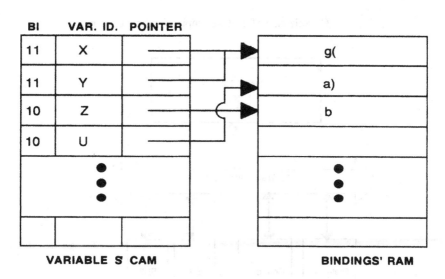

d) Binding Memory after X / g(U)

Fig. 12 (Continued)

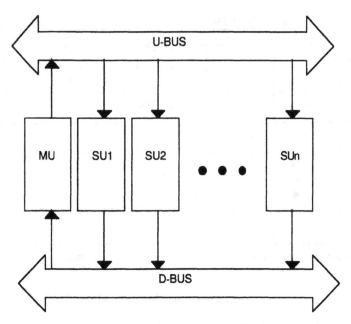

Fig. 13 Organization of the Overlapping Unification Array

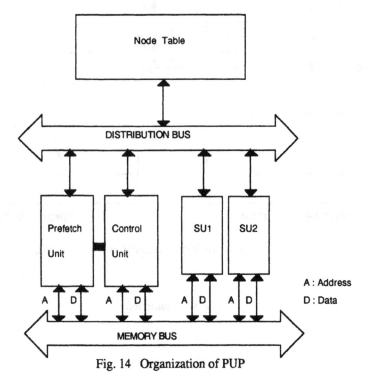

Fig. 14 Organization of PUP

References

[1]   Dwork , C. et al.,"On the Sequential Nature of Unification," *J. Logic Programming*, vol. 1(1), pp. 35-50, June 1984.

[2]   Yasuura, H.,"On Parallel Computational Complexity of Unification," *Proc. of the Int. Conf. on Fifth Generation Computer Systems*," Tokyo, Japan, pp. 235-248, Nov. 1984.

[3]   Citrin, W.,"Parallel Unification Scheduling in Prolog," Ph.D. Dissertation, EECS Dept., University of California, Berkeley, 1988.

[4]   Robinson, J.A.,"A Machine-Oriented Logic Based on the Resolution Principle," *J. of the ACM*, vol. 12 (1), pp. 23-41, Jan. 1965.

[5]   Knight, K.,"Unification:A Multidisciplinary Survey," *ACM Computing Surveys*, vol. 21 (1), pp. 93-124, March 1989.

[6]   Paterson, M. S., and Wegman, M. N.,"Linear Unification," *J. of Computer and Sys. Sciences*, vol. 16 (2), pp. 158-167, April 1978.

[7]   De Champeaux, Dennis,"About the Paterson-Wegman Linear Unification Algorithm," *J. of Computer and Sys.Sciences*, vol. 32 (1), pp. 79-90, Feb. 1986.

[8]   Martelli, A., and Montanari, U.,"An Efficient Unification Algorithm," *ACM Trans. on Prog. Lang. and Sys.*, vol. 4(2), pp. 258-282, April 1982.

[9]   Martelli, A., and Rossi, G., "Efficient Unification with Infinite Terms in Logic Programming," *Proc. International Conf. on Fifth Generation Computer Systems*, Tokyo, Japan, 1984.

[10]   Boriello, G., Cherenson, A., Danzig, P., and Nelson, M., "RISCs vs. CISCs for Prolog: A Case Study," *Proc. of 2nd Int. Conf. on Architectural Support for Prog. Lang. and Operating Sys.*, Palo Alto, CA, Oct. 1987, pp. 136-145.

[11]   Diel, H., Lenz, N., and Welsch, H.,"An Experimental Computer Architecture for Supporting Expert Systems and Logic Programming," *IBM J. of Research and Development*, vol. 30 (1), Jan. 1986.

[12]   Taki, K. et al., "Hardware Design and Implementation of the Personal Sequential Inference Machine (PSI)," *Proc. International Conf. on Fifth Generation Computer Systems*, Tokyo, Japan, 1984.

[13]   Carlsson, M., "A Microcoded Unifier for Lisp Machine Prolog," *Proc. of the 2nd Symp. on Logic programming*, July 1985.

[14]   Dobry, T., "A Prolog Machine Architecture," Ph.D. Dissertation, EECS Dept., University of California, Berkeley, May 1987. Also available as Tech. Report UCB/CSD 87/352.

[15]   Woo, N. S.,"A Hardware Unification Unit: Design and Analysis," *12th An. Int. Symp. on Computer Architecture*, Boston, MA, pp. 198-205, June 1985.

[16]   Woo, N. S.,"The Architecture of the Hardware Unification Unit and an Implementation," *Proc. 18th An. Workshop on Microprogramming*, Pacific Grove, CA, pp. 89-98, 1985.

[17] Chang, S.,"Towards a Theorem Proving Architecture," M.S. Thesis, CS Dept., California Institute of Technology, Pasadena, CA, 1981.

[18] Robinson, P.,"The SUM:An AI Coprocessor," *Byte*, vol. 10(6), pp. 169-180, June 1985.

[19] Gollakota, R.,"Design and Analysis of UNIFIC: A Coprocessor for the Unification Algorithm," M.S. Thesis, Dept. of EE, Texas A&M University, College Station, TX, August 1986.

[20] Parikh, P.,"VLSI Design of the Controller for the UNIFIC - A Prolog Unification Coprocessor," M.S. Thesis, Dept. of EE, Texas A&M University, College Station, TX, May 1987.

[21] Maluszynski, J., and Komorowski, H., "Unification-free execution of Horn-Clause Programs," *Proc. of 2nd Logic Programming Symp.*, N.Y., 1985.

[22] Ramesh, R. et al., "Term Matching on Parallel Computers," *J. Logic Programming*, vol. 6, pp. 213-228, 1989.

[23] Vitter, J., and Simons, R.,"New Classes for Parallel Complexity: A Study of Unification and Other Complete Problems for P," *IEEE Trans. on Comp.*, vol. C-35 (5), pp. 403-418, May 1986.

[24] Harland, J., and Jaffar, J., "On Parallel Unification for Prolog," *New Generation Comp.*, vol. 5, 1987.

[25] Robinson, J. A.,"Natural and Artificial Reasoning," in *Natural and Artificial Parallel Computation*, M. Arbib and J. A. Robinson, EDs., MIT Press, pp. 277-309, 1990.

[26] Sibai, Fadi N.,"A Parallel Machine for the Unification Algorithm: Design, Simulation, and Performance Evaluation," Ph.D. Dissertation, Dept. of EE, Texas A&M University, College Station, TX, December 1989.

[27] Sibai, F. N., Watson, K. L., and Lu, M. , "A Parallel Unification Machine," *IEEE MICRO*, Vol. 10 (4), pp.21-33, August 1990.

[28] Sibai, F. N.,"Parallel Unification with Distributed Memory," *The International Journal of Mini and Microcomputers*, Vol. 12 (3), pp.113-118, 1990.

[29] Sibai, F. N., "On Memory Organizations for Match Parallelism in Parallel Unification," submitted for publication.

[30] Kale, L. V., Ramkumar, B., and Shu, W., "A Memory Organization Independent Binding Environment for AND and OR Parallel Execution of Logic Programs," *Proc. of the fifth Int. Conf. and Symp. on Logic Programming*, vol. II, MIT Press, pp. 1223-1240, 1988.

[31] Robinson, Ian, "A Prolog Processor Based on a Pattern Matching Memory Device," *Proc. of 3rd Conf. on Logic Programming*," London, U.K., pp. 172-179, July 1986.

[32] Chang, J.,"High Performance Execution of Prolog Programs Based on a Static Data Dependency Analysis," Ph.D. Dissertation, EECS Dept., University of California, Berkeley, October 1985.

[33]   Delcher, A., and Kasif, S., "Some Results on the Complexity of Exploiting Data
        Dependency in Parallel Logic Programs," *J. Logic Programming*, vol. 6, pp. 229-
        241, 1989.

[34]   Singhal, A., and Patt, Y. N.,"A High Performance Prolog Processor with Multiple
        Function Units," *Proc. 16th AN. Int. Symp. on Comp. Architecture*, Jerusalem,
        pp. 195-202, 1989.

[35]   Singhal, A., and Patt, Y. N., "Unification Parallelism: How Much Can We Exploit ?,"
        Proc. of the North American Conf. on Logic Programming, vol. II, MIT Press, pp. 1135-
        1147, 1989.

[36]   Inagawa, M. et al.,"Unification Parallelism for Prolog Processing," *Sys. and Comp. in
        Japan*, vol. 19 (1), pp. 37-46, Jan. 1988.

[37]   Shobatake, Y., and Aiso, H.,"The Unification Processor Based on a Uniformly Structure
        Cellular Hardware," *Proc. 13th An. Int. Symp. on Comp. Architecture*, Tokyo, Japan,
        pp. 140-148, June 1986.

[38]   Shobatake, Y., and Aiso, H.,"A Prolog Machine Based on VLSI Algorithms," *Sys. and
        Comp. in Japan*, vol. 20 (2), pp. 15-24, 1989.

[39]   Chen, W., and Hsieh, K,"An overlapping Unification Algorithm and its Hardware
        Implementation," *Proc. Int. Conf. on Parallel Processing*, University Park, PA,
        pp. 803-805, 1987.

[40]   Singhal, A.,"PUP: An Architecture to Exploit Parallel Unification in Prolog," M.S. Thesis,
        EECS Dept., University of California, Berkeley, 1987.

[41]   Shih, Y., and Irani, K.,"Large Scale Unification Using a Mesh-Connected Array of
        Hardware Unifiers," *Proc. Int. Conf. on Parallel Processing*, University Park, PA,
        pp. 787-794, 1987.

[42]   Tanabe, M., and Aiso, H.,"The Unification Processor by Pipeline Method," in *Database
        Machines and Knowledge Base Machines*, M. Kitsuregawa and H. Tanaka, EDs., Kluwer
        Acad. Pub., Boston, MA, pp. 627-639, 1988.

[43]   Ito, N. et al.,"Data-Flow Based Execution Mechanisms of Parallel and Concurrent Prolog,"
        New Generation Comp., No. 3, pp. 15-41, 1985.

[44]   Beer, J., and Giloi, W.K., "POPE - A Parallel-Operating Prolog Engine," Tech. Report,
        GMD-FIRST/TU-Berlin.

[45]   Kogge, P. et al.,"VLSI and Rule-Based Systems," in *VLSI for Artificial Intelligence*, J.
        Delgado-Frias and W. Moore, EDs., Kluwer, Norwell, MA, pp. 95-108, 1989.

[46]   Ng, Y. et al.,"Unify with Active Memory,"in *VLSI for Artificial Intelligence*, J.
        Delgado-Frias and W. Moore, EDs., Kluwer, Norwell, MA, pp. 109-118, 1989.

Connectionist Inference Systems

Hans Werner Güsgen

Gesellschaft für Mathematik und Datenverarbeitung (GMD)

Schloß Birlinghoven

5205 Sankt Augustin 1

gmdzi!guesgen@uunet.uu.net

Steffen Hölldobler

FG Intellektik, FB Informatik, TH Darmstadt

Alexanderstraße 10

6100 Darmstadt

steffen@intellektik.informatik.th-darmstadt.de

Abstract

This paper presents a survey of connectionist inference systems.

1 Motivation

In almost all situations of our life we make decisions based on huge amounts of knowledge, which is often vague, incomplete, or even inconsistent. We have gathered the knowledge as well as the decision procedures in a long process of education and experience. In fact, the learning process never stops throughout our life. Many of our decisions can be viewed as inference processes, where we apply certain rules of inference to a given situation and to our aquired knowledge in order to achieve a certain goal. Humans can perform a wide variety of inferences extremely fast. The inference processes needed to solve object recognition, speech processing, story understanding, or commonsense reasoning tasks are just four examples.

On the first glance this observation is surprising as the main building block of the human nervous system, the neuron, is quite slow. Its computational speed is a few milliseconds and must account for the complex behavior carried out in a few hundred milliseconds [Posner, 1978]. This means that entire complex behaviors are carried out in less than a hundred time steps [Feldman and Ballard, 1982]. Within the field of Artificial Intelligence many attemps were made to model such complex behaviors. But current models need millions of time steps. Moreover, many of the problems that humans can solve almost instanteneously as if it were a reflex become intractable if modelled in a conventional way (cf., [Shastri, 1989a]). There seems to be only one possible conclusion. Massive parallelism must take place in the human nervous system.

Though the human nervous system is structured there is no central controller which supervises the activities of the various parts. Rather the neurons, which are interconnected through excitatory and inhibitory synapses, perform local operations only. These operations – like thresholding operations or spatial or temporal summation – seem to be quite simple. Moreover, neurons are not capable of transmitting significant amounts of symbolic information. All the knowledge seems to be encoded in the connections of the netrons and in the strength with which neurons excite or inhibit each other.

But our nervous system has more remarkable features. It is quite robust. Neurons are dying constantly. Nevertheless, this does not seem to hamper our skills unless our nervous system is injured in an accident or handicapped through a desease. Our nervous system can handle noisy input up to a certain level. It degrades gracefully if the noise level is increased. The nervous system is evidential in that it gathers information in order to make the *best* decision. It is also context-sensitive, and has general and powerful mechanisms for learning and generalization.

Recently, connectionist or artificial neural networks have received much attention as they were applied in models of behavior which match psychological data, are biological plausible and computationally efficient (cf., [Rumelhart *et al.*, 1986b]). These applications are mainly concerned with low-level cognitive tasks such as perception (cf., [McClelland and Rumelhart, 1981]), motor control, associative information retrieval (cf. [Hopfield, 1982]), or feature discovery (cf., [Rumelhart and Zipser, 1985]). Considerably less experience has been gathered so far in modelling high-level cognitive tasks using connectionist networks. How do we know that *pot* refers to *cooking-pot* in one context and to *marijuana* in a different context (cf., [Lange and Dyer, 1989a])? How do we understand stories? How are rules learned such that we can follow them almost immediately after they were told to us (cf., [Hadley, 1990])? How is knowledge represented and how do we reason about this knowledge?

To reason about knowledge is one of the main goals of the field of mathematical logic and deduction. Already G.W. Leibnitz (1646-1716) proposed the idea of a *lingua characteristica*, in which every possibly truth can be expressed, a *calculus ratiocanator*, in which every possible truth can be computed, and a *universal encyclopedia*, where all knowledge is represented. Though we know by now that there is neither a lingua characteristica nor a calculus ratiocanator in the sense of Leibnitz, we have gathered quite some experience in representing knowledge in a formal symbolic language such that conclusions can be drawn logically using a suitable inference mechanism.

The field of automated reasoning has mainly concentrated on mechanizing inference processes on a conventional computer and was not really concerned with the question of how humans reason. Automated reasoning systems are still rather slow in solving interesting problems. They have quite impressive power, but they are poor in exercising control over the reasoning process. They do not yet exhibit a reasonable form of *common sense*. They are not yet adequate in the sense that they should solve simpler problems faster than more difficult ones (cf., [Bibel, 1990]). Last but not least they are not adapted to massive parallelism.

The super computing community is convinced that by the year 2000 the fastest computers will be massively parallel. Hence, massive parallelism may serve as a vehicle to reconcile the research in the field of connectionism and the field of automated reasoning. We do not just want to build systems which show intelligent behavior, we also want to understand how humans do it. Both fields may profit from insights into connectionist inference systems. Automated reasoning systems may not only be more efficient, they may also be able to solve more interesting problems and may be more adequate. Conversely, the vast knowledge and techniques developed in the field of automated reasoning can be applied to model high-level inferences in a connectionist setting.

This article gives an overview of the state of the art in connectionist inference systems. Inference in this article is to be understood as a kind of *high-level* inference in the sense that conclusions are inferred from a given set of facts and rules. After a brief introduction into connectionist systems in the following section, we distinquish two classes of systems based on their principle mode of operation. Connectionist inference systems based on *energy minimization* are essentially symmetric networks of binary threshold units which compute by minimizing the energy encoded in the network (section 3). Connectionist inference systems based on *spreading of activation* are essentially structured networks, where patterns of activation are propagated through the network (section 4). In section 3 as well as in section 4 we will briefly describe the basic techniques followed by the systems based on these techniques. Section 5 gives a brief overview of two hybrid conventional and connectionist systems, where the conventional part is a PROLOG system and connectionist techniques were used to learn a heuristic from examples. An outlook to current research problems completes the article.

2 Connectionist Systems

Connectionist systems aim at modeling aspects of the animal and human nervous system on an abstract computational level (cf. [Feldman and Ballard, 1982; Rumelhart *et al.*, 1986b]). The central concept in a connectionist system is the individual *unit*. It models the functionality of a neuron or a group of neurons. Following [Feldman and Ballard, 1982] each unit is characterized by

- p the *potential*, which is a real number,
- v the *value*, which is an integer such that $0 \leq v \leq 9$, and
- i the input vector $i_1, \ldots, i_n$.

The potential p represents the action potential of a neuron. The value v represents the output of a firing neuron. The restriction of v to a finite number of integers is biologically motivated by the fact that the firing frequence of a neuron is between one and a few hundred impulses per second and that neurons react within 1/10-th of a second. Hence, the frequency can encode only a very limited amount of information. The input i represents the input received by a neuron either externally as the output of a receptor or internally as the weighted and possibly modified output of another unit.

The units are connected via a set of directed, weighted, and possibly modified links. The weight w_{kj} on a connection from unit j to unit k represents the strength with which a neuron excites or inhibits another neuron. A modifier may be either 1 or 0 and allows to quickly *turn* connections *on* and *off*. Hence, the input i_j received by unit k on its connection from unit j is determined by $w_{kj}m_jv_j$, where m_j is a modifier and v_j is the output of the j-th unit. Weights and modifiers are usually omitted if they are equal to 1.

The units in a connectionist network are updated synchronously or asynchronously. In each update the potential and value of a unit are computed by an *activation function f* and an *output function h* as

$$p \leftarrow f(\mathbf{i}, p)$$

and

$$v \leftarrow h(\mathbf{i}, p)$$

respectively, where $\leftarrow$ denotes assignment. The activation as well as the output function are *simple* functions like threshold or sigmoid functions. As an example consider a *binary threshold unit* k, whose potential and value are determined according to

$$p \leftarrow \sum_j w_{kj}v_j$$

and

$$v \leftarrow \begin{cases} 1 & \text{if } p > \theta \\ v & \text{if } p = \theta \\ 0 & \text{if } p < \theta, \end{cases}$$

where θ is a constant denoting the *threshold* of the unit.

Since units cannot transmit large amounts of information, almost all knowledge in a connectionist network must be encoded in the connections between the units. There is no central controller. All operations are performed locally. After an initial external activation units excite or inhibit each other. An obvious problem is how such a spreading of activation can be controlled such that a collection of locally operating units can together make a global decision.

Massive parallelism as such does not guarentee an efficient approach. One must ensure that the process of spreading activation converges quickly. In the ideal case, a connectionist system converges in a single sweep of spreading activation. This guarentees the computation of a result in time proportional to the diameter of the network. But we should keep in mind that an NP-hard problem remains NP-hard even if it is solved by a connectionist network.

3 Energy Minimization

Energy minimization is a technique to model the behavior of a certain class of connectionist networks. The technique was formally introduced by Hopfield [1982], who observed that there is a strong similarity between some statistical models for magnetic materials in physics and the behavior of so-called *symmetric networks*. Such a *symmetric network* consists of a set of binary threshold units, where each unit is connected to each other unit and each weight w_{ij} on a connection from unit j to unit i is equal to w_{ji}, ie., the weight on the connection from unit i to unit j. Figure 1 shows a small symmetric network. After an external activation of some of the units the network behaves according to the following procedure unless a *stable state* – ie., no unit changes its output anymore – is reached, where w_{ij} is the weight on the connection between unit j and i, v_i is the output of unit i, θ_i is the threshold of unit i and the sums range over the number of units in the network.

1. select an arbitrary unit i;

2. $v_i \leftarrow \begin{cases} 1 & \text{if } \sum_j w_{ij}v_j > \theta_i \\ v_i & \text{if } \sum_j w_{ij}v_j = \theta_i \\ 0 & \text{if } \sum_j w_{ij}v_j < \theta_i \end{cases}$

3. goto 1.

Figure 2(a) shows an example activation of the network depicted in figure 1. The network converges to one of the five possible stable states shown in figure 2(b) - (d) depending on the selection made in step 1 of the update procedure. For example, if unit 4 is selected, then it receives a total input of 6, which is larger than its threshold of 5. Hence, the unit is turned on and the net has received the stable state shown in figure 2(b).

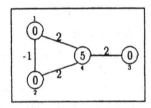

Figure 1: A small symmetric network. The numbers on the edges denote the weights, the numbers in the nodes denote the thresholds of the units, and the tiny numbers below or above each node are the numbers assigned to the units for further reference. Recall that $w_{ij} = w_{ji}$. Only connections with weight $w_{ij} \neq 0$ are shown. Hence, there are connections between the units 1 and 3 as well as between the units 2 and 3, but the weights on these connections is 0.

Hopfield showed that the state of a symmetric network can be described by the energy function

$$E = -\sum_{i<j} w_{ij}v_iv_j + \sum_i \theta_iv_i \qquad (1)$$

and that the energy of the network decreases whenever a unit changes its output. For the example shown in figure 1 we obtain

$$E^{(pl)} = v_1v_2 - 2v_1v_4 - 2v_2v_4 - 2v_3v_4 + 5v_4.$$

For the activation pattern in figure 2(a) we find that $E^{(pl)} = 1$. If we select unit 1 then, since the sum of its input is equal to -1 and is smaller than its threshold 0, the unit is

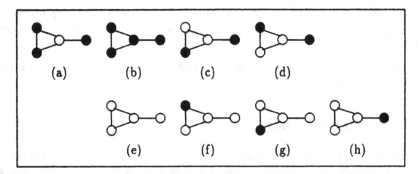

Figure 2: (a) An example activation. Units, which are activated, ie., which output 1, are shown as filled circles, whereas units who remain inactivated, ie., who output 0, are shown as open circles. (b) - (d) The stable states of the network which are reached from (a) depending on the selection made in step 1 of the update procedure. (e) - (h) The remaining stable states of the network reached by different initial activations.

turned off and we obtain the network shown in figure 2(c). One should observe that now the energy of the network is reduced to $E^{(pl)} = 0$. It is easy to see that in the example the value 0 defines a global minimum of the energy function.

The update procedure for symmetric network specifies a gradient descent on the energy function. Hence, it is not guaranteed that the procedure finds a global minimum, rather it may get stuck in a local minimum. This poses no problem unless we have to find a global minimum and in the examples discussed in the following subsection 3.1 this will be the case. To escape local minima Hinton and Sejnowski [1983] used again a result from statistical physics. The output of a unit is no longer computed deterministically, rather it changes with probability

$$P(v_i \leftarrow 1) = \frac{1}{1 + e^{(-\sum_j w_{ij} v_j + \theta_i)/T}}.$$

The parameter T is often called *pseudo temperature* – or *temperature* for short – since it relates to the temperature in statistical models of magnetic materials or gases in physics. For such *stochastic networks* it can be shown that, if the system is in equilibrium – ie., if the output of the units does not change over time anymore – then it is more likely that the system is in a state with low energy than that it is in a state with high energy.

But how can we drive a system into equilibrium? Obviously, the behavior of a stochastic network is equal to the behavior of a symmetric network if T approaches 0. Recall that in symmetric networks an equilibrium can be found quite easily and quickly by gradient descent. But such an equilibrium may be only a local minima. On the other hand, by a high temperature T it is very likely that the system finds a global minima, but it may take very long to reach it. To solve this dilemma Kirkpatrick etal. [1983] applied a technique called *simulated annealing* which was again taken from physics. They start with a large value for T and gradually decrease this value until it approaches 0. Geman and Geman [1984] were able to prove that this technique is guaranteed to find the global minima of an energy function if the steps by which the value of T is decreased are infinitesimal small. In other words, the time to find a global minima is exponential in the number of units in the network.

For a more detailed discussion of symmetric and stochastic networks the user is referred to [Hertz *et al.*, 1991].

3.1 Propositional Logic

Energy minimization has become an important technique in parallel distributed processing since many problems in Intellectics[1] can be rephrased as a problem of finding a global minima of an energy function. A typical example is the cube shown in figure 3. Our brain seems to be able to switch between two different spatial representations of the cube. In one representation the corner G is showing, whereas in the other representation the corner G is hidden. Feldman and Ballard [1982] showed that this observation can be modelled by a symmetric neural network, where the two possible representations are stable states of the network.

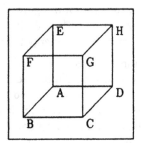

Figure 3: The Necker Cube

Since we are interested in inferencing, we would like to know what kind of inference problems can be computed by minimizing the energy of a symmetric or stochastic network. Pinkas [1990] has answered this question by formally showing that the problem of finding a global minima of an energy function is equivalent to the satisfiability problem in propositional logic. To illustrate Pinkas' results, we come back to the example in figure 2. The behavior of the network can be characterized by the propositional logic formula

$$F^{(pl)} \equiv \neg(v_1 \wedge v_2) \wedge \neg v_4 \ \vee \ v_1 \wedge v_2 \wedge v_3 \wedge v_4$$

in the sense that whenever an assignment for the variables $v_1, \ldots, v_4$ satisfies $F^{(pl)}$, then this assigment defines a global minimum for $E^{(pl)}$ and vice versa. Eg., under the assignment $\{v_1 \mapsto 1, \ v_2 \mapsto 0, \ v_3 \mapsto 1, \ v_4 \mapsto 0\}$ – which corresponds to the network in figure 2(d) – the formula $F^{(pl)}$ is evaluated to true.

Pinkas' proofs are constructive. Hence, for each propositional logic formula F we can define an *equivalent* energy function E in the form of (1) and vice versa. It is beyond the

---

[1] the field of Artificial Intelligence and Cognition [Bibel, to appear 1991]

scope of this paper to give the details of the transformation; they can be found in [Pinkas, 1990]. But it is worth to repeat that computing in a symmetric network is equivalent to computing in a propositional logic calculus.

Before we give some application and mention some related system, we want to point out that computation in a symmetric network usually means that some units of the network are externally activated and, then, the network converges to a stable state. In this sense we are interested in a stable state which is *close to* the initial activation. As mentioned in the previous subsection, to find a global minimum of an energy function by simulated annealing may take time exponential in the number of units in the network. In practical applications of simulated annealing, the steps by which the temperature is decreased are usually quite large and the network converges much faster. Such systems are not guaranteed to find a global minimum, but usually they converge to a stable state which is *close* to a local minima. In optimization problems (see subsection 3.2) this means often that the network does not find an optimal solution, but a suboptimal one. Formally, however, those systems trade soundness for time.

3.2   Applications and Related Systems

Optimization Problems   It is an immediate consequence of Pinkas' results, that symmetric neural networks can be applied to solve optimization problems. To illustrate such an application we consider the travelling salesman problem (TSP). The TSP is an NP-hard problem which has received considerable attention in the neural network community (cf., [Hopfield and Tank, 1985; Wilson and Pawley, 1988; Kamgar-Parsi and Kamgar-Parsi, 1990]). The formalisation presented herein is taken from [Brandt et al., 1988] and can be found in [Hertz et al., 1991] as well. A salesman has to visit n cities. To travel from city i to city j costs him the amount d_{ij}. The problem of the travelling salesman consists of finding a tour such that he visits each city once, returns to his starting point, and has minimal costs. To represent the problem we use binary threshold units v_{ik} with the interpretation that

$$v_{ik} = \begin{cases} 1 & \text{if the } k\text{-th stop is made in the } i\text{-th city} \\ 0 & \text{otherwise.} \end{cases}$$

Hence, we need n^2 units. The total costs of a tour can now be computed as

$$\frac{1}{2} \sum_{i,j,k} d_{ij} (v_{ik} v_{j,k+1} + v_{ik} v_{j,k-1}), \tag{2}$$

where the indices range from 0 to $n-1$ and are taken modulo n. A solution is obtained if each city is visited, ie., if

$$\forall i : \sum_k v_{ik} = 1 \tag{3}$$

holds, and if each stop is in only one city, ie., if

$$\forall k : \sum_i v_{ik} = 1 \tag{4}$$

holds. Equations (2), (3), and (4) can be combined into

$$E^{(TSP)} = \frac{1}{2} \sum_{i,j,k} d_{ij}(v_{ik}v_{j,k+1} + v_{ik}v_{j,k-1}) + \frac{\gamma}{2}[\sum_k (1 - \sum_i v_{ik})^2 + \sum_i (1 - \sum_k v_{ik})^2],$$

where γ is a scaling factor. Obviously, $E^{(TSP)}$ has a global minimum iff the assignment for the v_{ik}'s defines a solution for the TSP. Moreover, $E^{(TSP)}$ can easily be transformed into the form of (1). Thus, it can be represented by a symmetric network and a global minimum can be found by simulated annealing.

Constraint Satisfaction A special form of inference is realized by constraint satisfaction techniques, which has been applied successfully in many subfields of AI (such as computer vision [Waltz, 1972], circuit analysis [Stallman and Sussman, 1977], planning [Stefik, 1981], diagnosis [Davis, 1984] [Geffner and Pearl, 1987] [DeKleer and Williams, 1986], and logic programming [Jaffar and Lassez, 1987]) and among which are connectionist approaches as well.

Constraint satisfaction may be described as follows: given a set of variables and a set of constraining relations on subsets of these variables, find values from some given domains such that assigning them to the variables satisfies the constraints. More formally, constraint satisfaction and its related concepts are defined as follows:

1. A k-ary constraint C consists of variables $x_1, \ldots, x_k$ over domains $D_1, \ldots, D_k$ and a decidable relation $R \subseteq D_1 \times \cdots \times D_k$, ie., a k-ary relation the ith place of which is symbolized by x_i.

2. Different constraints are tied to constraint networks by sharing variables, ie., a constraint network on variables $x_1, \ldots, x_m$ consists of constraints $C_1, \ldots, C_n$, the variables of each C_i being a subset of $x_1, \ldots, x_m$.

3. A tuple $(a_1, \ldots, a_m)$ satisfies a constraint C_i if the subsequence of $(a_1, \ldots, a_m)$ that corresponds to the variables of C_i is an element of the relation of C_i.

4. A solution of a constraint network that is given by constraints $C_1, \ldots, C_n$ on variables $x_1, \ldots, x_m$ over domains $D_1, \ldots, D_m$ is a tuple $(a_1, \ldots, a_m) \in D_1 \times \cdots \times D_m$ that satisfies the constraints.

5. The task of finding one, some, or every solution of a constraint network is called constraint satisfaction problem (CSP).

6. A CSP consisting of unary and binary constraints only is called a binary CSP.

Each CSP can be transformed into a binary CSP in such a way that each solution of the binary CSP yields a solution of the original CSP. Thus, one can restrict oneself to binary CSPs without loss of generality, and so we will do in this paper.

There are a variety of algorithms for constraint satisfaction. Since constraint satisfaction in general is NP-hard, a special subclass of constraint satisfaction algorithms deserves our attention. These algorithms may be viewed as preprocessing methods which simplify the problem by transforming a given constraint network into an equivalent but easier-to-solve one. We will come back to these algorithms in section 4.1.

The approach for solving combinatorial search problems which appears to be the most promising one is to generate an initial *almost* solution and to repair this almost solution by applying some energy function. As Minton et al. [1990] have shown, this technique can be extended to constraint satisfaction problems. An initial assignment of values to the constraint variables is repaired until an assignment is found that violates none of the constraints. The repair method is guided by an ordering heuristic that selects a variable currently participating in a constraint violation and a value for this variable minimizing the number of outstanding constraint violations.

Minton et al.'s work was inspired by the Hubble Space Telescope scheduling problem, for which traditional programming methods failed: the initial scheduling system developed in FORTRAN was supposed to require more than three weeks to schedule one week of observations. As a consequence, a constraint-based system was developed, which is based on the Guarded Discrete Stochastic (GDS) network developed by Johnston and Adorf [1990].

The GDS network is a derivation of a Hopfield network, having a main network guarded by an auxilary network. This means in particular: Each constraint variable is represented by a set of nodes, each node in the set representing a value for the variable. This representation is in analogy to the one in [Güsgen, 1990]. A node has either value 0 or 1. In a solution state, exactly one node of each variable has value 1; the other nodes have value 0. The nodes with value 1 represent the assignment of values to the variables of the constraint network.

The constraint are represented in the GDS network by inhibitory connections between nodes. As opposed to [Hertzberg and Guesgen, 1991], an auxilary network ensures that a value is assigned to each variable. The auxilary network provides excitatory input that is large enough to turn on a node of each set of nodes belonging to the same variable. On the other hand, the connection weights are set in a way that makes turning on more than one node of each set unlikely.

The update of the network works as follows. A set of nodes that represents a variable is picked randomly. Then, that node of the set is selected whose state is *most inconsistent*, and the state of the node is flipped. If the states of all nodes are consistent, a solution is reached.

An analysis of the GDS network showed that its performance is much better than backtracking on certain tasks such as the n-queens problems. The reason lies in the following. When a node is chosen for update, this means

- either an inconsistent value is retracted ($1 \rightarrow 0$),

- or a new value is assgned that minimizes the number of variables it is inconstent with ($0 \rightarrow 1$).

This heuristic can be expressed as follows (cf., [Minton *et al.*, 1990]).

Min-Conflicts Heuristic

Given: A set of variables, a set of binary constraints, and an assignment specifying a value for each variable. Two variables *conflict* if their values violate a constraint.

Procedure: Select a variable that is in conflict, and assign it a value that minimizes the number of conflicts.

Minton et al. found out that the network's behavior can be approximated by a symbolic system that uses hill-climbing based on the min-conflicts heuristic. Similar to hill-climbing, the network may settle down in some local optimum, involving a group of unstable states among which it will oscillate. However, this does not cause problems in practice, since if the network fails to converge, it can be stopped and started again.

Unfortunately, the GDS network has shown to work effectively only on problems which have many solutions. It fails to solve problems which have few solutions or for which there are many local minima. Wang and Tsang [1991] have shown how to remedy this drawback. They have proposed a multilayer neural network and a learning rule that updates connection weights in order to escape from local optima.

An issue closely related to constraint satisfaction is constraint relaxation. It has turned out that many practical problems are inconsistent, ie., they do not have a solution. To handle these problems, the idea of constraint relaxation has developed, which assumes that not every constraint in a constraint network must be satisfied but only a subset of these. In many cases, the constraints are divided into *hard* constraints (the ones that must be satisfied) and *soft* constraints (the ones that may be violated).

In [Hertzberg and Guesgen, 1991], a neural-net approach is introduced for realizing both constraint satisfaction and constraint relaxation. The idea is to transform a constraint satisfaction problem into a Boltzmann machine in such a way that constraint relaxation is enabled if the problem is inconsistent. More than that, if the problem is inconsistent, the Boltzmann machine tends to converge towards the best *almost* solutions.

Restricted Unit Resolution Ballard [Ballard, 1986a; Ballard, 1986b] tried to construct a symmetric network such that the global minima of the corresponding energy function represent restricted unit resolution proofs. (See [Chang and Lee, 1973] for a definition of unit resolution.) In his system, the formulas and proofs are restricted in that only variables and constants are terms and that each clause can be used at most once in a proof. Consequently, the Herbrand universe underlying Ballard's logic is finite and the logic is decidable. Furthermore, the set of substitutions is finite. For a given formula a network is constructed such that there is a unit for each substitution. If there is a restricted unit resolution proof then, as soon as this proof has been discovered, the substitution units are activated, which represent the substitutions used in the proof.

Restricted First-Order Logic Pinkas [1991a] has lifted Ballard's restriction. He allows general first-order terms (including function symbols) and applies unrestricted resolution. From a given set of clauses and a query Pinkas compiles a symmetric network such that each global minima of the network – viz. the energy function encoded by the network – corresponds to a first-order resolution proof. The only remaining restriction is that the length of a proof is bound. In other words, if k is the bound on the length of a proof and for a given knowledge base and query there is a proof of length $k + 1$, then the system will not find this proof. But this is a kind of restriction that every automatic theorem prover has to obey.

FRAMEVILLE FRAMEVILLE is a connectionist frame system supporting the binding of variables, the allocation of frames, and equality [Anandan et al., 1989; Mjolsness et al., 1989]. The main operation in FRAMEVILLE is the matching of a term s with variables against a ground term t, where terms are represented as directed acyclic graphs (dags). In other words, FRAMEVILLE attempts to find a substitution σ such that the instance σs of s is equal to t. To find such a substitution a distance metric or objective function between dags is defined which specifies the mismatch between to dags. The objective function is equivalent to an energy function of the form (1) and the matcher σ corresponds to a global minimum of the energy function. Hence, a symmetric network can be used to represent the objective function and simulated annealing can be used to compute the matching substitution.

DCPS - A Distributed Connectionist Production System Touretzky's and Hinton's [1988] DCPS is a connectionist interpreter for a restricted class of production system based on distributed representations. A finite set of constants and essentially one variable comprise the set of terms. The hypothesis of each production rule consists of two triples of terms, which are either ground or of the form $\langle x\ a\ b \rangle$ and $\langle x\ c\ d \rangle$, where x is a variable and all other letters are constants. In other words, if the hypothesis of a rule contains variables at all, it contains only one variable and this one occurs as the first argument of the first and second triple. Touretzky's and Hinton's production system is further restricted by assuming that at any time only one hypothesis of a rule successfully matches against the content of the working memory. There is no conflict.

The working memory of the DCPS is a set of binary state units. It is coarse-coded such that each unit represents a set of triples. A certain triple is stored in the working memory by activating all units which vote – among others – for this triple. To find out which hypothesis of a production rule matches the working memory two so-called *clause spaces* are introduced. These are pullout networks in the sense of [Mozer, 1987], which pull out the first and second triple of the hypothesis of a production rule. The units in the clause spaces are copies of the units in the working memory. There is a bidirectional excitatory connection between the units of the working memory and the clause spaces. Similarly, rule units representing the triples in the hypothesis of the production rules are bidirectional excitatory connected with the respective units in the clause space. The weights on all these connections are set up such that exactly one triple is selected from the triples stored in the main memory. Thus, two atoms in the working memory which together form the hypothesis of a production rule activate via the clause spaces the respective rule and vice versa. Other solutions are suppressed by inhibitory connections between the units of the clause space and between the units representing different rules.

So far we have considered only ground production rules. The effect of using variables in Touretzky's and Hinton's production systems is to constrain the hypothesis of the rules such that the first constant in both triples is the same in order to fire the rule. Within the *bind space* the constants are coarse-coded and bidirectional excitatory connected to the respective units of the clause space. That is, a bind unit representing – among others – the constant a is connected to all units in the clause space who represent – among others – triples whose first element is the a.

Now, a matching rule is found if a minimum energy state is found. This can be done by simulated annealing if the production system is modeled by a symmetric network. As soon as a matching rule is discovered the action part of the rule is executed by storing new triples in or removing old triples from the working memory. For more details see [Touretzky and Hinton, 1988]. Dolan and Smolensky [1988] have given a formal account of the behavior of Dcps by using tensor product techniques [Smolensky, 1990].

The most interesting part of Dcps is the organization of the working memory and it is worth to mention its properties as they are not easily achieved by standard AI technologies. The working memory consists of 2000 units each representing 256 triples, ie., the em receptive field of each unit consists of 256 triples. Since the triples are built out of 25 constants, there are $25^3 = 15625$ different triples. These are distributed equally among the units in the working memory and, hence, each triple occurs in about 28 receptive fields. A triple is stored in the memory by activating all units whose receptive field contains this triple. But the units represent other triples as well. But this does not pose a problem as long as only few triples are actually stored in the memory. The stored triples will receive much more votes than the other triples. However, if too many triples are stored at the same time, then *ghosts* may occur, ie., triples may receive enough votes to be considered as present in the memory though they never were explicitly stored. On the other hand, a triple is deleted from the memory by inhibiting all units whose receptive fields contain this triple. Since the units represent more than one triple, this process may cause other stored triples to lose votes. Consequently, a triple must not have 28 votes to be considered as stored, 23 or 24 votes may suffice. However, if many triples are deleted, then previously stored triples may vanish though they never were explicitly deleted.

The techniques used in Dcps were applied in BoltzCONS [Touretzky, 1990] to show how structured objects like lists and trees can be distributively represented and associatively retrieved. The main idea to represent a list structure like the one shown in figure 4 by a set of triples

$$\{\langle a, b, c \rangle, \ \langle b, peter, d \rangle, \ \langle d, likes, d \rangle, \ \langle c, art, c \rangle\}$$

and to represent and manipulate these triples in the same way as triples are represented and manipulated in Dcps.

3.3 Propositional Non-Monotonic Reasoning

In the previous subsections we have examplified how the satisfiability problem of propositional logic can be mapped onto the energy minimization problem of a symmetric network and vice versa. But symmetric networks may be applied to propositional non-monotonic

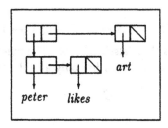

Figure 4: A simple CONS cell representation as used in LISP

reasoning as well [Pinkas, 1991b]. To illustrate the approach consider the *Meeting* example taken from [Brewka, 1989] and assume the following commonsense statements.

Usually one has to go to a project meeting.

This rule does not apply if somebody is sick, unless he or she has a cold.

The rule is also not applicable if somebody is on vacation.

These statements can be formalized by five propositional formulae, where M, S, C, and V have the obvious intended meaning.

$$
\begin{array}{ll}
M & 1 \\
S \rightarrow \neg M & 2 \\
C \rightarrow S & 4 \\
C \rightarrow M & 4 \\
V \rightarrow \neg M & 4
\end{array}
\tag{5}
$$

The positive real numbers associated with the formulae are regarded as *penalties*, which have to be *paid* by an assignment which does not satisfy the respective formulae. Intuitively, we prefer an assignment I_1 over an assignment I_2 iff the penalty to be paid by I_1 is less than the penalty to be paid by I_2. If we want to meet a person and know only (5), the assignment

$$\{M \mapsto 1, \ S \mapsto 0, \ C \mapsto 0, \ V \mapsto 0\}$$

is the most preferred one. All formulae in (5) are satisfied under this assignment and no penalty has to be paid. Any other assignment falsifies at least one formula in (5) and, thus, receives a higher penalty.

Now assume we learn that the person we are going to meet is sick. Formally, we add the fact

$$S \qquad \infty$$

to (5), where ∞ represents a real number which is much larger than any other penalty in (5). Informally, any assigment which falsifies S will have to pay an inacceptable penalty. It is easy to check that under these circumstances the assignments

$$\{M \mapsto 0, \ S \mapsto 1, \ C \mapsto 0, \ V \mapsto 0\}$$

and
$$\{M \mapsto 0, \ S \mapsto 1, \ C \mapsto 0, \ V \mapsto 1\}$$

are the most preferred ones as they falsify only M. The meeting has to be canceled. The situation changes again if the sick person has only a cold. After adding the fact

$$C \qquad \infty$$

the assignment
$$\{M \mapsto 1, \ S \mapsto 1, \ C \mapsto 1, \ V \mapsto 0\}$$

is the most preferred one and the meeting will take place. But if the person having a cold happens to be on vacation, the assignment

$$\{M \mapsto 0, \ S \mapsto 1, \ C \mapsto 1, \ V \mapsto 1\}$$

is most preferred and there is no chance to meet him or her.

Pinkas [1991b] showed that the problem of finding a most preferred assignment for a given set of propositional formulae can be encoded as minimization problem of an energy function and vice versa. The proofs are constructive and for (5) we obtain the function

$$E^{(m)} = 1 - M + 8C + 4VM - 4CS - 4CM + 2SM.$$

This function can be encoded in a symmetric network as shown in figure 5.[2] It is easy to see that the global minima of $E^{(m)}$ corresponds precisely to the most preferred assignment of (5). If simulated annealing is performed long enough, then the network will settle into the stable state where unit M is active and all other units are passive.

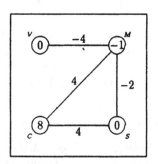

Figure 5: The symmetric network for the *Meeting* example

If we learn about a fact like the sickness of a person we simply clamp the unit S[3] and let the network settle down. The clamping of a unit v corresponds to the addition of a term $\infty - \infty v$ to the corresponding energy function, where ∞ is a real number larger than the maximal input received by v.

---

[2]Note that we may omit constants in an energy function if we are seeking for minima.

[3]A unit is clamped by externally activating the unit and keeping this activation throughout the computation. A clamped unit is always active.

μKLONE Derthick's [1990] μKLONE combines a frame-based language similar to KL-ONE [Brachman and Schmolze, 1985] with non-monotonic reasoning. As in Pinkas' approach, so-called *certainties* – viz. positive real numbers – are associated with each formulae and specify the *penalty* to be paid by an interpretation which does not satisfy the formulae. μKLONE searches for a most likely model for a given proposition. It believes a proposition if the proposition is true in one model of one extension with respect to the underlying default theory.

3.4 Summary

We have learned in previous subsections that, if the simulated annealing schedule is run too fast, a symmetric network may not settle into a global minima but into a local minima instead. In a propositional non-monotonic reasoning task this corresponds to the selection of an assignment which is not the most preferred one. But we can improve the selection, viz. escape the local minima, if we add more time to the annealing schedule. In other words, if time is a limited resource, then the network will make a decision. This is not necessarily the optimal one. But, as soon as more time is available, the network will have *second thoughts* and following this reconsideration will eventually make a better decision.

4 Spreading of Activation

In the previous section we have discussed inference systems based on energy minimization. There, the problem at hand was transformed into an energy function such that the (global) minima of the energy function correspond to the solutions of the problem. Thereafter, the energy function was encoded into a symmetric network of binary threshold units, which was driven into a stable state – viz. the minima of the energy function – by asynchronous updates of the units.

In this section we consider inference systems based on the spreading of activation metaphor. Here, a problem is encoded into a structured connectionist network, which is not necessarily symmetric. Thereafter, some input units are externally activated and this activation is spread through the network until some output units are excited or inhibited. As a simple example consider the feed-forward network of binary thrshold units shown in figure 6. If we externally excite unit 1, then after two steps unit 5 will be activated. Similarly, if we excite unit 2, then after two steps unit 5 will be activated and it is easy to see that the network encodes the XOR-function.

Networks of binary threshold units were already investigated by McCulloch and Pitts [1943]. They showed that such networks encode finite automata and, vice versa, that each finite automaton can be encoded by such a network. Hence, everything that can be done with a computer can be done with a network of binary threshold units.

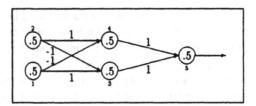

Figure 6: A connectionist network encoding the XOR-function

4.1 Constraint Satisfaction

In the previous section we have sketched how constraint satisfaction can be realized by energy minimization. Here, we describe an alternative that is based on a special subclass of constraint satisfaction algorithms. These algorithms are preprocessing methods, ie., they are not complete constraint satisfaction algorithms but methods computing some level of local consistency. Examples are the arc consistency algorithms in [Mackworth, 1977], the complexity of which is discussed in [Kasif, 1990]. These algorithms can be implemented in parallel very easily; moreover, there are connectionist approaches for computing arc consistency. We will introduce such an approach in the first part of this section, based on the work described in [Cooper and Swain, 1988]. We will then show in the second part of this section how the approach can be extended to compute global consistency rather than local consistency, ie., how connectionist networks can be designed to compute solutions of constraint satisfaction problems. This work has previously been published in [Güsgen, 1990].

The connectionist networks that are used here are in accordance with the unit/value principle (cf., [Feldman and Ballard, 1982]): a separate connectionist node is dedicated to each value of each variable and each tuple of each constraint of the constraint network. This approach is in analogy to the way deKleer represents constraint networks as propositional clauses [Kleer, 1989].

4.1.1 Computing Arc Consistency

Let V be the set of variables of a given CSP and, for the sake of simplicity, D be the union of all variable domains. In Cooper's approach, each variable-value pair $\langle x, a \rangle$, $x \in V$, $a \in D$, is represented by a connectionist node (v-node), which we will denote here by $v\langle x, a \rangle$.

A binary constraint on two variables consists of a set of pairs, each pair representing a consistent value assignment for the variables. Cooper introduces a connectionist node (c-node) for each quadruple $\langle x, y, a, b \rangle$ with $x, y \in V$ and $a, b \in D$. We will denote such a node by $c\langle x, y, a, b \rangle$. Because of symmetry, $c\langle x, y, a, b \rangle$ and $c\langle y, x, b, a \rangle$ denote the same node.

As it is shown in [Cooper and Swain, 1988], v-nodes and c-nodes can be connected in such a way that the resulting network computes an arc consistent solution for the

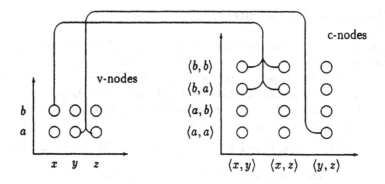

Figure 7: Scheme of a connectionist network for constraint satisfaction

corresponding constraint satisfaction problem (cf., figure 7). For that purpose, the nodes are initialized as follows:

- Each v-node obtains potential 1.

- A c-node $c\langle x, y, a, b\rangle$ obtains potential 1, if $\langle a, b\rangle$ is an admissible assignment of values for $\langle x, y\rangle$; else it obtains potential 0.

Since it is more convenient, we will use $v\langle x, a\rangle$, for example, for both: either for referring to the potential of a node or for denoting the node itself.

A v-node is reset to 0 if one cannot find at least one v-node for every other variable such that the constraint between this v-node and the given v-node is satisfied. This rule is called the arc consistency label discarding rule:

$$v\langle x, a\rangle \leftarrow \neg \bigwedge_{y \in V} \bigvee_{b \in D} (v\langle y, b\rangle \wedge c\langle x, y, a, b\rangle)$$

It is easy to verify that this is equivalent to the following, where sgn denotes the signum function[4]:

$$v\langle x, a\rangle \leftarrow \prod_{y \in V} \text{sgn} \left(\sum_{b \in D} v\langle y, b\rangle \cdot c\langle x, y, a, b\rangle \right)$$

A shortcoming of the label discarding rule is that it computes only arc consistency according to [Mackworth, 1987]. Although arc consistency may help to find a global solution by restricting the search space, one often needs additional mechanisms to obtain a globally consistent network. We will show in the next section how a connectionist network can be designed to compute global consistency. The approach described in that section may be compared with the one in [Lange and Dyer, 1989b], where signatures are used to maintain variable bindings.

$$^4\text{sgn}(z) = \begin{cases} 1 & \text{if } z > 0 \\ 0 & \text{if } z = 0 \\ -1 & \text{if } z < 0 \end{cases}$$

4.1.2 Towards Global Consistency

The idea is to apply the same communication scheme as in [Cooper and Swain, 1988] but to use the potential of a v-node to encode information about how the variable/value pair contributes to a solution (and not only whether or not it does so). The information is composed from the codings that are associated with the c-nodes. In particular, we encode each c-node by a prime number and denote this encoding by a function $e : V^2 \times D^2 \rightarrow P$ from the set of c-nodes to the set of prime numbers.

For example, let $V = \{x, y\}$ and $D = \{a, b\}$, then e may be defined as follows:

$$
\begin{array}{ll}
e\langle x, x, a, a\rangle = 2 & e\langle x, y, a, a\rangle = e\langle y, x, a, a\rangle = 11 \\
e\langle x, x, b, b\rangle = 3 & e\langle x, y, a, b\rangle = e\langle y, x, b, a\rangle = 13 \\
e\langle y, y, a, a\rangle = 5 & e\langle x, y, b, a\rangle = e\langle y, x, a, b\rangle = 17 \\
e\langle y, y, b, b\rangle = 7 & e\langle x, y, b, b\rangle = e\langle y, x, b, b\rangle = 19
\end{array}
$$

Nodes such as $c\langle x, x, a, b\rangle$ with $a \neq b$ do not make sense and therefore are omitted in the coding.

We will again use the same notation for a node and its potential, ie., the term $c\langle x, y, a, b\rangle$, for example, may denote the connectionist node representing the tuple $\langle a, b\rangle$ of the constraint between x and y, or may denote the potential of that node. It is determined by the context which meaning is intended.

The initial potentials of c-nodes are the same as in [Cooper, 1989]. A c-node $c\langle x, y, a, b\rangle$ is assigned the potential 1, if there is a pair $\langle a, b\rangle$ in the constraint between x and y; else it is 0. The initial potential of a v-node $v\langle x, a\rangle$ is determined by the product of the codes of all c-nodes except those that refer to the same variable as the given v-node but to a different value for that variable (ie., a factor $e\langle x, .., b, ..\rangle$ with $b \neq a$ does not occur in the product):

$$
\prod_{\substack{y \in V \\ b \in D}} e\langle x, y, a, b\rangle \prod_{\substack{y_1, y_2 \in V \setminus \{x\} \\ b_1, b_2 \in D}} \sqrt{e\langle y_1, y_2, b_1, b_2\rangle}
$$

The square root is due to the fact that $c\langle y_1, y_2, b_1, b_2\rangle$ and $c\langle y_2, y_1, b_2, b_1\rangle$ are identical nodes.

Unlike computing arc consistency (in which a v-node's potential is reset to 0 if it is inconsistent), we will perform here what is called graceful degradation:

1. A c-node receives the potentials of its v-nodes and computes their greatest common divisor (gcd).

2. The gcd is returned to the v-nodes if the c-node has potential 1; else 1 is returned.

3. A v-node computes the least common multiples (lcm) of data coming in from c-nodes that refer to the same variables and combines these by computing their gcd.

The idea is that the potentials of v-nodes shall reflect paths in the network that correspond to solutions of the constraint satisfaction problem. A v-node may be on the same path as another v-node if the c-node between them has potential 1. We start with allowing all paths among the v-nodes. Whenever a part of path is determined that is not admissible, ie., the corresponding c-node has potential 0, the path is deleted.

This means that global information about solution paths is held locally in the v-nodes of the network. To keep this information consistent, the c-nodes compute the gcd of the potentials of neighboring v-nodes. The gcd reflects that piece of information neighboring v-nodes can agree on. In order to consider alternatives, the v-nodes compute the lcm of data that comes in from c-nodes connecting to the same variable, and combine the results by applying the gcd operator. The alternation between the application of gcd and lcm directly corresponds to the semantics of constraints and their constituting tuples: a constraint network can be viewed as a conjunction of constraints (therefore gcd) wheras a constraint can be viewed as disjunction of tuples (therefore lcm).

More formally, the degradation rule can be denoted as follows:

$$v\langle x, a\rangle \leftarrow \gcd_{y \in V} \operatorname{lcm}_{b \in D} (\operatorname{out}(c\langle x, y, a, b\rangle)))$$

with

$$\operatorname{out}(c\langle x, y, a, b\rangle) = \begin{cases} \gcd(v\langle x, a\rangle, v\langle y, b\rangle) & \text{if } c\langle x, y, a, b\rangle = 1 \\ 1 & \text{else} \end{cases}$$

Since the degradation rule is monotonous and discrete, the network finally settles down. After that, the potentials of the v-nodes characterize the set of solutions of the given constraint satisfaction problem. In particular, a solution is given by a subset of v-nodes, W, for which the following holds.

1. Every variable occurs exactly once in W.

2. The potentials of the v-nodes in W are divisible by p, where:

$$p = \prod_{v\langle x,a\rangle, v\langle y,b\rangle \in W} \sqrt{e\langle x, y, a, b\rangle}$$

(Again, the square root is due to the fact that $c\langle x, y, a, b\rangle$ and $c\langle y, x, b, a\rangle$ are identical nodes.)

We will now show that our approach is sound and complete. For that purpose, we have to answer the following questions.

1. Does every subset W of v-nodes with

   (a) Every variable occurs exactly once in W.

   (b) The potentials of the v-nodes in W are divisible by p, where:

$$p = \prod_{v\langle x,a\rangle, v\langle y,b\rangle \in W} \sqrt{e\langle x, y, a, b\rangle}$$

   represent a solution, ie., does the degradation rule always converge to a solution, ie., is our approach sound?

2. Does a subset W of v-nodes with the above properties exist for each solution of the constraint satisfaction problem, ie., is our approach complete?

To answer the first question, let us assume that there is a subset of v-nodes, W, for which the above conditions hold but which does not represent a solution of the constraint satisfaction problem. This means that the tuple suggested by W violates at least one constraint of the network. Let $c\langle x, y, a, b\rangle$ be the c-node representing the tuple of the constraint that is violated, then the potential of $c\langle x, y, a, b\rangle$ is 0. Due to the initialization scheme, the potential of a node $v\langle x, a'\rangle$ with $a' \neq a$ does not contain the factor $e\langle x, y, a, b\rangle$; the same holds for $v\langle y, b'\rangle$ with $b' \neq b$. Since the potential of $c\langle x, y, a, b\rangle$ is 0 and since no neighboring node can provide the factor $e\langle x, y, a, b\rangle$, this factor is neither in the potential of $v\langle x, a\rangle$ nor in the potential of $v\langle y, b\rangle$, ie., these potentials are not divisible by $e\langle x, y, a, b\rangle$. Therefore, they are also not divisible by p (p defined as above). This, however, is in contradiction to the assumption, ie., every subset of v-nodes for which the above conditions hold represents a solution of the constraint satisfaction problem.

On the other hand, each solution of a given constraint satisfaction problem defines a subset of c-nodes, C, for which the following holds.

1. Each constraint is represented by exactly one c-node.

2. The potentials of the c-nodes are equal to 1.

Let W be the subset of v-nodes that are connected to c-nodes of C, ie.:

$$W = \{v\langle x, a\rangle \mid \exists y, b : c\langle x, y, a, b\rangle \in C\}$$

It is easy to see that W represents the given solution. Since the potentials of the c-nodes in C are equal to 1, the potentials of the v-nodes in W are divisible by the code of any c-node in C, ie., they are divisible by p, where p is the product of the codes of c-nodes in C. Thus, W satisfies the conditions proposed above.

With that, we have shown the soundness and completeness of our approach, ie., the one-to-one relationship between solutions of a given constraint satisfaction problem and special subsets of v-nodes in the corresponding connectionist network.

We will now discuss the space complexity of our approach. Let n be the number of variables of the given constraint satisfaction problem ($n = V$), and let m be the number of values in their domain ($m = D$). Then, the number of v-nodes and c-nodes can be estimated as follows.

Number of v-nodes:	$O(mn)$
Number of c-nodes:	$O(m^2n^2)$
Total number of nodes:	$O(m^2n^2)$

In addition, we have to consider the local space that is required for storing the Goedel numbers. Each v-node potential is the product of at most $O(m^2n^2)$ factors, corresponding to the c-nodes of the network. These factors could be represented by bit vectors, which facilitates the gcd and lcm operations, reducing them to intersection und union operations. This means that we need additional space of magnitude $O(m^2n^2)$ for each v-node, ie., $O(m^3n^3)$ additional space in total.

4.2 Limited Inference Systems

Humans are capable of performing a wide variety of cognitive tasks with extreme ease and efficiency. Shastri [1989a] has called such inferences *reflexive* since human react as if it were a reflex. On the other hand, in traditional AI systems, where these tasks are often modeled as inference problems, the same problems turn out to be intractable. This problem is even more serious as we intend to model common sense reasoning. There, we expect that a common sense knowledge base spanning human consensus knowledge may comprise as many as 10^8 rules and facts [Lenat *et al.*, 1990]. If we want to model reflexive reasoning in such an environment we have to discover inference processes which yield answers and make decisions within a time sublinear to the size of the knowledge base. Shastri's and Ajjanagadde's [1990a; 1990b] system performs such inferences.

But Shastri and Ajjanagadde were also inspired by a recent criticism of John McCarthy, who observed in a commentary to [Smolensky, 1988] that in the connectionist models which he has seen *the basic predicates are all unary and are even applied to a fixed object, and a concept is a propositional function of these predicates.* To overcome this *propositional fixation* and to allow multiplace predicates Shastri and Ajjanagadde had to solve the variable binding problem [Barnden, 1984], ie., the problem of dynamically binding values to variables.

Before we desribe Shastri's and Ajjanagadde's system in more detail, we should mention that the inference system ROBIN developed by Lange and Dyer [1989a; 1989b] is essentially equivalent to Shastri's and Ajjanagadde's system. They differ only in a small technical detail concerning the binding of variables, which we will discuss at the end of this subsection.

It is beyond the scope of this paper to present Shastri's and Ajjanagadde's system in detail. Rather we want to give a flavour of their system by showing an example. The data base of Shastri's and Ajjanagadde's inference system contains PROLOG-like clauses like

$$Owns(y, z) \Leftarrow Gives(x, y, z)$$
$$Owns(x, y) \Leftarrow Buys(x, y)$$
$$Can\text{-}sell(x, y) \Leftarrow Owns(x, y)$$
$$Gives(carl, josephine, book)$$
$$Buys(carl, x)$$
$$Owns(josephine, ball)$$

and is queried by goals like

$$\Leftarrow Owns(josephine, book)$$

or

$$\Leftarrow Owns(josephine, x).$$

For both queries we expect an answer *yes* or *no*, but in the second query we also expect a set of bindings for the variable x if the answer is *yes*.

Shastri's and Ajjanagadde's system can generate such answers if the following conditions are satisfied.

- Only constants and variables are terms.

- The body of a rule contains only variables as terms

- If in the body of a rule a variable occurs more than once than the variable is bound whenever thr rule is called.

- In a derivation each rule is instantiated at most once.[5]

For each set of program clauses Shastri and Ajjanagadde generate a structured connectionist network like the one shown in figure 8 for the *Josephine* example given above. Each predicate symbol occurring in a rule is represented by two *relais units* $\triangle$ and $\triangledown$ as well as *argument units* $\bigcirc$ for each argument. These units are interconnected as shown in figure 8. Eg. the connections from the $\triangle$-unit of *Owns* to the $\triangle$-unit of *Can-sell* and from the $\triangledown$, first, and second argument unit of *Can-sell* to the $\triangledown$, first, and second argument unit of *Owns*, respectively, represent the rule $Can\text{-}sell(x,y) \Leftarrow Owns(x,y)$. Each constant occurring in the program is represented by a *constant unit* $\bigcirc$. In the *Josephine* example we find constant units for *book*, *john*, *ball*, and *josephine*. Facts are represented by $\triangleright$-units. These units are interconnected with the units representing rules and constants as shown in figure 8. As an example consider the fact $Owns(josephine, ball)$. There is a connection from the $\triangledown$-unit of *Owns* to the $\triangleright$-unit of the fact and from the $\triangleright$ unit to the $\triangle$-unit of *Owns*. Furthermore, there are connections from the first and second argument of *Owns* which modify the connection from the $\triangledown$-unit of *Owns* to the $\triangleright$ unit. These connections are themselves modified by connections from the constant units for *josephine* and *ball*, respectively.

The variable binding problem is solved by Shastri and Ajjanagadde by introducing phases. A unit may be activated within a certain phase and eventually produces an output in the same phase. Similarly, modifiers are phase-sensitive. In other words, information encoded as phases can be sent along the connections in the network. A query like

$$\Leftarrow Can\text{-}sell(josephine, book)$$

will be answered as follows.

1. A unique phase is assigned to each constant in the query. Eg. the phases 1 and 2 may be assigned to *josephine* and *book*, respectively.

2. The constant units and the argument units of the predicate in the query are clamped on in the respective phases.

3. The $\triangledown$-unit of the predicate in the query is clamped on in all phases.

4. The activity is propagated through the net. Argument units are activated as soon as they are excited in a certain phase and output this phase. Relais and fact units are activated if they are excited in all phases. Modifiers are activated as soon as they are excited in a certain phase and *filter* this phase out of the connection which they modify.

---

[5]In the latest version of their system this condition is relaxed such that each rule is instantiated at most k times, where k is fixed.

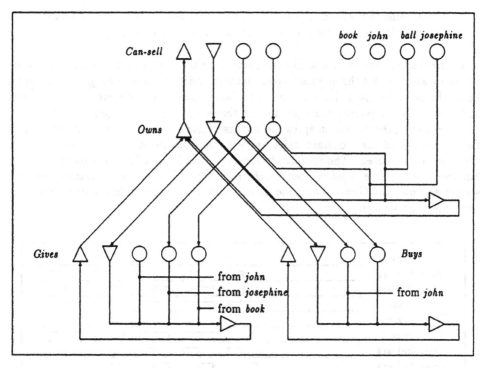

Figure 8: The connectionist network for the *Josephine* example

5. If after some (finite) time the △-unit of the predicate in the query is activated, then the query is answered by *yes*; otherwise it is answered by *no*.

Figure 9 shows the various activation patterns of the units in the *Josephine* network, where we assume that the units are synchronously updated. Since John gave Josephine a book, she owns a book and, hence, can sell a book. One should observe that the ▷-unit of *Gives* receives uninterrupted input though the second and third argument of *Gives* are activ. However, the activation spread from these units is blocked by the activation from the *josephine* and *book* constant units, respectively. On the other hand, the ▷-unit of *Owns* is not activated. The ▽-unit of *Owns* does send activation towards the ▷-unit, but the second phase is *filtered* out by the modifier which receives activation from the second argument of *Owns*. Thus, the ▷-unit does not receive uninterupted input and, hence remains passive.

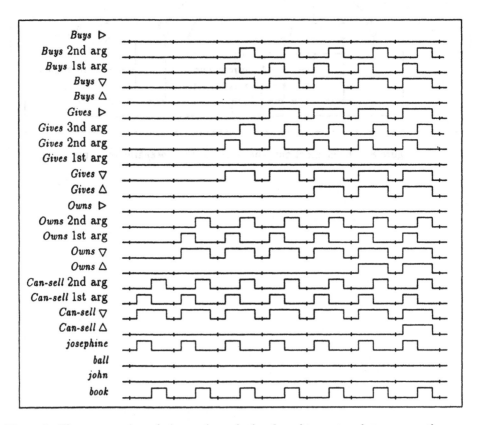

Figure 9: The propagation of phases through the *Josephine* network to answer the query whether Josephine can sell a book.

An argument of a predicate is bound to a certain constant if the unit representing the argument is activated in the same phase as the unit representing the constant is activated.

Eg. in figure 9 the first argument of *Can-sell* is bound to *josephine* and this binding is propagated to the first argument of *Owns* and from there to the first and second argument of *Buys* and *Gives*, respectively.

The answer is derived in time proportional to the depth of the search space since the activation of the ∇-unit of *Can-sell* has to travel to the $\triangleright$-unit of *Gives* and back to the $\triangle$-unit of *Can-sell*. This is a worst case result. If we ask whether Josephine can sell a ball, then the activation of the ∇-unit of *Can-sell* has only to travel to the $\triangleright$-unit of *Owns* and back to the $\triangle$-unit of *Can-sell*. Hence, the answer *yes* will be derived after 5 steps in this example.

The number of units as well as of connections is bound by the size of the knowledge base and, thus, is linear in the size of the knowledge base.

The network shown in figure 8 has to be extended slightly in order to compute answer susbtitutions, to allow a fixed number of compies of rules, to allow multiple literals in the body of a rule, to update the network asynchronously, or to built in a taxonomy. The details can be found in [Shastri and Ajjanagadde, 1990b]. Ajjanagadde [1990] shows how the inference system can be extended to handle some function symbols.

Lange's and Dyer's [1989a; 1989b] ROBIN differs from Shastri's and Ajjanagadde's inference system in that they use signatures instead of phases to encode variable bindings. Thus, the units in ROBINare *standard* units in the sense of eg. [Feldman and Ballard, 1982], but signatures are sent along the connections in the network.

The propagation of information along the connections of a neural network does not necessarily violate the condition that artificial neural networks should be biologically plausible. There is certain evidence that a limited amount of information can be propagated in a natural neural network (cf., [Churchland, 1986; Miller, 1956; Shastri and Ajjanagadde, 1990b]). In the inference systems presented in this section this means that as long as the number of different constant occurring in the initial query is restricted to about 7, the propagation of information is conform with findings in the animal and human brain.

From a logical point of view the restrictions imposed on formulae by Shastri and Ajjanagadde or Lange and Dyer are quite severe. They essentially do not unify terms, but propagate constants through a network; function symbols are usually not allowed; the conditions of a rule may contain only variables as terms; etc. On the other hand, answers are computed extremely fast and the size of the network is linear in the knowledge base. Thus, they are trading expressiveness for time and size.

4.3   CHCL

To overcome some of the limitations of the inference systems presented in the last subsection, CHCL has been developed. CHCL is a connectionist inference system for *H*orn based on Bibel's connection method and using *l*imited inferences [Hölldobler, 1990c; Hölldobler, 1990a]. It is the first connectionist inference system which can handle arbitrary first-order terms. The system is built around a connectionist unification algorithm for first-order terms [Hölldobler, 1990b]. We know from [Bibel, 1987] or [Stickel, 1987] that a proof for a formula is found if we can identify a *spanning* and *complementary* set of connections, where a connection consists of a positive and negative literal having the same predicate symbol.[6] Informally, the *spanning* conditions ensure that the connections in the set form a complete proof of the formula on the propositional level obtained by omitting all arguments of the predicates. Such a spanning set is *complementary* iff all connected literals are simultaneously unifiable. The search space can be reduced with the help of *reduction techniques* which are typically applied linearly in time and space. CHCL reduces a formula, generates the spanning sets one-by-one and simultaneously unifies all connected literals in such a set. CHCL is a connectionist system in the sense of [Feldman and Ballard, 1982] since each formula is represented by an artificial neural network and the (un-)satisfiability of the formula is determined by spreading of activation through the network. For more details see [Hölldobler and Kurfess, 1991] in this book.

4.4   Related Systems

CONPOSIT   In [Barnden, 1989], a neural net implementation that performs syllogistic reasoning based on some core aspects of Johnson-Laird's mental model theory [Johnson-Laird and Bara, 1984]. This theory states that a syllogistic inference like

> *Some athletes are beekepers.*
> *All beekeepers are chemists.*
> *Therefore, some athletes are chemists.*

is made in the following way. First, one or more mental models are constructed which conform with the premises. Then, a conclusion is tried to be read off a mental model.

A mental model is a data structure consisting of tokens and identity links between tokens. For example, there are tokens for athletes, beekeepers, and chemists. Beyond that, there are links between a proper non-empty set of athlete tokens and beekeeper tokens (the subset indicates that some but not all athletes are beekeepers), and there are links between all beekeeper tokens and chemist tokens. The conclusion that some athletes are chemists is indicated by the fact that there are chains of links from some (but not all) athlete tokens to chemist tokens.

The system introduced in [Barnden, 1989], CONPOSIT, constructs mental models from symbolic data structures that encode syllogism premises, and represents them in a configuration matrix. Such a matrix consists of registers, each register associated with a symbol and a vector of binary flags. The symbols denote, for example, classes like athletes, beekeepers, and chemists, individuals of these classes, or situations like overlapping classes. The flags denote relationships between neighboring registers, for example, the member relationship between a register representing an individual and a register representing a class.

CONPOSIT uses production rules to manipulate a configuration matrix. A production rule consists of a condition part that tests for the presence or absence of sprecific sorts

---

[6]Note that a connection in the sense of Bibel and Stickel is a pair of literals in a logical formula, whereas a connection in a neural network is a link between two units.

of state configuration in the configuration matrix. The action part of a production rule changes the symbols or the flags in the configuration matrix. By applying the production rules, syllogistic inferences are made, ie., a syllogism conclusion is deducted from the premises.

As Barnden points out, there is a neural-net implementation of the CONPOSIT register machine. The network consists of a subnetwork for each register, subnetworks for neighboring registers being connected. Beyond that, each subnetwork is connected to the so-called parallel distributor, which receives command signals from nodes corresponding to rule action parts.

To summarize, CONPOSIT represents Johnson-Laird's mental models in a straightforward way, and performs syllogistic inferences on the representations of these models. The system is able to maintain limited forms of variable bindings, for example, bindings such as the ones involved in the rule *if A loves B, B loves C, and C is not A, then A is jealous of C.*

Aspects of Johnson-Laird's approach that are not addressed in CONPOSIT are

1. the understanding or generation of natural language,

2. a thorough attempted-falsification process, and

3. negative premises and conclusions.

FMNN Tomabechi's and Kitanos' [1989] frequency modulation neural network FMNN is an extension of current neural models. Their heterogeneous network consists of various neuron ensembles each of which is capable of oscillating pulses. Information is represented and propagated using frequency modulation and superposition of pulses. The variable binding problem is solved by specifying where the oscillation was originated. Structures can be built up by modulating oscillations on top of received frequencies. Thus, the FMNN supports massively parallel models of structured marker, which were developed in the field of Intellectics to model human cognitive activities.

4.5 Evidential Reasoning

Knowledge is often represented in terms of concepts, their properties, and a hierarchical relationship between concepts (cf., [Quillian, 1968]). In such a hierarchy of concepts, property values are usually inherited from higher concepts as a *rule of thumb* unless specified otherwise. In a large hierarchy, where a concept has many anchesters with potentially conflicting property values, it is not at all obvious which property values a certain concept may have. Vice versa, if certain property values of an otherwise unknown concept are given, one would like to know which concept *best* matches the given property values. These two problems are often referred to as *inheritance* and *classification* problem.

In his thesis Shastri [1988b; 1988a; 1989b] showed how the inheritance and classification problem can be solved by selecting from a set of hypothesis the one, which is most likely – viz. for which the most evidence has been gathered. Operationally, the most likely hypothesis is computed by maximizing the entropy in the system. For example, suppose a rational agent has seen a fruit basket with three apples and knows that two apples are red, one is green, and that two apples are sweet and one is sour. If the agent picks an apple, what are the property values of this apple? More specifically, which is the best estimate for the number of red and sweet apples? In the given scenario, there are six possible models or *micro-configurations*, in which there is one red and sweet apple and only three possible micro-configurations, in which there are two red and sweet apples. Since none of the micro-configurations is more plausible than the other ones, the rational agent can only assume that the *macro-configuration*, where one apple is red and sweet is more likely than the macro-configuration, where two apples are red and sweet, as it is supported by more micro-configurations.

Shastri demonstrates how the most likely solutions for inheritance and classification problems can be solved in a structured connectionist setting. His emphasis is not to obtain the largest class for which these problems can be solved, rather he has devised a limited inference system in which the number of units is of the order of the size of the knowledge base and the time needed to find a solution is bound by the depth of the search space.

5 Strategy Learning

So far we have considered only purely connectionist approaches. But connectionist techniques may also supplement traditional AI systems in order to overcome their weaknesses. A theorem proving task can usually be divided into the logic of the problem and the control needed to find a proof [Kowalski, 1979]. Whereas it is comparatively easy to specify a problem as a logical formula, it is much more difficult to specify control knowledge as this kind of knowledge is often domain dependent. In most automated theorem provers and logic programming systems the programmer has to provide some rudimentary control knowledge, which in many applications is insufficient for finding short proofs.

Recently, Suttner and Ertel [1990] as well as Ultsch et.al. [1990] have applied connectionist learning techniques in order to learn control strategies for automated theorem provers. Whereas the former have considered the first-order theorem prover SETHEO [Letz *et al.*, 1992] the latter have considered the logic programming language PROLOG. In both cases a multi-layer feed-forward network was trained via backpropagation in order to select in each inference step the alternative which may lead to the shortest proof. The alternatives were classified by static as well as dynamic features such as the number of distinct variables occurring in a (part of a) clause or the total number of uses of a clause in the current derivation. Training examples were provided by optimal proofs obtained from SETHEO and PROLOG by computing all possible proofs and selecting the shortest ones. The results obtained so far are encouraging as the training resulted in a significant speed-up of SETHEO and PROLOG while the overhead for applying the learned strategies seems to be tolerable.

6 Outlook

In this article, we discussed a number of connectionist inference systems, and we tried to classify them. The presented systems are the first attempts to explore whether techniques and methods developed in the field of artificial neural networks can successfully merged with results obtained in the field of automated reasoning. Many of the systems perform operations which can be encoded as simple symbol manipulations within traditional AI. Nevertheless, they have a number of advantages that are not easily obtained in traditional AI systems.

- Connectionist systems are potentially fast as they exploit the massive parallelism inherent in reasoning. Limited inference systems like the ones presented in section 4.2 compute an answer to a given query in time proportial to the depth of the search space.

- As a kind of *natural* operation connectionist systems may gather evidence in order to make the *best* decision. For example, Shastri [1988b; 1988a; 1989b] has shown how certain classes of inheritance and classification problems can be solved in a connectionist setting by maximizing the entropy in the problem.

- Connectionist systems are potentially robust. Noise and damage up to a certain degree will not render a massively parallel system useless, rather the performance of these systems will degrade gracefully. The distributed production system DCPS presented in section 3.2 exhibits such properties by using a coarse-coding technique to represent objects.

- There are general and powerful learning algorithms for large classes of massively parallel systems. Connectionist models may recognize patterns of similarities and generalize from past experience. The experiments of Suttner and Ertel as well as Ultsch et.al. presented in section 5 show that connectionist learning algorithms can be successfully applied to obtain powerful heuristics for guiding the search in inference systems.

- Connectionist systems may base their decisions on a given context and may combine multiple cues. For example, the non-monotonic reasoning system presented in section 3.3 may revise its decisions whenever the context changes.

- Connectionist systems may give immediate responses if required but may have second thoughts and yield better conclusions whenever there is more time. The non-monotonic reasoning system presented in section 3.3 is such an example.

- Finally, connectionist models are more plausible from the biological point of view than traditional AI systems. The methods and techniques applied in artificial neural networks are based on findings in real neural networks. Most research in artificial neural networks has concentrated on high-level cognitive functions such as perception and speech performed by humans. Since reasoning is a typical human capability and which most of us believe can – at least in parts – be captured in a reasoning system, findings in these areas are of upmost importance for the field of automated reasoning and vice versa. Connectionist systems may serve as a vehicle to stimulate interdisciplary research bringing together people from areas such as cognition, psychology, biology, and artificial intelligence.

But the connectionist models of inference developed so far are quite simple and often there is only a single model which exhibits a certain desired property. This is not surprising as the field is just beginning to emerge. There is a variety of fundamental research problems.

General Problems[7]

The Learning Problem Whereas techniques such as backpropagation [Rumelhart *et al.*, 1986a], reinforcement learning [Barto *et al.*, 1983], or recruitment learning [Feldman, 1982; Diederich, 1988] have solved interesting problem, they have failed so far to demonstrate how complex structures needed for representing formulas can be learned. Moreover, the have failed to show how complex structures such as rules can be learned instantaneously, a capability that humans typically have [Hadley, 1990].

The Scaling Problem Connectionist models have so far been fairly small. Hopfield and Tank's [1985] attempted solution for the travelling salesman problem takes only 10 cities into account and scaling the solution up is a major problem [Wilson and Pawley, 1988; Kamgar-Parsi and Kamgar-Parsi, 1990].

The Merging Problem In this article we have seen solution for various parts of a deductive system. For example, Hölldobler has specified a connectionist unification algorithm [1990b] and the kernel of an inference system [1990a]. But the strategy for investigating the search space is fixed, whereas Suttner and Ertel [1990] demonstrate how heuristics can be automatically aquired. The representation of formulas is almost localist in [Hölldobler, 1990a], whereas Touretzky and Hinton [1988] distribute their formulas widely. This has the desired effects that less units have to be used, a best-match algorithm replaces the perfect match unification algorithm, the performance of the system degrades gracefully, etc. However, besides constants they do not allow function symbols, the occurrences and numbers of variables are fairly limited, and the distributed representation is artificial and not guided by semantic considerations. The last point can probably be overcome if we apply techniques developed by Jordan [1986] and Elman [1989]. Nevertheless we have to merge the various parts into a single system while retaining all the benevolent properties of the single system.

The Plausibility Problem Is a certain massively parallel model biologically plausible or does it violate established knowledge?

---

[7]Some of the research problems are taken from [McClelland *et al.*,], which deals with connectionist models in the much more general framework of cognitive science.

The Methodology Problem Massive parallel systems lack a design methodology. Are there connectionist counterparts to classical concepts like recursion, iteration, data structures, etc.?

Representation Problems

The Form Problem Shall the information be represented locally and/or distributed? Shall it be represented symbolically and/or sub-symbolically?

The Problem of Representing Relational Knowledge How should a system represent the propositions *John loves Mary, John hates Sue, Fred loves Sue*, and *Fred hates Mary* such that the system can retrieve the appropriate completion of a proposition from two of its constituents? The problem is equivalent to the XOR-problem [Minsky and Papert, 1972] and cannot be solved by pairwise connections between units representing *John, Fred, loves, hates, Sue*, and *Mary*. There is the trivial solution by assigning a unit to each possible triple. However, the number of units needed in this solution grows exponentially with the number of constituents.

The Cross-Talk Problem As soon as a coarse-coded representation is chosen the cross-talk problem may arise. *Ghosts*, ie., objects which were not explicitly stored, may suddendly appear as a result of superimposing various representations.

The Problem of Specifying the Domain Adequately Domain specific modelling reduces the number of units and connections in a massively parallel model (cf., [Cooper and Swain, 1988]). But what are the important properties of a given domain?

The Binding Problem How shall we bind variables to objects in a connectionist setting? If each possible binding is represented locally by an ensemble of units, an exponential number of units is required. If we restrict the number of units significantly by using a distributed representation, we run into the cross-talk problem.

The Control Problem Connectionist systems are generally autonomous. Input is clamped on, each unit computes locally and independently, and the whole system generates an output by activating certain units or going into a minimal energy state. However, inherent problems such as the variable-binding problem or the cross-talk problem either require to consider an unrealistic number of units or to focus attention on certain parts of the network, whereas other parts are ignored. Controlling the search space of a deductive systems also requires attention based on the problem at hand and vast experience.

Acknowledgement This article was started while both authors stayed at the International Computer Science Institute (ICSI) in Berkely, USA. We are indepted to Jerry

Feldman and his staff at the ICSI for providing such a stimulating environment. Thanks also to Franz Kurfeß and Christian Suttner.

References

[Adorf and Johnston, 1990] H. M. Adorf and M. D. Johnston. A discrete stochastic neural network algorithm for constraint satisfaction problems. In *Proceedings of the International Joint Conference on Neural Networks*, 1990.

[Ajjanagadde, 1990] V. Ajjanagadde. Reasoning with function symbols in a connecionist system. In *Proceedings of the Annual Conference of the Cognitive Science Society*, 1990.

[Anandan et al., 1989] P. Anandan, S. Letovsky, and E. Mjolsness. Connectionist variable-binding by optimization. In *Proceedings of the Annual Conference of the Cognitive Science Society*, pages 388–395, 1989.

[Ballard, 1986a] D. H. Ballard. Parallel logic inference and energy minimization. In *Proceedings of the AAAI National Conference on Artificial Intelligence*, pages 203 – 208, 1986.

[Ballard, 1986b] D. H. Ballard. Parallel logic inference and energy minimization. Technical Report TR 142, Computer Science Department, Univ. of Rochester, Rochester, NY 14627, 1986.

[Barnden, 1984] J. A. Barnden. On short term information processing in connectionist theories. *Cognition and Brain Theory*, 7:25–59, 1984.

[Barnden, 1989] J. A. Barnden. Neural-net implementation of complex symbol-processing in a mental model approach to syllogistic reasoning. In *Proceedings of the International Joint Conference on Artificial Intelligence*, pages 568–573, 1989.

[Barto et al., 1983] A. G. Barto, R. S. Sutton, and C. W. Anderson. Neuronlike adaptive elements that can solve difficult learning control problems. *IEEE Transactions on Systems, Man, and Cybernetics*, pages 835–846, 1983.

[Bibel, 1987] W. Bibel. *Automated Theorem Proving*. Vieweg Verlag, Braunschweig, second edition, 1987.

[Bibel, 1990] W. Bibel. Perspectives in automated deduction. In R. S. Boyer, editor, *Festschrift for W.W. Bledsoe*. Kluwer Academic, Utrecht, 1990.

[Bibel, to appear 1991] W. Bibel. Intellectics. In S. C. Shapiro, editor, *Encyclopedia of Artificial Intelligence*. John Wiley, New York, to appear 1991.

[Brachman and Schmolze, 1985] R. J. Brachman and J. G. Schmolze. An overview of the KL-ONE knowledge representation system. *Cognitive Science*, 9(2):171–216, 1985.

[Brandt et al., 1988] R. D. Brandt, Y. Wang, A. J. Laub, and S. K. Mitra. Alternative networks for solving the travelling salesman problem. In *IEEE International Conference on Neural Networks*, pages vol. II, 333–340, 1988.

[Brewka, 1989] G. Brewka. Preferred subtheories: An extended logical framework for default reasoning. In *Proceedings of the International Joint Conference on Artificial Intelligence*, pages 1043–1048, 1989.

[Chang and Lee, 1973] L. Chang and R. C. T. Lee. *Symbolic Logic and Mechanical Theorem Proving*. Academic Press, New York, 1973.

[Churchland, 1986] P. S. Churchland. *Neurophilosophy: Toward a Unified Science of Mind/Brain*. MIT Press, Cambridge, Ma., 1986.

[Cooper and Swain, 1988] P. R. Cooper and M. J. Swain. Parallelism and domain dependence in constraint satisfaction. Technical Report 255, Computer Science Department, Univ. of Rochester, 1988.

[Cooper, 1989] P. R. Cooper. Parallel object recognition from structure (the tinkertoy project). Technical Report TR 301, University of Rochester, Computer Science Department, 1989.

[Davis, 1984] R. Davis. Diagnostic reasoning based on structure and behavior. *Artificial Intelligence*, 24:347–410, 1984.

[DeKleer and Williams, 1986] J. DeKleer and B. C. Williams. Diagnosing multiple faults. In *Proceedings of the AAAI National Conference on Artificial Intelligence*, pages 132–139, 1986.

[Derthick, 1990] M. Derthick. Mundane reasoning by settling on a plausible model. *Artificial Intelligence*, 46:77–106, 1990.

[Diederich, 1988] J. Diederich. Connectionist recruitment learning. In *Proceedings of the European Conference on Artificial Intelligence*, pages 351–356, 1988.

[Dolan and Smolensky, 1988] C. P. Dolan and P. Smolensky. Implementing a connectionist production system using tensor products. In Touretzky, Hinton, and Sejnowski, editors, *Proceedings of the 1988 Connectionist Models Summer School*, pages 265 – 272. Morgan Kaufmann, 1988.

[Elman, 1989] J. L. Elman. Structured representations and connectionist models. In *Proceedings of the Annual Conference of the Cognitive Science Society*, pages 17–25, 1989.

[Feldman and Ballard, 1982] J. A. Feldman and D. H. Ballard. Connectionist models and their properties. *Cognitive Science*, 6(3):205–254, 1982.

[Feldman, 1982] J. A. Feldman. Dynamic connections in neural networks. *Biological Cybernetics*, 46:27–39, 1982.

[Geffner and Pearl, 1987] H. Geffner and J. Pearl. An improved constraint-propagation algorithm for diagnosis. In *Proceedings of the International Joint Conference on Artificial Intelligence*, pages 1105–1111, 1987.

[Geman and Geman, 1984] S. Geman and D. Geman. Stochastic relaxation, gibbs distribution, and the bayesian restoration of images. *IEEE Transactions on Pattern Analysis and Machine Intelligence*, 6:721–741, 1984.

[Güsgen, 1990] H. W. Güsgen. Connectionist networks for constraint satisfaction. In *Proceedings of the ISMM International Conference on Parallel and Distributed Computing, and Systems*, pages 12–16, 1990.

[Hadley, 1990] R. F. Hadley. Connectionism, rule following, and symbolic manipulation. In *Proceedings of the AAAI National Conference on Artificial Intelligence*, pages 579–586, 1990.

[Hertz et al., 1991] J. Hertz, A. Krogh, and R. G. Palmer. *Introduction to the Theory of Neural Computation*. Addison-Wesley Publishing Company, 1991.

[Hertzberg and Guesgen, 1991] J. Hertzberg and H.W. Guesgen. Transforming constraint relaxation networks into Boltzmann machines. In *Proceedings of the German Workshop on Artificial Intelligence*, pages 244–253. Springer, 1991.

[Hinton and Sejnowski, 1983] G. E. Hinton and T. J. Sejnowski. Optimal perceptual inference. In *Proceedings of the IEEE Conference on Computer Vision and Recognition*, pages 448–453, 1983.

[Hölldobler and Kurfess, 1991] S. Hölldobler and F. Kurfess. CHCL – A connectionist inference system. In B. Fronhöfer and G. Wrightson, editors, *Parallelization in Inference Systems*. Springer, 1991. (to appear).

[Hölldobler, 1990a] S. Hölldobler. CHCL - A connectionist inference system for a limited class of Horn clauses based on the connection method. Technical Report TR-90-042, International Computer Science Institute, Berkeley, CA, 1990.

[Hölldobler, 1990b] S. Hölldobler. A structured connectionist unification algorithm. In *Proceedings of the AAAI National Conference on Artificial Intelligence*, pages 587–593, 1990. A long version appeared as Technical Report TR-90-012, International Computer Science Institute, Berkeley, California.

[Hölldobler, 1990c] S. Hölldobler. Towards a connectionist inference system. In *Proceedings of the International Symposium on Computational Intelligence*, 1990.

[Hopfield and Tank, 1985] J. J. Hopfield and D. W. Tank. Neural computation of decisions in optimization problems. *Biological Cybernetics*, 52:141 – 152, 1985.

[Hopfield, 1982] J. J. Hopfield. Neural networks and physical systems with emergent collective computational abilities. In *Proceedings of the National Academy of Sciences USA*, pages 2554 – 2558, 1982.

[Jaffar and Lassez, 1987] J. Jaffar and J-L. Lassez. Constraint logic programming. In *Proceedings of the ACM Symposium on Principles of Programming Languages*, pages 111–119, 1987.

[Johnson-Laird and Bara, 1984] P.N. Johnson-Laird and B.G. Bara. Syllogistic inference. *Cognition*, 16(1):1–61, 1984.

[Jordan, 1986] M. I. Jordan. Attractor dynamics and parallelism in a connectionist sequential machine. In *Proceedings of the Annual Conference of the Cognitive Science Society*, 1986.

[Kamgar-Parsi and Kamgar-Parsi, 1990] B. Kamgar-Parsi and B. Kamgar-Parsi. On problem solving with hopfield neural nets. *Biological Cybernetics*, 62:415 – 423, 1990.

[Kasif, 1990] S. Kasif. On the parallel complexity of discrete relaxation in constraint satisfaction networks. *Artificial Intelligence*, 45(3):275–286, 1990.

[Kirkpatrick et al., 1983] S. Kirkpatrick, C. D. Gelatt Jr., and M. P. Vecchi. Optimization by simulated annealing. *Science*, 220:671–680, 1983.

[Kleer, 1989] J. De Kleer. A comparison of ATMS and CSP techniques. In *Proceedings of the International Joint Conference on Artificial Intelligence*, pages 290–296, 1989.

[Kowalski, 1979] R. A. Kowalski. Algorithm = logic + control. *Communications of the ACM*, 22:424–436, 1979.

[Lange and Dyer, 1989a] T. E. Lange and M. G. Dyer. Frame selection in a connectionist model of high-level inferencing. In *Proceedings of the Annual Conference of the Cognitive Science Society*, pages 706–713, 1989.

[Lange and Dyer, 1989b] T. E. Lange and M. G. Dyer. High-level inferencing in a connectionist network. *Connection Science*, 1:181 – 217, 1989.

[Lenat et al., 1990] D. B. Lenat, R. V. Guha, K. Pittman, D. Pratt, and M. Shepard. Cyc: Toward programming with common sense. *Communications of the ACM*, 33(8):30–49, 1990.

[Letz et al., 1992] R. Letz, S. Bayerl, J. Schumann, and W. Bibel. SETHEO: A high-performance theorem prover. *Journal of Automated Reasonsing*, 1992. *to appear*.

[Mackworth, 1977] A. K. Mackworth. Consistency in networks of relations. *Artificial Intelligence*, 8:99–118, 1977.

[Mackworth, 1987] A. Mackworth. Constraint satisfaction. In Shapiro, editor, *Encyclopedia of Artificial Intelligence*, pages 205–211. John Wiley & Sons, 1987.

[McClelland and Rumelhart, 1981] J. L. McClelland and D. E. Rumelhart. An interactive activation model of the effect of context in perception: Part 1. *Psychological Review*, 88:375–405, 1981.

[McClelland et al.,] J. L. McClelland, J. Feldman, G. Bower, and D. McDermott. Connectionist models and cognitive science: Goals, directions and implications.

[McCulloch and Pitts, 1943] W. S. McCulloch and W. Pitts. A logical calculus and the ideas immanent in nervous activity. *Bulletin of Mathematical Biophysics*, 5:115–133, 1943.

[Miller, 1956] G. A. Miller. The magical number seven, plus or minus two: Some limits on our capacity for processing information. *The Psychological Review*, 63(2):81–97, 1956.

[Minsky and Papert, 1972] M. Minsky and S. Papert. *Perceptrons*. MIT Press, 1972.

[Minton et al., 1990] S. Minton, M. D. Johnston, A. B. Philips, and P. Laird. Solving large-scale constraint-satisfaction and scheduling problems using a heuristic repair method. In *Proceedings of the AAAI National Conference on Artificial Intelligence*, pages 17–24, 1990.

[Mjolsness et al., 1989] E. Mjolsness, G. Gindi, and P. Anandan. Optimization in model matching and perceptual organization. *Neural Computation*, 1:218–229, 1989.

[Mozer, 1987] M. C. Mozer. *The Perception of Multiple Objects: A Parallel, Distributed Proceesing Approach*. PhD thesis, University of California, San Diego, 1987.

[Pinkas, 1990] G. Pinkas. The equivalence of energy minimization and propositional calculus satisfiability. Technical Report WUCS-90-03, Washington University, 1990.

[Pinkas, 1991a] G. Pinkas. Expressing first-order logic in symmetric connectionist networks. In L. N. Kanal and C. B. Suttner, editors, *Informal Proceedings of the International Workshop on Parallel Processing for AI*, pages 155–160, Sydney, Australia, August 1991 1991.

[Pinkas, 1991b] G. Pinkas. Propositional non-monotonic reasoning and inconsistency in symmetrical neural networks. In *Proceedings of the International Joint Conference on Artificial Intelligence*, 1991.

[Posner, 1978] M. I. Posner. *Chronometric Explorations of the Mind*. Lawrence Erlbaum Associates, 1978.

[Quillian, 1968] R. M. Quillian. Semantic memory. In Minsky, editor, *Semantic Information Processing*, pages 216–270. MIT Press, 1968.

[Rumelhart and Zipser, 1985] D. E. Rumelhart and D. Zipser. Feature discovery by competitive learning. *Cognitive Science*, 9:75–112, 1985.

[Rumelhart et al., 1986a] D. E. Rumelhart, G. E. Hinton, and R. J. Williams. Learning internal representations by error propagation. In *Parallel Distributed Processing*. MIT Press, 1986.

[Rumelhart et al., 1986b] D. E. Rumelhart, J. L. McClelland, and the PDP Research Group. *Parallel Distributed Processing*. The MIT Press, 1986.

[Shastri and Ajjanagadde, 1990a] L. Shastri and V. Ajjanagadde. From associations to systematic reasoning: A connectionist representation of rules, variables and dynamic bindings. Technical Report MS-CIS-90-05, Department of Computer and Information Science, University of Pennsylvania, Philadelphia, School of Engineering and Applied Science, PA 19104-6389, 1990.

[Shastri and Ajjanagadde, 1990b] L. Shastri and V. Ajjanagadde. An optimally efficient limited inference system. In *Proceedings of the AAAI National Conference on Artificial Intelligence*, pages 563-570, 1990.

[Shastri, 1988a] L. Shastri. A connectionist approach to knowledge representation and limited inference. *Cognitive Science*, 12(3), 1988.

[Shastri, 1988b] L. Shastri. *Semantic Networks: An Evidential Formalization and its Connectionist Realization*. Research notes in Artificial Intelligence. Pitman, London, 1988.

[Shastri, 1989a] L. Shastri. Connectionism, knowledge representation, and effective reasoning. In Brauer und Freksa, editor, *Proceedings of the International GI Congress on Knowledge-Based Systems*, pages 186 - 195, 1989.

[Shastri, 1989b] L. Shastri. Default reasoning in semantic networks: A formalization of recognition and inheritance. *Artificial Intelligence*, 39:283-355, 1989.

[Smolensky, 1988] P. Smolensky. On the proper treatment of connectionism. *Behavioral and Brain Sciences*, 11:1-74, 1988.

[Smolensky, 1990] P. Smolensky. Tensor product variable binding and the representation of symbolic structures in connectionist systems. *Artificial Intelligence*, 46:159-216, 1990.

[Stallman and Sussman, 1977] R. M. Stallman and G. J. Sussman. Forward reasoning and dependency-directed backtracking in a system for computer-aided circuit analysis. *Artificial Intelligence*, 9:135-196, 1977.

[Stefik, 1981] M. Stefik. Planning with constraints (molgen: part 1). *Artificial Intelligence*, 16:111-140, 1981.

[Stickel, 1987] M. E. Stickel. An introduction to automated deduction. In W. Bibel and P. Jorrand, editors, *Fundamentals of Artificial Intelligence*, pages 75 - 132. Springer, 1987.

[Suttner and Ertel, 1990] C. B. Suttner and W. Ertel. Using connectionist networks for guiding the search of a theorem prover. *Journal of Neural Networks Research and Application*, 1990.

[Tomabechi and Kitano, 1989] H. Tomabechi and H. Kitano. Beyond PDP: The frequency modulation neural network architecture. In *Proceedings of the International Joint Conference on Artificial Intelligence*, pages 186 - 192, 1989.

[Touretzky and Hinton, 1988] D. S. Touretzky and G. E. Hinton. A distributed connectionist production system. *Cognitive Science*, 12:423 – 466, 1988.

[Touretzky, 1990] D. S. Touretzky. BoltzCONS: Dynamic symbol structures in a connectionist network. *Artificial Intelligence*, 46:5–46, 1990.

[Ultsch et al., 1990] A. Ultsch, R. Hannuschka, U. Hartmann, and V. Weber. Learning of control knowledge for symbolic proofs with backpropagation networks. In R. Eckmiller, G. Hartmann, and G. Hauske, editors, *Parallel Processing in Neural Systems and Computers*, pages 499–502. Elsevier, 1990.

[Waltz, 1972] D. L. Waltz. Generating semantic descriptions from drawings of scenes with shadows. Technical Report AI-TR-271, Massachusetts Institute of Technology, Cambridge, Massachusetts, 1972.

[Wang and Tsang, 1991] C. J. Wang and E. P. K. Tsang. Solving constraint satisfaction problems using neural networks. Department of Computer Science, University of Essex, 1991.

[Wilson and Pawley, 1988] G. V. Wilson and G. S. Pawley. On the stability of the travelling salesman problem algorithm of Hopfield and Tank. *Biological Cybernetics*, 58:63 – 70, 1988.

PART II

PAPERS SECTION

Implementing Parallel Rewriting*†

Claude Kirchner   Patrick Viry

INRIA Lorraine & CRIN
615 Rue du Jardin Botanique, BP101
54600 Villers les Nancy, France
E-mail: {ckirchner,viry}@loria.fr

Abstract

Rewriting is a computation paradigm that allows to implement directly an equational specification (eg. an abstract data type). Much work has been done about theoretical aspects of rewriting, which has made this technique of practical interest for programming. The next step is now to provide an efficient implementation. We present in this paper an implementation technique of rewriting on any loosely-coupled parallel architectures. Restricted to one processor, its efficiency is in the same order of magnitude as those of functional languages such as interpreted LISP or ML, and we expect an almost linear increase of the efficiency when increasing the number of processors.

This approach allows parallel execution of programs directly from their equationally axiomatized specification, without having at all to explicit the potential parallelism, thus providing a simple and precise operational semantics.

1 Introduction

Rewriting is a computational paradigm that is now widely recognized and used. As a mathematical object, rewrite systems have been studied for more than ten years, and the reader may find in [18] and [3] general surveys describing properties and applications either in theorem proving or in programming languages. Theorem proving oriented rewriting implementations are numerous and a survey of most of them is made in [14]. Rewriting for computing has been developing for several years [9, 26, 2]. It is in particular used as an operational semantics in many programming languages like OBJ [6], ASF [13] or SLOG [5] among many others.

1.1 Motivations

The reasons for seeking a parallel implementation of rewriting are numerous:

- It is crucial, in order to get realistic performances, to have efficient implementations. Several alternatives have been explored. A first one is to compile rewriting either using abstract machines like in [26, 17, 1] or using a functional language like in [15, 21]. A second (possibly complementary) one, on which [23] and this paper are based, is to implement rewriting on parallel machines.

*This is the revised version of a paper presented at the PLILP'90 conference [22].

†This research has been partially supported by the *GRECO de Programmation of CNRS*, the Basic Research Workshop COMPASS of the CEC and contract MRT 89P0423.

- Parallelism is not a fashion effect: rewriting is really a computational paradigm that specifies the actions and not the control (though strategies may be added if explicit control is needed, see [8]), so it can be *directly* implemented on a parallel machine. Since no explicit parallelization directives are to be given, the same program may run on a sequential or a parallel machine. This may be the beginning of a solution to the difficult problem of programming parallel architectures.

- Parallelism is not only a property of our implementation, but is inherent to the abstract model we are using, namely the concurrent rewriting relation [8]: *A rewrite program is a parallel specification.* It is shown in [25] how concurrent rewriting nicely generalizes most of the known concurrency semantics (e.g. CCS, Petri Nets, and many others). This also allows to state formal properties, such as for example "parallel complexity" or "parallel termination". Our study of such properties shows that much more powerful results than for sequential rewriting can be elaborated for concurrent rewriting [28].

- Rewriting does not introduce any intermediate steps between the program description and its implementation: an implementation of rewriting is an implementation of an operational semantics of abstract data types.

These are already main concepts in the rewrite rule machine project [7, 10] which goal is to design a hardware having a rewrite rules machine code and whose model of computation is concurrent rewriting [8]. Our purpose here is quite different, since it consists in implementing rewriting on *existing* parallel machines. The implementation we describe here is tuned for MIMD (loosely-coupled) architectures, like transputer networks, but the same principles would also apply to SIMD architectures, such as the connection machine.

1.2   Intuition

In order to implement term rewriting, several steps are involved. Let us take as example the following rewrite program specifying the computation of the length of a list of integers:

op	nil	:	$\longrightarrow$ ListInt	length(nil)	$\rightarrow$	0
op	_._	: Int, ListInt	$\longrightarrow$ ListInt	length(n.L)	$\rightarrow$	length(L) + 1
op	length	: ListInt	$\longrightarrow$ Nat			

where we assume known the usual operations on integers. These rules will be directly used to compute the length of the list 1.2.3.nil by applying them on the term length(1.2.3.nil). No intermediate compilation neither of the term nor of the rewrite rules will be necessary.

In order to perform these computations, a pattern has first to be *matched* against the term to be reduced. For example, the left-hand side length(n.L) matches the term length(1.2.3.nil) (which is then called a *redex*), and the *substitution* allowing the match, in this case $\{n \mapsto 1, L \mapsto 2.3.nil\}$, is computed. Then the right-hand side of the rule is *instantiated* with the matching substitution: here length(L) + 1 is instantiated into length(2.3.nil) + 1. Finally the redex has to be *replaced* by the instantiated right-hand side: in the example length(1.2.3.nil) is replaced by length(2.3.nil) + 1. And the same process can be iterated until possibly an irreducible term is obtained.

The crucial idea is that if one wants to reduce the term length(1.2.nil) + length(3.4.nil), the computations can be performed independently on the subterms length(1.2.nil) and length(3.4.nil). This parallelism is *inherent* to the rewrite system, and can freely be used by an implementation. We define in section 2 the *concurrent rewriting relation*, that formalizes the one-step rewriting of multiple *disjoint* redexes, and thus captures all the potential parallelism of a computation.

1.3 Overview

This concurrent rewriting relation is the one we aim to implement, but this implementation is not straightforward because of two points: First, computing a set of disjoint redexes is a costly operation, that moreover needs a global knowledge of the term. Second, this relation describes a step-by-step computation, implying some kind of synchronization between each steps.

We address the first point in section 2, where we show that when representing the term by a DAG (Directed Acyclic Graph) and applying the rules appropriately, one does not need anymore to compute sets of disjoint redexes.

The second point would not be a problem on SIMD parallel architectures, but our target is a distributed one where global synchronization is very costly. Let us describe the abstract model of our implementation, and see later how it solves this problem: we represent the term to be reduced by a DAG, whose nodes may be distributed among processors. Each node is considered as an independently running process, containing local informations, and able to exchange messages with the other processes through communication channels following the edges of the DAG:

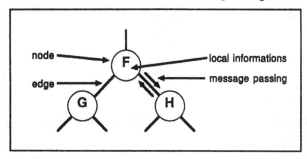

What we are aiming at is to be able to apply a rule at some node (corresponding to some occurrence in the term) by using only the *local* informations contained in that node:

The first idea is to use *bottom-up matching*, that we describe in section 3. Each node stores a *matching state* which is computed only from the states of neighboring nodes. This works in an event-driven way, i.e. without any read request, thus avoiding synchronization or locking problems. We show that we are able to compute the set of rules applyable at some node knowing only this local recorded state.

The second idea is to store locally to each node the *substitution* corresponding to the current matching state, so that applying a rule only requires this local information. Since ongoing reductions may have modified other parts of the term, this recorded substitution may be no more up to date with respect to the rest of this term, but we show in section 4 how this provides a correct implementation for concurrent rewriting. In other words, there is no need for a *global state*.

We finally address in section 5 implementation specific questions.

We do not recall the formal definitions of the concepts needed in rewriting systems and refer to [3, 18, 8]. In particular we suppose the reader familiar with the notions of term, position (or occurrence) and overlap.

2   The Concurrent Rewriting Relation

The concurrent rewriting relation on terms has been introduced in [8] to formalize the idea that many redexes in a term may be rewritten simultaneously while keeping the semantics of rewriting.

2.1 Definition

Let us give an example: the following term may be rewritten by the right-associativity rule $(x + y) + z \to x + (y + z)$ at the three positions (redexes) numbered 1, 2, 3. We would like to rewrite in a single step the redexes 1 and 3, giving the same result as rewriting successively the positions 1 then 3, or 3 then 1. But we can see that it would have no sense to rewrite in a single step 1 and 2, because after rewriting redex 1, the redex 2 disappears.

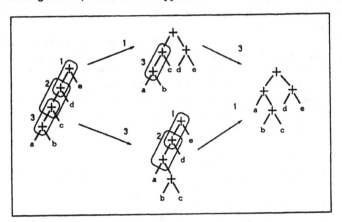

So in order to formally define concurrent rewriting, we have to introduce the notion of non-overlapping set of redexes:

Definition 1 *Let t be a term and R a term rewriting system. Let $R(t) = \{(p_i, l_i, r_i)\}$ be the set of all the redexes in t under R; i.e.*

$$(p_i, l_i, r_i) \in R(t) \Leftrightarrow l_i \to r_i \in R \text{ and } \exists \sigma \text{ such that } t_{|p_i} = \sigma(l_i)$$

A subset W of $R(t)$ is said to be **nonoverlapping** *iff for any redexes (p, l, r) and (p', l', r') in W,*

- *p and p' are incomparable (none is a prefix of the other)*

- *or p is a prefix of p' and there exists a variable position q in l such that $p.q$ is a prefix of p'*

- *if l is non-linear for the variable x and if there exists a position q of x in l such that $p' = p.q.r$ for some r, then $(p.q'.r) \in W$ for all positions q' of x in l.*

The third condition comes from the fact that if a non left-linear rule is applyable, then some subterms have to be equal. If such a rule is applied concurrently with some others, it should be checked that the redexes occurring in the subterms corresponding to the same variable are reduced in the same rewrite step. Otherwise concurrent rewriting would not be correct.

We can now define the concurrent rewriting relation: let $\Delta(t)$ be the set of all nonoverlapping subsets of redexes in t.

Definition 2 *The relation $\to^{R}$ of concurrent rewriting is then defined by*

$$t \to_W^R t' \Leftrightarrow \begin{cases} W = \{(p_i, l_i, r_i) | 1 \le i \le n\} \in \Delta(t) \\ \text{and} \\ i < j \Rightarrow p_i \not< p_j \\ \text{and} \\ t \to_{[p_1, l_1, r_1]}^R t_1 \to \dots \to_{[p_n, l_n, r_n]}^R t' \end{cases}$$

The second condition is only a technical trick that allows a simple expression of the third one. It can be dropped by using the notion of residuals [17].

The concurrent rewriting relation provides a simple mathematical semantics to the parallel execution of rewriting: if sequential rewriting always terminates giving a unique result, so will concurrent rewriting [8] (notice that the converse is false). This ensures the correctness of concurrent rewriting as an implementation of Abstract Data Types. When W is chosen with the maximal number of elements, we talk of *maximal concurrent rewriting*: this relation captures the greatest amount of concurrency that could possibly be achieved in one step. For instance, computing $fibonacci(n)$ using sequential rewriting needs exponential time, while only *linear* time when using maximal concurrent rewriting.

2.2 Implementation

Implementing concurrent rewriting straightforwardly from its definition means repeatedly computing a set of non-overlapping redexes of a term, then rewriting it according to this set; this would lead to a very poor and most probably quite inefficient implementation. The solution that we propose here is twofold. First, in order to avoid testing for overlapping redexes, terms should be represented by DAGs, as already stated in [8]. Second, the operations of matching, substitution and replacement should be performed independently for each redex in the term as it will be explained below. This results in a new rewriting relation that we call parallel rewriting.

Terms are abstract objects that may be implemented as trees or as DAGs. A DAG is a Directed Acyclic Graph, where nodes are labeled with function symbols or variable names, which is compatible with the signature, ie. every node labeled with a symbol of arity k has exactly k ordered outgoing edges. Given a DAG D and a node n in it, the term represented by D at n is defined by:

$$term_D(n) = f(term_D(n_1), \ldots, term_D(n_k)) \text{ if } n \text{ is labeled with the function symbol } f \text{ of arity } k,$$
$$\text{where } n_i \text{ is the target node of the } i\text{-th outgoing edge, or}$$
$$= x \text{ if } n \text{ is labeled with the variable } x$$

We will always assume that each DAG has a distinguished node called *root*, and say that *the* term represented by the DAG D is $term_D(root_D)$. Since there is a canonical mapping from nodes in a DAG to positions of the represented term, we will often identify nodes and positions.

Many DAGs may represent the same term. A node may have many ingoing edges, so some equal subterms may be shared in a DAG implementation. There may also exist nodes without any incoming edge: they are not joinable from the root and are called "garbage" nodes, since they do not act in defining the represented term. The reader may find in [11] a summary about trees versus DAGs for term representation.

The garbage nodes are usually destroyed when performing a rewrite step (ie. the right-hand side of a rule *replaces* the corresponding left-hand side). The key for implementing concurrent rewriting is to keep these nodes, because they may be needed for another simultaneous rewrite step. We can rewrite this way *all* redexes without taking care of overlapping. We just build the right-hand sides and redirect edges as needed, and possibly destroy garbage nodes only after all redirections have taken place. This is shown in the following picture:

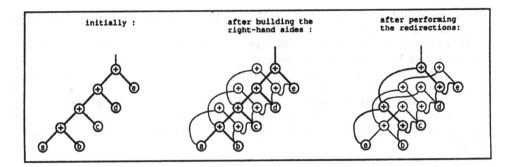

Notice that a DAG structure is mandatory here because some nodes need to be shared. If we now reclaim the garbage nodes (this is not at all mandatory, and in fact we won't do this eagerly), the result is the same as what we would have obtained by rewriting only redexes 1 and 3 (which are non-overlapping):

In our implementation, redirection will be the only atomic operation.

3   The Matching Process

Matching, the operation of finding redexes, is the first step of a rewriting process. We present in this section an efficient concurrent matching algorithm, that needs only constant (low) parallel time, able to match in a single step a term against a (fixed) set of patterns. We use a bottom-up approach which is often more efficient than the top-down one (though it requires a preprocessing phase). It has, moreover, the advantage in a parallel environment to avoid locking and synchronization problems due to read requests.

Bottom-up matching is an old recurrent idea that has been widely studied and improved for special cases. The reader may find a survey on matching algorithms in [16]. The principle of this algorithm is the same as that of the bottom-up algorithm described in [16]. Its originality is that it has been specially designed for allowing an event-driven parallel implementation, needing neither global store nor global control, and to be compatible with parallel rewriting.

In this section, we will only address the case of linear patterns. How to deal with non left-linear rules is explained in Section 4.2.

3.1   Principle of bottom-up matching

Problem 1 (The Matching Problem) *Given a fixed set $L = \{l_1, \ldots, l_n\}$ of linear terms, called patterns (actually the left-hand sides of rewrite rules), and a term t (we will always assume that the variables in L and t are disjoint), determine all the subsets L_p of L such that $l_i \in L_p$ iff there exists a substitution σ such that $\sigma(l_i) \leq t|_p$ (if $l_i \in L_p$, then t may be rewritten at the position p using the rule $l_i \to r_i$).*

We will interleave formal description of the algorithm with its application to the following sample matching problem:

Example 1 *Let R be the rewrite system (over the signature $\{+, F, 0\}$):*

$$\begin{cases} 1: & F(x) + F(y) & \to & F(x+y) \\ 2: & x + (y+z) & \to & (x+y) + z \\ 3: & (x + F(y)) + F(z) & \to & x + F(y+z) \\ 4: & F(0) & \to & 0 \\ 5: & 0 + x & \to & x \\ 6: & x + 0 & \to & x \end{cases}$$

This system may be used, for example, for code optimization (if F is a more costly operation than $+$, this system replaces multiple applications of F by additions). It is canonical, ie. every computation terminates giving a unique result. L is the set of the left-hand sides (notice that all terms in L are linear).

Let the "linear matching" relation $\sqsubseteq$ over terms be defined by $s \sqsubseteq t$ if s is a variable or if $s = f(s_1, \ldots, s_n), t = f(t_1, \ldots, t_n)$, and $s_i \sqsubseteq t_i$ for all $1 \le i \le arity(f)$.

If s is linear, then $s \sqsubseteq t$ if and only if there exists a substitution σ such that $\sigma(s) = t$ (see [17]), so we restate Problem 1 as:

Problem 2 *Given a fixed set $L = \{l_1, \ldots, l_n\}$ of linear patterns, determine all the subsets L_p of L such that $l \in L_p \Leftrightarrow l \sqsubseteq t|_p$.*

Using this formulation, the name of the variables in the patterns does not matter, so we will manipulate these patterns modulo variable renaming, and we introduce the symbol $\perp$ meaning any variable; for example, the set of patterns $\{x + 0, y + 0\}$ becomes $\{\perp + 0\}$ modulo renaming.

For better understanding, we give the graphical (tree) representation of the elements of L. Since we treat the patterns modulo renaming, we do not print the variable's names, but represent them as pending lines:

Example (Continued) *The set L of patterns (modulo renaming) is*

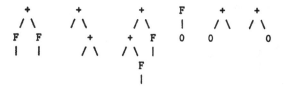

Since a variable pattern matches any term, we will suppose all the patterns to be nonvariable. From the definition of $\sqsubseteq$, the problem of determining L_p is then

$$l \in L_p \Leftrightarrow l \sqsubseteq t|_p \Leftrightarrow l(\epsilon) = t(p) \text{ and } l|_i \sqsubseteq t|_{p.i} \text{ for } 1 \le i \le arity(t(p)) \tag{1}$$

If all $l|_i$ were in L, the subproblems $l|_i \sqsubseteq t|_{p.i}$ would be equivalent to $l|_i \in L_{p.i}$. We can replace Problem 2 by a more general problem were this equivalence always holds:

Problem 3 *Given a fixed set $L = \{l_1, \ldots, l_n\}$ of linear patterns, let $L' = \{l|_p, l \in L, p \in occ(l)\}$ be the set of all subterms of the patterns, called subpatterns, determine all the subsets L'_p of L' such that $l \in L'_p \Leftrightarrow l \sqsubseteq t|_p$.*

Example (Continued) *The set L' of subpatterns is*

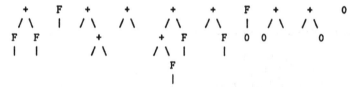

Now we have:

$$l \in L'_p \Leftrightarrow l(\varepsilon) = t(p) \text{ and } l|_i \in L'_{p,i} \text{ for } 1 \leq i \leq arity(t(p)) \qquad (2)$$

and an algorithm for solving Problem 3 becomes straightforward: compute step by step in a bottom-up way each set L'_p from the previously computed $L'_{p,i}$'s, using the relation (2).

We see from relation (2) that each L'_p only depends on the nodes located under p at a distance bounded by the height H of the biggest pattern [16]. When a local change is made in the input term, it is enough to recompute the L'_p's for the changed part and some ancestors of this changed part. So after applying a rewriting step, very few recomputation is needed. Also, when computing the L'_p's in parallel, at most H steps are needed.

3.2 Parallel matching

As formulated, the bottom-up matching algorithm works, but is very costly since we have to store sets of terms and test for membership. But we can improve this algorithm in the following way:

Let S^f be the set

$$S^f = \overline{\{l|_i, l \in L', l(\varepsilon) = f \text{ for } 1 \leq i \leq arity(f)\}} \cup \{\bot\}$$

where $\overline{E}$ denotes the *sup-closure* of the set E with respect to $\sqsubseteq$, ie. $\overline{E}$ is the smallest set containing E such that $e_1, e_2 \in \overline{E} \Rightarrow sup(e_1, e_2) \in \overline{E}$. S^f contains all the subpatterns that a node, labeled f, needs to know whether they match at some son (relation (2)).

Example (Continued) *The sets S^+, S^F and S^0 all contain the term $\bot$ (numbered 0) and the following elements (numbered from 1):*

+					F		0
(1)	(2)	(3)	(4)		(1)		
+	+	F	0		0		
/ \	/ \	|					
	F						
	|						

Now, following relation (2), we can represent each set L'_p by a tuple $S_p = (s_1, \ldots, s_k)$, where $s_i = max\{s \in S^f \mid s \sqsubseteq t|_{p,i}\}$. L'_p is uniquely defined from S_p by

$$L'_p = \{f(s'_1, \ldots, s'_k) \mid s'_i \in S^f, s'_i \sqsubseteq s_i\} \cap L'$$

We can then associate to each position p a tuple S_p, hereafter called the *state* of p, and use a precomputed table to find the corresponding L'_p; we thus avoid storing sets. Actually, we are not interested in the whole L'_p, but only in is subset included in L, ie. the left-hand sides of the rewrite rules, so the table we use is (one for each symbol f with arity k)

$$table^f_1 : (S^f)^k \longrightarrow \mathcal{P}(L)$$
$$(s_1, \ldots, s_k) \longmapsto \{l \in L, l \sqsubseteq f(s_1, \ldots, s_k)\}$$

f	$s = (s_1,\ldots,s_k)$	$table_1^f(s)$	$table_2^f(g,s)$ g 0	f	$+$
0	$()$	$\{\}$	0	1	4
F	(0)	$\{\}$	0	0	3
	(1)	$\{4\}$	0	0	3
$+$	$(0,0)$	$\{\}$	0	0	1
	$(0,1)$	$\{2\}$	0	0	1
	$(0,2)$	$\{2\}$	0	0	1
	$(0,3)$	$\{\}$	0	0	2
	$(0,4)$	$\{6\}$	0	0	1
	$(1,0)$	$\{\}$	0	0	1
	$(1,1)$	$\{2\}$	0	0	1
	$(1,2)$	$\{2\}$	0	0	1
	$(1,3)$	$\{\}$	0	0	2
	$(1,4)$	$\{6\}$	0	0	1
	$(2,0)$	$\{\}$	0	0	1

f	$s = (s_1,\ldots,s_k)$	$table_1^f(s)$	$table_2^f(g,s)$ g 0	f	$+$
$+$	$(2,1)$	$\{2\}$	0	0	1
	$(2,2)$	$\{2\}$	0	0	1
	$(2,3)$	$\{3\}$	0	0	2
	$(2,4)$	$\{6\}$	0	0	1
	$(3,0)$	$\{\}$	0	0	1
	$(3,1)$	$\{2\}$	0	0	1
	$(3,2)$	$\{2\}$	0	0	1
	$(3,3)$	$\{1\}$	0	0	2
	$(3,4)$	$\{6\}$	0	0	1
	$(4,0)$	$\{5\}$	0	0	1
	$(4,1)$	$\{5,2\}$	0	0	1
	$(4,2)$	$\{5,2\}$	0	0	1
	$(4,3)$	$\{5\}$	0	0	2
	$(4,4)$	$\{5,6\}$	0	0	1

Figure 1: $table_1$ and $table_2$ for our example. See the sample execution in the following.

Now we can use a second precomputed table giving the biggest term of S^g matching $t|_{p.i}$ when $t(p.i) = f$ and $S_{p,i} = (s_1,\ldots,s_k)$ (one for each f):

$$table_2^f \ : \ F \times (S^g)^k \ \longrightarrow \ S^f$$
$$(g,(s_1,\ldots,s_k)) \ \longmapsto \ s = max\{s \in S^f | s \sqsubseteq g(s_1,\ldots,s_k)\}$$

The tables for our example are shown in Figure 1. Using $table_2$, we are able to compute each S_p in a bottom-up way from the previously computed $S_{p,i}$'s.

The size of $table_2^f$ grows exponentially with the arity of f, but since its content is very regular, it can be stored using few place.

The matching algorithm, using those tables, is the following:

- (sequential version)

$state(p) = (s_1,\ldots,s_k)$ where
$\qquad t(p) = f,\ arity(f) = k,$
$\qquad s_i =$ if $t(p.i)$ is a variable
$\qquad\qquad$ then 0 (assuming $\perp$ is always coded by 0 as in the example)
$\qquad\qquad$ else $table_2^f(g, s_i')$ where
$\qquad\qquad\qquad g = t(p.i)$ and $s_i' = state(p.i)$

The L_p's are then found by looking up $table_1$. This algorithm clearly needs $O(n)$ time, where n is the number of nonvariable positions in the input term. Notice that the time unit is only a table lookup, plus the overhead for tree traversal.

- (parallel version) A property of this algorithm is that each field of a state $(s_1,\ldots,s_k)$ can be computed independently, so it can work in a fully asynchronous way. This is not the case in [16], since when matching a pattern $f(a,b)$, one has to know simultaneously that the left son matches a and the right son matches b. Here we are ensured that there exist intermediate states corresponding to the knowledge of only one son. Moreover, a state needs to be updated only when a successor's state changes, so the algorithm can work in an event-driven way (ie. without read requests).

Suppose that a process is associated to each node, and can communicate through channels with the ancestor(s) and successors of this node. The algorithm for each process (node labeled f with arity k) is:

initially:
  $s = (0, \ldots, 0)$
  send (f, s) to all ancestors

each time a message (f', s') is received from son i:
  $s_i = table_2^f(f', s')$
  if s_i has changed, send (f, s) to all ancestors

Then, assuming a fairness hypothesis, the algorithm will eventually stop with all the states S_p such that $l \sqsubseteq t|_p \Leftrightarrow l \in table_1^f(S_p)$ (it is correct and complete). We have no way to detect termination, but this is not needed since we aim to use this algorithm for rewriting: as soon as there is enough information in a state for knowing that l_i matches at some node, we are allowed to apply the rule $l_i \longrightarrow r_i$ to that node. We need only to detect termination of the whole rewriting process, which can be done by managing a normal form flag in each node.

Example (Continued)*Here is a sample execution of this algorithm. The term to match is $(F(x) + F(y)) + F(0)$. We write beside each function symbol the corresponding state once it has been computed (in parentheses). We compute step by step each state after all states below it have been computed:*

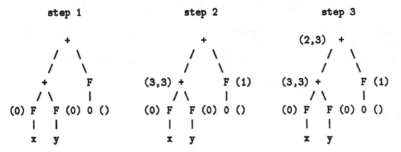

For example, in the third step, we compute the state of the topmost $+$ symbol. Its state is a tuple (s_1, s_2) (arity$(+) = 2$):

- *its left son is labeled $+$ and has state $(3,3)$, so we look into $table_2^+$ and we find*
  $s_1 = table_2^+(+, (3,3)) = 2$

- *its right son is labeled F and has state (1), so we look into $table_2^F$ and we find*
  $s_2 = table_2^F(+, (1)) = 3$

Now we look into table₁ to find the applyable rules with respect to the computed states. We write them between braces:

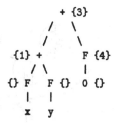

```
                          + {3}
                         /  \
                        /    \
              {1}  +           F {4}
                   / \         |
             {} F   F {}    o {}
                |   |
                x   y
```

For example, the topmost symbol is + and we computed for it the state $(2,3)$, so we look into $table_1^+$ and find $table_1^+((2,3)) = \{3\}$.

Notice that we presented this algorithm for *term* matching, but it extends in a straightforward way to DAGs.

4 Parallel Rewriting

4.1 Linear case

We have seen in section 2 how a DAG representation allows not to compute a set of non-overlapping redexes: this was for one given concurrent rewriting step. Now, since our target architecture is loosely-coupled, we would like to avoid the need of a global state, and consider each node being an independently running process, exchanging informations only through message-passing (see picture page 3). We do no more consider "global" or "synchronous" concurrent rewriting steps, but rather independent "asynchronous" single rewriting steps.

Each node then needs to be able to determine if a rule is applyable and to possibly apply it, using only the locally recorded informations. We have already seen in the previous section a matching algorithm solving the first problem. Now, what is needed for applying a rule is the matching *substitution*, telling how to bind the variable nodes of the newly build right-hand side (a substitution, which is a mapping from variables to terms in the term realm, is implemented by a mapping from variable nodes to *specific* nodes of the DAG).

The solution is to send the substitution informations together with the matching messages. Each node has to record the structure of a part of the DAG located below it, bound in depth by the maximal height of the left-hand sides, say D (deeper nodes cannot be involved in a substitution). This can be done through channels in a bottom-up way, as for matching: each node records locally the node IDs of its successors until the depth D, and sends to its ancestors its own ID and the recorded node IDs until depth $D - 1$.

But, since reductions may take place place everywhere at any time, the recorded substitutions may be no more up to date. This is not a problem; the key point is that match states and substitutions be updated simultaneously, so that the local data are coherent.

Let us see an example. We denote the recorded substitution of the *topmost* node (and only this one, for simplicity of the picture) by dashed lines, the recorded states of all nodes in parentheses and the applicable rules (according to state) in braces. Suppose the initial DAG is as shown in Figure 2 (left). Since the state recorded in node 2 shows that rule 1 may be applied, this node may decide to rewrite (Figure 2, right). Notice that the recorded substitution in node 1 did not change.

Then the newly created node 9 will eventually send a message to node 1 for updating its state and substitution. But node 1 also may perform a rewrite, since its state shows that rule 3 may be applied. Two cases may then arise, depending on which of the two following actions takes place first:

1. If node 1 decides to rewrite before having received the message, it performs the rewriting *according to the substitution it had recorded* (it acts as if the rewriting at node 2 had never occurred, since it does not yet know this). The result is shown in Figure 3, left.

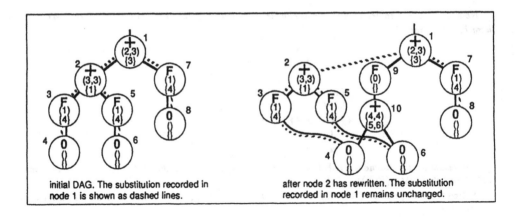

initial DAG. The substitution recorded in node 1 is shown as dashed lines.

after node 2 has rewritten. The substitution recorded in node 1 remains unchanged.

Figure 2

2. If the message is received before node 1 "decides" to rewrite, it updates its state and substitution according to the message. The rewrite at node 2 has now been taken into consideration by node 1; its new state shows that rule 3 can no more be applied (Figure 3, right).

Of course, nodes should not be considered garbage as long as they are referenced in the substitution field of other nodes, since they may still be needed for binding right-hand sides variables. In the figures, we didn't remove the nodes unjoinable from the root: the rule is that a node may be removed when no DAG edges come to it *and* it is no more referenced in a substitution. Removing the "garbage" is not mandatory, but in a distributed environment, the garbage nodes will continue to work and perform rewritings. An eager garbage collection is needed to avoid unnecessary computations.

4.2 Dealing with non left-linear rules

Matching a non left-linear rule is equivalent with matching a linearized version of the same rule and then checking for equality of some instantiated subterms. We already know how to do the first part.

Now, in order to allow non left-linear rules for parallel rewriting, we need to test for subDAGs equality. The only way that we know is to examine nodes in a top-down way. The arising problem is that if the part of the DAG already examined changes (due to parallel rewriting) before the equality test had been completed, then this test would have no sense. Thus we have to ensure that no such rewriting takes place.

Rather than doing some locking on the nodes, our solution is to delay the application of a non left-linear rule at a node until no more linear rule can be applied in the subDAG beginning at that node. This is easy to manage by using a "linear normal form flag" indicating that no linear rule can be applied. This flag is maintained as the normal form flag. When it is set, we are ensured than no rewriting can take place in the subDAG, and we allow the application of non linear rules (ie. equality check).

This solution imposes an implicit bottom-up strategy for the application of non linear rules. This could be a drawback only in very few pathological cases, such as when rewriting $fibonacci(1000) - fibonacci(1000)$, but it is useful in most cases, since the probability of two equivalent terms to be syntactically equal is very low if they are not both in normal form.

When an equality test has succeeded, we are allowed to share the two equal subDAGs. We will of course do it whenever possible for saving space.

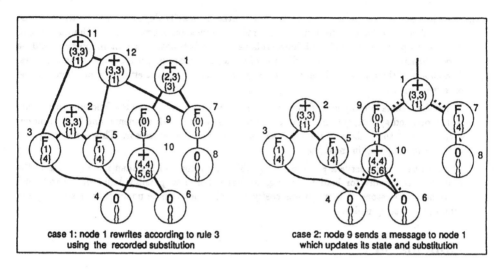

case 1: node 1 rewrites according to rule 3
using the recorded substitution

case 2: node 9 sends a message to node 1
which updates its state and substitution

Figure 3

Another different solution for non linear rules could be to maintain always a fully shared DAG: testing subDAGs equality is only checking the equality of two pointers, and there is no need to lock rewriting. Maintaining a fully shared DAG seems expensive in a distributed environment, but it would be interesting to evaluate this solution in an effective implementation.

5 Implementation issues

A parallel implementation of parallel rewriting is currently under development on a transputer-based machine "T-Node", which is an industrial version of the prototype developed within the European ESPRIT project "Supernode", running the "Trollius 2.1" system [24, 4]. A sequential simulation of parallel rewriting is already running. It consists of two parts, both written in C++. The first builds the matching tables from a given rewrite system, and the second uses those tables for performing parallel rewriting.

We present now a synthetical description of our implementation. In the theoretical description of parallel rewriting we considered each node as a process. On a large-grain architecture, we have to map many processes (nodes) on the same processor. The most important implementation-specific questions are then related to mapping nodes onto processors:

1. When many nodes are located on the same processor, we better process them sequentially. This allows to not record substitutions, except those involving remote nodes, thus saving much space. In fact, we memorize substitutions at the channel level for all outgoing remote channels.

2. Within the same processor, the nodes are implemented using double linked structures (links to successors and ancestors) containing fields for the label, the state and the reference count. We simulate parallel rewriting using a linked list of active nodes, ie. nodes that may possibly be rewritten. Once a node has been examined (and perhaps rewritten), it is removed from the list. It may become active again only when the state of one of its successors changes. This allows to reduce drastically the number of nodes to be checked for rewriting, and would provide an efficient implementation of rewriting even on sequential machines. Also, this implements some kind of *maximal* concurrent rewriting, which has shown to be an interesting strategy, owning nice properties, that we plan to study further.

3. The time and space efficiency of this implementation heavily depends on the ratio between the number of nodes and the number of remote channels on a processor. So the mapping of nodes onto processors should minimize this ratio. Unfortunately, a best mapping would be very expensive to maintain. We will try to get a good mapping, using some heuristic rules. The choice of these rules will need of course to be checked against efficiency, but here are the ones we propose.

When the term is initially loaded on the processor, map it according to the following rule: write it in a prefixed syntax, cut the obtained string into equal length segments, and load all nodes corresponding to symbols in the same segment on the same processor. This seems to give a good initial mapping in most cases.

Then we have to preserve a good mapping while rewriting. Rather than moving parts of the DAG between nodes for load balancing, we have chosen to possibly build right-hand sides on remote processors: it is much less costly to build once remote nodes than destroying and rebuilding existing nodes.

6 Conclusion

We have described in this paper parallel rewriting as a way to efficiently implement concurrent rewriting. The main advantages of our approach are:

- to allow parallel implementation of rewriting on existing parallel architectures,

- to have an implementation backed by a simple but powerful semantics,

- to propose and manage solutions involving only local computations, at least for left-linear rules.

Concurrent rewriting can then provide a programming paradigm allowing efficient parallel execution of programs without any explicit parallel directive. It can also be the kernel of simplification based theorem provers provided we further investigate its interaction, from the concurrency point of view, with the others components of such provers.

Of course the performances of the implementation principles proposed here have to be verified on different kinds of architectures: we plan to run our implementation on a connection machine and an implementation on a transputer based machine is currently under development.

Next in the developments of this work come the generalization of the ideas presented here to the two main extensions of rewriting. On one hand narrowing, which is a powerful equation solving method [20], used as operational semantics for logic-functional languages, for example [5, 12]. In particular the works of [27] and [23, 19] have to be pursued. On the other hand equational rewriting, especially rewriting modulo associativity and commutativity which is shown in [25] to be useful for implementing many known parallelism languages such as Petri nets, CCS, Actors, UNITY.

Acknowledgements: We thank M. Hermann and Hélène Kirchner for their helpful comments about a first version this paper.

References

[1] G. Boudol. Computational semantics of term rewriting systems. In M. Nivat and J. Reynolds, editors, *Application of Algebra to Language definition and Compilation*. Prentice Hall, 1985. Also INRIA research report 192 (1983).

[2] N. Dershowitz. Computing with rewrite systems. *Information and Control*, 65(2/3):122–157, 1985.

[3] N. Dershowitz and J.-P. Jouannaud. Rewrite Systems. In J. van Leuven, editor, *Handbook of Theoretical Computer Science*, chapter 6, pages 244–320. Elsevier Science, 1990.

[4] Gregory Burns et al. Trillium operating system. In *Proc. Third Conference on Hypercube Concurrent Computers and Applications*, pages 374–376. ACM, 1988.

[5] L. Fribourg. SLOG : A logic programming language intepreter based on clausal superposition and rewriting. In *Proceedings of the IEEE Symposium on Logic Programming*, pages 172–184, Boston, MA, July 1985.

[6] J. Goguen, C. Kirchner, H. Kirchner, A. Megrelis, J. Meseguer, and T. Winkler. An introduction to OBJ-3. In J.-P. Jouannaud and S. Kaplan, editors, *Proceedings 1st International Workshop on Conditional Term Rewriting Systems, Orsay (France)*, volume 308 of *Lecture Notes in Computer Science*, pages 258–263. Springer-Verlag, 1988. Also as internal report CRIN: 88-R-001.

[7] J. Goguen, C. Kirchner, S. Leinwand, J. Meseguer, and T. Winkler. Progress report on the rewrite rule machine. *IEEE Computer Architecture Technical Commitee Newsletter*, pages 7–21, March 1986.

[8] J. Goguen, C. Kirchner, and J. Meseguer. Concurrent term rewriting as a model of computation. In R. Keller and J. Fasel, editors, *Proceedings of Graph Reduction Workshop*, volume 279 of *Lecture Notes in Computer Science*, pages 53–93. Springer-Verlag, 1987.

[9] J. A. Goguen and J. Tardo. OBJ-0 preliminary users manual. Semantics and theory of computation report no. 10, UCLA, 1977.

[10] J.A. Goguen. The rewrite rule machine project. In *Proceedings of the second international conference on supercomputing*, Santa Clara, California, May 1987.

[11] J.A. Goguen, C. Kirchner, and J. Meseguer. Models of computation for the rewrite rule machine. Technical report, Rapport CRIN 86-R-104, 1986.

[12] J.A. Goguen and J. Meseguer. EQLOG: Equality, types and generic modules for logic programming. In D. DeGroot and G. Lindstrom, editors, *Logic Programming. Funstions, relations and equations*. Prentice Hall, 1986.

[13] P.R.H. Hendriks. Asf system user's guide. internal report CS-R8823, Centre for Mathematics and Computer Science, PO BOX 4079, 1009 AB Amsterdam, Netherlands, May 1988.

[14] M. Hermann, C. Kirchner, and H. Kirchner. Implementations of term rewriting systems. Technical Report 89-R-218, Centre de Recherche en Informatique de Nancy, 1989. To appear in the *Computer Journal*, British Computer Society.

[15] T. Heuillard. Compiling conditional rewriting systems. In S. Kaplan and J.-P. Jouannaud, editors, *Proceedings 1st International Workshop on Conditional Term Rewriting Systems, Orsay (France)*, volume 308 of *Lecture Notes in Computer Science*, pages 111–128. Springer-Verlag, 1987.

[16] C. Hoffmann and M.J. O'Donnell. Pattern matching in trees. *Journal of the Association for Computing Machinery*, 29(1):68–95, 1982.

[17] G. Huet and J.-J. Levy. Call by need computations in non-ambiguous linear term rewriting systems. Research report 359, INRIA, August 1979.

[18] G. Huet and D. Oppen. Equations and rewrite rules: A survey. In R. Book, editor, *Formal Language Theory: Perspectives and Open Problems*, pages 349–405. Academic Press, New York, 1980.

[19] N. Alan Josephson and Nachum Dershowitz. An implementation of narrowing. *J. of Logic Programming*, 6(1&2):57–77, March 1989.

[20] J.-P. Jouannaud and C. Kirchner. Solving equations in abstract algebras: a rule-based survey of unification. Research report, CRIN, 1990. To appear in *Festschrift for Robinson*, J.-L. Lassez and G. Plotkin, editors, MIT Press.

[21] S. Kaplan. A compiler for conditional term rewriting system. In P. Lescanne, editor, *Proceedings 2nd Conference on Rewriting Techniques and Applications, Bordeaux (France)*, volume 256 of *Lecture Notes in Computer Science*, pages 25–41, Bordeaux (France), May 1987. Springer-Verlag.

[22] C. Kirchner and P. Viry. Implementing parallel rewriting. In P. Deransart and J. Maluszynski, editors, *Proceedings of PLILP'90*, volume 456 of *Lecture Notes in Computer Science*, pages 1–15, Linköping (Sweden), August 1990. Springer-Verlag.

[23] N. Lindenstrauss. A parallel implementation of rewriting and narrowing. In *Proceedings 3rd Conference on Rewriting Techniques and Applications, Chapel Hill, (North Carolina, USA)*, volume 35 of *Lecture Notes in Computer Science*, pages 569–573, Chapel Hill, NC, April 1989. Springer-Verlag.

[24] M. Loi and B. Tourancheau. Trollius 2.0. Technical report, Ecole Normale Supérieure de Lyon, 1990. In french.

[25] José Meseguer. Rewriting as a unified model of concurrency. Technical Report SRI-CSL-90-02, SRI International, Computer Science Laboratory, February 1990.

[26] M. J. O'Donnell. *Computing in Systems Described by Equations*, volume 58 of *Lecture Notes in Computer Science*. Springer-Verlag, 1977.

[27] P. Viry. Implantation parallèle de la surréduction et de la réécriture. Rapport de DEA de l'université de Nancy I, September 1989.

[28] P. Viry. Properties of concurrent rewriting. Technical report, Centre de Recherche en Informatique de Nancy, 1991. In preparation.

Experiments with ROO, a Parallel Automated Deduction System*

Ewing L. Lusk
William W. McCune

Mathematics and Computer Science Division
Argonne National Laboratory

lusk@mcs.anl.gov
mccune@mcs.anl.gov

1 Introduction

The automated theorem prover OTTER[12, 14] represents the state of the art in high-speed, general purpose theorem provers. One way to increase OTTER's speed further is through the exploitation of parallelism. A general, parallel algorithm for the computing the closure of a set under an operation was presented in [18]. Since OTTER's fundamental algorithm can be viewed as a closure computation, this algorithm can be applied to OTTER. The result is ROO, a parallel theorem prover compatible with OTTER that runs on shared-memory multiprocessors.

ROO itself is described in [8] and [9]. For completeness we present a summary of the basic algorithm in Section 2. Compared with the numerical applications typically run on today's multiprocessors, ROO's behavior is considerably more complex. Its algorithm performs well in general, but in certain situations does badly. Some of these situations reflect only certain phases of runs on particular problems. Sometimes ROO, even with only one process, outperforms OTTER, and sometimes it does much worse. Speedups are often roughly linear, which is why we are well-satisfied with ROO. Sometimes they are far below linear, and sometimes startlingly superlinear. In general, a full appreciation of the subtleties of parallel computation in this application area can only be obtained by looking closely at the behavior of ROO on a wide variety of theorem-proving problems.

The purpose of this paper is to provide such a detailed look. After summarizing the algorithms of OTTER and ROO in Section 2, we present a series of experiments taken from a wide variety of test problems. These show ROO both at its best and its worst and exhibit a number of surprising features. Since the problems themselves are of interest, we provide (except in one rather tedious case) the complete set of input clauses that make up the problem. For each problem we exhibit the performance of ROO and analyze the results.

Finally, the non-deterministic nature of parallel algorithms means that consecutive runs of the same input file, on the same number of processes, can produce different results. In Section 4 we address the question of the stability and reproducibility of the results we have reported for ROO.

*This work was supported by the Applied Mathematical Sciences subprogram of the Office of Energy Research, U.S. Department of Energy, under Contract W-31-109-Eng-38.

2 Algorithms

2.1 A Sequential Theorem Proving Algorithm without Deletion

We present here a simplified form of the theorem-proving algorithm that has been used in Argonne systems over the years[23, 11, 12]. For an introduction to the approach, see [21]. We assume that the goal is to prove a set of clauses unsatisfiable. We assume further that the input clauses are divided into two sets, which we call *Usable* and *Set of support* (SOS), in such a way that the Usable set is satisfiable. (If the input clauses make this difficult to do, then the Usable set may be chosen to be the empty set.) Thus we will be using the "set-of-support strategy" first described in [22].

```
While (the null clause has not been produced and SOS is not empty)
        Choose a clause from the set of support, call it the given clause, and move it to
                the Usable set
        Generate all clauses that can be deduced from the given clause and
                other clauses in the Usable set
        For each new generated clause
                Process it (rewrite to canonical form, merge literals, etc.)
                Test if it is subsumed by any existing clause (in either Usable or SOS)
                Test if it is too heavy
                If the new clause survives
                        Add it to SOS
                end if
        end for
end while
```

Figure 1: Sequential Theorem-Proving Algorithm without Deletion (Algorithm 1)

The algorithm given in Figure 1 can complete with the empty clause found (giving a proof that the input clause set is unsatisfiable), compete without the empty clause being found (no proof), or it can fail to terminate with the constraints of time and memory. If the filtering mechanism applied is appropriately chosen, then this scheme is complete: that is, if the algorithm terminates without finding the empty clause, then the original set of clauses is satisfiable.

The currently most effective implementation of this algorithm is OTTER[12]. OTTER has a wide variety of inference rules and control parameters for adapting this algorithm to a particular problem and sophisticated indexing methods to make each of the operations quite fast, even when the set of kept clauses has grown to a hundred thousand clauses or more.

This particular approach contrasts with some more recent "Prolog technology" theorem provers[19, 17], which use the compilation techniques from WAM-based Prolog implementations to achieve extremely high inference rates, at a cost of possibly redundant computations. The "closure" approach taken here is based on the expectation that a clause deduced and processed is worth keeping as a filter for preventing the deduction and subsequent use of duplicate or weaker clauses. Experience is on the side of the closure approach; although certain small problems can be done very quickly with the Prolog-technology approach, many

large problems done years ago with the closure approach remain out of reach of even the
best Prolog technology systems. An example is given in Section 3.1 below.

2.2 ROO Without Deletion

In this section we present the parallel version of Algorithm 1 and its implementation based
on OTTER.

An early attempt to parallelize Algorithm 1 focused on the inner "for" loop. This is
relatively straightforward, since the rewriting, subsumption, and filtering of one new clause
is independent from that of another, as long as one finishes up the loop by checking for
subsumption among members of the batch. The problem with this approach is that even
when there are large numbers of clauses in each batch, the barrier at the end of the loop
meant that many processes were temporarily idle.

The key idea here is to parallelize the outer "while" loop instead. That is, we will
consider multiple "given" clauses simultaneously. This both increases the grain size of the
parallel computation and removes any barriers. The difficulty, of course, is that without
some care, two copies of the same clause might enter the permanent clause space, each
deduced and post-processed by a different process. We will also need to solve technical
problems associated with adding clauses to the clause space while it is in use by other
clauses.

Our approach is to use an intermediate holding area, which we will call (arbitrarily)
K. New clauses are first put in K, from which they are removed by a single process which
repeats the post-processing of the clause before adding it to the clause database. Thus we
break down the work to be done into two tasks: A and B. At any moment multiple processes
will be executing Task A, but at most one process will be executing Task B. Each instance
of Task A is associated with a given clause. Task B is only executed when the set K is
non-empty.

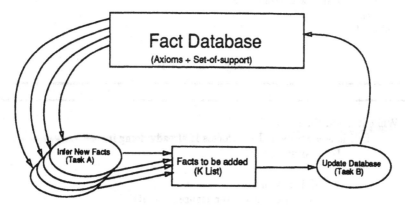

Figure 2: Flow of Data in Simplified ROO

Note that there is not a separate process dedicated to Task B. Rather, we create a
uniform pool of processes, each of which performs the loop shown in Figure 5.

The loop continues until some process detects unit conflict or until the set of support is
empty and all processes are waiting for a clause to appear there.

```
Task A(given clause):
     Generate new clauses
     For each new clause
          Rewrite it
          Subsumption test
          Filter
          If it survives
               Lock K
               Put new clause in K
               Unlock K
          end if
     end for
```

Figure 3: Task A

```
Task B:
     While K is not empty
          Lock K
          Choose a clause from K
          Unlock K
          Redo rewrite, subsumption test, filter
          If it survives
               Integrate new clause into database
               Put new clause in SOS
          end if
     end while
```

Figure 4: Task B

```
While it is not time to stop
     If K is non-empty and no process is already doing it
          Do Task B
     else
          If SOS is not empty
               Choose a new given clause from SOS
               Do Task A(given clause)
          end if
     end if
end while
```

Figure 5: Main loop performed by all processes

2.3   The Complete Roo Algorithm

In Section 2.2 we described a simplified version of OTTER's algorithm, in which no clauses are deleted from the database once they have been added. In the complete version, back subsumption tests are done on newly-derived clauses, causing deletions, and new rewrite rules may be derived in the course of the run. These new rewrite rules are immediately applied to existing clauses in the database, causing both deletions and new additions. Coping with deletions complexifies Roo since we do not want to interfere with the generation of new clauses when deleting. It turns out that this problem can be solved by having Task B handle actual deletions. Back subsumption and back demodulation processes can run in parallel with all other processes, but instead of actually deleting clauses from the database, they place their identifiers in shared lists where Task B (executed by only one process at a time) can find them and carry out the actual deletions. This algorithm is shown schematically in Figure 6.

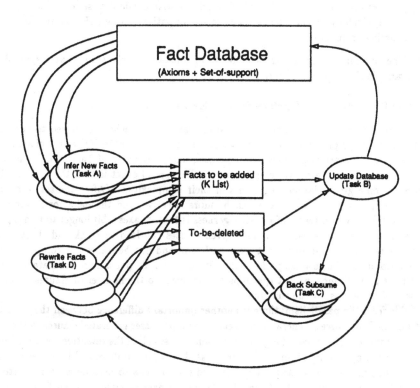

Figure 6: Flow of Data in Roo

The clause lists are held in shared memory with Otter's elaborate data structures for indexing. This makes the above algorithm very much a shared-memory parallel algorithm.

2.4 Some Important Features of OTTER and ROO

In order to understand the experiments, it is necessary to be familiar with at least a few of the many OTTER and ROO features for controlling the algorithms given in this section.

1. The user must select one or more inference rules. Each of the experiments presented here uses one of the inference rules hyperresolution, binary resolution, or paramodulation.

2. The default method for selecting the next given clause is by weight—to take one with the fewest number of symbols. An alternative is to use the SOS list as a queue, which results in a breadth-first search. The ratio strategy combines those two methods: The user specifies a ratio n, with n given clauses selected by weight for each selected because it is first in SOS.

3. The Knuth-Bendix option causes OTTER or ROO to use its paramodulation and demodulation as in the Knuth-Bendix completion method. With that option, the program can find refutations as well as terminate with a complete set of reductions. The user typically uses the lexicographic recursive path ordering (LRPO) and assigns an ordering on function symbols.

4. The rule for distinguishing variables from constants in clauses is that a symbol is a variable if and only if it starts with u–z.

2.5 Differences that Surface in the Experiments

The parallelism of ROO can significantly alter search spaces when compared to analogous OTTER runs. Both programs by default select the simplest clause in SOS as the given clause. However, at the start of parallel ROO searches, many instances of Task A demand given clauses before there are many to select from. The typical effect is that the first few kept clauses become given clauses, regardless of their complexities. (After the set of support has had a chance to grow, Task A can be more selective, and the behavior is similar to OTTER's.) The typical result of ROO's eagerness is that it takes a bit longer to find a proof; but in some cases those early, complex given clauses can lead to quick and short proofs, which are reflected in speedups that are superlinear, and in other cases, the complex clauses can lead to prolific but useless paths in the search space. To give a more accurate picture of the ROO's performance, we list speedups with respect to the number of clauses generated per second as well as for the run time.

Aside from the parallelism, there is another important difference between the ways that OTTER and ROO process generated clauses. OTTER processes generated clauses in the order in which they are generated. If a generated clause passes all of the retention tests, including forward subsumption, it is immediately integrated into the database and becomes available to subsume the next generated clause. In addition, if it is to become a demodulator, it does so immediately and is able to rewrite the next generated clause. When ROO's Task A generates a clause which passes the retention tests, the clause goes into limbo in the K list, and is not available to subsume or rewrite the next generated clause. ROO's Task B removes clauses from the K list shortest-first and integrates those that pass the second application of the retention tests. OTTER can perform better in some cases, because ROO must reapply retention tests, and ROO can perform better in other cases, because it integrates simple clauses before complex clauses. This behavior occurs in one-processor ROO searches as well as in parallel searches.

3 Experiments

The following experiments come from a variety of areas: lattice theory, semigroup theory, group theory, Boolean algebra, circuit design, calculus, non-classical logic, and robotics. They include several standard theorem prover test problems from the literature as well as some more exotic ones.

The tests were conducted on the 26-processor, 32 megabyte Sequent Symmetry in the Advanced Computing Research Facility at Argonne National laboratory. We give results for OTTER as well as for ROO, (1) so that speedups can be measured against the best known sequential algorithm, as they should be, (2) to show that the parallel algorithm with one process is in general comparable to that of OTTER, and (3) to illustrate the occasional differences between OTTER and ROO with one process.

We give statistics not only for elapsed time (in seconds) but also for the number of clauses generated, because it is a rough measure of how much work was done during the run. We aim for regular and predictable speedups in the amount of work done per unit of time, even when the rearrangement of the search space caused by nondeterminism causes sudden changes in the time ROO takes to discover a proof.

3.1 SAM's Lemma

SAM's Lemma, a problem in lattice theory named after the first theorem prover that proved it, is a standard problem for evaluating theorem provers. It was one of the first non-trivial problems done by an automated system. It was first described in [3]. Although its solution was reported more than twenty years ago, it still remains beyond the reach of most current systems. The main reason is common to many problems in algebra: there are many paths to each derived clause, so any system that does not employ subsumption will explore a much larger search space than is necessary. (Clauses 1–20 below are not a full axiomatization of modular lattice theory.)

Clauses for SAM's Lemma

Input Usable Clauses

1   $join(1, x, 1)$.
2   $join(x, 1, 1)$.
3   $join(0, x, x)$.
4   $join(x, 0, x)$.
5   $meet(0, x, 0)$.
6   $meet(x, 0, 0)$.
7   $meet(1, x, x)$.
8   $meet(x, 1, x)$.
9   $meet(x, x, x)$.
10 $join(x, x, x)$.
11 $\neg meet(x, y, z) \mid meet(y, x, z)$.
12 $\neg join(x, y, z) \mid join(y, x, z)$.
13 $\neg meet(x, y, z) \mid join(x, z, x)$.
14 $\neg join(x, y, z) \mid meet(x, z, x)$.
15 $\neg meet(x, y, xy) \mid \neg meet(y, z, yz) \mid \neg meet(x, yz, xyz) \mid meet(xy, z, xyz)$.
16 $\neg meet(x, y, xy) \mid \neg meet(y, z, yz) \mid \neg meet(xy, z, xyz) \mid meet(x, yz, xyz)$.

17   $\neg join(x, y, xy) \mid \neg join(y, z, yz) \mid \neg join(x, yz, xyz) \mid join(xy, z, xyz).$
18   $\neg join(x, y, xy) \mid \neg join(y, z, yz) \mid \neg join(xy, z, xyz) \mid join(x, yz, xyz).$
19   $\neg meet(x, z, x) \mid \neg join(x, y, x1) \mid \neg meet(y, z, y1) \mid \neg meet(z, x1, z1) \mid join(x, y1, z1).$
20   $\neg meet(x, z, x) \mid \neg join(x, y, x1) \mid \neg meet(y, z, y1) \mid \neg join(x, y1, z1) \mid meet(z, x1, z1).$

Input Set of Support Clauses

21   $meet(a, b, c).$
22   $join(c, r2, 1).$
23   $meet(c, r2, 0).$
24   $meet(r2, b, e).$
25   $join(a, b, c2).$
26   $join(c2, r1, 1).$
27   $meet(c2, r1, 0).$
28   $meet(r2, a, d).$
29   $join(r1, e, a2).$
30   $join(r1, d, b2).$
31   $\neg meet(a2, b2, r1).$

Strategy for SAM's Lemma

The inference rule was hyperresolution, and forward subsumption (but not back subsumption) was applied.

Results for SAM's Lemma

	OTTER	Roo-1	Roo-4	Roo-8	Roo-12	Roo-16	Roo-20	Roo-24
Run time	30.70	32.04	7.91	4.37	2.57	2.85	1.98	1.62
Generated	5924	5981	5977	6079	6022	6208	6143	5837
Kept	134	134	131	131	130	130	129	124
Memory (K)	95	159	220	344	468	592	716	840
Gen/sec	192	186	755	1391	2343	2178	3102	3603
Speedups:								
Proof	1.0	1.0	3.9	7.0	11.9	10.8	15.5	19.0
Gen/sec	1.0	1.0	3.9	7.2	12.2	11.3	16.2	18.8

Notes on SAM's Lemma

The performance of Roo is excellent with up to 12 processes, because of the simple and uniform nature of the clauses. Speedups with more than 12 processes are less than linear because the problem is so short.

3.2   Imp-4

This problem in the implicational propositional calculus was first brought to our attention in [15]. Clause 2 below is a single axiom (due to Lukasiewicz) for the calculus, clause 3 denies the law of hypothetical syllogism, and clause 1 is the representation of condensed detachment. Any refutation of these three clauses shows that law of hypothetical syllogism can be derived by condensed detachment from the single axiom.

Clauses for Imp-4

Input Usable Clauses

1   $\neg P(x) \mid \neg P(i(x,y)) \mid P(y)$.

Input Set of Support Clauses

2   $P(i(i(i(x,y),z),i(i(z,x),i(u,x))))$.
3   $\neg P(i(i(a,b),i(i(b,c),i(a,c))))$.

Strategy for Imp-4

The inference rule was hyperresolution, and forward subsumption (but not back subsumption) was applied. In addition, to conserve memory, generated clauses with more than 20 symbols were discarded.

Results for Imp-4

	OTTER	Roo-1	Roo-4	Roo-8	Roo-12	Roo-16	Roo-20	Roo-24
Run time	29098.32	29984.67	7180.29	3440.89	2462.52	1844.03	1492.35	1269.28
Generated	6706380	6668046	6413924	6208570	6649996	6662397	6826296	7108289
Kept	20410	20342	20309	20242	20438	18281	19534	18759
Memory (K)	7185	7791	8653	9737	13119	14235	17109	19498
Gen/sec	230	222	893	1804	2700	3612	4574	5600
Speedups:								
Proof	1.0	1.0	4.1	8.5	11.8	15.8	19.5	22.9
Gen/sec	1.0	1.0	3.9	7.8	11.7	15.7	19.9	24.3

Notes on Imp-4

Roo obtains nearly linear speedups on Imp-4. Note that with 24 processes, more clauses are generated, but fewer are kept than in most other cases.

3.3   F3B2

It is possible for a free semigroup to be known to be finite yet for its size to remain unknown. The semigroup can be represented in terms of generators and an operation, in which the semigroup itself is the closure of the set of generators under that operation. OTTER's (and therefore Roo's) basic algorithm can thus be used to compute the size of the semigroup. It is only necessary to describe the semigroup operation in terms of hyperresolution. this process is described in detail in [10] for the case of the semigroup F2B2. The semigroup F3B2 is larger, and potentially contains 5^{125} elements. The fact that there are actually only 1435 elements was first discovered by ITP, OTTER's predecessor[7, 6]. Again, this problem relies heavily on subsumption.

Clauses for F3B2

The elements of F3B2 are 125-tuples of elements of the Bradt semigroup B2, whose multiplication table is as follows:

	0	e	f	a	b
0	0	0	0	0	0
e	0	e	0	a	0
f	0	0	f	0	b
a	0	0	a	0	e
b	0	b	0	f	0

Multiplication in F3B2 is componentwise. The generators of F3B2 can be written as

$$g_1 = 0^5 e^5 f^5 a^5 b^5$$
$$g_2 = (0efab)^5$$
$$h_1 = 0^5 e^5 f^5 b^5 a^5$$
$$h_2 = (0efba)^5$$

To find the size of F3B2, we use clauses (1) that say that these are the generators, (2) that say that generators are elements of the semigroup, and (3) that say that the product of a generator and an element is an element, where the product is defined by demodulators. The complete set of clauses is a straightforward extension of the clauses given in [10] for F2B2.

Strategy for F3B2

The inference rule was hyperresolution, and forward subsumption (but not back subsumption) was applied. No refutation is expected—the run terminates when the SOS list is exhausted.

Results for F3B2

	OTTER	Roo-1	Roo-4	Roo-8	Roo-12	Roo-16	Roo-20
Run time	1056.74	1062.74	277.06	142.83	98.62	77.80	65.97
Generated	8616	8616	8616	8616	8616	8616	8616
Kept	1435	1435	1435	1435	1435	1435	1435
Memory (K)	6642	6706	8716	11270	14652	18096	23139
Gen/sec	8	8	31	60	87	110	130
Speedups:							
Run time	1.0	1.0	3.8	7.4	10.7	13.6	16.0
Gen/sec	1.0	1.0	3.9	7.5	10.9	13.8	16.3

Notes on F3B2

Performance of Roo is very regular, but we have not yet determined why the speedups are not closer to being linear.

3.4   2-Inverter Problem

Is it possible to construct a 3-input, 3-output binary circuit, consisting of any number of AND gates and OR gates, but only two NOT gates, in which each output is the inversion of the corresponding input? This is a pleasing circuit design puzzle, described in [21] and in [16]. The trick is to keep track not of every circuit that can be built, but only of the output patterns that can be constructed, and the use of the inverters. An interesting result derived by OTTER is that any solution of this problem (of which there are many) must use the two inverters in the same way; that is, to invert the same signals.

Clauses for 2-Inverter Problem

Input Usable Clauses

1 $\neg function(x, v) \mid \neg function(y, v) \mid function(\$BIT\_AND(x, y), v)$.
2 $\neg function(x, v) \mid \neg function(y, v) \mid function(\$BIT\_OR(x, y), v)$.
3 $\neg function(x, v) \mid function(\$BIT\_AND(255, \$BIT\_NOT(x))$,
                 $addinv(v, invtab(\$BIT\_AND(255, \$BIT\_NOT(x)))))$.
4 $\neg function(240, v) \mid \neg function(204, v) \mid \neg function(170, v)$.

Input Set of Support Clauses

5 $function(15, v)$.
6 $function(51, v)$.
7 $function(85, v)$.

Input Demodulators

8 $(addinv(l(x, y), z) = l(x, addinv(y, z)))$.
9 $\$CONDITIONAL(\$VAR(x), addinv(x, y), l(y, x))$.

Strategy for 2-Inverter Problem

The clauses for this problem use several built-in functions (those that start with $\$BIT$) to perform bitwise operations. Boolean functions are encoded as integers, and demodulation evaluates the built-in functions. Demodulators 8 and 9 manage the list of inverted signals. $\$CONDITIONAL(\alpha, \beta, \gamma)$ means "if α, then rewrite β to γ".

The inference rule was hyperresolution, and forward subsumption (but not back subsumption) was applied. Generated clauses representing circuits with more than two inverters were discarded by weighting.

Results for 2-Inverter Problem

	OTTER	Roo-1	Roo-4	Roo-8	Roo-12	Roo-16	Roo-20	Roo-24
Run time	47235.57	47704.68	12376.65	6219.20	4402.19	3141.14	2586.23	2236.77
Generated	6323644	6324501	6313683	6050605	6340536	6099702	5978269	6351410
Kept	21342	21343	21343	21343	21344	21343	21343	21343
Memory (K)	5588	5875	6033	6256	6762	6959	16184	18736
Gen/sec	133	132	510	972	1440	1941	2311	2839
Speedups:								
Proof	1.0	1.0	3.8	7.6	10.7	15.0	18.3	21.1
Gen/sec	1.0	1.0	3.8	7.3	10.8	14.6	17.4	21.3

Notes on 2-Inverter Problem

Performance of Roo is regular, with excellent speedups.

3.5 Bledsoe-P1

This is first (easiest) of a sequence of five challenge problems from W. Bledsoe[1]. All of the five problems are variants of the theorem that the sum of continuous functions is continuous.

Clauses for Bledsoe-P1

Input Usable Clauses

1   $\neg LE(0, xE) \mid LE(0, D1(xE))$.
2   $\neg LE(0, xE) \mid LE(0, D2(xE))$.
3   $\neg LE(0, xE) \mid \neg LE(abs(+(x, \neg(A))), D1(xE)) \mid LE(abs(+(F(x), \neg(F(A)))), xE)$.
4   $\neg LE(0, xE) \mid \neg LE(abs(+(x, \neg(A))), D2(xE)) \mid LE(abs(+(G(x), \neg(G(A)))), xE)$.
5   $LE(0, E0)$.
6   $\neg LE(0, xD) \mid LE(abs(+(XS(xD), \neg(A))), xD)$.
7   $\neg LE(z, MIN(x, y)) \mid LE(z, x)$.
8   $\neg LE(z, MIN(x, y)) \mid LE(z, y)$.
9   $\neg LE(0, x) \mid \neg LE(0, y) \mid LE(0, MIN(x, y))$.
10   $\neg LE(x, HALF(z)) \mid \neg LE(y, HALF(z)) \mid LE(+(x, y), z)$.
11   $\neg LE(0, x) \mid LE(0, HALF(x))$.

Input Set of Support Clauses

12   $\neg LE(0, xD) \mid$
     $\neg LE(+(abs(+(F(XS(xD)), \neg(F(A)))), abs(+(G(XS(xD)), \neg(G(A))))), E0)$.

Strategy for Bledsoe-P1

The inference rule was binary resolution with factoring. (Factoring is not required). Forward subsumption (but not back subsumption) was applied. Generated clauses with more than 40 symbols were discarded, and generated clauses in which any of the function symbols *HALF*, *abs*, *MIN*, +, *D1*, or *D2* was nested with itself were discarded.

Results for Bledsoe-P1

	OTTER	ROO-1	ROO-4	ROO-8	ROO-12	ROO-16	ROO-20	ROO-24
Run time	49.63	66.67	18.04	11.37	11.41	11.19	11.89	12.37
Generated	2594	2338	3056	3235	3136	3156	3143	3122
Kept	756	704	652	523	523	524	524	522
Memory (K)	510	574	1372	1880	1940	2000	2028	2216
Gen/sec	52	35	169	284	274	282	264	252
Speedups from OTTER:								
Proof	1.0	0.7	2.8	4.4	4.3	4.4	4.2	4.0
Gen/sec	1.0	0.7	3.3	5.5	5.3	5.4	5.1	4.9
Speedups from ROO-1:								
Proof	1.3	1.0	3.7	5.9	5.8	6.0	5.6	5.4
Gen/sec	1.5	1.0	4.8	8.1	7.9	8.1	7.6	7.2

Notes on Bledsoe-P1

The difference in performance between OTTER and ROO-1 results from extra forward subsumption tests done by ROO-1. Generated clauses were typically nonunit, and subsumption with nonunit clauses is very expensive. Statistics in the output files showed that Task B was a bottleneck, requiring more than 10 seconds in each of the ROO runs, which is reflected the poor speedups.

3.6 CD-12

Problem CD-12 is from the two-valued sentential calculus. Clauses 2–4 below are Lukasiewicz's axiomatization of the calculus, clause 5 denies a form of the law of syllogism, and clause 1 encodes condensed detachment. The symbols i and n can be interpreted as implication and negation, respectively.

Clauses for CD-12

Input Usable Clauses

1    $\neg P(i(x,y)) \mid \neg P(x) \mid P(y)$.

Input Set of Support Clauses

2    $P(i(i(x,y), i(i(y,z), i(x,z))))$.
3    $P(i(i(n(x),x),x))$.
4    $P(i(x, i(n(x),y)))$.
5    $\neg P(i(i(b,c), i(i(a,b), i(a,c))))$.

Strategy for CD-12

The inference rule was hyperresolution, and both forward and back subsumption were applied. Generated clauses with more than 20 symbols were discarded.

Results for CD-12

	OTTER	ROO-1	ROO-4	ROO-8	ROO-12	ROO-16	ROO-20	ROO-24
Run time	373.96	398.19	108.89	54.30	27.13	24.82	8.42	8.15
Generated	78301	78303	79323	84353	67595	80796	31972	30692
Kept	7220	7122	7451	5183	2951	2480	803	612
Memory (K)	3576	3768	5459	7309	6668	8998	6188	6312
Gen/sec	209	196	728	1553	2491	3255	3797	3765
Speedups:								
Proof	1.0	0.9	3.4	6.9	13.8	15.1	44.4	45.9
Gen/sec	1.0	0.9	3.5	7.4	11.9	15.6	18.2	18.0

Notes on CD-12

Performance of ROO appears to be regular with up to 16 processes. ROO-20 and ROO-24 apparently found shortcuts in the search spaces. (See Sections 2.5 and 4).

3.7 CD-13

Problem CD-13 is similar to CD-12, except that the goal is to prove Peirce's law (denied in clause 5 below) rather than the syllogism law.

Clauses for CD-13

Input Usable Clauses

1 $\neg P(i(x,y)) \mid \neg P(x) \mid P(y)$.

Input Set of Support Clauses

2 $P(i(i(x,y), i(i(y,z), i(x,z))))$.
3 $P(i(i(n(x),x),x))$.
4 $P(i(x, i(n(x),y)))$.
5 $\neg P(i(i(i(a,b),a),a))$.

Strategy for CD-13

The inference rule was hyperresolution, and both forward and subsumption were applied. Generated clauses with more than 20 symbols were discarded.

Results for CD-13

	OTTER	ROO-1	ROO-4	ROO-8	ROO-12	ROO-16	ROO-20	ROO-24
Run time	373.07	416.12	104.20	58.68	34.21	9.38	7.62	18.78
Generated	78624	78773	80606	88026	83701	29850	29385	90541
Kept	7324	7292	7149	5270	3546	1016	739	1533
Memory (K)	3608	3800	5171	8138	8649	5615	5836	12220
Gen/sec	210	189	773	1500	2446	3182	3856	4821
Speedups:								
Proof	1.0	0.9	3.6	6.4	10.9	39.8	49.0	19.9
Gen/sec	1.0	0.9	3.7	7.1	11.7	15.2	18.4	23.0

Notes on CD-13

Performance of ROO appears to be regular with up to 12 processes, but ROO-16 and ROO-20 apparently found shortcuts in the search spaces, and ROO-24 had to explore more of the space. (See Sections 2.5 and 4).

3.8 CD-90

Problem CD-90, which is in the left group calculus[4], is to show a dependence in one of J. Kalman's original axiomatizations of the calculus[13]. The symbols P and e can be interpreted as "is the identity" and left division in groups.

Clauses for CD-90

Input Usable Clauses

1 $\neg P(e(x,y)) \mid \neg P(x) \mid P(y)$.

Input Set of Support Clauses

2    $P(e(e(e(e(e(e(x,y),e(x,z)),e(y,z)),u),u))$.
3    $P(e(e(e(e(e(e(e(x,y),e(x,z)),u),e(e(y,z),u)),v),v))$.
4    $\neg P(e(e(e(e(e(a,b),c),d),e(e(e(a,p),c),e(e(b,p),d))))$.

Strategy for CD-90

The inference rule was hyperresolution, and both forward and subsumption were applied. Generated clauses with more than 20 symbols were discarded.

Results for CD-90

	OTTER	Roo-1	Roo-4	Roo-8	Roo-12	Roo-16	Roo-20
Run time	825.46	867.62	221.31	120.80	156.27	146.37	160.18
Generated	149798	149806	151714	153693	261292	380548	542331
Kept	5909	5909	5951	5981	6047	6091	6100
Memory (K)	3097	3257	3766	6191	10309	14396	16821
Gen/sec	181	172	685	1272	1672	2599	3385
Speedups:							
Proof	1.0	1.0	3.7	6.8	5.3	5.6	5.2
Gen/sec	1.0	1.0	3.8	7.0	9.2	14.4	18.7

Notes on CD-90

Performance of Roo appears to be regular with up to 8 processes, but with more processes, Roo's eagerness appears to have led it down fruitless paths.

3.9 Apabhp

This is the "blind hand problem", a standard problem from the area of robotics. It is included in many theorem prover test suites.

Clauses for Apabhp

Input Set of Support Clauses

1    $\neg a(m(x),z,d(g(z),y)) \mid a(m(x),z,y) \mid i(m(x),y)$.
2    $\neg a(m(x),z,y) \mid \neg a(h,z,y) \mid i(m(k(y)),d(p,y))$.
3    $\neg a(h,z,y) \mid a(m(x),z,y) \mid \neg i(m(x),y)$.
4    $\neg a(m(x),z,y) \mid a(h,z,y) \mid \neg i(m(x),y)$.
5    $\neg a(x,t,y) \mid c(y) \mid \neg r(x)$.
6    $\neg a(m(x),z,y) \mid a(m(x),z,d(g(z),y))$.
7    $\neg i(m(x),y) \mid i(m(x),d(g(z),y))$.
8    $\neg a(h,z,y) \mid a(m(k(y)),z,y)$.
9    $\neg a(x,z,y) \mid a(x,z,d(p,y))$.
10   $\neg a(x,z,y) \mid a(x,z,d(l,y))$.
11   $\neg a(x,z,d(l,y)) \mid a(x,z,y)$.
12   $\neg a(x,e,n) \mid r(x)$.
13   $\neg c(y)$.
14   $\neg a(x,e,y) \mid \neg a(x,t,y)$.

15   $\neg i(m(x), d(l, y))$.

16   $\neg r(h)$.

17   $a(h, z, d(g(z), y))$.

18   $a(m(s), e, n)$.

Strategy for Apabhp

The inference rule was hyperresolution, and both forward and subsumption were applied. Given clauses were selected with ratio 3 (Section 2.4).

Results for Apabhp

	OTTER	Roo-1	Roo-4	Roo-8	Roo-12	Roo-16	Roo-20	Roo-24
Run time	55.55	46.94	13.10	5.48	5.22	5.72	5.00	5.37
Generated	3103	2312	2485	2639	2583	2554	2564	2565
Kept	1621	1285	1403	583	495	493	494	494
Memory (K)	894	798	2329	2584	2580	2576	2732	2856
Gen/sec	55	49	189	481	494	446	512	477
Speedups:								
Proof	1.0	1.2	4.2	10.1	10.6	9.7	11.1	10.3
Gen/sec	1.0	0.9	3.4	8.8	9.0	8.1	9.3	8.7

Notes on Apabhp

The reason Roo-1 performs better than Otter is that generated clauses from a given clause are integrated smallest-first in Roo, and in this problem, given clauses generate many clauses that properly subsume one another. The integration of smaller (more general) clauses first prevents the integration of larger clauses they subsume.

Speedups are limited by Task B, which requires at least 4.2 seconds in each of the runs.

3.10   Robbins

A proof for this problem shows that if the hypothesis $\exists x, x + x = x$ is added to a Robbins algebra, then the resulting algebra is Boolean[20]. Clauses 2–4 axiomatize Robbins algebra, clause 5 asserts the hypotheses, and clause 6 denies Huntington's axiom. (Huntington's axiom together with clauses 2 and 3 axiomatize Boolean algebra.)

Clauses for Robbins

Input Usable Clauses

1   $(x = x)$.

2   $(+(x, y) = +(y, x))$.

3   $(+(+(x, y), z) = +(x, +(y, z)))$.

Input Set of Support Clauses

4   $(n(+(n(+(x, y)), n(+(x, n(y))))) = x)$.

5   $(+(C, C) = C)$.

6   $(+(n(+(A, n(B))), n(+(n(A), n(B)))) \neq B)$.

Strategy for Robbins

The Knuth-Bendix option was used, with LRPO ($+ > n > C > B > A$, and $+$ with LR status). Generated and simplified clauses with more than 20 symbols were discarded. Two sets of experiments were run: (1) selecting given clauses by symbol count, and (2) selecting given clauses with ratio 3 (Section 2.4).

Results for Robbins (without Ratio)

	OTTER	Roo-1	Roo-4	Roo-8	Roo-12	Roo-16	Roo-20	Roo-24
Run time	349.17	320.41	72.94	10.60	9.93	11.23	10.89	14.82
Generated	8272	8874	11430	2961	4725	7567	10271	17366
Kept	456	401	451	257	263	274	236	385
Memory (K)	638	734	1116	1016	1396	1776	2284	2952
Gen/sec	23	27	156	279	475	673	943	1171
Speedups:								
Proof	1.0	1.1	4.8	32.9	35.2	31.1	32.1	23.6
Gen/sec	1.0	1.2	6.8	12.1	20.7	29.3	41.0	50.9

Results for Robbins (with Ratio 3)

	OTTER	Roo-1	Roo-4	Roo-8	Roo-12	Roo-16	Roo-20	Roo-24
Run time	104.57	156.73	28.77	23.88	26.20	19.53	21.69	15.73
Generated	3543	4867	4302	7354	13717	13665	18793	17698
Kept	315	351	301	390	428	425	436	363
Memory (K)	479	670	892	1336	1972	2192	2508	2664
Gen/sec	33	31	149	307	523	699	866	1125
Speedups:								
Proof	1.0	0.7	3.6	4.4	4.0	5.4	4.8	6.6
Gen/sec	1.0	0.9	4.5	9.3	15.9	21.2	26.3	34.1

Notes on Robbins

Note that the poor speedups in the ratio 3 experiments when compared to the experiments without ratio are due mostly to the improvement in OTTER performance.

3.11 Z22

This is a problem in combinatorial group theory first brought to our attention by J. Kalman. It is one of a family of problems to determine the structure of certain groups, called Fibonacci groups, defined by a symmetric set of relations. Some of these problems are still open. It illustrates the performance of Roo on a Knuth-Bendix completion problem. The problem is to show that the group on five generators with the five given relations (clauses 12–16) is the cyclic group of order 22. We use a notation in which multiplication on the left is expressed as the application of a function, and $a1, b1 \ldots$ represent the inverses of $a, b, \ldots$.

Clauses for Z22

Input Usable Clauses

   1   $(x = x)$.

Input Set of Support Clauses

2 $(a(a1(x)) = x)$.
3 $(a1(a(x)) = x)$.
4 $(b(b1(x)) = x)$.
5 $(b1(b(x)) = x)$.
6 $(c(c1(x)) = x)$.
7 $(c1(c(x)) = x)$.
8 $(d(d1(x)) = x)$.
9 $(d1(d(x)) = x)$.
10 $(h(h1(x)) = x)$.
11 $(h1(h(x)) = x)$.
12 $(a(b(c(x))) = d(x))$.
13 $(b(c(d(x))) = h(x))$.
14 $(c(d(h(x))) = a(x))$.
15 $(d(h(a(x))) = b(x))$.
16 $(h(a(b(x))) = c(x))$.

Strategy for Z22

The Knuth-Bendix option was used, with LRPO ($a > a1 > b > b1 > c > c1 > d > d1 > h > h1$). A refutation was not expected; rather we derive a set of equations in which each generator is expressed in terms of $h1$ and $h1^{22}(x) = x$.

Results for Z22

	OTTER	Roo-1	Roo-4	Roo-8	Roo-12	Roo-16	Roo-20	Roo-24
Run time	398.38	274.19	144.29	418.55	328.30	491.96	400.89	543.02
Generated	2260	2438	2224	4491	3064	5273	4917	6405
Kept	2742	2058	573	501	293	339	310	378
Memory (K)	4885	4502	3767	7502	5522	8587	7305	9892
Gen/sec	5	8	15	10	9	10	12	11
Speedups:								
Proof	1.0	1.5	2.8	1.0	1.2	0.8	1.0	0.7
Gen/sec	1.0	1.6	2.7	1.9	1.6	1.9	2.2	2.1

Notes on Z22

Extracting new demoulators from the K List by symbol count (Section 2.5) caused Roo-1 to perform better than OTTER. However, due to extensive back demoduation, Task B was a serious bottleneck in parallel Roo runs, which resulted in very poor speedups.

3.12 Luka-5

This problem is the equational (Wajsberg algebra) version of a problem in the many-valued sentential calculus $L_{\aleph_0}$ of Lukasiewicz[5]. Equalities 2–5 axiomatize the logic, and clause 6 denies an equality that was included in the first axiomatizations of the logic.

Clauses for Luka-5

Input Usable Clauses

1   $(x = x)$.

Input Set of Support Clauses

2   $(i(T, x) = x)$.
3   $(i(i(x, y), i(i(y, z), i(x, z))) = T)$.
4   $(i(i(x, y), y) = i(i(y, x), x))$.
5   $(i(i(n(x), n(y)), i(y, x)) = T)$.
6   $(i(i(i(a, b), i(b, a)), i(b, a)) \neq T)$.

Strategy for Luka-5

The Knuth-Bendix option was used, with LRPO ($i > n > T$). Back subsumption was not applied.

Results for Luka-5

	OTTER	ROO-1	ROO-4	ROO-8	ROO-12	ROO-16	ROO-20	ROO-24
Run time	4871.68	3596.68	869.33	480.30	317.32	243.71	210.89	180.10
Generated	538329	533705	531348	578189	578895	592728	642889	624213
Kept	2496	2449	2460	2432	2415	2423	2420	2388
Memory (K)	3065	3161	3479	4149	5713	7595	9923	13879
Gen/sec	110	148	611	1203	1824	2432	3048	3465
Speedups from OTTER:								
Proof	1.0	1.4	5.6	10.1	15.4	20.0	23.1	27.0
Gen/sec	1.0	1.3	5.6	10.9	16.6	22.1	27.7	31.5
Speedups from ROO-1:								
Proof	0.7	1.0	4.1	7.5	11.3	14.8	17.1	20.0
Gen/sec	0.7	1.0	4.1	8.1	12.3	16.4	20.6	23.4

Notes on Luka-5

The similarity in the number of generated and kept clauses in the Luka-5 searches indicates that the search spaces were similar. The superlinear speedups are thus not explained by the differences in the search spaces. However, the time difference between OTTER and ROO-1 hint at an explanation. The statistics in the output files show that OTTER spent approximately 1300 more seconds rewriting than ROO-1 did. We have not yet determined the precise reason for the difference.

3.13   JimC-8

This problem was brought to our attention by J. Christian[2], who used it as a benchmark for HIPER, his high-performance Knuth-Bendix completion program. The problem is to find a complete set of reductions for an associative system with 24 left identities and 24 right inverses.

Clauses for JimC-8

Input Set of Support Clauses

1 $(x = x)$.
2 $(f(f(x, y), z) = f(x, f(y, z)))$.
3 $(f(e1, x) = x)$.
$\vdots$
26 $(f(e24, x) = x)$.
27 $(f(x, g1(x)) = e1)$.
$\vdots$
50 $(f(x, g24(x)) = e24)$.

Strategy for JimC-8

The Knuth-Bendix option was used, with LRPO ($g24 > \ldots > g1 > f > e24 > \ldots > e1$, and f with LR status).

Results for JimC-8

	OTTER	ROO-1	ROO-4	ROO-8	ROO-12	ROO-16	ROO-20	ROO-24
Run time	778.58	797.51	129.32	110.37	127.78	103.14	139.47	131.36
Generated	37495	37499	37339	48541	72881	54840	67275	75927
Kept	15802	15476	5767	2999	3230	2016	2201	1996
Memory (K)	10793	11879	10951	9447	11940	8617	10885	11780
Gen/sec	48	47	288	439	570	531	482	578
Speedups:								
Run time	1.0	1.0	6.0	7.1	6.1	7.5	5.6	5.9
Gen/sec	1.0	1.0	6.0	9.2	11.9	11.1	10.0	12.0

Notes on JimC-8

Note the great disparity in the amount of work done (clauses generated) in the various runs. Memory use, on the other hand, remains constant.

3.14 Problems Not Included

Some well-known test problems such as Wos-10 and Schubert's Steamroller are not represented in the list of problems, because they are done by OTTER in a few seconds and thus are simply not difficult enough to warrant the use of ROO.

4 Stability of Experiments

The nondeterminism introduced by parallelism gives rise to the question of how repeatable the experiments are. It is indeed true that ROO, unlike OTTER, does not run the same way every time, even with the same input file and the same number of processes. In this section we report on some experiments to measure, at least on a limited sample of examples, the extent of this phenomenon. We do this by running the very same problem ten times with the same number of processes, and comparing the results.

We choose two problems that illustrate the dependence of stability on the input data. The dots in the following graphs show the results of ten runs of CD-12. the line indicates the curve of normal perfect speedup. The dots below the line for 16 and 20 processes thus illustrate superlinear speedups. The widest distribution of times is from 8.11 to 28.13 seconds with 16 processes, which correspond to speedups between 49 and 14. This is an unfortunate feature of Roo, but a direct consequence of the self-scheduling nature of the algorithm.

Stability of CD-12

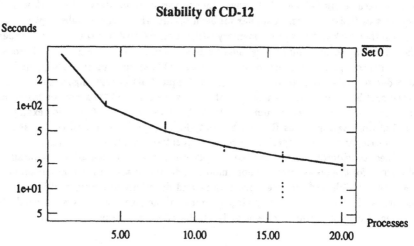

The following graph shows eight runs of SAM's Lemma. Here the close vertical spacing (within about 1 second) of the dots for each number of processes indicates reliably reproducible results.

Stability of SAM's Lemma

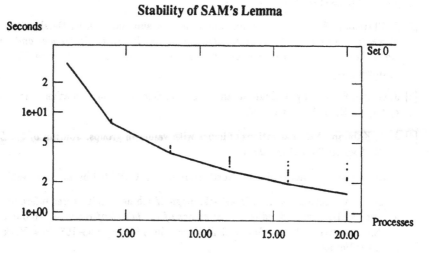

5 Conclusions

Roo is an implementation of a complex parallel algorithm, and it exhibits complex behavior when given difficult problems. We have tried to illustrate this wide range of behaviors by documenting ROO's performance on a set of interesting problems.

Despite considerably variability in behavior, ROO is the fastest theorem prover of its type in the world, and on the largest problems it performs best. This speed, coupled with its compatibility with OTTER, make it a valuable research tool for automated theorem proving.

One task remaining is to continue to try to squeeze more parallelism out of Task B. In the examples in which ROO performs poorly, the reason is usually that Task B does become a bottleneck. In particular, Knuth-Bendix problems in which a lot of back demodulation occurs, such as JimC-8 and Z22, cause other processes to be starved for work while Task B reprocesses K-list clauses. A similar problem occurs when nonunit subsumption happens.

Another task is to improve memory utilization relative to OTTER. Most experiments show that the total memory consumed by ROO increases with the number of processes.

Our speedups with respect to OTTER were for OTTER running on the Sequent Symmetry, in order to make comparisons between the (sequential) OTTER algorithm and the (one-processor) ROO algorithm, which are not exactly the same. OTTER runs on faster machines than the Intel 386–based Symmetry. It is about twelve times faster, for example, on an HP-720 workstation. Thus ROO with twenty-four processes is only twice as fast as OTTER in this case, and in price/performance the sequential program is the winner.

These considerations lead us to contemplate next the implementation of a parallel version of OTTER for the distributed-memory model. This would allow us to take advantage of both networks of high-performance workstations and distributed-memory multicomputers with hundreds of processors and very large amounts of memory. Such a system would be quite different from ROO, which relies heavily on shared data structures.

References

[1] W. Bledsoe. Challenge problems in elementary calculus. *Journal of Automated Reasoning*, 6(3):341–359, 1990.

[2] J. Christian. Fast Knuth-Bendix completion: A summary. In N. Dershowitz, editor, *Proceedings of the 3rd International Conference on Rewriting Techniques and Applications, Lecture Notes in Computer Science, Vol. 355*, pages 551–555, New York, 1989. Springer-Verlag.

[3] J. Guard, F. Oglesby, J. Bennett, and L. Settle. Semi-automated mathematics. *Journal of the ACM*, 16(1):49–62, 1969.

[4] J. A. Kalman. Axiomatizations of logics with values in groups. *Journal of the London Math. Society*, 2(14):193–199, 1975.

[5] J. Lukasiewicz. *Selected Works*. North-Holland, 1970. Edited by L. Borkowski.

[6] E. Lusk, W. McCune, and R. Overbeek. Logic Machine Architecture: Inference mechanisms. In D. Loveland, editor, *Proceedings of the 6th Conference on Automated Deduction, Lecture Notes in Computer Science, Vol. 138*, pages 85–108, New York, 1982. Springer-Verlag.

[7] E. Lusk, W. McCune, and R. Overbeek. Logic Machine Architecture: Kernel functions. In D. Loveland, editor, *Proceedings of the 6th Conference on Automated Deduction, Lecture Notes in Computer Science, Vol. 138*, pages 70–84, New York, 1982. Springer-Verlag.

[8] E. Lusk, W. McCune, and J. Slaney. High-performance parallel theorem proving for shared-memory multiprocessors. Preprint, Mathematics and Computer Science Division, Argonne National Laboratory, Argonne, IL, 1991. In preparation.

[9] E. Lusk, W. McCune, and J. Slaney. ROO—a parallel theorem prover. Tech. Memo. MCS-TM-149, Mathematics and Computer Science Division, Argonne National Laboratory, Argonne, IL, 1991. To appear.

[10] E. Lusk and R. McFadden. Using automated reasoning tools: A study of the semigroup F2B2. *Semigroup Forum*, 36(1):75–88, 1987.

[11] E. Lusk and R. Overbeek. The automated reasoning system ITP. Tech. Report ANL-84/27, Argonne National Laboratory, Argonne, IL, April 1984.

[12] W. McCune. OTTER 2.0 Users Guide. Tech. Report ANL-90/9, Argonne National Laboratory, Argonne, IL, March 1990.

[13] W. McCune. Single axioms for the left group and right group calculi. Preprint MCS-P219-0391, Mathematics and Computer Science Division, Argonne National Laboratory, Argonne, IL, 1991.

[14] W. McCune. What's new in OTTER 2.2. Tech. Memo. ANL/MCS-TM-153, Mathematics and Computer Science Division, Argonne National Laboratory, Argonne, IL, July 1991.

[15] F. Pfenning. Single axioms in the implicational propositional calculus. In E. Lusk and R. Overbeek, editors, *Proceedings of the 9th International Conference on Automated Deduction, Lecture Notes in Computer Science, Vol. 310*, pages 710–713, New York, 1988. Springer-Verlag.

[16] L. Sallows. A curious new result in switching theory. *The Mathematical Intelligencer*, 12(1):21–32, 1990.

[17] J. Schumann and R. Letz. PARTHEO: A high-performance parallel theorem prover. In M. Stickel, editor, *Proceedings of the 10th International Conference on Automated Deduction, Lecture Notes in Artificial Intelligence, Vol. 449*, pages 40–56, New York, July 1990. Springer–Verlag.

[18] J. Slaney and E. Lusk. Parallelizing the closure computation in automated deduction. In M. Stickel, editor, *Proceedings of the 10th International Conference on Automated Deduction, Lecture Notes in Artificial Intelligence, Vol. 449*, pages 28–39, New York, July 1990. Springer-Verlag.

[19] M. Stickel. A Prolog Technology Theorem Prover: Implementation by an extended Prolog compiler. *Journal of Automated Reasoning*, 4(4):353–380, 1988.

[20] S. Winker. Robbins algebra: Conditions that make a near-boolean algebra boolean. *Journal of Automated Reasoning*, 6(4):465–489, 1990.

[21] L. Wos, R. Overbeek, E. Lusk, and J. Boyle. *Automated Reasoning: Introduction and Applications*. Prentice-Hall, Englewood Cliffs, NJ, 1984.

[22] L. Wos, G. Robinson, and D. Carson. Efficiency and completeness of the set of support strategy in theorem proving. *J. ACM*, 12(4):536–541, 1965.

[23] L. Wos, S. Winker, and E. Lusk. An automated reasoning system. In *Proceedings of the National Computer Conference*, pages 697–702. AFIPS, 1981.

A Process Algebra over the Herbrand Universe : Application to Parallelism in Automated Deduction

Mounira Belmesk
Zineb Habbas
Philippe Jorrand

Institut IMAG - LIFIA
46, avenue Félix Viallet
38000 Grenoble - France
e-mail : jorrand@lifia.imag.fr

Abstract

We present a process algebra, HAL (Herbrand Agent Language), aimed at abstract and concise descriptions of a large class of complex parallel machines. In HAL, an atomic action is a set of synchronous communications, where each communication is achieved by unification of terms offered by agents. Two semantics of HAL are defined. We introduce first the "ground semantics", where only ground terms can be exchanged among agents. We then extend it to "non ground semantics" by allowing non ground terms to be exchanged. We give both an operational and an algebraic definitions of the semantics in the ground case and an operational one in the non ground case. Both operational definitions associate transition systems with HAL agents and the algebraic definition maps HAL agents into a domain of communication trees. These definitions of the semantics induce equivalence relations among HAL agents : for the ground case and for the non ground case, we prove that the operational definitions are respectively fully abstract and correct with respect to the algebraic definition of the ground semantics.

With communication by unification, and with its non ground semantics, HAL has the expressiveness of logic and algebraic languages. Machines where computation is based on deduction can be described very concisely, like for example parallel interpretors of logic and equational languages. We illustrate the use of HAL by translating Horn clause programs into HAL agents and we prove the correctness of this translation. This example also exhibits a new programming paradigm introduced by HAL, where computations can be described entirely by means of synchronous communications among memory-less agents.

1   INTRODUCTION

Our purpose is to design a tool for describing parallel machines, allowing concise descriptions of rather complex parallel computations. Typical applications of such a tool are the description of parallelism in term rewriting and in logical deduction. For this purpose, we have generalized the notions of synchronization and communication available in process algebras like CCS [Milner 80] and FP2 [Schnoebelen and Jorrand 89].

In CCS, synchronization involves exactly two processes, communication is directed from one sender to one receiver, and only "ground" data can be exchanged. In FP2, n-party synchronization and multidirectional communication are possible, but only ground data (ground terms of the Herbrand Universe) can be exchanged and, unlike CCS, no recursive, dynamically evolving, communication topologies among processes can be described, which is a severe limitation to expressiveness.

The introduction of parallelism in term rewriting and logical deduction shows the need for expressive linguistic tools where n-party synchronization, multidirectional communication, exchange of non ground data and recursive communication topologies with dynamic creation of processes are easy to describe. For example :

- The subterms of a term should be reduced or narrowed in parallel, the subgoals of a Horn clause body should be solved in parallel. This implies that a set of rewrite rules with left sides matching or unifiable with the subterms, a set of clauses with heads unifiable with the subgoals, should be applied in parallel : when doing this with communicating processes, the process in charge of the reduction, narrowing or deduction task should invoke synchronously all the processes representing these rules or clauses.

- While solving a goal in Horn clause logic, most general unifiers of subgoals and clause heads are computed. When doing this with communicating processes, this implies bidirectional communication between the process containing the subgoals and each process containing corresponding unifiable clause heads. Furthermore, when variables are shared among subgoals, communication becomes multidirectional among the processes containing the subgoals and the processes chosen for solving them. A similar situation occurs in narrowing.

- The most general unifiers which are computed during narrowing or deduction are not necessarily ground. When doing this with communicating processes, this means that non ground data will be exchanged between the process in charge of the narrowing or deduction task and the processes representing the applied rules or clauses.

- Finally, the number of applications of a given rewrite rule during reduction or narrowing, the number of instances of a clause during deduction, cannot be determined statically. These instances must be created dynamically, when required during reduction, narrowing or deduction. If rules and clauses are represented by processes, dynamic process creation will occur.

None of the process algebras like CCS, CSP [Hoare 78] and FP2 offer means of expression which satisfy all of these requirements, at least in any concise way. A process algebra described in [Pletat 86] makes an operational junction between algebraic data types and CCS-like process algebras : this proposal contains an interesting generalization of the notion of communication by having it done through unification (which was an idea already present in FP2, but with a rather static view). But it does not allow n-party synchronization nor multidirectional communication and ground terms only can be exchanged among processes.

We present here a process algebra named HAL, for "Herbrand Agent Language". HAL agents (or processes) are described by means of a rather classical set of operators of a process algebra. The essential difference with algebras like CCS lies in the notion of what atomic actions are :

- A CCS process $p = a(x).p'$ offers on its port a to receive a value into its variable x from a process $q = \bar{a}(v).q'$, which offers on its port $\bar{a}$ to send a value v. In their composition $p \mid q$, they become able to share these offers : v can be communicated from q to p. If this communication occurs, the composition of the two offers is the invisible action τ, and the next possible actions are those of $p'[v/x] \mid q'$.

- An HAL agent $p = a_1(t_1)\, a_2(t_2)\, ... \,a_k(t_k).p'$ makes k synchronous offers : the terms t_i, of a free term algebra $T_{C,X}$ (C is a set of constructor names and X is a set of variable names) are offered on the ports a_i ($i = 1..k$). Similarly for an HAL agent $q = b_1(u_1)\, b_2(u_2)\, ... \,b_l(u_l).q'$, with the terms u_j synchronously offered on the ports b_j ($j = 1..l$). In their composition $p\ //\ q\ [a_i, b_j]$ (read : p in parallel with q, where a_i is connected to b_j), they become able to share their offers of t_i and u_j on a_i and b_j respectively, and only these two offers, provided that t_i and u_j are unifiable, with $s = mgu(t_i, u_j)$: if t_i and u_j are non ground, subterms can circulate between p and q, in directions defined by s. If this (generalized) communication occurs, the composition of the two sets of offers is $s(a_1(t_1)...a_{i-1}(t_{i-1})\, a_{i+1}(t_{i+1})...a_k(t_k)$ $b_1(u_1)...b_{j-1}(u_{j-1})\, b_{j+1}(u_{j+1})...b_l(u_l))$, and the next possible events are those of $s(p'\,//\,q'\,[a_i, b_j])$.

This mechanism for synchronization and communication generalizes what is proposed in CCS : with $p = a(x).p'$ and $q = b(v).q'$, where v is a ground term, we get the same situation as in CCS, with the composition $p\ //\ q\ [a, b]$. It also takes care naturally of communication of non ground terms. Furthermore, synchronization without exchange of values is merely a special case, as in the case of agents $p = a(t).p'$ and $q = b(t).q'$, where t is a ground term : with the same composition as above, there is simply an empty substitution. Finally, having atomic actions composed of sets of synchronous offers enables n-party synchronization and communication. If we have a third agent $r = c_1(v_1)\, c_2(v_2)\, ... \,c_m(v_m).r'$, we could build $p\ //\ q\ //\ r\ [a_i, b_j][a_n, c_p]$, where the three agents are synchronized and where the directions of communications are defined by the composition of the two substitutions $mgu(t_i, u_j)$ and $mgu(t_n, v_p)$: six different directions are possible, and all of them may be used when the action occurs.

In the rest of this paper, we define the syntax and semantics of HAL and we present an application. The syntax of HAL is introduced in section 2. We define the ground semantics of HAL in section 3, where ground terms only can be exchanged among agents : it is defined first as an operational semantics, by means of inference rules in the style of [Plotkin 81] which associate a transition system with every HAL agent, then as an algebraic semantics, by means of a mapping of HAL agents into an extended form of the comunications· trees of [Milner 80]. Both the operational and the algebraic definitions induce equivalence relations among HAL agents : by proving that these equivalence are the same, we show that, in the ground case, the operational semantics is fully abstract with respect to the algebraic semantics.

In section 4, we extend the ground operational semantics to non ground operational semantics, where it is no longer required that the terms exchanged among processes be ground. We prove that this semantics is correct with respect to the ground semantics, in the sense that if two agents are equivalent, according to this non ground semantics, they are also equivalent in the ground semantics.

An application of HAL to the description of parallel deduction in Horn clause logic is presented in section 5 : we translate Horn clause programs into HAL agents. We prove that this translation is correct by showing that the least Herbrand model of any Horn clause program is isomorphic to the set of terms that can be offered by the agent resulting of the translation. This application also exhibits a new programming paradigm introduced by HAL, where computations can be described entirely by means of synchronous communications among memory-less agents. We suggest some directions for future work based on this algebra in the last section.

2 SYNTACTIC DOMAIN

HAL is a process algebra, where processes (called "agents" in HAL) are built by means of process combining operators. This approach is classical : CSP [Hoare 78], CCS [Milner 80], ACP [Bergstra and Klop 85], Lotos [ISO 85], FP2 [Schnoebelen and Jorrand 89] and [Pletat 86] are examples of process algebras. However, none of these process algebras provide satisfactory answers to the requirements defined in the introduction. HAL differs from these algebras by using unification for generalizing the classical notion of communication, by having atomic actions as sets of synchronous communications and by a slightly different set of operators.

2.1 Atomic actions

An atomic action performed by an HAL agent is a finite, possibly empty, set of synchronous communications. In the syntax for describing an agent, each atomic action is described as a set of offers made by this agent, where each offer consists of a term, possibly non ground, offered on a port of the agent.

Terms : Given a set C of function symbols called constructors, a family X of variable names, $T_{C,X}$ is the set of terms over C and X, contructed in the usual way. T_C is the set of ground terms, a subset of $T_{C,X}$.

Ports : K is a familly of port names, which are simply denoted by identifiers. If k is a port name, k' ("k *prime*") is also a port name.

Offers : The offer of term t on port k is denoted by $k(t)$.

Sets of offers : Let $k_1, k_2, ..., k_n$ be n distinct port names and $t_1, t_2, ..., t_n$ be terms. The list $k_1(t_1) \, k_2(t_2) ... k_n(t_n)$ denotes the set of n synchronous offers of t_i on k_i ($i = 1..n$). We denote by $E_{K,T_{C,X}}$ the domain of sets of offers of terms of $T_{C,X}$ on finite subsets of K. In general, we shall leave $T_{C,X}$ implicit and simply write E_K. The empty set of offers is denoted by τ.

Formally, a set of offers e is a partial function from K into $T_{C,X}$: we denote by $\mathbf{dom}(e)$ the set of port names used by e. If e is a set of offers, e' is also a set of offers where, if k is in $\mathbf{dom}(e)$, then k' is in $\mathbf{dom}(e')$ and $e'(k') = e(k)$.

2.2 Agents

There are seven operators in the algebra of HAL agents. They are used within agent expressions written according to the following grammar, where p and q are agent expressions, e is a set of offers, k and l are port names and id is an identifier :

$$p, q ::= Nil \ | \ e.p \ | \ p+q \ | \ p \, / / \, q \ | \ p[k,l] \ | \ p \backslash k \ | \ p' \ | \ id$$

Parentheses can be used within expressions to make unambiguous to which operands the operators apply. HAL agents perform sequences of atomic actions :

Inactive agent : *Nil* denotes the inactive agent : it can perform no action.

Prefixing : *e.p* denotes an agent which starts by making the set of offers denoted by *e*. It is able to perform an atomic action which is an instance of *e*, provided that its environment (i.e. other agents whose ports are connected to the ports in **dom**(*e*)) is ready to participate in this atomic action : we say that the environment has accepted the offer *e*. Once this atomic action has taken place, *e.p* behaves like *p*, with some variables in the offers of *p* possibly instanciated by the atomic action.

Non deterministic choice : *p+q* behaves either like *p* or like *q*, depending on whose offers have been accepted by the environment of *p+q*.

Parallel composition : each atomic action of *p // q* is an atomic action *e* of *p*, or an atomic action *f* of *q*, or the union *e+f* (sum of two functions with disjoint domains) of two atomic actions, one of *p* and one of *q*. This means that, at each step, *p // q* can behave either like *p* or *q* asynchronously, or like *p* and *q* synchronously. Agents *p* and *q* must use distinct port names (but relabelling is always possible).

Connection : *p[k,l]* is agent *p* where ports *k* and *l* have been connected. It can perform all actions that were possible in *p*. In addition, for all actions of *p* described by sets of offers of the form *e* + {*k(t)*,*l(u)*}, then *p[k,l]* can perform actions described by sets of offers of the form *s(e)*, where *s* = **mgu**(*t,u*), iff *t* and *u* are unifiable. Typically, connection is used for connecting ports of parallel agents, but its definition is more general since, in *p[k,l]*, agent *p* is not necessarily a parallel composition.

Restriction : *p\k* is agent *p* without port *k*. It can perform all actions described by sets of offers *e* made by *p*, provided that *k* is not in **dom**(*e*).

Relabelling : *p'* behaves exactly like *p*, but in *p'* sets of offers *e* of *p* have been replaced by *e'*. Relabelling distributes across the other operators of the algebra, including connection and restriction, where it "primes" the port names.

Agent name : *id* denotes the agent associated with it by an agent definition (see below).

2.3 Agent definitions

Agent definitions are written *id* <= *p*, where *id* is an identifier and *p* is an agent expression. We assume, without further explanation, that an environment is built by such agent definitions, giving access, through the identifier *id*, to the agent denoted by *p*, thus making possible the use of *id* within agent expressions.

2.4 Examples

Let *X* = {*x,y,z*} be a set of variable names and *0, s(0),* ... be the integers. We define :

Buffer, a one place buffer, with ports *I* and *O* (for "*Input*" and "*Output*") :

> *Buffer* <= *I(z) . O(z) . Buffer*

Possible behavior of *Buffer* : if *I(s(0))* is its first action, it becomes *O(s(0)).Buffer*, where the only possible action is *O(s(0))*. Then it becomes *Buffer* again, and is ready to accept a new value on *I*, etc. Notice that Buffer has a "memory" : when accepting *s(0)* on *I*, it "stores" that value in *O(s(0)).Buffer*, for future use in the next action.

For the other examples, we choose $C = \{0,s,p\}$ as set of constructors, for zero, successor and predecessor. We have $T_C = \{(s+p)^n(0) \mid n{\geq}0\}$. We shall compute predecessors of natural integers, considering that the predecessor of 0 is 0 (which implies, for example, that $p(s(0))$ is 0, whereas $s(p(0))$ is $s(0)$).

Remove-one-p, a rather naive agent, with ports E and R (for "*Expression*" and "*Result*"). It accepts any term of T_C on its port E and, within the same action, if this term is of the form $p(s(x))$ or $p(0)$, the agent offers respectively x or 0 on its port R, otherwise it just returns the term :

$$
\begin{aligned}
\textit{Remove-one-p} \quad <= \quad & E(0)\ R(0)\ .\ \textit{Nil} \\
+ \ & E(p(s(x)))\ R(x)\ .\ \textit{Nil} \\
+ \ & E(p(0))\ R(0)\ .\ \textit{Nil} \\
+ \ & E(s(x))\ R(s(x))\ .\ \textit{Nil}
\end{aligned}
$$

This agent does not compute predecessors (it only removes the top "p", if any, from the expression it accepts, the result may still contain p's). It is presented to serve as an introduction to the next example :

Predecessor, an agent which computes predecessors. It removes all p's, and the corresponding inner s's to which they apply, if any, from a term of T_C. It returns a term of the form $s^m(0)$, $m{\geq}0$.

$$
\begin{aligned}
\textit{Predecessor} \ <= \quad & E(0)\ R(0)\ .\ \textit{Nil} && (1) \\
+\ (\ \ (\ \ (\ \ & E(p(x))\ F(x)\ Q(s(y))\ R(y)\ .\ \textit{Nil} && (2) \\
+\ & E(p(x))\ F(x)\ Q(0)\ R(0)\ .\ \textit{Nil} && (3) \\
+\ & E(s(x))\ F(x)\ Q(y)\ R(s(y))\ .\ \textit{Nil}\ ) && (4) \\
// \ & \textit{Predecessor'}\ )\ [F,E']\ [Q,R']\ \backslash\ F\ \backslash\ Q\ \backslash\ E'\ \backslash\ R'\ )
\end{aligned}
$$

This agent has only two ports, E and R, since all other ports (F, Q, E', F', R', ..., E''', etc.) have been removed by restriction operators after having been connected.

Assume that it accepts $s(p(p(s(0))))$ (we shall abbreviate to $spps0$) on its port E : this corresponds necessarily to the action of branch (4) in the non deterministic choice. Within the same action, it offers $pps0$ through its port F to the port E' of *Predecessor'*, which itself offers $ps0$ through its port F' to the port E'' of *Predecessor''*. *Predecessor'* and *Predecessor''* do this within actions in branches (2) or (3), we shall see which ones later. These actions are synchronous with the action of *Predecessor*, since they contain communications between F and E' and between F' and E''. *Predecessor''* offers $s0$ to *Predecessor'''* which, by applying (4), offers 0 to *Predecessor''''*. This last agent performs the action in branch (1) : synchronously with all the rest, it offers 0 through its port R'''' back to the port Q''' of *Predecessor'''*. Since *Predecessor'''* is applying (4), it offers $s0$ back to the port Q'' of *Predecessor''*, which therefore is applying (2) : it offers 0 back to the port Q' of *Predecessor'*, which therefore is applying (3). Finally, 0 is accepted at the port Q of *Predecessor*, which offers $s0$ on its port R, since it is applying (4).

Notice that, unlike the agent *Buffer*, none of the agents in this construction do have a "memory", in the sense that none of the values that they accept are copied into future offers made by these agents. As a corollary, all the computation performed by *Predecessor* has been achieved within a single atomic action : the computation is entirely performed by a composition of synchronous communications among memory-less agents.

3 GROUND SEMANTICS

The ground semantics of HAL is concerned with the case where ground terms only can be exchanged among agents. We define first the ground operational semantics, which associates a transition system with every well formed agent expression. We then define the ground algebraic semantics, by means of an homomorphism which maps agents expressions into a domain of extended communication trees. We finally show that these two semantics identify the same agents through the equivalence relations that they induce.

3.1 Ground operational semantics

The semantics of HAL is defined operationally in terms of transition systems. This operational semantics defines the behavior of HAL agents. It induces an equivalence relation among agents : we prove that this equivalence is a congruence with respect to the operators of the algebra.

3.1.1 Transition systems

A transition system is a 4-tuple $S = <Q, A, -->, q_0>$ where :

- Q is a non empty set of agents ;
- A is a set of actions ;
- $-->$ is a transition relation, a subset of $QxAxQ$;
- q_0 is an agent in Q, the initial agent of S.

We denote by $p--a-->r$ the membership of $<p,a,r>$ in $-->$. Among the classical definitions and properties relevant to transition systems, we only recall here the definition of an equivalence relation $\approx$ among transition systems. This definition is similar to definitions given in [Milner 80].

Given a transition system $S = <Q, A, -->, q_0>$ and two agents p and q in Q, we first define a family of relations $\{\approx_n\}$ in QxQ as follows :

- $p \approx_0 q$ always
- $p \approx_{n+1} q$ iff for all a in A : - if $p--a-->r$, then there is s s.t. $q--a-->s$ and $r \approx_n s$
                                            - if $q--a-->s$, then there is r s.t. $p--a-->r$ and $r \approx_n s$

The equivalence $\approx$ among two agents is then :

- $p \approx q$ iff $p \approx_n q$ for all $n \geq 0$

If $S_1 = <Q_1, A_1, -->_1, q_{01}>$ and $S_2 = <Q_2, A_2, -->_2, q_{02}>$ are transition systems with Q_1 and Q_2 disjoint (we can always assume this), consider their union $S = <Q, A, -->, q_0>$, where Q, A and $-->$ are the unions of the corresponding elements of S_1 and S_2 and q_0 is an arbitrary agent. We say that $S_1 \approx S_2$ iff $q_{01} \approx q_{02}$ in S.

3.1.2 Ground inference rules

We use the technique of definition of [Plotkin 81], which consists of building an inference system, with axioms and rules defined by cases on the syntactic structure of the language. In this definition, p, q, r and s are agent expressions, e is a set of offers, a and b are actions, that is ground instances of sets of offers, k and l are port names.

Inactive agent :

There is no a and no p such that $Nil\text{--}a\text{--}>p$.

Prefixing :

$$\tau.p\text{--}\tau\text{--}>p \qquad\qquad e.p\text{--}s(e)\text{--}>s(p)$$

where s is a ground substitution for the variables in e.

Non deterministic choice :

$$\frac{p\text{--}a\text{--}>r}{p+q\text{--}a\text{--}>r} \qquad\qquad \frac{q\text{--}b\text{--}>s}{p+q\text{--}b\text{--}>s}$$

Parallel composition :

$$\frac{p\text{--}a\text{--}>r}{p//q\text{--}a\text{--}>r//q} \qquad \frac{q\text{--}b\text{--}>s}{p//q\text{--}b\text{--}>p//s} \qquad \frac{p\text{--}a\text{--}>r \,,\, q\text{--}b\text{--}>s}{p//q\text{--}a+b\text{--}>r//s}$$

In $p//q$, it is required that p and q do not use any common port name.

Connection :

$$\frac{p\text{--}a\text{--}>r}{p[k,l]\text{--}a\text{--}>r[k,l]} \qquad \frac{p\text{--}a+(k(t),l(t))\text{--}>r}{p[k,l]\text{--}a\text{--}>r[k,l]}$$

Restriction :

$$\frac{p\text{--}a\text{--}>r}{p\backslash k\text{--}a\text{--}>r\backslash k} \qquad\qquad \text{if } k \text{ is not in } \mathbf{dom}(a).$$

Relabelling :

$$\frac{p\text{--}a\text{--}>r}{p'\text{--}a'\text{--}>r'}$$

Agent name :

$$\frac{p\text{--}a\text{--}>r}{id\text{--}a\text{--}>r} \qquad\qquad \text{if there is a definition } id <= p.$$

3.1.3 Congruence induced by operational semantics

Clearly, associating transition systems with HAL agent expressions induces the equivalence relation $\approx$ of transition systems over HAL agents. We have the following property :

Theorem 1. The equivalence relation $\approx$ is a congruence with respect to the operators of the algebra of HAL agents. That is , with agents p, q and t, set of offers e and port names k and l :

$$p \approx q \;\Rightarrow\; \begin{aligned} &e.p \approx e.q \\ &p+t \approx q+t \\ &p//t \approx q//t \\ &p[k,l] \approx q[k,l] \\ &p \backslash k \approx q \backslash k \\ &p' \approx q' \end{aligned}$$

Proof. We only prove the most complex case, which is parallel composition. The proof is done by induction on n in the family of equivalence relations $(\approx_n)$. The case n=0 is trivial. For the induction step, we assume that $p \approx_n q \;\Rightarrow\; p//t \approx_n q//t$ and we want to prove that $p \approx_{n+1} q \;\Rightarrow\; p//t \approx_{n+1} q//t$. There are three cases, corresponding to the three inference rules for parallel composition :

Case 1. We know that $p \approx_{n+1} q$ iff, for all action a, if $p\text{--}a\text{-->}r$, then there is s such that $q\text{--}a\text{-->}s$ and $r \approx_n s$. The first inference rule indicates that with $p\text{--}a\text{-->}r$ and $q\text{--}a\text{-->}s$, we have both $p//t\text{--}a\text{-->}r//t$ and $q//t\text{--}a\text{-->}s//t$. With $r \approx_n s$ and the induction hypothesis, we have $r//t \approx_n s//t$. Thus, using the definition of $\approx_{n+1}$, we get $p//t \approx_{n+1} q//t$.

Case 2. The second inference rule indicates that with $t\text{--}b\text{-->}u$, we have both $p//t\text{--}b\text{-->}p//u$ and $q//t\text{--}b\text{-->}q//u$. With the induction hypothesis, $p//u \approx_n q//u$. Using the definition of $\approx_{n+1}$, we get $p//t \approx_{n+1} q//t$.

Case 3. We compose cases 1 and 2. With $p \approx_{n+1} q$, we have, for all action a : $p\text{--}a\text{-->}r$, $q\text{--}a\text{-->}s$ and $r \approx_n s$. Thus, if we also have $t\text{--}b\text{-->}u$, the third inference rule indicates that we have both $p//t\text{--}a+b\text{-->}r//u$ and $q//t\text{--}a+b\text{-->}s//u$. With $r \approx_n s$ and the induction hypothesis, we have $r//u \approx_n s//u$. Therefore, $p//t \approx_{n+1} q//t$.

3.2 Ground algebraic semantics

The algebraic semantics defines a domain of mathematical objects which are denoted by HAL agent expressions. These objects are extended forms of the communication trees of [Milner 80]. They form an algebra, with an equivalence relation which is a congruence for the operators of this algebra.

The semantic function is an homomorphism from the algebra of HAL agents into the algebra of communication trees.

3.2.1 An algebra of communication trees

In [Milner 80], communication trees have been used for the semantics of CCS. We take a similar approach for the algebraic semantics of HAL but, because of our more general notion of atomic actions, we have to use an extended form of communication trees.

The elementary ingredients for building our communication trees are :

- K, a set of port names. H and L will denote finite subsets of K.
- V, a set of values

The set of atomic actions is A_K, the set of partial functions with finite domains from K into V. A_H and A_L denote the sets of atomic actions with domains contained in H and L respectively. Clearly, both A_H and A_L are subsets of A_K.

The set of all communication trees is called CT. A communication tree P is a finite multiset of pairs :

$$P = \{<H,f> \mid H \text{ finite subset of } K, f : A_H->CT, \text{ a partial function}\}$$

The intuition behind this structure is clear : at each node, a choice is possible among a finite set of branches, where each branch is represented by a pair $<H,f>$ and deals with actions involving port names in H. On a branch, a possibly infinite set A_H of different actions are possible on these port names, since a possibly infinite number of different values may be used on each port. After an action a in A_H, we go down to the root of the next tree $f(a)$.

There is a natural partial ordering "$\leq$" among communication trees, which reflects the inclusion of a tree into another one. Let P and Q be two communication trees :

$P \leq Q$ iff   for all $<H,f>$ in P, there is $<L,g>$ in Q, such that :
- $H = L$
- $dom(f)$ is a subset of $dom(g)$
- for all action a in $dom(f)$, $f(a)=g(a)$

The algebra of communication trees has seven operators :

Empty tree : $\emptyset$ is the empty communication tree.

Prefixing : $A_H.P$ is the communication tree $\{<H,f>\}$, where $f : A_H->CT$ is an arbitrary function such that for all action a in A_H, $f(a) \leq P$.

Non deterministic choice : $P \pm Q$ is the union of P and Q.

Parallel composition : we assume that for all pairs $<H,f>$ in P and $<L,g>$ in Q, H and L are disjoint. Then $P//Q$ is a communication tree containing all pairs of the form $<H,f//Q>$, $<L,P//g>$ and $<H+L,f//g>$, where :
- for all action a in A_H, $(f//Q)(a) = f(a)//Q$
- for all action b in A_L, $(P//g)(b) = P//g(b)$
- for all action a in A_H and b in A_L, $(f//g)(a+b) = f(a)//g(b)$

Connection : $P[k,l]$ is a communication tree which, in addition to all the pairs already in P, contains a pair of the form $<H,f[k,l]>$ for each pair of the form $<H+(k,l),f>$ in P, where $f[k,l] : A_H->CT$ is such that, for all action $a = b+(k(v),l(v))$ in $\text{dom}(f)$, $(f[k,l])(b)=f(a)[k,l]$.

Restriction : $P\backslash k$ is a communication tree containing a pair of the form $<H,f\backslash k>$ for each pair $<H,f>$ in P where k is not in H and where $(f\backslash k)(a)=f(a)\backslash k$ for all action a in $\text{dom}(f)$.

Relabelling : P' is a communication tree containing a pair $<H',f'>$ for each pair $<H,f>$ in P, where H' is H with all port names primed and where $(f')(a')=f(a)'$ for all action a in $\text{dom}(f)$.

3.2.2 Congruence relation over communication trees

We consider that two communication trees are equivalent if they have the same branching structure. This is the same notion as the notion of observational equivalence found in [Park 81].

Given a communication tree $P=\{<H,f>\}$, a step of P is a triple $<P,a,f(a)>$ for all a in $\text{dom}(f)$: we denote by P—a—$>R$ the membership of $<P,a,R>$ among the steps of P. The definition of the equivalence $\approx$ over CT is then similar to the definition of the equivalence over transition systems. Let P and Q be communication trees :

- $P \approx_0 Q$ always
- $P \approx_{n+1} Q$ iff for all a in A_K :
  - if P—a—$>R$, then there is S s.t. Q—a—$>S$ and $R \approx_n S$
  - if Q—a—$>S$, then there is R s.t. P—a—$>R$ and $R \approx_n S$
- $P \approx Q$ iff $P \approx_n Q$ for all $n \geq 0$

We then have the following, expected, result :

Theorem 2. The equivalence relation $\approx$ is a congruence with respect to the operators of the algebra of communication trees.

Proof. By induction on n in the familly of relations $(\approx_n)$, for every operator of the algebra : similar to the proof of congruence for the equivalence induced by the operational semantics.

3.2.3 Semantic function

The semantic function is denoted by $[.] : HAL -> CT$, where HAL is the set of HAL agent expressions and CT the set of communication trees. This function is the homomorphism defined as follows :

- $[Nil] = \emptyset$
- $[e.p] = \{<H,f>\}$, where : - $H=\text{dom}(e)$
  - $f: E_{H,Tc} -> CT$, a partial function with $f(a)=[q]$ such that $a=s(e)$ and $q=s(p)$ for all ground substitutions s for the variables of e

- $[p+q] = [p] \pm [q]$
- $[p//q] = [p] \; \underline{//} \; [q]$
- $[p[k,l]] = [p] [k,l]$
- $[p \backslash k] = [p] \underline{\backslash} k$
- $[p'] = [p] \; \underline{'}$

3.3 Full abstraction

We now come to the essential property of this definition of the ground semantics of HAL. The operational and algebraic semantics, through the equivalences that they induce, identify exactly the same agents : the operational semantics is fully abstract with respect to the algebraic semantics.

For proving full abstraction, we shall need the following two lemmas, which relate transition systems with communication trees in the ground semantics of HAL. Let p and q be two agent expressions, a be an atomic action and P be a communication tree :

Lemma 1. If p--a-->q in the transition system associated with p by the operational semantics, then $[p]$—a—>$[q]$ in the communication tree $[p]$ defined by the algebraic semantics.

Lemma 2. If $[p]$—a—>P in the communication tree $[p]$ defined by the algebraic semantics, then there exists an agent expression q such that $P = [q]$ and p--a-->q in the transition system associated with p by the operational semantics.

Proof. We prove lemma 1. The proof of lemma 2 is similar, and rather tedious. The proof is by induction on the structure of agent expressions.

Inactive agent : $p = Nil$. Trivial.

Prefixing : $p = e.q$. We want to show that $e.q$--$s(e)$-->$s(q)$ => $[e.q]$—$s(e)$—>$[s(q)]$, where s is a ground substitution for the variables of e. This is a direct consequence of the definition of $[e.q]$.

Non deterministic choice : $p = q+r$. According to the inference rules in the operational semantics, we can have $q+r$--a-->s only if we have either q--a-->s or r--a-->s. Assume that we have q--a-->s : from the induction hypothesis, we also have $[q]$—a—>$[s]$. Since $[q+r]$ includes $[q]$, we also have $[q+r]$—a—>$[s]$. Same proof when we assume r--a-->s.

Parallel composition : $p = q \; // \; r$. We have three cases, one for each inference rule. With the first rule, we may have $q//r$--a-->$s//r$ if q--a-->s : with the induction hypothesis, we also have $[q]$—a—>$[s]$. Therefore, using the first case in the definition of parallel composition of communication trees, we have $[q//r]$—a—>$[s//r]$. Same proof with the second inference rule. With the third rule, we may have $q//r$--$a+b$-->$s//t$ if both q--a-->s and r--b-->t hold. The induction hypothesis gives us both $[q]$—a—>$[s]$ and $[r]$—b—>$[t]$ and the parallel composition of communication trees shows that we get $[q//r]$—$a+b$—>$[s//t]$.

Connection : $p = q[k,l]$. There are two cases. First, we can have $q[k,l]$--a-->$s[k,l]$ if we have q--a-->s : we get $[q]$—a—>$[s]$ by induction hypothesis and, since $[q]$ is included in $[q[k,l]]$, we also have $[q[k,l]]$—a—>$[s[k,l]]$. Second, we can have $q[k,l]$--a-->$s[k,l]$ if we have q--$a+(k(v),l(v))$-->s : we get $[q]$—$a+(k(v),l(v))$—>$[s]$ by induction hypothesis and $[q[k,l]]$—a—>$[s[k,l]]$ from the definition of the connection operator on communication trees.

Restriction : $p = q \backslash k$. Straighforward from the inference rule, the induction hypothesis and the definition of restriction on communication trees.

Relabelling : $p = q'$. Straighforward from the inference rule, the induction hypothesis and the definition of relabelling on communication trees.

Theorem 3. The ground operational semantics is fully abstract with respect to the ground algebraic semantics : $p \approx q \iff [p] \simeq [q]$.

Proof. The "=>" part relies on lemma 1 and the "<=" part on lemma 2. We show the proof of the "=>" part. The other part is not much different.

The proof is by induction on the two families of relations $\{\approx_n\}$ and $\{\simeq_n\}$. The case n=0 is trivial. We then assume $p \approx_n q \Rightarrow [p] \simeq_n [q]$ and we prove $p \approx_{n+1} q \Rightarrow [p] \simeq_{n+1} [q]$. We have $p \approx_{n+1} q$ iff when p--a-->r, then there is s such that q--a-->s, when q--a-->s, then there is r such that p--a-->r and, in both cases, $r \approx_n s$. From lemma 1, we know that p--a-->$r \Rightarrow [p]$—a—>$[r]$ and q--a-->$s \Rightarrow [q]$—a—>$[s]$. Using the induction hypothesis, we also get $r \approx_n s \Rightarrow [r] \simeq_n [s]$. Therefore, from the definition of $\simeq_{n+1}$, we finally obtain $[p] \simeq_{n+1} [q]$.

4 NON GROUND SEMANTICS

The ground semantics of HAL allows ground terms only to be exchanged among agents. With this "ground" HAL, it is already possible to describe a wide range of parallel computations : the agent *Predecessor* defined in section 2 was an example of the kind of ground computations that can be described.

In fact, more generally, it can be shown that the ground semantics allows the parallel evaluation of any function defined by unconditional term rewriting rules, and that these computations can always be performed entirely by compositions of synchronous communications among memory-less agents.

But the ground semantics does not yet give to HAL the full expressiveness of logic languages, since it does not allow the manipulation of non ground terms within communications. This limitation is overcome by the non ground semantics of HAL. We limit ourselves to a definition of the non ground operational semantics, which is a natural extension of the ground semantics. We then prove that this extension is correct with respect to the ground semantics.

4.1 Non ground operational semantics

As in the case of the ground semantics, the non ground operational semantics is defined by means of inference rules which associate a transition system with every agent expression. In the ground case, an action $a=s(e)$ was a ground instance of a set of offers e : in the non ground case, it is no longer required that s be a ground substitution for the variables of e. To distinguish them from the ground case, where they were written p--a-->q, transitions in the non ground transition system are written p--a--»q, where a is a possibly non ground action.

All inference rules in the non ground semantics have exactly the same format as in the ground case, except for prefixing, where they become :

$\tau.p$--τ--»p $\qquad$ $e.p$--$s(e)$--»$s(p)$
$\qquad\qquad\qquad\qquad\qquad$ where s is a substitution for the variables in e.

Agents may now exchange terms which are no longer necessarily ground. Such an extension suggests that the ground semantics is merely a special case of the non ground semantics. This is emphasized by the following lemma, which tells that non ground actions can be viewed as abstractions of all their ground instances :

Lemma 3. For all non ground action a and all ground substitution s on the variables of a : p--a--»q => p--$s(a)$-->$s(q)$.

Proof. By structural induction over agent expressions. We show the proof for non deterministic choice and parallel composition.

Non deterministic choice : $p = q+r$. We can have $q+r$--a--»s only if we have either q--a--»s or r--a--»s. Assume that we have q--a--»s : from the induction hypothesis, we get q--$s(a)$-->$s(s)$, for all ground substitution s on the variables of a. Therefore, we also have $q+r$--$s(a)$-->$s(s)$. Same proof when we assume r--a--»s.

Parallel composition : $p = q // r$. There are three cases, one for each inference rule. With the first rule, we may have $q//r$--a--»$s//r$ if q--a--»s. We get q--$s(a)$-->$s(s)$ by induction hypothesis, hence $q//r$--$s(a)$-->$s(s)//r$, which can also be written $q//r$--$s(a)$-->$s(s//r)$, since we may always assume that agents s and r use distinct sets of variable names and s is a ground substitution. Same proof with the second inference rule. With the third rule, we may have $q//r$--$a+b$--»$s//t$ if both q--a--»s and r--b--»t hold. The induction hypothesis gives us both q--$s_1(a)$-->$s_1(s)$ and r--$s_2(b)$-->$s_1(t)$. We can infer $q//r$--$s(a+b)$-->$s(s//t)$, with $s=s_1+s_2$, the composition of two ground substitutions with distinct domains.

4.2 Correctness

The operational semantics of the non ground case induces an equivalence relation "$\approx$" among agents : using non ground transitions of the form p--a--»q, its definition has the same format as in the ground case.

Theorem 4. The non ground operational semantics is correct with respect to the ground algebraic semantics : $p{\approx}q$ => $[\![p]\!]{\sim}[\![q]\!]$.

Proof. Has a structure similar to the "=>" part of the proof of full abstraction, where it uses lemma 3 to go from $\approx$ to $\sim$ and full abstraction to go from $\sim$ to $\approx$.

5 APPLICATION

HAL is an expressive language for the description of parallel machines interpreting functional and logic languages. These descriptions are of a rather abstract nature, but, using an extended version of the expansion theorem of [Milner 80], they are executable. The application presented here is concerned with the parallel interpretation of Horn Clause Logic (HCL) programs.

The technique which is used amounts to translate HCL programs into HAL agent definitions. We give a general definition of this translation and we prove its correctness. But, in order to provide some preliminary intuition about the principles of the translation, we start with a very simple example.

5.1 Example

We consider an HCL program $P=\{C_1,C_2\}$ for computing the sum of two natural integers, where the program clauses C_1 and C_2 are :

$$S(0,u,u) <- \qquad\qquad\qquad\qquad C_1$$
$$S(s(x),y,s(z)) <- S(x,y,z) \qquad\qquad C_2$$

The classical way of defining the semantics of a set of program clauses $P=\{C_i|i=..n\}$ is by mapping P into its least Herbrand model M(P). Here, we have :

$$M(\{C_1,C_2\}) = \{S(k,l,m) \mid m=k+l, \text{ with } k, l, m \text{ in } T_{(0,s)} \}$$

(we allow ourselves some abuse of notation when we write "+", but it is clear what we mean).

It is well known [Lloyd 84] that M(P) is equal to the success set of P, that is, to the set of all atoms A of the Herbrand base of P such that $P\cup\{<- A\}$ has an SLD-refutation (a refutation procedure based on the resolution inference rule, which is a refinement of the original procedure of [Robinson 65]). The success set is the procedural counterpart of the least Herbrand model. With this procedural view, each clause C_i contributes for a subset $m(\{C_i\})$ of the success set M(P). In our example, computing $m(\{C_1\})$ is trivial : it is simply the set of ground instances of S(0,u,u). Computing $m(\{C_2\})$ is taking the heads of all ground instances of C2, the body of which is either in $m(\{C1\})$ or is already a member of $m(\{C2\})$. It is rather easy to see that we get :

$$m(\{C_1\}) = \{S(0,m,m) \mid m \text{ in } T_{(0,s)} \}$$
$$m(\{C_2\}) = \{S(s(k),l,s(m)) \mid m=k+l, \text{ with } k, l, m \text{ in } T_{(0,s)} \}$$

Clearly, we have $M(\{C_1,C_2\}) = m(\{C_1\}) \cup m(\{C_2\})$.

We consider now an HAL agent C_1, obtained from clause C_1 :

$C_1 = H_1(S(0,u,u))$. *Nil*

where H_1 is a port name standing for "head of clause C_1". The ground operational semantics of HAL associates a transition system with agent C_1. Given this transition system, we can build the set $E(C_1)$ of all executions of C_1, that is, the set of all chains of transitions starting with agent C_1. In general, executions of arbitrary agents may be finite or infinite. In the case of C_1, and of all agents C_i considered in this application, they always have a length of only one transition and they always terminate on agent *Nil* : they are all of the form $C_i\text{--}H_i(A)\text{-->}Nil$, where A is an atom in the Herbrand base. We get :

$E(C_1) = \{C_1\text{--}H_1(S(0,m,m))\text{-->}Nil \mid m \text{ in } T_{(0,s)}\}$

Clearly, this set is isomorphic to $m(\{C_1\})$: $E(C_1) \sim m(\{C_1\})$.

Then, we consider an agent C_2, obtained from clause C_2. For computing $m(\{C_2\})$, clause C_1 and instances of clause C_2 are used. Similarly, agent C_2 makes use of agent C_1 and of instances $C_2', C_2'', \ldots$ of agent C_2 :

$C_2 = H_2(S(s(x),y,s(z)))\ B_{21}(S(x,y,z))$. *Nil* $// C_1\ [B_{21},H_1]$
   $// C_2'\ [B_{21},H_2']$
   $\setminus B_{21} \setminus H_1 \setminus H_2'$

In agent C_2, port B_{21} (read : "body of clause C_2, 1st atom"), is connected to port H_1 of agent C_1 and to port H_2' of another instance C_2' of agent C_2. Then, these ports are removed by restriction operators and H_2 remains as the only port through which C_2 may communicate with its environment : all its executions will have the form $C_2\text{--}H_2(S(s(k),l,s(m)))\text{-->}Nil$. But C_2 will accept offers of the form $S(s(k),l,s(m))$ on its port H_2 iff, within the same action, the offer of $S(k,l,m)$ that it makes on its port B_{21} is also accepted, either by C_1 or by C_2'. By induction on the structure of C_2, we get :

$E(C_2) = \{C_2\text{--}H_2(S(s(k),l,s(m)))\text{-->}Nil \mid m=k+l, \text{ with } k, l, m \text{ in } T_{(0,s)}\}$

Once again, $E(C_2) \sim m(\{C_2\})$. Finally, we have the property : $E(C_1+C_2) \sim M(\{C1,C_2\})$. To conclude on this introductory example, assume we want to solve a goal G :

$\text{<-}\ S(s(s(0)),v,s(s(s(0))))$ G

We create the agent :

$G = G_1(S(s(s(0)),v,s(s(s(0)))))\ ANSW(v)$. *Nil* $// C_2\ [G_1,H_2] \setminus G_1 \setminus H_2$

The reader can verify that, using only synchronous communications and no other means of computation, G returns the answer in a single transition :

$G\text{--}ANSW(s(0))\text{-->}Nil$

5.2 Translation HCL program -> HAL agent

We consider the two forms of Horn clauses which can appear in a program $P=\{C_i|i=1..n\}$, which are unit clauses, with an empty body, and program clauses, with a non empty body :

$$L_j <-$$
$$L_k <- M_{k1}\ M_{k2}\ ...\ M_{kp}$$

$$C_j$$
$$C_k$$

where L_j, L_k, M_{k1}, ..., M_{kp} are atoms. The respective translations of C_j and C_k are :

$$C_j = H_j(L_j)\ .\ Nil$$
$$C_k = H_k(L_k)\ B_{k1}(M_{k1})\ ...\ B_{kp}(M_{kp})\ .\ Nil\ //\ S_{k1}\ //\ ...\ //\ S_{kp}$$

where each sub-expression S_{kl} $(l=1..p)$ has a form which depends on the corresponding atom M_{kl} in the body of clause C_k. It is possible to decide statically that M_{kl} is unifiable with the heads of only a subset $\{C_{lq},...,C_{lr}\}$ of P. Then, S_{kl} is of the form :

$$C_{lq}\ //\ ...\ //\ C_{lr}\ [B_{kl},H_{lq}]\ ...\ [B_{kl},H_{lr}]\ \backslash\ B_{kl}\ \backslash\ H_{lq}\ \backslash\ ...\ \backslash\ H_{lr}$$

where, if C_k itself belongs to $\{C_{lq},...,C_{lr}\}$, C_k' represents it in S_{kl} (with head port H_k').

Notice that this "compilation", which selects a relevant subset of clauses for each atom in the body of a program clause is not necessary from the point of view of semantics. We could have kept all C_i's in the program for each M_{kl}, and connected each B_{kl} with all H_i's : the semantics of the connexion operator of the algebra would make a selection among the same subset of clauses. But we chose to include it for producing a simpler resulting agent expression.

Furthermore, this translation with compilation has also the property to be a direct and operational encoding of the connexion method of [Bibel 87], where "connexions" relate pairs of complementary and unifiable literals.

Finally, the translation of a complete HCL program $P=\{C_i|i=1..n\}$ is the HAL agent P composed of the non deterministic sum of all clause agents :

$$P=\sum_{i=1..n}C_i$$

5.3 Correctness of the translation

Given the HCL program $P=\{C_i|i=1..n\}$ and its translation $P=\sum_{i=1..n}C_i$, we must prove that P computes exactly the success set of P.

Given an agent C_i for a clause C_i, we define its set of possible ground offers $O(C_i)$:

$$O(C_i) = \{A\ |\ C_i\text{--}H_i(A)\text{-->}Nil\ \text{is a possible transition in}\ E(C_i)\}$$

Theorem 5. With the above scheme of translation, the set of possible ground offers of P is isomorphic to the least Herbrand model of P : $O(\sum_{i=1..n} C_i) \sim M(\{C_i | i=1..n\})$.

Proof. By induction on the depth of proofs for atoms of the success set.

Given an atom of the success set, the depth of its proof is 0 if it is a ground instance of a unit clause. The depth of its proof is $d+1$ if it is the head of a ground instance of a program clause and all atoms in the body of that instance of that clause are provable with depth at most d.

The base case for induction concerns proofs of depth 0, which use agents C_j corresponding to unit clauses C_j, and shows that $O(C_j) \sim m(C_j)$. The induction hypothesis assumes that the correctness property "holds up to depth $d<N$" for an agent C_i corresponding to a unit or program clause C_i, that is, whenever C_i is at the root of any proof of depth $d<N$. The induction step considers and agent C_k corresponding to a program clause C_k and shows that the correctness property holds up to depth $d \leq N$. Hence we get $O(C_k) \sim m(C_k)$.

Base case. Consider the unit clause agent $C_j = H_j(L_j).Nil$. For proofs of depth 0, we
   have : $O(C_j) = \{s(L_j) \mid s$ is a ground substitution$\}$. Clearly, $O(C_j) \sim m(C_j)$.

Induction step. Consider the program clause agent :

   $C_k = H_k(L_k) B_{k1}(M_{k1}) \dots B_{kp}(M_{kp})$. $Nil \parallel S_{k1} \parallel \dots \parallel S_{kp}$ where each S_{kl}
   $(l=1..p)$ has the form $C_{lq} \parallel \dots \parallel C_{lr} [B_{kl}, H_{lq}] \dots [B_{kl}, H_{lr}] \setminus B_{kl} \setminus H_{lq} \setminus \dots \setminus H_{lr}$
   and where at most one of the agent names $C_{lq} \dots C_{lr}$ in each S_{kl} may be C_k'.

The ground operational semantics tells us that :

   $O(C_k) = \{s(L_k) \mid s$ is a ground substitution
                and for all M_{kl}, $l=1..p$, there exists C_{ls} with s in $\{q,...,r\}$
                                        and $s(M_{kl})=s(L_{ls})\}$

We consider proofs of depth at most N rooted in C_k : they include only subproofs of depth $d<N$ rooted in $C_{lq}, \dots, C_{lr}$, for $l=1..p$. In the above definition of $O(C_k)$, for $l=1..p$, if all $s(M_{kl})=s(L_{ls})$, for some s in $\{q,...,r\}$, correspond to atoms in the success set with proofs of depth $d<N$, then all elements $s(L_k)$ correspond to atoms provable by proofs of depth at most N : $O(C_k)$ is sound up to N. Furthermore, by induction hypothesis, we know that the correctness property holds for all agents C_i, but is restricted to the subset of the success set provable by proofs of depth $d<N$. This holds for agents $C_{lq}, \dots, C_{lr}, l=1..p$, including for C_k, thus also for C_k' : $O(C_k)$ is complete up to N. Therefore, $O(C_k) \sim m(C_k)$.

Final step of the proof : $O(\sum_{i=1..n} C_i) = \bigcup_{i=1..n} O(C_i) \sim \bigcup_{i=1..n} m(Ci) = M(\{C_i | i=1..n\})$.

6 CONCLUSION

Similarly to the application to Horn clause logic, other machines can be built, which use the same kind computation mechanism, by means of synchronous communications among memory-less agents : function evaluation by term rewriting, equation solving by narrowing. The application to Horn clause logic can be generalized to a larger subset of first order logic, where the same architectural principles apply to the encoding of the connexion method of [Bibel 87]. A number of further developments of the algebra are of interest. A non ground algebraic semantics can be designed, where ideas from [Falashi, Levi, Martelli and Palamedissi 88] could be applied to HAL. Extensions of the language itself can also be introduced, like parameterized agent definitions similar to [Pletat 86] and equational function definitions like those of FP2 [Schnoebelen and Jorrand 89].

REFERENCES

[Bergstra and Klop 85] J. A. Bergstra and J. W. Klop. Algebra of Communicating Processes. In J. W. de Bakker et al., editors, *Proceedings of CWI Symposium on Mathematics and Computer Science*. North-Holland, 1985.

[Bibel 87] W. Bibel. *Automated Theorem Proving*. Vieweg, second edition, 1987.

[Falashi, Levi, Martelli and Palamedissi 88] M. Falashi, G. Levi, M. Martelli and C. Palamedissi. A new Declarative Semantics for Logic Languages. In *Proceedings International Symposium and Conference on Logic Programming*, 1988.

[Hoare 78] C. A. R. Hoare. Communicating Sequential Processes. *Communications of the ACM*, 21 (8), pages 666-677, 1978.

[ISO 85] *LOTOS, a Formal Description Technique Based on the Temporal Ordering of Observational Behavior*. Information Processing Systems, Open Systems Interconnection, 1985.

[Lloyd 84] J. W. Lloyd. *Foundations of Logic Programming*. Springer-Verlag, 1984.

[Milner 80] R. Milner. *A Calculus of Communicating Systems*. LNCS 92, Springer-Verlag, 1980.

[Park 81] D. Park. Concurrency and Automata on Infinite Sequences. In *Proceedings of 5th GI Conference*, LNCS 104, pages 167-183. Springer-Verlag, 1981.

[Pletat 86] U. Pletat. Algebraic Specification of Abstract Data Types and CCS : an Operational Junction. In *Proceedings of 6th IFIP Workshop on Protocol Specification, Testing and Verification*. Montreal, 1986.

[Plotkin 81] G. Plotkin. *A Structural Approach to Operational Semantics*. Lecture Notes, Aarhus University, 1981.

[Robinson 65] J.A. Robinson. A Machine Oriented Logic Based on the Resolution Principle. *Journal of the ACM*, 12, 1, pages 23-41, 1965.

[Schnoebelen and Jorrand 89] Ph. Schnoebelen and Ph. Jorrand. Principles of FP2. Term Algebras for Specification of Parallel Machines. In J.W. de Bakker, editor, *Languages for Parallel Architectures : Design, Semantics, Implementation*

Using the Reform Inference System for Parallel Prolog

Håkan Millroth

Computing Science Dept., Uppsala University
Box 520, S-751 20 Uppsala, Sweden
Electronic mail: hakanm@csd.uu.se

Abstract. We show how a new method for parallel logic programming, based on compilation of Tärnlund's inference system Reform, can be applied to the logic programming language Prolog. We retain the sequential left-to-right depth-first backtracking scheme with one exception: the recursion levels of a recursive program, including the head unifications at each level, are computed in parallel. We discuss criteria for when a program is amenable to this kind of parallel processing and describe parallel Reform Prolog solutions of some programming problems.

1. INTRODUCTION

Previous attempts at developing parallel Prolog systems have focused on exploiting AND-parallelism, or OR-parallelism, or both. In this work we parallelize Prolog by exploiting parallelism in its fundamental control structure: recursion.

Our basic idea is that parallelization takes place across recursion levels: the recursion levels of a program, including the head unifications at each level, are computed in parallel. The sequential left-to-right depth-first backtracking scheme of Prolog is retained within each recursion level.

We compile structural recursion to bounded iteration (Millroth, 1990). The iterative programs are parallelized by standard methods developed for imperative programs. The technique is based on an analysis of the unification patterns of recursive programs.

This approach has a number of appealing consequences:

1. It gives the parallel program a natural and easy-to-understand parallel reading. The programmer can write efficient parallel programs by obeying some simple rules of programming.

2. It gives a natural partitioning of the computation and its data, since nondeterminism and producer-consumer relationships are often local to each recursion level. Nondeterminism and data dependencies *within* each recursion level does not impede parallelization, since we run the each level sequentially.

3. There is a simple mapping of the program onto a parallel machine whose processors are organized in, e.g., a ring: adjacent recursion levels are mapped to adjacent processors. The inter-processor communication on such a machine will mostly be between neighboring processors, since it is unusual that data is passed between nonadjacent recursion levels in a logic program. We thus achieve predominantly local communication, which is crucial on a distributed memory machine.

4. The workload will automatically be spread evenly among the parallel processors, assuming that each recursion level of the program requires approximately

the same amount of work. This assumption seems reasonable for most Prolog programs.

2. COMPILED REFORM COMPUTATIONS

In this section we briefly describe our method for compiling a program, using structural recursion, to a program that uses bounded iteration. The compilation technique makes use of Tärnlund's (1991) inference system Reform.

2.1. Reform

We shall define Reform for the special case of linear recursion. Let $R = (H \leftarrow \Psi \wedge T \wedge \Phi)$ be a clause. We enumerate its variants as:

$$R_i = (H_i \leftarrow \Psi_i \wedge T_i \wedge \Phi_i), \qquad i \geq 1.$$

The nth *reforment* $(n > 1)$ is defined as:

$$R^n = (H_1 \leftarrow \Psi_1 \wedge \cdots \wedge \Psi_n \wedge T_n \wedge \Phi_n \wedge \cdots \wedge \Phi_1)(\sigma_1 * \cdots * \sigma_{n-1}),$$

where

$$\sigma_i = \mathrm{mgu}(H_{i+1}, T_i) \qquad \text{and} \qquad \sigma_i * \sigma_j = \mathrm{mgu}(\sigma_i, \sigma_j).$$

Let G_0 be an (initial) goal. Resolving R^n with G_0 gives

$$G_n = (\leftarrow \Psi_1 \wedge \cdots \wedge \Psi_n \wedge T_n \wedge \Phi_n \wedge \cdots \wedge \Phi_1)\theta,$$

where

$$\theta = \mathrm{mgu}(G_0, H_1(\sigma_1 * \cdots * \sigma_{n-1})).$$

It can be shown that G_n can be derived from the clause R and the initial goal G_0 in $\lceil \log n \rceil + 1$ steps. Note that G_n is the resolvent derived in n SLD-resolution steps from R and G_0. The derivation is thus significantly shorter with Reform.

Example. Consider the program for scaling each element of a list by a factor Y:

```
scale([], Y, []).
scale([X|Xs], Y, [Z|Zs]) :-
    Z is X*Y,
    scale(Xs, Y, Zs).
```

Assume that we have the following goal, where $n = 4$.

```
scale([1,2,3,4], 10, W)
```

We may derive the $4th$ reforment of the program in two steps as follows. First, we unfold the recursive call, obtaining:

```
scale([X1,X2|Xs], Y, [Z1,Z2|Zs]) :-
    Z1 is X1*Y,
    Z2 is X2*Y,
    scale(Xs, Y, Zs).
```

Unfolding the recursive call of this clause (using the clause itself) now yeilds the 4*th* reforment:

```
scale([X1,X2,X3,X4|Xs], Y, [Z1,Z2,Z3,Z4|Zs]) :-
    Z1 is X1*Y,
    Z2 is X2*Y,
    Z3 is X3*Y,
    Z4 is X4*Y,
    scale(Xs, Y, Zs).
```

We can now resolve the goal with this clause in a single, direct step. This step opens up for parallelism: the first two list can be matched in parallel, the third list can be constructed in parallel, and the multiplications can be performed in parallel.

2.2. Compiling Reform

Carrying out the Reform transformation at run-time might impose considerable overhead. The question is thus: How do we obtain the parallel algorithm, represented by the nth reforment, at *compile-time*?

Let $\mu_n = \sigma_1 * \cdots * \sigma_{n-1}$, where σ_i $(1 \leq i \leq n)$ are defined in Section 2.1. Consider a variable x and its variant variables $x_1, \ldots, x_n$ (these correspond to the new variables created in each recursive invocation of the program in SLD-resolution). The *Reform series* of x is then the sequence

$$x_1 \mu_n, \ldots, x_n \mu_n.$$

We have shown that the Reform series of a variable can be inferred from information available in the first unifier σ_1. Closed-form expressions for the Reform series can be inferred for different classes of variables. Hence explicit Reform transformation is not needed for determining the variable bindings obtained by Reform (Millroth, 1990; 1991*a*).

Let us see how this can be useful in compilation of linear recursion. Consider a recursive clause $H \leftarrow \Psi \wedge T \wedge \Phi$ and a goal G. Let $H(i)$, $\Psi(i)$, $T(i)$, and $\Phi(i)$ denote H, Ψ, T, and Φ, respectively, with all variables replaced by the ith elements of the corresponding Reform series. The compiled program can then schematically be described, in a parametric form, as:

```
unify H(1) with G
for i=1 to n do call Ψ(i)
call T(n)
for i=n to 1 do call Φ(i)
```

(In some cases, the recursive call $T(n)$ can be unfolded against the base clause. In the general case, however, this call can match both the base clause and the recursive clause.)

Example (continued). The code for the recursive scale clause is:

```
n := length(arg1);
xs[1] := arg1;
```

```
y[1] := arg2;
for i = 1 to n+1
   zs[i] := new_variable();
endfor
bind arg3 to zs[1];
for i = 1 to n
   xs[i+1] := tail(xs[i]);
   y[i+1] := arg2;
endfor
for i = 1 to n
   x[i] := head(xs[i]);
   z[i] := x[i]*y[i];
   zs[i] := cons(z[i],zs[i+1]);
endfor
call scale(xs[n+1],y[n+1],zs[n+1]);
```

The first and third loop are parallel whereas the second loop is sequential. (In the actual implementation the second loop distributes data to the third.)

2.3. Scope of the method

Our compilation method is applicable to *structural* recursion: The 'step' function (how the recursion argument is decomposed or composed) of the recursion must be derivable from the program text and not be dependent on input data. Moreover, this step function must be the same in all recursive clauses of the predicate.

For other data structures than lists and integers (of which we assume the compiler to be aware) the compiler must have type information available.

Compilation of nonlinear structural recursion follows the same principles as in the linear case. This is possible since a temporary linear representation of the recursion tree is obtained in the single large head unification that replaces the smaller unifications of a traditional system (Millroth, 1990).

We shall limit the discussion in this paper to linear recursion.

3. REFORM PROGRAMMING IN PROLOG

We now apply Reform to the logic programming language Prolog. The idea is to retain the usual left-to-right depth-first backtracking scheme with one exception: the recursion levels of a recursive program, including the unifications at each level, are computed in parallel.

An attractive consequence of this idea is that the nondeterminism of the language does not impede efficient parallelization in most cases, assuming that nondeterminism most often occurs locally *within* recursion levels. This assumption seems reasonable for most Prolog programs.

3.1. Criteria for running in parallel

Let us refer to variables shared between recursion levels as *global* variables. (Which variables are shared between recursion levels is easily seen by doing one or a few Reform transformation steps: they are the ones that get bound in the transformation.)

We shall now give two conditions for running the different recursion levels efficiently in parallel.

1. *Each recursion level is deterministic with respect to the bindings made to the global variables.*

We say that the recursion levels are *binding deterministic* (Naish, 1988) with respect to the global variables, if this condition is fulfilled. Note that the concept of binding determinism is different from the concept of data dependency in programming languages lacking logical variables. As an example, in the context of traditional AND-parallelism, consider appending three lists x, y and z to form a new list w. Given the logic program

```
append([], Y, Y).
append([E|X] ,Y, [E|Z]) :- append(X, Y, Z).
```

we can do this with the query

```
?- append(Y, Z, YZ), append(X, YZ, W).
```

The two calls in this query can be computed in parallel, since unification allows us to use the result of a computation (the variable YZ in our example) before it is actually computed.

In order to achieve binding determinism with respect to global variables, it must be assured that such variables are bound only after it has been determined which clause of the recursive program to use. Hence one must be careful not to bind any global variables before tests or before *cut* in a clause. Consequently, one must sometimes defer output unification to the clause body. We observe that it would be convenient to do this program transformation automatically. The declarations used in Parallel NU-Prolog (Naish, 1988) seems to be adequate for this purpose.

What happens if we try to run the recursion levels in parallel when the condition of binding determinism is violated? The computation will toggle back and forth between recursion levels by means of backtracking until appropriate bindings of the global variables are found. This is clearly a very inefficient method of control.

2. *There is no cross-level dereferencing.*

(Dereferencing is the process of following variable-to-variable bindings until a non-variable term, or an unbound variable, is found. In effect, it amounts to retreiving the value of the variable.) Cross-level dereferencing amounts to dereferencing a global variable bound to a variable or term on another recursion level; we will see in Section 4 how the programmer easily can detect this situation.

Consider, as an example, the following program which computes the sum of the elements of a list using an accumulating parameter (initialized to zero).

```
sum_list([], Y, Y).
sum_list([X|Xs], Y, Z) :-
    W is X+Y,
    sum_list(Xs, W, Z).
```

Here Y is a global variable, and binding W requires dereferencing Y. Hence the recursion levels must be computed in sequence, although they are deterministic. Let us now contrast this program with a slightly contrived variant of the usual list reversal program using an accumulating parameter:

```
rev([], Y, Y).
rev([X|Xs], Y, Z) :-
    W = [X|Y],
    rev(Xs, W, Z).
```

This program is very similar in structure to the sum_list program. The difference is that instead of binding W to the evaluated value of X+Y, we bind W to the list [X | Y]. We may put it like this: sum_list *uses* Y whereas rev *mentions* it (the distinction between use and mention is a nice feature of logical variables). Mentioning Y does not enforce dereferencing and all recursion levels of rev can run in parallel.

Assume now that a recursion level that performs a cross-level dereferencing suspends execution until the dereferenced value is obtained. Then, if we try to run recursion levels in parallel and the condition of no cross-level dereferencing is violated, the effect is that the recursions level are *synchronized*. Of course, this does not mean that such programs always lack potential for parallel speed-up. Although the recursion levels are synchronized, they may overlap in time to smaller or larger extent.

Let us summarize. If condition 1 (binding determinism) is violated, then the parallel computation may be very ineffcient. If condition 2 (no cross-level dereferencing) is violated, then the computation is more or less sequentialized due to synchronization.

4. EXECUTION MODEL

In this section we describe an execution model for parallel Prolog, suitable for a large-scale distributed memory multiprocessor. The idea is to increase performance of a restricted, yet interesting, class of predicates with parallelism, running other predicates sequentially.

The sequential and parallel parts of a Prolog program interact as follows. The sequential predicates of the program run on a *root processor*. When a parallel predicate is called, control is transferred to a network of parallel *node processors*. Upon termination, the parallel predicate returns control to the root which continues sequential execution or invokes another parallel predicate.

A parallel computation is thus initiated by calling a parallel predicate on the root processor. The parallel computation can then conceptually be divided into three phases (in reality, they may overlap in time):

1. Supplying the input data to the node processors.
2. Computing one instance of the body of the recursive clause on each node processor.
3. Returning control to the root processor.

The parallel abstract machine used in the Reform project at Uppsala University (Tärnlund *et al.*, 1991) has an inter-processor topology incorporating both a ring and a binary tree. The ring is used for communication between adjacent recursion levels of a parallel predicate whereas the tree is used for transmitting data between the sequential and the parallel parts of the computation.

Example. Consider the following program for partitioning a list X of numbers with respect to a particular pivot number P. Those elements of X that are less than or equal to P are collected in a list Y, and those elements that are greater than P in a list Z.

```
split([], _, [], []).
split([U|X], P, Y, Z) :-
   (   U =< P ->
       Y = [U|S], Z = T
   ;   Y = S,    Z = [U|T]
   ),
   split(X, P, S, T).
```

A few steps of Reform transformation yield the following clause:

```
split([U1,U2,U3|X], P, Y1, Z1) :-
   (   U1 =< P ->
       Y1 = [U1|Y2], Z1 = Z2
   ;   Y1 = Y2,    Z1 = [U1|Z2]
   ),
   (   U2 =< P ->
       Y2 = [U2|Y3], Z2 = Z3
   ;   Y2 = Y3,    Z2 = [U2|Z3]
   ),
   (   U3 =< P ->
       Y3 = [U3|Y3], Z3 = T
   ;   Y3 = S,    Z3 = [U3|T]
   ),
   split(X, P, S, T).
```

By studying the transformed clause we can get an accurate view of what will happen when we run the program in parallel. Although explicit Reform transformation is not used in the system, this can be a convenient method for the programmer to understand the parallel program. The clause obtained after one or a few Reform transformation steps can tell us if bindings to global variables are deterministic, if there is any cross-level dereferencing, if backtracking across recursion levels may occur, etc.

So what happens more exactly at the node processors when we we run the split program? Once the ith node processor has received its input data (one element Ui of the input list and the pivot number P), it can start computing the ith instance of split's body. Assuming we have an input list of length n and n node processors, the processors run the following code (each processor employs the sequential computation rule of standard Prolog):

Node 1:	Node 2:	Node n:
(U1 =< P ->	(U2 =< P ->	(Un =< P ->
Y1 = [U1|Y2],	Y2 = [U2|Y3],	Yn = [Un|S],
Z1 = Z2	Z2 = Z3	Zn = T
; Y1 = Y2	; Y2 = Y3	; Yn = S
Z1 = [U1|Z2]	Z2 = [U2|Z3]	Zn = [Un|T]
)	)	)

If we bind Y1 ← [U1 | Y2] on processor 1, we can simultaneously bind Y2 ← [U2 | Y3] on processor 2, since the action taken on processor 1 does not require Y2 to be dereferenced. The situation is analogous on the other processors. Hence the second condition of Section 3.1 is fulfilled: no cross-level dereferencing takes place.

The first condition is also fulfilled, since the bindings are deterministic. Hence we can run the recursion levels efficiently in parallel.

5. PROGRAM EXAMPLES

In this section we describe parallel Reform Prolog solutions of some programming problems.

In the first example all work is done by head unification. Such programs can exploit parallel unification (Barklund, 1990) with our method, but are hard to parallelize efficiently in other parallel models.

Since mutual recursion cannot be handled directly with our compilation technique it must be, automatically or manually, transformed to straight recursion. Our second example illustrates this.

In the third example we discuss a program which allows parallelism in head unification and execution of the left-body, but has a sequential right-body.

5.1. Parentheses matching

We shall first consider an example proposed by Shapiro (1983). We are given a list of left and right parentheses of two kinds. The task is to check that the parentheses are balanced.

```
balanced(L) :-
   balanced(L, Ss),
   stack(Ss, []).

balanced([], []).
balanced(['('|Ins], [push('(')|Outs]) :-
   balanced(Ins, Outs).
balanced(['{'|Ins], [push('{')|Outs]) :-
   balanced(Ins, Outs).
balanced([')'|Ins], [pop('(')|Outs]) :-
   balanced(Ins,Outs).
```

```
balanced([']'|Ins], [pop('{')|Outs]) :-
   balanced(Ins, Outs).

stack([], []).
stack([push(X)|Ss], S) :-
   stack(Ss, [X|S]).
stack([pop(X)|Ss], [X|S]) :-
   stack(Ss, S).
```

Let us consider running this program with Reform parallelism. In `balanced/1`, we run the calls to `balanced/2` and `stack/2` in sequence. However, both `balanced/2` and `stack/2` can exploit Reform parallelism. That is, all recursion levels of each of these predicates are computed simultaneously. Since neither predicate has any goals in the residual body, this amounts to two large parallel head unifications.

It is interesting to compare Reform with other paradigms of parallel logic programming with respect to this program:

1. The program cannot benefit from traditional AND-parallelism: running `balanced/2` in parallel with `stack/2` is not possible unless some notion of communicating processes is adapted. Neither `balanced/2` nor `stack/2` are, by themselves, amenable for traditional AND-parallelism since each clause contains at most one literal.

2. In a concurrent logic programming language, like Parlog (Clark & Gregory, 1983) or GHC (Ueda, 1986), the `balanced/2` and `stack/2` calls can run as concurrent processes. The variable Ss acts as a communication channel on which `balanced/2` writes messages to be consumed by `stack/2`. However, it is unlikely that this program will be accelerated by concurrent execution in this manner when run on parallel machine. The reason is simple, yet quite typical: the concurrent processes are too small to make the overhead associated with spawning parallel processes worthwhile.

When considering this example, the reader may wonder how programs which have more than one recursive clause are handled by the compiler. The answer is that in a preprocessing step such programs are transformed into equivalent programs having only one recursive clause (this is called *clause fusing*). For example, the `stack` program is transformed to:

```
stack([], []).
stack([Y|Ss], U) :-
   s(Y, U, W),
   stack(Ss, W).
s(push(X), S, [X|S]).
s(pop(X), [X|S], S).
```

5.2. Dutch national flag

We shall now consider the following program, adapted from O'Keefe (1990), for solving Dijkstra's Dutch national flag problem. The problem reads: "Given a list of elements coloured red, white, and blue, reorder the list so that all the red elements appear first, then all the white elements, followed by the blue elements. This reordering should preserve the original relative order of elements of the same colour." For clarity, we modify O'Keefe's program to represent each d-list explicitly rather than as a pair of lists.

```
dutch_national_flag(Input, Output) :-
    dnf(Input, Output-X, X-Y, Y-[]).

dnf([], R-R, W-W, B-B).
dnf([Item|Items], R0-R, W0-W, B0-B) :-
    colour(Item, Colour),
    dnf(Colour, R0-R, W0-W, B0-B, Item, Items).

dnf(red, [Item|R1-R], W0-W, B0-B, Item, Items) :-
    dnf(Items, R1-R, W0-W, B0-B).
dnf(white, R0-R, [Item|W1-W], B0-B,Item, Items) :-
    dnf(Items, R0-R, W1-W, B0-B).
dnf(blue, R0-R, W0-W, [Item|B1-B], Item, Items) :-
    dnf(Items, R0-R, W0-W, B1-B).
```

We transform the program to use straight recursion. First we merge the three clauses of dnf/6 to one clause by introducing an auxiliary predicate dnf_branch/5:

```
dnf(Colour, R0-R, W0-W, B0-B, Item, Items) :-
    dnf_branch(Colour, R0-R1, W0-W1, B0-B1, Item),
    dnf(Items, R1-R, W1-W, B1-B).

dnf_branch(red, [Item|R1-R1], W0-W0, B0-B0, Item).
dnf_branch(white, R0-R0, [Item|W1-W1], B0-B0, Item).
dnf_branch(blue, R0-R0, W0-W0, [Item|B1-B1], Item).
```

Now we can unfold the call to dnf/6 in dnf/4, thereby obtaining a program using straight recursion. The resulting procedure for dnf/4 is:

```
dnf([], R-R, W-W, B-B).
dnf([Item|Items], R0-R, W0-W, B0-B) :-
    colour(Item, Colour),
    dnf_branch(Colour, R0-R1, W0-W1, B0-B1, Item),
    dnf(Items, R1-R, W1-W, B1-B).
```

This program is amenable to Reform parallel execution: Traversal of the input list, construction of the output lists, and all calls to colour/2 and dnf_branch/5 can be computed in parallel. That gives a very high degree of parallelism to this seemingly sequential program.

5.3. Linear regression

The presentation of our next example is adopted from Press et al. (1989). The problem is to fit a set of n data points (x_i, y_i) to a straight line $y = a + bx$. We assume that the uncertainty σ_i associated with each data y_i is known, and that the $x_i's$ (values of the dependent variable) are known exactly.

Let us first define the following sums.

$$S = \sum_{i=1}^{n} 1/\sigma_i^2 \quad S_x = \sum_{i=1}^{n} x_i/\sigma_i^2 \quad S_y = \sum_{i=1}^{n} y_i/\sigma_i^2$$

$$S_{xx} = \sum_{i=1}^{n} x_i^2/\sigma_i^2 \quad S_{xy} = \sum_{i=1}^{n} x_i y_i/\sigma_i^2$$

The coefficients a and b of the straight-line equation can now be computed as:

$$\Delta = SS_{xx} - (S_x)^2$$
$$a = \frac{S_{xx}S_y - S_x S_{xy}}{\Delta}$$
$$b = \frac{SS_{xy} - S_x S_y}{\Delta}$$

The following is a Prolog program for computing the five sums needed in the calculation of a and b.

```
lin_regr_sums([], [], [], 0, 0, 0, 0, 0).
lin_regr_sums([X|Xs], [Y|Ys], [E|Es], S, Sx, Sy, Sxx, Sxy) :-
    E1 is 1/(E*E), X1 is X*E1, Y1 is Y*E1,
    XX is X*X1, XY is X*Y1,
    lin_regr_sums(Xs, Ys, Es, S1, Sx1, Sy1, Sxx1, Sxy1),
    S is S1+E1, Sx is Sx1+X1, Sy is Sy1+Y1,
    Sxx is Sxx1+XX, Sxy is Sxy1+XY.
```

We have broken up the arithmetic calculations in the body in two parts: The parallel operations are done in the left-body, and all calculations which are dependent on earlier recursion levels are done in the right-body.

Notice that we could, of course, have used accumulating parameters for the five sum-arguments, and thus obtained a tail-recursive version of the program. This would have been a good idea if we intended the program to run sequentially. However, we would then have missed most opportunities for parallelism.

6. RELATED WORK ON PARALLELIZATION OF RECURSION

The idea of running the goals of a conjunction concurrently was described by Kowalski (1974) in his seminal paper on predicate logic as a programming language. This kind of parallel processing was later coined AND-parallelism.

Let us consider running a recursive logic program in AND-parallel mode. Assume that, at each recursion level, the recursive call and the other body calls are made in parallel. Then the different recursion levels are initiated one after the other but their work may overlap in time. Clearly, this kind of parallel processing can only speed up the computation of recursive programs with a constant factor: it takes $O(n)$ time to spawn all n recursion levels.

In our model, the time complexity for getting all recursion levels into work is bounded only by the time it takes to distribute the input data of the program. This may take logarithmic time on, for example, a machine with tree topology. On a shared-memory machine (or on a distributed-memory machine where the input data is already distributed) work on all recursion levels can be initiated simultaneously.

Now, let us look outside the logic programming world. A parallelization technique for recursion in Lisp, which gives essentially the same degree of parallelism as with AND-parallelism, is described by Larus (1991).

PARCEL (Harrison, 1989) is a compiler, for the Lisp-dialect Scheme, that parallelizes recursion for execution on shared-memory multiprocessors. This work addresses the same problem as we do: compiling recursion to parallel iteration. Let us point out some notable differences in the solutions.

In the first place, PARCEL does not parallelize programs that use other data structures than lists (a nonstandard, vector-like, representation of lists is employed). Our compilation method is neither restricted to any particular data structure, nor to linear recursion. The only restriction is that the 'step' function of the recursion must be independent of input data.

Secondly, PARCEL does not parallelize programs that destructively modify list structures. The Prolog counterparts of such programs use difference lists which allow constant-time concatenation. The use of difference lists does not impede parallelization with our method. On the contrary, difference lists offer a very efficient way of constructing lists in parallel, as is shown in Section 5.2.

Thirdly, PARCEL depends on solving (at run-time) recurrences which gives expressions corresponding to our Reform series. Our classification of variables and derived expressions for Reform series allow us to determine the bindings of the variables involved in the recursion at compile-time (modulo the particular input data of the call).

7. CONCLUSIONS

The important issues in parallel computation on large-scale distributed memory machines are programming simplicity, locality of reference, and workload balance. We have described a method which successfully addresses these questions for a class of recursive Prolog programs.

Locality of reference is assured by the natural mapping of parallel programs to a ring of parallel processors. Adjacent recursion levels are mapped to adjacent processors on such a machine. Thus, inter-processor communication is local for the majority of Prolog programs which do not pass data between nonadjacent recursion levels.

Even workload among processors is assured (without dynamic load balancing) if the recursion levels of the parallel program contain approximately the same amount of work. This is the case for many Prolog programs.

Reform offers a conceptually simple model of parallelism for the Prolog programmer: the operational behaviour of a parallel program is no more complex than the corresponding sequential program. Here it is interesting to draw an analogy between our parallelization of recursion and parallelization (or vectorization) of iteration in Fortran. In both cases one starts from a sequential program and parallelizes it by exploiting parallelism in the language construct for repetition. In the Fortran case, this is often a very complicated procedure which requires expertise (Fox, 1990). In our case, a few simple rules of programming is sufficient for writing efficient parallel programs.

ACKNOWLEDGEMENT

Jonas Barklund, Johan Bevemyr, Thomas Lindgren and Margus Veanes gave valuable comments on earlier drafts of this paper.

REFERENCES

BARKLUND, J. (1990) *Parallel Unification*, Ph.D. Thesis, Computing Science Dept., Uppsala University.

CLARK, K. L. & S. GREGORY (1983) PARLOG: a parallel logic programming language. Research report DOC 83/5, Dept. of Computing, Imperial College, London.

FOX, G. (1990) Talk given at a workshop on Massively Parallel Reasoning Systems, Syracuse, New York, December 1990.

HARRISON III, W. L. (1989) The interprocedural analysis and automatic parallelization of Scheme programs. *Lisp and Symbolic Computation* 2, No. 3/4, 179–396.

KOWALSKI, R. A. (1974) Predicate logic as a computer language. In *Information Processing 74*, pp. 569–574. North-Holland, Amsterdam.

LARUS, J. R. (1991) Compiling Lisp programs for parallel execution. *Lisp and Symbolic Computation* 4, No. 1, 29–99.

MILLROTH, H. (1990) *Reforming Compilation of Logic Programs*, Ph.D. Thesis, Computing Science Dept., Uppsala University. (Summary to appear at Int. Logic Programming Symp., San Diego, CA., October 1991)

MILLROTH, H. (1991) Compiling Reform, (to appear in) *Massively Parallel Reasoning Systems* (eds. J. A. Robinson & E. E. Siebert), MIT Press.

MYCROFT, A. & R. A. O'KEEFE (1984) A Polymorphic Type System for Prolog. *Artificial Intelligence* 23, No. 3, 295–307.

NAISH, L. (1988) Parallelizing NU-Prolog. *Proc. 5th Int. Conf./Symp. Logic Programming* (eds. K. A. Bowen & R. A. Kowalski), Seattle, Washington.

O'KEEFE, R. A. (1990) *The Craft of Prolog*. MIT Press, Cambridge, Mass.

PRESS, W. H. *et al.* (1989) *Numerical Recepies. The Art of Scientific Computing.* Cambridge U. P., Cambridge.

SHAPIRO, E. Y. (1983) *A Subset of Concurrent Prolog and its Interpreter*. Technical report TR-003, ICOT, Tokyo.

TÄRNLUND, S.-Å. (1991) Reform, (to appear in) *Massively Parallel Reasoning Systems* (eds. J. A. Robinson & E. E. Siebert), MIT Press.

TÄRNLUND, S.-Å, H. MILLROTH, J. BEVEMYR, T. LINDGREN & M. VEANES (1991) Perform: a Parallel Reform Machine, submitted for publication.

UEDA, K. (1986) *Guarded Horn Clauses*, Eng.D. Thesis, University of Tokyo.

Random Competition:
A Simple, but Efficient Method for Parallelizing Inference Systems

Wolfgang Ertel

Institut für Informatik
Technische Universität München
Augustenstraße 46 Rgb.
D-8000 München 2
email: ertel@informatik.tu-muenchen.de

Abstract

We present a very simple parallel execution model suitable for inference systems with nondeterministic choices (OR-branching points). All the parallel processors solve the same task without any communication. Their programs only differ in the initialization of the random number generator used for branch selection in depth first backtracking search. This model, called random competition, permits us to calculate analytically the parallel performance for arbitrary numbers of processors. This can be done exactly and without any experiments on a parallel machine. Finally, due to their simplicity, competition architectures are easy (and therefore low-priced) to build.

As an application of this systematic approach we compute speedup expressions for specific problem classes defined by their run-time distributions. The results vary from a speedup of 1 for linearly degenerate search trees up to clearly "superlinear" speedup for strongly imbalanced search trees. Moreover, we are able to give estimates for the potential degree of OR-parallelism inherent in the different problem classes. Such an estimate is very important for the design of particular parallel inference machines, since spedups strongly depend upon the application domain.

1 Introduction

Many parallel search procedures have been developed in the last few years. Implementations on parallel machines with a small number of processors show promising results. But how can these results be extrapolated to very high numbers of processors? This is an important question since for most of the combinatorial search problems in AI computation times increase exponentially or even worse with the problem size and currently only very small problems can be solved. Therefore, apart from heuristic techniques highly parallel architectures are of great importance in this field. Experiments on highly parallel machines are expensive and time consuming. Thus mathematical models of parallel architectures for inference in AI are necessary. Since most of these parallel architectures use sophisticated load balancing mechanisms or share data in a global memory, mathematical models of such systems are hard to derive.

A promising approach to qualitative performance models of parallel depth first search based on the term of isoefficiency is presented in [KR90]. In [Ali87] a parallel Prolog execution

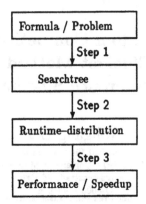

Figure 1: *Procedure for computing the competition performance. Step 3, the computation of the parallel speedup from sequential performance figures, is described in this paper.*

model with very loosely coupled sequential processors is described, but without any detailed performance analysis.

In the present paper we introduce an even more simple, non interacting, parallel search architecture called *random competition* for which we derive a statistical performance model. This model enables us to compute exact parallel performance figures for arbitrary high numbers of processors without any parallel experiments. A similar theoretical study for parallel Prolog, based on different classes of random trees was described in [JAM87]. Compared with this study, the present work emphasizes the interpretation of theoretical results and their application to particular inference systems and problem domains. In [FK87] an extension of the competition model, called Cooperative Competition, is proposed which probably leads to even higher speedups than the model presented here.

An important question in this context is: How high is the speedup of a specific random competitive search procedure when applied to a certain problem? To answer this question we propose a three step procedure (see Figure 1). In the first, and hardest, step, the structure of the search tree must be derived from the problem. From this search tree the frequency distribution of the run-time is computed in the second step.[1]

In the following (Section 3) we will focus on step three for computing parallel speedup figures from sequential run-time frequency distributions. In Section 4 this formalism is applied to some example distributions.

First, however, in Section 2 we introduce the parallel execution model.

2 The Competitive Parallel Execution Model

In many cases there exists a number of different algorithms[2] for solving a problem, where each algorithm consumes a different amount of time for execution. If it is known in advance which algorithm is the best, only one processor is necessary to execute this algorithm. In

---

[1]Step 2 is currently under investigation, whereas step 1 is a goal of future research.

[2]Examples for different search algorithms are: depth first search with leftmost selection, depth first search with rightmost selection, breadth first search, $A*$ with different heuristic evaluation functions.

many artificial intelligence applications, however, this is not known. In this case a gain in computation time is achieved if the different algorithms are executed competitively in parallel. We will show that the larger the difference between the minimal and the average run-time the larger the speedup of the competitive system will be.

In our competition model the task to be solved is not partitioned among the processors like in most other parallel architectures. Rather, each processor gets an identical copy of the whole problem. This works as follows (see Fig. 2):

1. **Startup phase**
   The host sends the whole task to all the worker processors.

2. **Working phase (Competitive Search)**
   On each of the worker processors runs a *different* program (algorithm) for solving the whole task.

3. **Termination**
   If a processor finds a solution for the task, or if he fails[3] to find a solution, he sends a message (with the solution in case of success) to the host. If the host receives such a message, he stops all the workers and outputs the result.[4]

In the rest of this paper we will neglect the time consumed by the startup and termination phases since for most problems of interest in parallel computing these times can be neglected as compared to the working time.

Obviously, during the whole working phase no communication between the processors is necessary. As a consequence no idle times occur and load is perfectly balanced all the time. Due to its simplicity, such a competitive system is very easy to implement on almost every parallel MIMD computer. The number of parallel processors is bounded by the number of different algorithms available for the given computation task.

A typical hardware for competition needs only a broadcasting medium connecting the host to all the workers, where every message (start message containing task, termination message containing the solution) from the host or a worker is sent to all the other processors.

The run-time T_k of the parallel system is the minimum of all the sequential run-times t_i $(i=1,...,k)$ of the k different algorithms.[5]

To define the speedup S of competition for a specific task we need a sequential run-time which we define as the mean value $\langle T_{seq} \rangle$ of the run-time for the different sequential algorithms. With the definitions

$$\langle T_{seq} \rangle = \frac{1}{k} \cdot \sum_{i=1}^{k} t_i \qquad \text{and} \qquad T_k = \min\{t_1,\ldots,t_k\}$$

---

[3]A processor reports a fail to the host if he has found no solution after exploring the whole search tree.

[4]If the underlying hardware allows broadcasting, the workers can also be stopped by the message of the first terminating processor himself.

[5]Please note the difference between T_i and t_i. t_i stands for the sequential run-time of algorithm number i, whereas T_i denotes the run-time of the competitive parallel system with i parallel processors (i.e. i different algorithms).

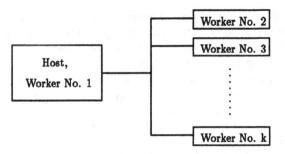

Figure 2: *A possible hardware architecture required for competition consists of $k + 1$ fast processors and a broadcasting medium connecting the host to the k worker processors.*

the speedup S evaluates to

$$S := \frac{\langle T_{seq} \rangle}{T_k} = \frac{\sum\limits_{i=1}^{k} t_i}{k \cdot \min\{t_1, \ldots, t_k\}}$$

It is easy to see that

$$1 \leq S \leq \frac{1}{k} + \frac{(k-1) \cdot \max\{t_1, \ldots, t_k\}}{k \cdot \min\{t_1, \ldots, t_k\}}$$

holds. S is equal to the upper bound if one processor has a short time and all the others have the same long time. In this case the speedup with k processors can become much larger than k. This justifies the intuition that strongly scattering run-times are a prerequisite for good competitive performance. On the other hand, if all run-times are equal, the speedup equals one, since $k - 1$ of k processors do redundant work.

The requirement of strongly scattering run-times is often fulfilled for heuristic search algorithms (e.g. A^*) with a number of different possible heuristic evaluation functions and missing knowledge about which heuristic will perform best for a given task.

If there exist no or only a few heuristics for a given search task, the number of competitive parallel processors is very small. In this case random competition offers a much higher potential for parallelism.

2.1 Random Competition

The model described so far is adaptable to any kind of problem for which different algorithms exist. In the following we will specialize on combinatorial search problems, which also fall into this category. In particular we focus on such domains for which no good search guiding heuristics exist.[6] The search space of most search problems in the fields of planning, robotics, theorem proving, game theory and problem solving can be represented as OR-tree or AND-OR-tree, where different branches at a choice point stand for independent alternatives. If one of these independent alternatives is successful, none of the others need to be expanded.

---

[6]Even with heuristics a big part of the search space may remain which has to be searched by an uninformed algorithm.

In our model we use depth-first backtracking search. If the search tree is infinite, global bounds have to be imposed which in case of failure are iteratively increased ([Kor85]). At each choice point one of the open branches is selected at random.[7] This sequential search procedure, which we call *random search*, is the same on all the processors. According to the general competition model described before, the task to be solved is the same for all the processors. The only difference between the programs running on the worker processors is the initialization of their random number generators which are used for random branch selection. The processor number can be used for this purpose, i.e. worker number i uses i as initial random number what produces different sequences of random numbers.[8] For determining the branch to be expanded the following modulo operation is applied on the integer random number

No. of selected branch = (random number *modulo* actual branching factor) + 1.

Since the programs running on the different processors are identical and no communication occurs during the working phase, this model is ideally suited for implementation on highly parallel SIMD machines with arbitrarily high numbers of processors. The number of processors is only restricted by the problem size as evaluated in Section 3.

The difference between this model and other OR-parallel models (e.g. [SL90], [KPB+89]) can be illustrated informally with the following scenario. Suppose a needle is lost in a big hay stack and ten persons together want to search this needle. One possibility to organize their search is to assign individuals to small parts of the stack which they treat exclusively. During the evolution of the search process it may become necessary to repartition the remaining stack from time to time if some searchers have no more work. The reason for this is that the hay stack (search space) is too large and complex to be partitioned it into equal parts before starting to explore it.

The other possibility is *not* to organize the search. Every searcher goes his own (random) way without being disturbed by the others. This method saves all the organization overhead, but redundant work is being done. The details about the efficiency of this method will be discussed in the following Section.

3 Analytical Computation of Performance

The goal of this Section is to compute with methods of elementary statistics an analytical expression for the speedup $S(k)$ of random competition with k parallel processors, which we define as

$$S(k) = \frac{\langle T_1 \rangle}{\langle T_k \rangle},$$

where $\langle T_k \rangle$ $_{(k=1,2,...)}$ stands for the mean value (expected value) of the run-time T_k with k processors. T_k is a stochastic variable with values $t \in I\!R^+$ and probability density $p_k(t)$. In order to obtain objective parallel speedup figures, $\langle T_k \rangle$ must be computed from a representative set of random search runs. If for $k = 1$ a single deterministic sequential search

---

[7]In case of backtracking, if a choice point is encountered more than once, the branch selection (among the remaining branches) again is done at random.

[8]In terms of the general competitive model these different sequences of random numbers represent the required different search algorithms (strategies).

procedure is used, the only run-time which can be obtained may be by chance very short or very long, depending on the location of the solution(s) in the search space.[9] With statistic sampling of random-search runs this effect can be avoided. For such a set of samples $\langle T_k \rangle$ is defined as[10]

$$\langle T_k \rangle = \int_0^\infty p_k(t) \cdot t \ dt \qquad (1)$$

where $p_k(t)$ stands for the probability density of the competitive parallel system with $k \geq 1$ processors. The probability for observing a sequential run-time in an infinitesimally small interval of width dt located at t is $p_1(t)dt$. The rest of this Section is devoted to compute $p_k(t)$ starting from the sequential run-times, i.e. from $p_1(t)$.

The basis for the performance analysis are sequential frequency distributions $n(t)$ for the run-time, which denote the number of times a run-time t occurs in a set of samples. An empirical frequency distribution of run-times obtained with the automated theorem prover SETHEO [LSBB91] is shown in Figure 3.

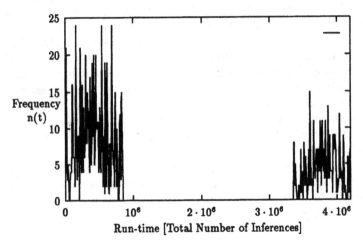

Figure 3: *Distribution of the search effort (tot. no. of inferences) of SETHEO applied to the theorem IP_1 ([Pfe88]) in random search mode. The graph splits into two clusters, separated by a region of times which were not observed ($n(t) = 0$). The total number of runs (samples) is 1402.*

The probability for observing the (sequential) run-time t is

$$p_1(t) = \frac{1}{N} \cdot n(t), \qquad \text{where} \quad N = \int_0^\infty n(t)dt. \qquad (2)$$

---

[9]In fact, many researchers wonder about very strongly scattering experimental speedup results, even if they do extensive sampling of parallel runs. The reason for this is that they do no sampling of sequential runs with a random selection function.

[10]In case of empirical data, which are discrete in time, it is better to define the expected values by summation over the possible times, where we get e.g. $\langle T_{seq} \rangle = \langle T_1 \rangle$. In the following, however, we aim at analytical computation of the speedup for (piecewise) continuous probability density functions.

Figure 4: *The parallel probability density p_k is obtained from p_1 via a three step detour.*

The computation of $p_k(t)$ now is done in three steps via the distribution functions $P_k(t)$ as shown in Figure 4. The probability $P_1(t)$ for the sequential algorithm to terminate in a time less or equal to t evaluates to

$$P_1(t) = \int_0^t p_1(t')dt' \tag{3}$$

Suppose we know this probability P_1. Since our k competitive processors are independent we can now apply the laws of probability and compute the probability $P_k(t)$ for our random competition system with k parallel processors to terminate in a time less or equal to t.

$$
\begin{aligned}
P_1(t) &= \text{Probability for one processor to terminate in a} \\
&\quad \text{time } T_1 \leq t. \\
1 - P_1(t) &= \text{Probability for one processor \textbf{not} to terminate in} \\
&\quad \text{a time } T_1 \leq t. \\
(1 - P_1(t))^k &= \text{Probability for k independent processors \textbf{not} to} \\
&\quad \text{terminate in a time } T_k \leq t.^{11} \\
1 - (1 - P_1(t))^k &= \text{Probability for at least one of k independent pro-} \\
&\quad \text{cessors to terminate in a time } T_k \leq t.^{12}
\end{aligned}
$$

As a consequence

$$P_k(t) = 1 - (1 - P_1(t))^k. \tag{4}$$

This formula is the key for the step from sequential to parallel performance figures. In order to calculate $\langle T \rangle_k$ with equation (1) we need the parallel probability density $p_k(t)$ which we obtain from

$$P_k(t) = \int_0^t p_k(t')dt' \tag{5}$$

as

$$
\begin{aligned}
p_k(t) &= \frac{d}{dt}P_k(t) \tag{6} \\
&= k \cdot (1 - P_1(t))^{k-1} \cdot \frac{d}{dt}P_1(t) \tag{7} \\
&= k \cdot \left(1 - \int_0^t p_1(t')dt'\right)^{k-1} \cdot p_1(t) \tag{8}
\end{aligned}
$$

---

[11]Here we made use of the fact that $P(A \wedge B) = P(A) \cdot P(B)$ for independent events A and B.

[12]This derivation via the probabilities of the complement is much easier than the direct way where we would have to sum over all the different cases for one of k processors to terminate in a time $T \leq t$.

The last equation together with (2) enables us to compute the parallel probability density for every given sequential frequency distribution $n(t)$. If we use experimentally derived distributions which are given numerically, the integrals over t in the derived formulas change into sums over the discrete observed time values $t_1, \ldots, t_m$. In the next Section, however we will compute the speedup analytically for functionally given probability density functions. This is mathematically much easier by integration over continuous distributions, rather than by summation.

3.1 Maximum OR-Parallel Speedup

From an OR-parallel search algorithm one expects an increase of performance with increasing number of processors. For each problem, however, there exists an upper bound for the speedup since there is a lower bound for the parallel run-time $\langle T \rangle_k$ which is the same for all OR-parallel algorithms. This lower bound is equal to the shortest possible sequential run-time t_0 with random search. This case happens if one processor immediately without backtracking or communication finds a solution. Therefore

$$\lim_{k \to \infty} S(k) = \frac{\lim_{k \to \infty} \langle T_1 \rangle}{\lim_{k \to \infty} \langle T_k \rangle} \leq \frac{\int_0^\infty p_1(t) t \, dt}{t_0} \tag{9}$$

for all OR-parallel architectures. Now we show that for random competition this inequality becomes an equality. From equation (4) we get

$$\lim_{k \to \infty} P_k(t) = \begin{cases} 1 & \text{if } t > t_0 \\ 0 & \text{if } t \leq t_0 \end{cases} \tag{10}$$

since $P_1(t) > 0$ iff $t > t_0$. Now we use equation (6) to compute $p_k(t)$. Although P_k is not differentiable at $t = t_0$ we can apply the theory of distributions and get $p_k(t) = \delta(t - t_0)$, where δ is the Dirac delta function. With (1) we get $\lim_{k \to \infty} \langle T \rangle_k = t_0$ which is the optimal possible OR-parallel execution time.

The reason for this optimal asymptotic result of competition is that no communication and idle times occur. Although this is a promising result, it is of minor practical interest since the efficiency $S(k)/k$ becomes very small for $k \to \infty$.

4 Particular Distributions

In this Section we compute the speedup for some mathematically treatable probability density functions. This allows us to make propositions about the asymptotic behaviour of the competitive system. With these results we are able to derive upper bounds for the degree of parallelism possible with any OR-parallel system.

4.1 Exponential Distribution

First we consider the exponential distribution $p_1(t) = \lambda \cdot e^{-\lambda t}$. Applying the formalism of Section 3, a simple computation yields linear speedup:

$$\langle T \rangle_k = \frac{1}{k \cdot \lambda} \quad \text{and} \quad \boxed{S(k) = k}$$

4.2 Twofold uniform distribution

In some of our theorem proving examples like that of Figure 3 we observed distributions with two separate clusters. This type of distribution is produced by search in trees consisting of two subtrees with different size and one solution in the smaller subtree.[13] As an approximation of this type of distribution we use the density function

$$p_1(t) = \begin{cases} \frac{1}{2a} & \text{if } l \le t \le l+a \\ 0 & \text{if } l+a < t < L-a \\ \frac{1}{2a} & \text{if } L-a \le t \le L \end{cases}$$

the graph of which is

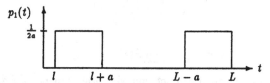

It consists of two separated uniform distributions with same height ($\frac{1}{2a}$) and same width a. The procedure of Section 3 results in (see Appendix)

$$S(k) = \frac{(r+1)(k+1)2^{k-1}}{(k+1)(r-1)(1-2b) + 2^k(k+1+(r-1)2b)} \tag{11}$$

where $r = \frac{L}{l}$ and $b = \frac{a}{L-l}$.

Two graphs of this speedup expression for different values of the parameters r and b are shown in Figures 5 and 6. The whole spectrum from sublinear and bounded up to highly superlinear speedups is possible with competition, depending on the distribution of the run-times.

In the asymptotic limit ($k \to \infty$) we get the (not surprising) result

$$\lim_{k \to \infty} \langle T \rangle_k = l \quad \text{and} \quad \lim_{k \to \infty} S(k) = \frac{r+1}{2} = \frac{L+l}{2 \cdot l}$$

which could also directly be obtained from equation (9). This is the upper bound for every OR-parallel search procedure.

If $b = 0$ (i.e. $a = 0$), the distribution consists of only two run-times l and L and $S(k)$ is

$$S(k, b = 0) = \frac{r+1}{2 \cdot [1 + (r-1) \cdot (1/2)^k]}$$

This equation shows that for large r (i.e. $L \gg l$) and small k the speedup grows exponentially as $S(k) \approx 2^{k-1}$. This superlinear behaviour of the speedup is due to the strongly

---

[13]This results from current work on step 2 of the procedure depicted in Figure 1.

imbalanced structure of search trees which causse the given run-time distribution for large r. Many researchers argue that significantly superlinear speedups like in these figures should not (can not) occur. In case of OR-parallel depth first search, however, parallelization introduces a breadth first component which is not present in the sequential algorithm. In many (not all) of these superlinear cases the use of breadth first search for computing $\langle T_1 \rangle$ would lower the speedup results below the line $S(k) = k$. An other way of eliminating this superlinear speedup behaviour – and thus a way of enhancing the underlying sequential algorithm – is to simulate (e.g. time-slice) the competitive search (or more general: parallel search) on a sequential computer. For such a simulation one should use that value of k for which the parallel efficiency $E(k) := S(k)/k$ is maximal. For our example distribution and $b = 0$, $k = 1000$ (see Fig. 5) the maximum of $E(k)$ lies at $k_{max} \approx 13$ and $E(13) = 34.3$. Thus, the sequential simulation with $k = 13$ is about 34 times faster than with $k = 1$. For $b = 0$, $k = 200$ we have $k_{max} \approx 10$ and $E(10) = 8.4$.

In case of $b = 1/2$ (single uniform distribution) we get

$$S(k) = \frac{(r+1)(k+1)}{2(r+k)} \tag{12}$$

and $$\lim_{r \to \infty} S(k) = \frac{k+1}{2}$$

Figure 6 allows a comparison of competition with other OR-parallel architectures since $b = 1/2$ represents the uniform distribution which results from balanced search trees with constant branching factor and one solution. For large search problems r becomes very large and $S(k)$ therefore is nearly linear ($S(k) \approx (k+1)/2$) even for large numbers of processors.

Typical search problems which touch the limits of todays computers produce search trees with a size between 10^6 and 10^9 nodes to be explored. If we assume an exponential tree with 10^7 nodes and a constant branching factor of 10, we get $r = 1.11 \cdot 10^7/7 = 1.59 \cdot 10^6$. From equation (12) we obtain a speedup of 4969 with 10000 processors. This result is not optimal, but it is realistic since it is exact and the parallel implementation causes no overhead.

4.3 Application of Results to a Realistic Frequency Distribution

In Figure 7 the exact speedup curve for the experimental distribution of the IP_1 runs (Figure 3) is plotted. This has been obtained by applying the formalism of Section 3 (discrete variant) directly (numerically) to the distribution of Figure 3. As a main result one can see that the speedup is linear up to about 120 processors. This gives a good estimate for the size of a hardware architecture which is well suited for problems of this size and class. Performing such computations for a class of problems representative for a particular application domain is therefore very helpful in designing special purpose parallel hardware.

We are now ready to apply equation (11) to the experimental distribution of the IP_1 runs (Figure 3) with $r = 524$ and $b = 0.2$, i.e. to approximate the experimentally derived distribution by the analytically treatable twofold uniform distribution.[14] The resulting speedup curve is shown as the thin line in Figure 7.

Although the approximation of the distribution by a twofold uniform distribution is very rough, the speedup results are quite similar. The higher speedup of the exact curve

---

[14]From the data plotted in Figure 3 we extract: $l = 8000$, $L = 4192000$, $a = 836000$

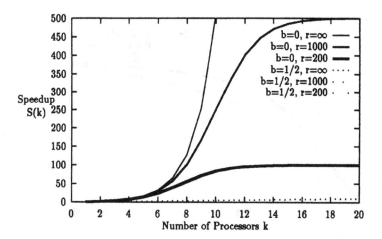

Figure 5: *Speedup figures of the simple distribution with only two different run-times (b = 0). The two graphs r = 200 and r = 1000 show a strongly superlinear behaviour for up to 15 processors and are bounded by the limits of $\frac{r+1}{2}$. The graph r = ∞, which represents the case that the shorter of the two run-times l is zero, grows exponentially with k.*

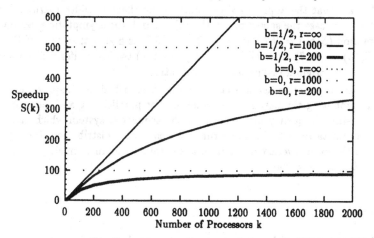

Figure 6: *Speedup figures of the uniform distribution (b = 1/2). If the shortest run-time is zero (r = ∞) the speedup behaves linear (S(k) = (k + 1)/2). Otherwise the graphs are sublinear and again bounded by $\frac{r+1}{2}$.*

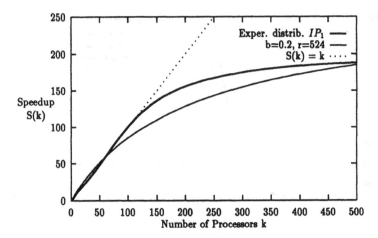

Figure 7: *Speedup figures for the experimental distribution of Figure 3. The exact numerically derived results (Label: Theorem IP_1) are compared with the approximation through a twofold uniform distribution.*

is caused by the fact that the approximation enlarges the effective width (variance) of the two clusters what decreases the speedup. On the other hand, the asymptotic speedup value of the approximation ($S(\infty) = 262.5$ for $r = 524$, $b = 0.2$) is higher than that of the exact computation ($S(\infty) = 191.7$) since $\langle T_1 \rangle$ of the (symmetric) twofold uniform distribution is larger than that of the original (asymmetric) distribution.

Finally, we want to mention again, that the method described here requires no parallel experiments for computing the parallel performance. For parallelizing an inference system one needs the run-time frequency distribution of the sequential system which can be obtained from a representative set of sample runs. Given such a distribution, the described method computes the exact average speedup of the parallel random competition system for an arbitrary number of processors.

5   Conclusion

We introduced random competition, a parallel search procedure which we analyzed with a statistical method. This provides a means for transforming sequential performance measurements into exact speedup values of the competitive parallel system.

The performance figures computed for some example distributions show that random competition is efficient (often superlinear) in case of imbalanced search trees, for which the variance of run-times is high. The general upper bound (which is the same for all OR-parallel systems) for the speedup together with the maximum of $S(k)/k$ provides the user of a search procedure or of an inference system with an estimate of the number of processors required for efficient parallel execution of problems in specific application domains. As part of our future work we are aiming at an extension of this method and its application to other parallel search procedures.

Finally, random competition is easy to implement on most parallel computers as well as on (large) local area networks since there is no communication between the processors.

References

[Ali87]   K. A. M. Ali. Or-parallel execution of PROLOG on a multi-sequential machine. *Int. Journal of Parallel Programming*, 15(3):189–214, 1987.

[BS81]   I. N. Bronstein and K. A. Semendjajew. *Taschenbuch der Mathematik*. Harri Deutsch, Thun, Frankfurt, 1981.

[FK87]   B. Fronhöfer and F. Kurfeß. Cooperative competition: A modest proposal concerning the use of multi-processor systems for automated reasoning. Technical Report ATP–74–VII–87, Institut für Informatik, Technische Universität München, 1987.

[JAM87]   V. K. Janakiram, D. P. Agrawal, and R. Mehrotra. Randomized parallel algorithms for Prolog programs and backtracking applications. In *Int. Conf. on Parallel Processing*, pages 278 – 281, 1987.

[Kor85]   R. E. Korf. Depth-first iterative-deepening: An optimal admissible tree search. *Artificial Intelligence*, 27:97–109, 1985.

[KPB+89]   F. Kurfeß, X. Pandolfi, Z. Belmesk, W. Ertel, R. Letz, and J. Schumann. PARTHEO and FP2: Design of a Parallel Inference Machine. In Ph. Treleaven, editor, *Parallel Computers: Object-Oriented, Functional, Logic*, chapter 9, pages 259–297. Wiley & Sons, Chichester, 1989.

[KR90]   Vipin Kumar and V. Nageshwara Rao. Scalable parallel formulations of depth-first search. In P.S. Gopalakrishnan Vipin Kumar and Laveen N. Kanal, editors, *Parallel Algorithmus for Maschine Intelligence and Vision*, pages 1–41. Springer Verlag, New York, 1990.

[LSBB91]   R. Letz, J. Schumann, S. Bayerl, and W. Bibel. SETHEO, A High–Performance Theorem Prover. *to appear in Journal of Automated Reasoning*, 1991. available as Technical Report TUM–I9008 from Technical University Munich.

[Pfe88]   F. Pfenning. Single axioms in the implicational propositional calculus. In *9th Int. Conf. on Automated Deduction*, pages 710 – 713, Berlin, 1988. Springer.

[SL90]   J. K. Slaney and E. L. Lusk. Parallelizing the closure computation in automated deduction. In *10th Int. Conf. on Automated Deduction*, pages 28–39, Berlin, Heidelberg, 1990. Springer.

Appendix: Evaluation of the Integral for the Twofold Uniform Distribution

$$p_k(t) = k(1 - \int_0^t p_1(t')dt')^{k-1}p_1(t) \qquad \langle T \rangle_k = \int_0^\infty p_k(t) \cdot t \; dt \quad = \quad I_1 + I_2 + I_3$$

where $\quad I_1 = \int_l^{l+a} p_k(t) \cdot t \; dt, \quad I_2 = \int_{l+a}^{L-a} p_k(t) \cdot t \; dt, \quad I_3 = \int_{L-a}^{L} p_k(t) \cdot t \; dt$

1.) $l \le t \le l + a$: $\quad p_1(t) = \dfrac{1}{2a} \implies \int_l^t p_1(t')dt' = \dfrac{1}{2a}[(t-l)]$

$$p_k(t) = \frac{k}{2a}(1 - \frac{1}{2a}(t-l))^{k-1} = \frac{k}{(2a)^k}\int_l^{l+a}(2a - t + l)^{k-1}$$

$$I_1 = \int_l^{l+a} p_k(t) \cdot t dt = \frac{k}{(2a)^k}\int_l^{l+a}(2a - t + l)^{k-1} \cdot t dt$$

For evaluating this integral we used equation (3) p. 87 in [BS81] what results in:

$$\begin{aligned}
I_1 &= \frac{k}{(2a)^k}\left[\frac{1}{k+1}(2a - t + l)^{k+1} - \frac{2a+l}{k}(2a - t + l)^k\right]_l^{l+a} \\
&= \frac{1}{(2a)^k(k+1)}\left[k(2a - t + l)^{k+1} - (k+1)(2a+l)(2a - t + l)^k\right]_l^{l+a} \\
&= \frac{1}{(2a)^k(k+1)}\left[ka^{k+1} - (k+1)(2a+l)a^k - k(2a)^{k+1} + (k+1)(2a+l)(2a)^k\right] \\
&= \frac{1}{2^k(k+1)}\left[ka(1 - 2^{k+1}) + (k+1)(2a+l)(2^k - 1)\right] \\
&= \frac{1}{2^k(k+1)}\left[ka - ka2^{k+1} + 2^k(2ak + kl + 2a + l) - 2ak - kl - 2a - l\right] \\
&= \frac{1}{2^k(k+1)}\left[-ak + (2^k - 1)(kl + 2a + l)\right]
\end{aligned}$$

2.) $l + a < t < L - a \qquad p_1(t) = 0 \implies I_2 = 0$

3.) $L - a \le t \le L \qquad p_1(t) = \dfrac{1}{2a}$

$$p_1(t) = \int_0^t p_1(t')dt' = \frac{1}{2} + \left[\frac{t'}{2a}\right]_{L-a}^t = 1 + \frac{1}{2a}(t - L)$$

$$p_k(t) = k\left(1 - 1 - \frac{1}{2a}(t - L)\right)^{k-1}\frac{1}{2a} = \frac{k}{(2a)^k}(L - t)^{(k-1)}$$

$$I_3 = \frac{k}{2a^k}\int_{L-a}^{L}(L - t)^{k-1} \cdot t dt$$

Again we use equation (3) p. 87 in [BS81] and get:

$$I_3 = \frac{k}{(2a)^k}\left[\frac{1}{k+1}(L-t)^{k+1} - \frac{1}{k}(L-t)^k L\right]_{L-a}^{L}$$

$$= \frac{1}{(2a)^k(k+1)}\left[0-0-ka^{k+1}+(k+1)a^k L\right] = \frac{1}{2^k(k+1)}(kL+L-ka)$$

$$\langle T\rangle_k = I_1+I_3 = \frac{1}{2^k(k+1)}\left[-ak+2^k(kl+2a+l)-kl-2a-l+kL+L-ka\right]$$

$$= \frac{1}{2^k(k+1)}\left[-(k+1)2a-(k+1)l+(k+1)L+2^k((k+1)l+2a)\right]$$

$$\langle T\rangle_1 = \frac{1}{4}\left[-a+2(2l+2a)-l-2a-l+L+L-a\right] = \frac{l+L}{2}$$

$$S(k) = \frac{\langle T\rangle_1}{\langle T\rangle_k} = \frac{(L+l)2^{k-1}(k+1)}{(k+1)(L-l-2a)+2^k((k+1)l+2a)}$$

with $a := b(L-l)$ we get

$$S(k) = \frac{(L+l)(k+1)2^{k-1}}{(k+1)(L-l)(1-2b)+2^k((k+1)l+2b(L-l))}$$

$$= \frac{(r+1)(k+1)2^{k-1}}{(k+1)(r-1)(1-2b)+2^k(k+1+(r-1)2b)}$$

where $r := \frac{L}{l}$ $\quad 1 \le r < \infty$

Parallel and Efficient Implementation
of the
Compartmentalized Connection Graph Proof Procedure:
Resolution to Unification

David M. W. Powers[1]
Universität Kaiserslautern
W-6750 KAISERSLAUTERN FRG

powers@informatik.uni-kl.de

Abstract

This paper documents aspects of the development of a logic programming paradigm with implicit control, based in a compartmentalized connection graph theorem prover. Whilst the research has as it main goal the development of a language in which programs can be written with much less explicit control than PROLOG and its existing successors, a secondary goal is to exploit the immense parallelism inherent in the connection graph. This is what is in focus in this presentation.

We focus initially on analysis of the extent of the parallelism inherent in the proof procedure. We characterize six different forms of parallelism These various forms of parallelism can be further classified into two classes: those associated with the performance of resolution steps, and those which are more concerned with unification.

Unification is thus also a major topic of this report, and is identified as a major source of the cost of executing a logic program or proving a theorem. It turns out that deferring unification is the one of the best ways of dealing with it: hashing to perform it, and indexing to avoid it.

Indexing and hashing, therefore, are our third topic.

Introduction

Our previous papers and reports [Powe88,90,91; Wise84] discussed the advantages and disadvantages of PROLOG, focussing particularly on logic and control — the advantages of a clean declarative semantics and the disadvantages of a rigid predetermined control. We then presented some of the advantages and possibilities of logic programming in an automated theorem prover without cuts, annotations, builtins and other embellishments of clausal logic: in particular advantages relating to efficient treatment of recursion and examples of programming around major classes of builtin predicates. These goals were achieved either directly in the compartmentalized connection graph theorem prover or in combination with preprocessing transformations.

---

[1] The work reported here was in the main undertaken while the author was at Macquarie University NSW 2009 AUSTRALIA, and was supported in part by IMPACT Ltd, PETERSHAM NSW 2049 AUSTRALIA, the Australian Telecommunications and Electronics Research Board, and the Australian Research Council (Grant No. A48615954). The author is currently supported under ESPRIT BRA 3012: COMPULOG.

The most common generalizations of PROLOG have held fast to its general control regime, whilst allowing relaxation as well. In particular, the parallel or concurrent PROLOG systems generally fall into this category. Most generalizations also tend to adhere largely to the Horn clause paradigm, while perhaps allowing more general forms with some specific model.

This work has approached logic programming from the opposite extreme, a completely general clausal theorem prover without control — we seek to understand the behaviour of logic programs expressed in such an environment, including how efficiently to implement the environment, and whether it is possible to use general search heuristics and learning techniques rather than an explicit control paradigm. The CONG system [Powe88] for CONcurrent logic programming is based on a CONnection Graph theorem prover and can accept pure PROLOG programs (cutless Horn clauses without builtin predicates) as well as general clause form theorems.

This paper moves on to address some of the efficiency issues which remain. Clearly the heuristics will be major determiners of efficiency, and even efficacy, and [Powe90] showed that given appropriate heuristics CONG can achieve enormous reduction in proof length compared with PROLOG. We, moreover, characterized the complexity of the proof as being of order by $c*n*d$ operations, where the number of literals in the program is n, the maximum depth of any term is d, and the maximum number of copies of any clause is c. This reflects the subdivision of labour between (recursive) copying, (unit) resolution of (ground) Horn clauses, and instantiation (unification testing) of the proof. In the following sections we address the cost of these three components in parallel and/or sequential implementations.

Our techniques (detailed more fully in our technical report [Powe90]) demonstrate that in a theorem prover it is possible to reduce the number of recursive resolution steps to the logarithm of that of either PROLOG or a standard connection graph theorem prover — using clause doubling by resolution on *pseudo-links* (hence, *pseudo-resolution*). But the number of copies of the terms of a clause is still in general c, so the work in unification can remain of order $c*n*d$ operations.

Whilst PROLOG traditionally measures speed of PROLOG implementations in LIPS (Logical Inferences Per Second), or resolutions per second, this hides the cost of unification inherent in the problem, and the benchmarks with trivial unification will demonstrate far greater speeds than those with complex unification characteristics. Indeed, the unification can be optimized away by a compiler in the trivial cases, but never in the complex problems where complex unification is inherent in the nature and purpose of the program.

Similarly with CONG, trivial unifications will not slow the resolution and pseudoresolution processes. But although the number of recursive resolution steps can be reduced from $o(c)$ to $o(\log c)$, mostly an unification operation linear in c will be required at the point where a pseudoresolvent is resolved non-recursively. But in a parallel context, the most common examples should be unifiable in unit time on $o(c)$ processors. In a typical complex logic program this may grow to logarithmic time, whilst in the most artfully constructed automated reasoning problems it may remain linear.

We have therefore identified unification as the major remaining bottleneck. In this paper we explore the complexity characterization of unification and provides examples with the various behaviours just outlined. We further examine the feasibility of avoiding and delaying unification where the unifiability is not yet known or unifier is not yet required. In particular, we note the separability of unifiability testing and unifier determination.

The above calculations were also based on a direct deterministic discovery of the proof — whether guided by oracle, heuristics or control. In an Artificial Intelligence application with blind search characteristics, most unifications will fail, or at least the proof strand of which they form a part will fail. In these cases the time expended on accurate unifiability testing and unifier determination is totally wasted. We therefore explore the possibility of trial unification in which unification work is undertaken in a way designed to expedite the detection of failure, allowing the proof to proceed with only a certain likelihood of the eventual success of the unification. This allows also the concept of a trial proof in which unifiability and unifiers are only finally accurately determined when it appears that a proof has been found.

The relative importance of unification also emerges when we characterize the various sorts of parallelism which are achievable in CONG.

Proof Algorithm

Compartmentalized Connection Graph

We now recapitulate the algorithm used by CONG as presented in [Powe90], with references back to the differences from the original algorithm of [Kowa79].

Unification

In the following, unless specifically stated otherwise, *unifiable* and *unifier*, refer respectively to *weak unification* and the resulting *most general unifier*. In PROLOG terminology, these are unification in distinct environments and the unifying substitution. Weak unification can also be described in terms of unifiability after renaming.

Links

A set of clauses to be proven inconsistent are linked into a graph by connecting distinct clauses with a *link* whenever they have unifiable complementary literals. A link may at times most conveniently be regarded as two connecting clauses, at other times as connecting the two literals which gave rise to it. However, they actually indicate potential resolutions, or equally well potential resolvents. The substitution giving rise to the most general unifier of the linked literals is associated with the link.

Resolution links

Under this above definition a link is formally defined only between distinct clauses, although loosely used it may, when the context permits, include internal links. In certain syntactic contexts all forms of links, including even links between non-complementary unifiable literals may be intended. When we want be absolutely clear we can refer to the links between complementary literals of distinct clauses as *resolution links*.

Pseudolinks

Additional connections between unifiable literals of opposite sign within a single clause are added and are termed *pseudolinks*. These internal links represent the potential for copies of the clause to resolve, but are themselves never actually resolved on. They may thus also be referred to as *self-resolving links*. The substitution giving rise to the most general unifier of the linked literals is associated with the pseudolink.

Initial graph

The graph resulting from the addition of resolution links and pseudolinks to a set of clauses is called the *initial graph*. Figure 1 shows the initial graph and substitutions for a simple append example.

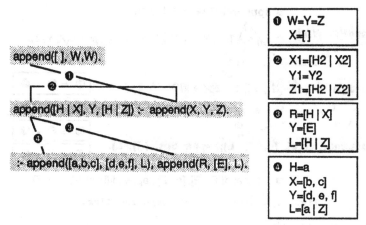

Fig. 1. *Initial graph for* append

Resolution rule

A link may be resolved upon by resolving upon the linked clauses (the *parents*) and *replacing* the link by a new clause (the *resolvent*) obtained from the union of terms of the two clauses excluding the linked terms with the application of the associated substitution.

In the compartmentalized connection graph a constraint is added, that neither of the parent clauses may contain a pseudolink. But a complementary constraint is lifted, in that pseudolinks may themselves be resolved upon as if it linked two separate copies of its parent clause. The terms of the resolvent are said to have *inherited* from its parents.

In fact, this leads to alternating phases: a *static* phase where clauses without pseudolins are resolved, and a *dynamic* phase where pseudolinks are resolved. The clauses with and without pseudolinks are said to belong to different (*static* or *dynamic*) *compartments*.

Inheritance rule

Upon resolution, links and pseudolinks impinging on the inheriting terms of the parent also inherit to give new links and pseudolinks attached to the inherited terms which have the composition of the resolving link's substitution and that of the original links, and will be a resolution link or a pseudolink according to whether the link connects distinct clauses or is internal to one clause, respectively.

We define the composition operator as performing unification of the substituted variables occuring in two link substitutions. That is, when the substitutions both instantiate the same variable, the bound structures are unified.

Figure 2 shows the results of resolving on each of the four links of Fig. 1 and in the case of the clause ❶ (resulting from link ❶) the inherited links are also shown. Note that the evaluation of the new substitutions associated with the may be carried out in a lazy manner, and in particular composition of substitutions associated with new pseudo-links is deferred to the dynamic phase.

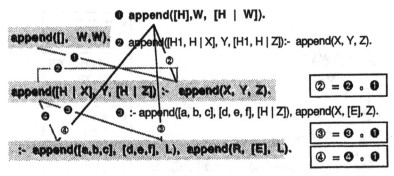

Fig. 2. *Inheriting and Composing Links*

Positive-to-parent rule

In the compartmentalized connection graph, pseudolinks will not be inherited *from* during a link resolution, as a consequences of the restriction against parents containing pseudolinks (in the static phase). However they may be inherited from during a pseudoresolution (in the dynamic phase). In this case, the pseudolink currently being resolved could give rise to a new pseudolink and two new links connecting the parent clause and the resolvent, as the parent clause is playing a dual role and resolving with a copy of itself producing a redundant link [Eisi88]. As illustrated in Fig. 3, this is resolved arbitrarily by the *positive-to-parent* rule [Powe90] which says that, apart from the pseudolink, only the resolution link connecting the *positive* literal of the resolvent *to* (the negative literal of) the *parent* clause is inherited from the pseudolink undergoing pseudoresolution (which is in the process of being processed and removed).

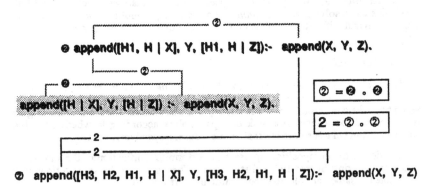

Fig. 3. *The Doubling Effect and Pseudoinheritance*

The pseudoresolution operation leads to particularly efficient handling of recursion through the doubling effect, reaching a point in the logarithm of the number of steps required by link-resolution, as can be seen in Fig. 3 where the number of explicit heads increase 1, 2, 4, ...

Factoring, purity, tautology and subsumption rules

Applied to general clauses (unrestricted to Horn), resolution is incomplete without factoring (or merging). Also there are various optimizations whereby certain clauses which are inessential to the proof may be deleted. These considerations are irrelevant to this paper and the rules are therefore not presented. See [Eisi88; Powe90].

Ordering and restriction filters

Certain heuristics may be used to further specify the selection of links, which are left considerable latitude under both the original and the compartmentalized connection graph procedures. In fact, strong completeness cannot be assured without such filters, and even with filters no proofs of strong completeness have yet survived scrutiny [Eisi88].

This is again not an issue for the Horn case, where strong completeness is assured by a variety of strategies. Filters recommend include unit resolution, hyperresolution and orphaning [Eisi88; Powe90]. The standard and compartmentalized connection graph procedures presented may also be seen as the results of applying particular filters to the generalized procedure of [Eisi88], in which no restrictions are applied to when or whether one can resolve on particular types of links (viz. resolution links or pseudolinks).

The compartmentalized filter was specifically designed to take advantage of the power of treating recursion separately and in view of apparent strong completeness properties in combination with the *parent-before-child* (orphaning) and other filters – a draft proof exists but has not yet been subject to sufficiently rigourous examination.

Handling Recursion

Doubling

The doubling effect of pseudo-resolution as provided for in the compartmentalized connection graph algorithm has the effect of reducing the number of resolution operations dramatically, logarithmically in the depth of recursion. This has the effect of reducing the number of separate (sequential) unifications required and increasing the size and number of the (parallel) unification problems involved in these steps during the composition processes involved in inheritance. If this doubling technique can be exploited, the actual cost of resolution becomes insignificant in comparison with the cost of the unification.

However, the doubling technique can only be use when recursion is *explicitly* represented in a clause with pseudo-links. This is the reason that the *parent-before-child* filter has been built into the compartmentalization procedure. Moreover, the completeness proof also makes use of the strict compartmentalization which ensues when all recursion is made *explicit*.

It is therefore appropriate to show how this *explication* process operates.

The doubling effect is useful when it skips intermediate steps in producing a large macro-expanded clause of a predicate *and this expanded clause forms a part of the end proof*. However, when a predicate has multiple recursion, and in particular multiple recursive clauses with cross-links, resolution on all pseudo-links and cross-links produces new recursive clauses. This results in an exponential increase in the *number* of clauses, as well as the *size* of the clauses.

However, once again the problem can be transformed so as to avoid this problem by converting explicitly multiple-recursive predicates into singly recursive predicates. We illustrate this as well. In fact, the two problems are related as the cross-links actually represent *implicit* recursion until they have inherited to *explicit* pseudo-links.

Example of Explication

We illustrate with a set of Horn clauses which is beyond the power of PROLOG and which has this property of *implicit multiple recursion*. Below we will provide a virtually identical example which has no *explicit recursion..*

```
q(g(f(g(f(g(f(a))))))).
q(X) :- q(f(X)).
q(Y) :- q(g(Y)).
:- q(a).
```

Note that if the positive and negative terms were interchanged, so that the query was complex and the unit clause simple, it would run under PROLOG. But as it stands PROLOG will only search for unit clauses of the form q(f(f(..f(a)..))), which include no g functors.

Resolving on a pseudolink produces the next clause in a family of recursive clauses containing exclusively one functor or the other. But resolving on a cross-link between the two recursive clauses produce the first of one of two families with alternating functors. Confluence and completeness guarantees that CONG can succeed in finding the proof in this way. But the explosion in the number of families is exponential.

We noted that the problem was the implicit recursion which was not already expressed by pseudolinks, and that such recursion can also occur in clauses which are not directly recursive, but only indirectly or *implicitly*. If we make a slight modification to the above algorithm we will see such an example.

```
q(g(f(g(f(g(f(a))))))).
q(X) :- p(f(X)).
p(Y) :- q(g(Y)).
:- q(a).
```

We would like to make this recursion *explicit* so that we may deal with it efficiently. Careful *ordering* of our choice of links in the compartmentalized connection graph can *explicate* such recursion.

Consider what happens if we use straight forward goal directed search as PROLOG does. We generate a sequence of goals:

```
p(f(a)). q(g(f(a))). p(f(g(f(a))))...
```

This will eventually find the unit clause in this case. If we used unit resolution in a data driven way we would produce a similar but reducing set of positive unit clauses. In both cases the process is linear in the size of the complex term. If we could *explicate* the recursion and then use *doubling* it could be done in a logarithmic number of steps.

We can achieve explication very simply in the static phase of the algorithm: we have introduced the *parent-before-child* rule, technically an *ordering strategy*, which prohibits resolving on a link before its parent link (that is the link it was inherited from) is resolved upon. This stops the above unit resolution series after the first step. The generated unit clause has a link only because it was inherited from somewhere — one of the cross-links. This forces resolving on the parent of the new link first, on a cross-link, and forces generation of an explicitly recursive clause containing a pseudolink.

Example of Canonization

We wish however to prevent the explosion which would result from the first of the above examples under the compartmentalized connection graph procedure. We do this by requiring that, at the beginning of the static phase, multiply recursive predicates are transformed to singly recursive predicates in such a way that the removed recursion is not simply made *implicit* . This means that only one pseudo-link involving a predicate may exist in the entire graph. We can achieve this effect with a canonical form in which a recursive predicate has one recursive clause and one non-recursive clause, where the recursive clause contain exactly one positive and exactly one negative instance of the predicate, the non-recursive clause contains exactly one instance of the predicate, and both clauses contain at most one additional literal which is not an instance of the predicate.

We show how the above example of multiple recursion may be represented in this canonical form:

```
q(g(f(g(f(g(f(a)))))).
q(X) :- q(Z), p(Z,X).
p(f(Y),Y).
p(g(Y),Y).
:- q(a).
```

The requirement that the canonical recursive clause has at most one other literal minimizes the effect of the doubling of the number of non-recursive terms during pseudo-resolution.

Elimination of multiple recursive goals

The case where there is multiple recursion in one clause will also cause explosion even where there is only one recursive clause, because in general a new clause will be generated for each pseudo-link resolved on (indeed for each combination of pseudo-links resolved on). Although these could be reduced to one multiply recursive clause straightforwardly using the above technique, that does not eliminate the explosion as the predicate introduced would reflect the number of pseudo-links or combinations of pseuo-links, and the number of pseudo-links would also be increasing.

Hence we would also like to reduce such examples to the canonical form.

A typical case where two recursive calls seem to be required in the same clause is in quicksort. The partition predicate is similar to the find predicate, acting to create a tree (non-nil partitions). The sort predicate itself is naturally expressed with double recursion and append. (We don't bother showing choice of pivot — it isn't necessary in CONG. And the part predicate is omitted — it is treated like the previous example of multiple singly recursive clauses)

```
qsort([],[]).
qsort([H],[H]).
qsort(LI,LO):- part(LI,LLI,LRI),
               qsort(LLI,LLO), qsort(LRI,LRO),
               append(LLO,LRO,LO).
```

We can distinguish four stages in the processing of the recursive clause: partition, left_recurse, right_recurse, append. However using dummy predicates with such names would only hide the recursion, which would later reappear in all its glory (making implicit recursion explicit) or simply prevent exploitation of doubling of self-recursive clauses (without the use of a technique to expose recursion).

Can we flatten out this extra recursion?

Yes, by means of a simulated stack! Instead of giving qsort a list to sort, we give it a list of lists to sort & append:

```
qflatten([],[]).
qflatten([H|T],L):- part(H,HH,HT), qflatten([HH,HT|T],L).
qflatten([[A]|T],[A|L]):- qflatten(T,L).
```

```
fqsort([],[]).
fqsort(X,Y):- qflatten([X],Y).
```

Note that this form of quicksort is actually more efficient than the original — as we happen to have got rid of the `append` as a side-effect of canonization. It is moreover simpler than the difference list version, and it is tail recursive. The two recursive clauses can be combined using the technique of the previous subsection to achieve the canonical form.

Elimination of arbitrary multiple recursion

This method is completely general: `part` & `append` here are simply the literals which do not participate directly in the recursion (any implicit recursion will eventually be*explicated* independently). Note that the order of these literal is of no significance without SLD control.

This defines implicitly a linear deterministic algorithm to reduce arbitrary recursive predicates to exactly one singly-recursive 3-literal form. We also reduce predicates composed of unit clauses to a single clause with database access link. Although, we are here concerned primarily with logic programming and Horn predicates, a technique similar to our explication of multiple singly recursive clauses can be used to deal straightforwardly with multiple recursive heads: we simply introduce a new predicate and a single non-recursive clause which defines it disjunctively. Consider:

```
a(f(X)), a(g(X)):- p(Z,X), a(Z,X).
```

This becomes:

```
a(Y):- b(Y,X), p(Z,X), a(Z,X).
```

```
b(f(X),X), b(g(X),X).
```

At this point we have not formally frozen and implemented the preprocessing algorithms, and the examples in this "Heuristics and Control" section are hand-crafted.

Latent Parallelism

While the primary motivation for choosing to consider Logic Programming in the context of a Connection Graph Theorem Prover was to allow escape from the strictness of PROLOG control and the possibility of concurrent solving of independent parts of the problem (e.g. working around unknowns in Machine Learning and Natural Language applications), a secondary motivation was that this allowed not only application level parallelism, but the fine grained parallelism of a graph in which all links could in principle be resolved in parallel.

Therefore, in addition to application level (coroutine or process) parallelism which emerges straightforwardly in any parallel regime, we now look at half a dozen possible ways of exploiting parallelism within the connection graph formalism itself. We start by considering the system from the traditional Parallel Logic Programming perspective.

OR-Parallelism

√: Links totally Independent

Fig. 4. *Or-Parallelism*

The concept of OR-parallelism in relation to PROLOG encompasses the idea that given a (sub)goal, all matching clauses can be pursued in parallel – and indeed a set of (partial) solutions is returned. In the PROLOG context, this set of parallel solutions can be carried forward independently, effectively replacing backtracking.

OR-parallelism is trivially modelled in the connection graph by resolving all links associated with a term in parallel, producing independent resolvents, and inheriting links straightforwardly (Fig. 4).

AND-Parallelism

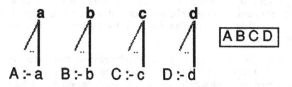

X: Can't remove links – links not used up
?: Compose combination of substitutions

Fig. 5. *And-Parallelism*

AND-Parallelism in PROLOG involves solving the present set of subgoals in parallel. This incurs the difficulty that substitutions must later be composed, and that those which might have been far more tightly specified (e.g. deterministically instantiated) with the PROLOG goal ordering may now find many irrelevant bindings.

In CONG the difficulty manifests itself in that the indexing function of the links cannot be maintained, as links are only partially used. The substitutions on the set of selected links must be composed to produce the resolvent and inherited links. The additional overhead required to index the partial use of links negates the point of the graphical marking of work to be done, unless it is part of a complete elimination of the clause.

CLAUSE Parallelism

But the most effective use of AND-Parallelism in CONG comes about when one eliminates the whole clause in parallel. This eliminates the problem of indexing which combination of links has been used — or uses sub-indexing of highly linked clauses in a progressive way which precludes redundancy. And it combines OR-Parallelism into the solution as progress is being made through resolution with every matching clause for every term of the target clause, as illustrated in Fig. 6.

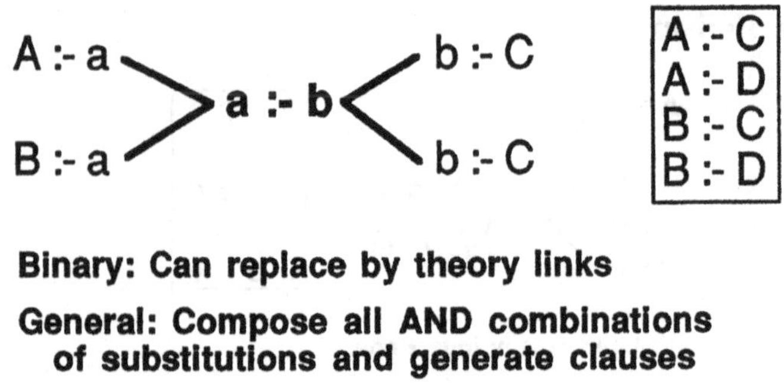

$$A :- a$$
$$B :- a$$
$$a :- b$$
$$b :- C$$
$$b :- C$$

$$
\begin{array}{l}
A :- C \\
A :- D \\
B :- C \\
B :- D
\end{array}
$$

Binary: Can replace by theory links

General: Compose all AND combinations of substitutions and generate clauses

Fig. 6. Clause Parallelism

Note that, where clauses are multiply linked, that is in the one pair of clauses there is more than one distinct pair of linked terms, new links would normally be inherited back from terms between which pseudo-links occur in the resolvent (making explicit the recursion). This problem is avoided by the combination of orphaning and compartmentalization which gradually eliminates the implicit recursion, and in the meantime prohibits further resolution using the new pseudo-linked clauses. Thus the new links are in general not legal and need not be considered in the present static phase. (In fact, for technical reasons, we don't check composition of the pseudo-links until the dynamic phase.)

The composition operation on new resolution-links logically takes place before further work on deepening the search, and many of the resulting combinations tend to be incompatible — that is the unification of substitutions during composition fails. This acts to prune the search.

As a further special case, binary clauses can be eliminated in a totally different way by compilation into theory links [Ohlb90], extending the definition of unification with a theory represented as a substitution tree. In combination with unit resolution and reformulation into at most ternary clauses, whole Horn programs can be compiled into unification. This approach is presently being investigated in combination with other optimizations of representation.

LINK Parallelism

The application level parallelism, that evident through having completely independent problem parts, or at least parts linked through a very well defined and relatively small interface, is available by the straightforward observation that if two links have no clause in common, there is no possibility of interference with the creation of the resolvent, the inheritance of the new links, or the removal of old links.

Note that this parallelism involving independent links can be combined with clause parallelism with the independence condition being modified so as to allow parallel clause elimination only where the sets of clauses linked with each pair of clauses are disjoint. Again this makes best sense in combination with compartmentalization.

General: Any set of links with no clauses in common may be resolved in parallel without any interference with link removal or inheritance processes

Corollary: Gross application level parallelism may be exploited

Fig. 7. Link Parallelism

Inheritance Parallelism

The introduction of a graph, however, introduces a form of indexing overhead which is itself parallelizable. As illustrated in Fig. 8, the inheritance, and the composition and unification involved, can be performed in parallel. However, we can do better still by looking at the decomposition of this work of inheritance.

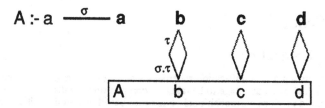

√: Inheritance of new links can always be done independently in parallel

Fig. 8. Inheritance Parallelism

Composition Parallelism

The actual work involved in resolution on links is primarily the inheriting of new links, which in turn involves composition of substitutions using unification. Thus the parallelism represented in the AND- and OR- parallelism can be combined into Clause Parallelism and can be multiplied by taking advantage of Link Parallelism, which results in a multiplied plethora of Inheritance Parallelism. This boils down to us doing a lot of unification in parallel.

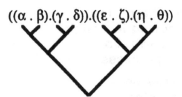

α . β . γ . δ . ε . ζ . η . θ

$(((((((\alpha.\beta).\gamma).\delta).\epsilon).\zeta).\eta).\theta)$

Substitutions are by default composed sequentially and are thus left associated

$((\alpha . \beta).(\gamma . \delta)).((\epsilon . \zeta).(\eta . \theta))$

If associated pairwise substitutions can be composed with only logarithmic delay

Subcompositions are reusable

Fig. 9. *Composition Parallelism*

But there are dependencies within the composition and unification work which cut across the other forms of parallelism. In PROLOG and its concurrent and parallel variants, composition would tend to be done sequentially, but as shown in Fig. 9, it can best be done in a pairwise parallel fashion. Clause Parallelism already allows this, because the AND-Parallel composition admits precisely this form of parallelization. Link Parallelism excludes direct dependency. But a sequence of such parallel steps would still tend to be combining (composed) substitutions in a linear way.

Trial Proofs

Delayed Unification

By introducing a lazy unification scheme, we can allow composition to be delayed in ways which allows advantage to be taken of composition parallelism. One extreme is that we could produce a propositional-style proof based just on the initial graph (viz. without further composition of substitutions), and then check this *trial-proof*, once found, by using efficient composition parallelism.

A blind implementation of this extreme scheme, however, eliminates the possibility of pruning on the way through. Whilst for some programs this may not be a problem, in others an explosion could occur in cases which should be deterministic. In such programs, most unification attempts actually fail. We want to have the failure information as soon as possible, but to delay the full unification expense as long as possible, and minimize the total expense as much as possible.

This leads to the concept of *trial unification* as an extension of clause indexing [Powe88]. If we can eliminate 99% of the non-unifiable cases with 1% of the expense, we will make a huge saving in those cases where the failure information is important, both in terms of our *trial proof* and our eventual unification bill. If we can further use the information gained in the *trial unification* to gain a head start with the actual unification, so much the better. And ideally as we find ourselves searching more and more explosive paths, it would be nice to be able to become increasingly certain that we are not predicating our search on a *false drop*.

If this *trial unification* can be done in a way which both extends to *full unification* (and appropriately represented substitutions) and is consistent with our pairwise *composition parallelism* ideal, then we can achieve several orders of magnitude improvement, quite apart from the speedup directly due to parallelism.

Trial unification requires the obtaining of some sort of approximate indication of unifiability based on incomplete samples or inexact associations. Fast unification requires some way of quickly identifying which atomic subterms need to be compared.

We show below how these can be achieved using indexing and hashing techniques respectively.

Intersected Composition

As we have defined it, our composition operator is not only associative but commutative.

Composition parallelism exploits associativity by taking the original links, the first level of (*weight* 1) substitutions, and combining them pairwise to form the *double weight* substitutions of the next level, repeating until the single substitution representing the composition of the multiple composition task has been obtained. In general, not all of these paired substitutions correspond to actual links in the graph, although usually one multiple composition (e.g. *trial proof* or *AND-combination*) will have significant overlap with others.

Thus it would be advantageous also to choose pairs to compose which are subsets of other required compositions. In the case of *AND-combinations*, this is automatic. In the case of *trial proofs*, it may be advantageous to exploit the commutativity of composition so that the precise choice of which pairs to unify can be selected to be those which are useful in more compositions. However, again given the sequential component and tree structuring in the growth of partial proofs, some advantage may be had from intermediate substitutions found simply by the heuristic of combining substitutions of similar *weight* as they become available.

A composition failure or substitution produced in one context can thus be made available for re-use when, via some other path through the graph, the same initial links are again brought into a multiple composition — which can itself be restructured to take advantage of existing compositions. Moreover, the failed compositions may be used to identify and prune incompatible links. Any attempt to make use of this preexisting unification and composition information will only be reasonable if links and compositions are efficiently indexed and/or sorted.

The result of using information from intersecting or subset compositions would be that information obtained in the checking of one trial proof could prune away part of the remaining resolution search space, or act as a non-link substitution at the beginning of subsequent parallel compositions.

If all sub-compositions of a multiple composition were available, this would clearly have more potential for effective pruning than if only *power-of-two weight* compositions are performed through the use of pairwise composition to obtain composition parallelism. Whilst additional processors could be allocated to check other combinations, or in particular, other initial compositions, it is most productive to have the allocation guided by other parts of the connection graph procedure, and processors are therefore better allocated to discovering other, preferably related, trial proofs.

Trial Unification

Superimposed Code Words

The key to trial unification is indexing in a way which allows a selection of bits cutting across the terms structure to be used to assess the potential for a match. This type of approach was originally introduced for database search with superimposed codes.

Here we use a special form of hashing, the *Superimposed Code Word (SCW)*, to overlay hash type codes in a word, and use a subset operation to determine if the code for the key we are seeking has been ordered in. This is fine for databases, but we need to handle both variables and term position information. Hence we have defined a special variant for Logic Programming applications [Wise84; Powe88].

Interestingly, indexing with SCWs can itself be construed as exploiting the parallelism inherent in even a single sequential processor. A processor with 32-bit data paths and logical operations gains advantage from superimposed coding in part because it allows 32 logical operations to precede in parallel. Alternatively, we can note that an n-processor SIMD machine is equivalent to a sequential machine with $o(n)$ data paths, and that an MIMD can be interpreted on an SIMD machine.

Field Encoded Words

In the *Field Encoded Words (FEWs)*, we retain the subset operation, but allocate fields of the word to subterms down to a certain depth, and use a ternary tree for each functor to index into terms. This is illustrated in Fig. 10, showing the saving achieved by using this technique on a particular set of benchmarks (about 20 subterms down to depth 5).

a(b,c):	a	b	c	
active:	01011001110101100	10010110	11010001	A1
passive:	01011001110101100	10010110	11010001	P1

a(X,c):	a	X	c	
active:	01011001110101100	10010110	11010001	A2
passive:	01011001110101100	10010110	11010001	P2

Quick Unification Check: $(A1 \subseteq B2)$ & $(A2 \subseteq B1)$
Quick 3-Tree Indexing: left: $(A1 < B2)$ right: $(A2 < B1)$ mid: *rest*

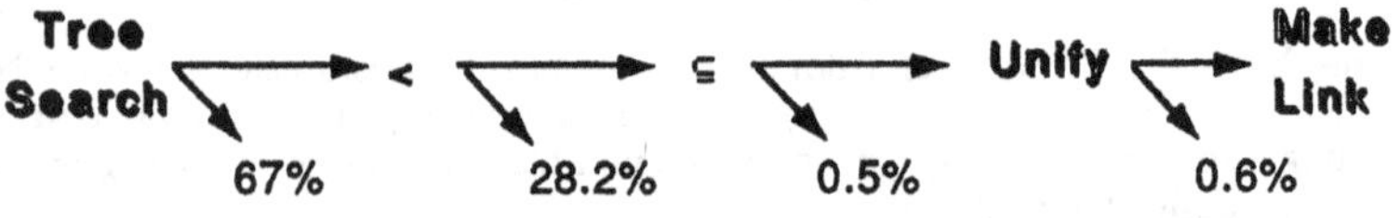

Tree Search → $<$ 67% → $<$ 28.2% → $\subseteq$ 0.5% → Unify → Make Link 0.6%

Fig. 10. *Field Encoded Words & Tree Indexing*

We now need to consider how to extend it usefully to deeper structures, and in particular linear structures. We should also note that by keeping the fields as powers of two, it is possible to do variable substitution totally with the codes.

Unification Algorithm

We now go on to report on some preliminary investigations on the application of hashing and indexing techniques to full unification. In particular, we sketch a unification algorithm (not yet fully implemented or specified) which has the potential for expected unit-time unification on an expected linear number of processors. Unit time is trivially achieved if we allow cubic order processors. We need very careful hashing if we hope to achieve near unit unification on linear processors or unit unification on near linear processors.

In trying to develop an algorithm for unit-time unification on a number of processors linear in the size of the problem, we are dealing with a task which seems to be impossible in the general case [Dwor84] — which even in the cases which are not pathological still requires careful treatment.

In the following we spend some time exploring the possibilities for hashing and show that given perfect hashing we can find some simple characterizations of the conditions under which parallel unification exhibits particular worst case orders. We further show how to develop a hashing function which we would expect to provide unit-time association on regular logic programming examples, leading to an "expected" unit-time unification algorithm (in the sense that pathological examples are by definition "unexpected", but without defining how we would characterize the probability of a particular term structure).

Hashed Unification

The answer to the problem of deep and linear structures is to use another form of hashing: hashing of the terms into field positions of the FEW. This extends the capability to an extent. To go further would clearly require more bits, as we simply don't have enough information. When we add the capability of extension, of adding these extra bits, we have the possibility of extending to exact unification. Or looking at in from the point of view of parallel unification, if we can hash our terms into processor space so that subterms in corresponding positions hash into the same (or a corresponding) processor, we have the capability of performing a large class of unifications in unit time, and another large class in logarithmic time. Or looking at it yet another way, we want to associate corresponding heap addresses for the two terms (or sequences of lefts and rights).

If we can do this association in unit time, then in unit time we can do simple matching of ground structures or terms without repeated variables. The problems related to association or hashing are illustrated in Fig. 11 and the inherent linear and logarithmic nature of some unification problems are illustrated Fig. 12.

Problem: Term skeletons of order N may take many forms and several may match the same tree of order exp(N).

|7|　　a(X, b(Y, c(Z, d))) *and* a(b(c(d, Z), Y), X)
　　　　　　　　　　　both match

|15|　　a(b(c(d,d), c(d,d)), b(c(d, d), c(d,d)))

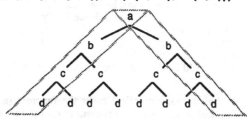

Fig. 11. *Worst Case Example for Unification Hashing*

In Fig. 11, we see the problems of attempting to hash terms simply by depth. If the actual bit determining whether a left or right position is being occupied occurs either in the addressing or the content of a hash entry, unambiguous matching of degenerate (viz list) structures is possible. However, all of these degenerate structures can also match against the balanced structure of the same depth. Thus we want to match a term linear in the depth of the tree with another term exponential in the depth of the tree, and in general mapping, even superimposing, the balanced tree into a table bounded according to its depth loses too much information.

But not always! Note that if the b's, c's and d's in Fig. 11 are actually the same, folding to the same hash position is no clash. But, if even just the d's are distinct we must use some method such as a common index and replace them by pointers (instantiated variables) to an overflow area. If we do this at every level we have no gain over descending the term normally.

Another alternative is to hash into a balanced tree structure linear in the size of the term, but then terms of degenerate structures won't have addresses in the hash table which correspond to those to which occur in the same position in the balanced tree of the same depth. In both schemes, the worst cases involve a mismatch of the order of the table and the tree we are trying to hash into it.

Note that empty matches, where a node in one structure meets a vacuum in the matching structure, may be safely treated as successful. Such an empty match can only occur if the corresponding subtree in the other term was terminated earlier with either a constant or a variable. In the latter case, the binding will be made at the higher level, and the substructure is irrelevant (till we consider the repeated variable case for full unification). In the former case, the constant must match unsuccessully against some term with non-zero arity and the whole match will fail in any case.

The big problem is that any attempt to *associate* keys based on the sequences of lefts and rights (or indexes into a virtual heap) must recognize that the length of these keys (or virtual) addresses is linear in the case of a degenerate or very sparse term, and that we may no longer hide behind the charitable assumption that we can manipulate addresses in unit time — as we do without comment when they are logarithmic in the size of our data structures, as is the case with the balanced tree. An associative memory looks for one key amongst n in unit time, and involves n active memory units in doing so. To match n such keys simultaneously requires n of these groups, and by the time we take into account that the match involves n bits, we are up to a n^3 processing units in a CRCW PRAM!

The linear length of our keys or labels is of course still a problem even if we were to use special hardware and/or language features (à la Linda).

Even during hashing, we must be careful that we don't try to use an n bit quantity, and have to take account of the actual time required for hashing. The association of terms with the same label can also be accomplished by merging or sorting (in o(log n) time on n processors), except that again we must take into account the o(n) bit labels in the degenerate cases.

In view of all of these pitfalls, we must be very careful to choose a hash function which is perfect for the sort of structures which are likely to occur. Moreover, we would like to ensure that dependencies between addresses in a structure are minimized by ensuring that a clash at one point in the tree doesn't imply it continues for all descendants of a node. But unless we take into account every bit of the address key, the bit which is omitted could be the only one which is different between two keys, and all subtrees subtended by them.

Note, moreover, that in many practical cases the functors (and arities) of the interior nodes are identical, and it is thus sufficient to ensure that the leaves can be matched effectively. Indeed, any structure can be mapped into a binary tree, thus ensuring satisfaction of the condition for such leaf matching.

Furthermore, not only must different size structures be able to match specified parts of the different sized hash tables, but the unifying substitutions and/or the unified terms must be made available in hash table form for subsequent use by the algorithm. In the first case, this limits the extent to which we can pervert the actual values for the depth of a term, if we aim at hashing into a table linear in depth. In the second case, there is the problem of the redundant representation upon instantiation of multiple variables (as we have given up the advantages of a DAG). We look at this later on.

As a final comment on the question of hashing and association, we note that it is possible to superimpose the entries destined for a hash address in the event of a clash, and to have additional structures which store the clashing terms for checking if the imprecise subset-matching unification succeeds — viz. applying ideas from FEWs again. If we introduced tables of double the size after each clash, we would end up with a number of passes logarithmic in the maximum number of clashes at any one hash address, and an squared order worst case memory overhead.

Sliced Unification

But before we turn to the development of a hash function, let us look at the other use we want to make of these hash tables. We not only want to perform full unification in unit time (when the processor resources are available and the problem complexity allows), but (when the number of processes is limited) to do *trial unification* which gives a first approximation of unifiability and aims to detect *unification failure* as soon as possible.

By actually using only one random bit of each row of the tree in Fig. 11, a *bit slice*, we achieve matching of two degenerate ground structures (like the |7| examples). with a probability of not detecting nonunifiability which reduces exponentially in the depth of the tree. This probability itself reduces exponentially with each subsequent bit slice we take. Thus with depth d and taking b bits the probability of detecting an inequality is $(1-2^{bd})$. When b actually is the full number of bits required to represent the symbols, the probability is that of them not actually being equal, and failure to detect an inequality therefore is a guarantee of unifiability (remembering that in this ground case life is not complicated by multiple variables and occur checks).

Thus providing we can *slice* through the terms, we can approach full matching as closely as desired. With enough processors, linear in the total number of bits in the terms, we can establish the match in unit time. Where there are variables, by adopting the same technique as for variables in the FEWs, we can again have a match in unit time. Since we can also establish the proposed bindings for variables, we can then continue with a pairwise unification of repeated variables as illustrated in Fig. 12.

Characterization of Unification

Given that the hashed matching problem can be solved in unit (expected) time, these hashed unification and sliced unification algorithms leads to unit, logarithmic and linear parallel unification complexity for the algorithm, depending on various features of the terms which we now proceed to characterize.

p(X, X, X, X)		&	p(a(...), a(...), a(...), a(...)).			*Log Case*
p	X		X	X	X	
p	a...		a...	a...	a...	

p(X, X)		&	p(f(Y, Y), f(g(Z, Z), g(a,b)).			*Linear Case*
p	X		X			
p	f	Y	Y	f	g Z Z g a b	

Fig. 12. *Log and Linear Cases with Perfect Hash*

In general, the algorithm will be worst case unit if there are no repeated variables, logarithmic in the maximum number of repetitions of a variable and linear in the number of distinct repeated variables, as illustrated in the example of Fig. 12. The logarithmic results arises from the possibility of dealing with the multiple instances of a variable pairwise as separate unification problems. The linear limit is a sequential result, and the example of Fig. 12 show that this algorithm does exhibit linear behaviour on this case. The unit result in the absence of repeated variables is a trivial consequence of perfect hashing — but note that some schemes introduce additional pointers when the hashing is not perfect.

The hashing and matching schemes explained below (see Fig. 13) have been designed so as to be perfect for most common, and in particular regular, sparse (towards degenerate) or dense (towards balanced) subterm allocations.

We should however note that we must distinguish between the size of the "hash table" and the number of processors used. The hash size is significant primarily in terms of the number of *bits* used for the addresses, which we would prefer to be $o(\log n)$ rather than $o(n)$. The number of processors can be significantly smaller than the hash address space if we use a low load factor, which *is* still an allocation problem if we don't want them to be idle, and we don't have other independent tasks to perform. Even a constant factor overhead, let alone polynomial or exponential, is undesirable if the unaddressed processors are left idle.

However, in our present application, there is plenty of parallelism, and we therefore want to exploit parallelism as cheaply and efficiently as possible, moving to less optimal algorithms only when unused resources are available.

Assuming that the amount of parallelism vastly exceeds the resources available, and that different unification problems can be executed in parallel, we can overlay the address spaces for different subproblems with different offsets or mapping functions. Moreover, following the sliced unification technique, we want to *resequentialize* some of the unification parallelism in a different way which will decrease the overheads in determining failure.

Development of a Hash Function

The first observation to be drawn from our discussion above is that a hashing function which is optimized for sparse trees will be worst case for balanced trees, and vice-versa. But our superimposing concept allows us still to derive some information in either of these mismatch situations. Furthermore it is straightforward to add an additional bit to warn of a clash, or a field to track the number of clashes, or even an overflow list as in traditional hash tables.

But failure to detect a clash means that matching of the hash tables is completely reliable. Thus if we hash into two tables, one optimized for the more balanced tree, and one for the more degenerate, we know that if *either* fails to note a clash, the unification has been reliable.

But note too, that if a structure is close to one or other extreme, the ratio of the actual size of the tree to the size of either the degenerate or balanced tree must be close to 1. If we allocate space for a table generously whenever the ratio is bounded by some constant, then (given an appropriate hash function) the most common and regular structures should avoid clashes in that table. Furthermore, if overflow structures are developed in the form of addition of new variables, local balance or linearity can be taken into account at the cost of an additional time step (for each level of nested overflow).

Heap addresses				Left-0 Right-1 addresses				Sum Hash (Left-Right)			
	1				0				0		
10		11		00		01		0		1	
100	101	110	111	000	001	010	011	0	1	1	2

4 × Sum + Depth Hash				4 × Depth + Sum Hash				Depth Hash			
	1				4				0		
2		6		8		9		1		1	
3	7	7	11	12	13	13	14	2	2	2	2

Fig. 13. *Examples of hash function for unification*

This optimization process is illustrated in Fig. 13, working towards a list optimal hash function. Here we note that allocation of a key either as an index into a heap or as a left-right string is equivalent – within a bit. In the first case the first bit is always a 1, in the second a 0. The first gives all positions distinct for a balanced tree, the second all leaves distinct. The sum of the bits is the same ± 1 (taking into account the first bit). One obvious hash function with some merit is to weight each of the bits of the table with different weights from 1 upto order n. This however distributes the clashes in a way which does not bias for or against particular types of structure. With any hash function there will be pathological cases. We would like these to be the rare cases rather than the common data structures of logic programming. So we analyze some other possibilities.

Using the sum as hash function, the number of clashes in the leaves is distributed normally (the number of clashes is given by the binomial coefficients), and there are also additional clashes taking interior nodes into account. The depth hash has all leaves clashing, indeed all leaves at the same depth but none between different depths.

The example continues with the supposition that the structure actually contains about four times as many elements as the depth, and shows two ways of combining the basic hashes so as to combine the favourable features. We cannot expect to eliminate clashes amongst the elements of a level in this way, as the number of clashes in a level is still basically exponential in its depth and hence the size of the table. However, note that (within the size of the table represented) all lists can be represented without clash (for either interior or exterior nodes), and that the most likely cases of bifurcating degeneracy can also be represented (viz. both second level positions can subtend lists of the same type).

This compromise is good for the typical case of a term with a fairly flat initial structure, but a couple of list arguments a few levels down. It also substitutes well as the hash for a given position can be added to (resp. subtracted from) that of all positions of the substituted (resp. bound) subtree. Viz. the processors doing the work make us of a fixed offset.

To handle the need for compatibility among different sized structures, as well as rapid copying and expansion upon substitution, it is necessary to store parameters (in $\log(n)$ space) which uniquely identify the hash function used, and it is helpful to increase the allocated size to a power of two.as we did with the FEW [Wise84]. This introduces at most a factor of two additional overhead and allows compatibility to be ensured with simple shift operations. If we allocate copies at all smaller powers of two, with clashes superimposed, then we have for the cost of another factor of two a family of faster approximations, and compatibility with all smaller structures. Or we can simply define matching routines which virtually reduce the table to the appropriate size for a given match using shifts. We can similarly arrange for slices of these tables to be obtained virtually for trial unification.

Finally, we point out that the number of processors required for the detection of the occasional clash and its resolution, along with the logarithmic and linear overheads resulting from examples with multiple variable, usually do not require the full order of processors for their completion, and that this can be performed in parallel with other work not dependent on full knowledge of the resulting substitution.

Hybrid Hashing

The way we are using hash functions is a little more complicated than usual. The use of overflow structures is not unusual, nor are the techniques for resizing a hash table as it grow beyond its bounds. However we have proposed also storing smaller tables for use in matching against smaller terms. An alternative is for each processor in one structure to dynamically rehash itself into the hash address space of another. This introduces a sequential overhead which is typically linear in the size of the hash label, and even if groups of parallel processors are allocated would typically be logarithmic. Hence it is important that the hashing of unified terms is achieved within the existing overheads for the matching. We discuss this in the following section briefly. Here we we wish to present some of alternatives to pure hashing which have been considered.

For this purpose we introduce a number of definitions which are intended to capture substructures which are near to one or other of the degenerate or balanced streams, each of which can independently be handled efficiently.

We present this material for completness, although in fact we prefer not to have even the additional constant factor overheads in the expected case, and increased total work, only to achieve a better worst case bound for certain cases. This preference is again a consequence of us wanting to exploit the massive cheap parallelism before the brute-force faster but more processor expensive/intensive parallelism.

Maximal Balanced Subtree

Defn. A maximal balanced subtree (mbs) is a balanced subtree (all nodes above the lowest level have arity descendants, arity=2 by an earlier assumption) such that no containing subtree is balanced.

Note. The structure of the tree is fully captured by the labels (see Fig. 13) and the heights of the mbs's.

Maximal Degenerate Subtree

Defn. A maximal degenerate subtree (mds) is a linear subtree (all nodes above the lowest level have one descendant) such that no containing subtree is degenerate.

Note. The root and leaf of a mds are also part of mbs's (which are distinct if root and leaf are distinct). The leaf of an mds need not be a leaf of the full tree, any more than the root the root. The branches of the mbs's and mds's are distinct; the union of their nodes is the set of all nodes in the tree.

Maximal Approximately Balanced Subtree

Defn. A approximately balanced subtree (abs) has at least $2^{h/k}$ nodes at level h (the root is level 0, and k is a constant, k=2 unless otherwise specified).

Defn. A maximal approximately balanced subtree (mabs) is an approximately balanced subtree such that no containing subtree is approximately balanced.

Note. The structure of the tree is fully captured by the labels (see Fig. 13) and the heights of the mbs's.

Leaf Path

Defn. A leaf path (lp) is the sequences of branches and nodes between a leaf and the root of the tree. It is specified by the label of the leaf as a series of left and rights commencing at the root (the root is node 1 as in Fig. 13).

Summary of hybrid techniques and efficiency

Here we indicate the worst case time, processor and address space requirements for various approaches to the *matching*, and outline the basis of the algorithms.

Naive 1:	o(1) time	o(n) procs	o(exp n) proc. addr. space.
Naive 2:	o(1) time	o(n^3) procs	o(n^3) proc. addr. space.
Sum+Depth:	o(n) time	o(n) procs	(n) proc. addr. space.
Leaf Path:	o(1) time	o(n^2) procs	o(n^2) proc. addr. space.
Leaf Path + mabs:	o(1) time	o($n^{1.5}$) procs	o(n^2) proc. addr. space.
Max Subtrees:	o(log n) time	o(n) procs	o(n^2) proc. addr. space.

The first thing to observe is that the naive approaches have either too large an address space (label length) or processor overhead. The standard hashing approach produces o(1) time only for the cases it has been designed to be good for, and allows pathological cases in which no significant advantage from the parallel processors is achieved (but without wasting processors either).

With leaf paths, we avoid the problem of the long label by distributing it along the leaf path, and then compare all pairs of leaf paths. If we are not careful, and do use a CRCW PRAM model available, we pay a penalty that the interior nodes occur on multiple leaf paths. However, since we are only trying to establish a match at this stage, it suffices for each node to concurrently write to the root if the match fails, in which case the single bit of left-right information and the content information can be matched in unit time even in interior nodes, as the same comparison is required for each of the path it is contained on.

Moreover, if the tree is a maximal approximate subtree, and we treat this as if it were actually balanced, with a quadratic address space, the remaining cases can be handled on a o($n\sqrt{n}$) number of processes as the total number of leaves, and hence leaf trees, will be o($\sqrt{n}$) and the number of pairs is o(n). The non-optimality of these result is renders it not particularly useful when we have other more efficiently exploitable sources of parallelism.

With the mds, mbs and mabs approaches, no satisfactory approach has been specified, but we can show that the number of mds's subtended by a mabs is at most about a third of the nodes in the mabs and always less than half, or conversely, that the number of nodes in subtending mabs is at least about three times the breadth across the mds. (For k=2 in the definition of the mabs, the ratio here is actually worst case $\sqrt{8}$.)

We are thus able to apply the mabs technique until an o(1) match is achieved, and this will involve at most o(log n) stages. The mabs's and mds's of the two terms being matched will not necessarily match up at any point, but will overlap requiring a calculation using the stored depths as to where the match should take place.

This outline is very sketchy, representing work in progress, or indeed promising approaches which were shelved to concentrate on those more appropriate for the particular aims of trial unification and prioritizing of the different types of parallelism.

Hashed Composition

Now the question is whether we can handle composition and ensure that results of the unification are presented in a form appropriate to subsequent unification. The case where the unified term is no larger than its parents is straight forward, as processors have already been allocated.to these terms. When it grows, we need to ensure that the appropriate copying takes place. This, like the original set up of the terms, requires that the information about where subterms will end up reaches the appropriate processors for copying. Because we deal with multiple unifications pairwise, we can be sure that each term will not need to be multiply copied because of repeated variables. And the propagation through multiple variables is already linear. Thus the copying can be achieved without worsening the order of the algorithm.

Asking Uncle

The parallel traversing and *in situ* placement of the elements of an arbitrary tree structure can be performed by linear order processors in logarithmic time. This is by application of techniques well known in parallelism for dealing with linked lists.

This algorithm involves having each algorithm pass back or forward information successively to its immediate parent, (one generation), its grandparent (two generations), and all its other ancestors a power of two removed. This information includes the number of known levels of descendants/ancestors, and whether that information is complete. Thus after time logarithmic in the depth of the tree (that is, if degenerate logarithmic in the size of the structure, and if balanced logarithmic in the logarithm of that size), the number of levels of descendants/ancestors is known.

In the case of a CONG term, there is the possibility of termination in a variable as well as termination with an atom (such as *nil*). Thus there are three cases which can be stored in a trit called *UNCLE*: *UNComputed*, *Longer* (variable termination) and *Exact* (nil termination). It is recommended that this trit, along with the number of descendants currently known, be not only calculated during hashing, but stored permanently with subterms and variable bindings.

This not only allows faster determination of composed structures, but is useful itself as a quick unification check, the UNCLE check. In this check, two constraints are available for quick determination: *Exact* pairs must compare exactly; *Exact* terms must be at least as long as *Longer* terms (or *UNComputed* terms).

This check is extremely useful in the Compartmentalized Connection Graph as it is usually sufficient to prevent Pseudoresolution proceeding beyond what is necessary for the problems at hand.

Application

The Compartmentalized Connection Graph has been applied, as presently implemented, to a small number of standard PROLOG benchmarks. Furthermore some of these benchmarks have been analyzed in relation to their behaviour under the further techniques of this paper – in particular the ability to match lists in unit time and unfold recursion in unit time.

One of these standard algorithms is QuickSort. As no standard sequential sorting algorithm was known to be amenable to optimal speed up through parallelization, it was a surprise to discover that our analyses predicted that running QuickSort on CONG using the techniques described here will in fact produce linear speedup given linear processors. To verify this quickly, in the absence of a version of CONG implementing the parallel unification, the predicted behaviour was further analyzed and used to design a conventional *in situ* style parallel sorting algorithm which did indeed demonstrate this behaviour [Powe89].

Further analysis, tracing through the maze of unifications, developed an even more efficient version based on linked lists [Powe91]. We will report on the analysis of the CONG performance of QuickSort in due course.

Acknowledgements

I wish to acknowledge the participation of Graham Wrightson, Deborah Meagher, Lazaro Davila, David Menzies, Martin Wheeler, Graham Epps, Richard Buckland and Philip Nettleton in the MARPIA project at Macquarie University, and their varying contributions to the development of CONG. Laz Davila wrote the first version of the present incarnation of CONG. Debbie Meagher has been responsible for its further development including the addition of compartmentalization.

In addition I thank Norbert Eisinger and Hans Jürgen Ohlbach for helpful discussions during my time in Kaiserslautern.

References

[Bark90] Jonas Barklund, "Parallel Unification", doctoral dissertation, UPMAIL, Uppsala University, Sweden (October 1990).

[Dwor84] C. Dwork, P.C. Kanellakis and J. Mitchell, "On the Sequential Nature of Unification", J. Logic Programming 1, pp35-50 (1984).

[Eisi88] Norbert Eisinger, "Completeness, Confluence and Related Properties of Clause Graph Resolution", Doctoral Dissertation, SEKI Report SR-88-07, FB Informatik, University of Kaiserslautern FRG (1988)

[Eisi89] Norbert Eisinger, "A Note on the completeness of resolution without self-resolution.", Information Processing Letters 31, pp323-326 (1989)

[Kowa79] Robert Kowalski, "Logic for Problem Solving", North Holland (1979)

[Mill90] Håkan Millroth, "Reforming Compilation of Logic Programs", doctoral dissertation, UPMAIL, Uppsala University, Sweden (October 1990).

[Ohlb90] Hans-Jürgen Ohlbach, "Compilation of Recursive Two-Literal Clauses into Unification Algorithms", Proceedings of AIMSA 1990, Albena, Bulgaria, (Wiley 1990).

[Powe88] David M. W. Powers, Lazaro Davila and Graham Wrightson, "Implementing Connection Graphs for Logic Programming", Cybernetics and Systems '88 (R. Trappl, Ed), Kluwer (April 1988)

[Powe89] David M. W. Powers, "Parallelized QuickSort with Optimal Speedup", submitted. An expanded version is available as SEKI Report-90-09, University of Kaiserslautern FRG.

[Powe90] David M. W. Powers, "Compartmentalized Connection Graphs for Concurrent Logic Programming I: Compartmentalization, Transformation and Examples", SEKI Report SR-90-16, University of Kaiserslautern FRG (1990).

[Powe91] David M. W. Powers, "Optimal Parallel Speedup of QuickSort and RadixSort both in situ and in Lists", to be submitted. An earlier version is available as SEKI Report-90-09, University of Kaiserslautern FRG.

[Wise84] Michael J. Wise and David M. W. Powers, "Indexing PROLOG Clauses via Superimposed Code Words and Field Encode Words", Proc. Int'l Symp. on Logic Programming, IEE Computer Society, pp203-210 (1984).

Constraint satisfaction via partially parallel propagation steps

Walter Hower
Institut für Informatik
Fachbereich 4
Universität Koblenz-Landau
Rheinau 3–4
D–W-5400 Koblenz
Federal Republic of Germany
walter@uni-koblenz.de

Abstract

The constraint satisfaction problem (CSP) deals with the assignment of values to variables according to existing constraints. Given n variables with their finite domains, the admissible combinations of values form a set of n-tuples which represents the globally consistent solution.
This article presents a parallel approach to global constraint satisfaction.

0   Introduction

The constraint satisfaction problem (CSP) deals with the assignment of values to variables according to existing constraints. Given n variables with their finite domains, the admissible combinations of values form a set of n-tuples which represents the globally consistent solution.
The kind of consistency wherein only a small subset of the potentially possible constraints is taken into consideration is briefly presented in the subsequent section (because a lot of papers just deal with this so-called "local

consistency"). Section 2 points to the main topic "global consistency". In both sections an evaluation of the sequential complexity is discussed in order to provide a common basis for considerations upon a parallel approach. In section 3 some additional suggestions are made. The references are listed in section 4.

1 Local consistency

Binary constraint satisfaction achieves a kind of ("local") consistency where just binary constraints (concerning pairs of variables) are considered.[1]

1.0 Sequential processing

The sequential complexity of binary constraint satisfaction ("arc consistency") is $O(e)$ wherein e denotes the number of edges (binary constraints) in the constraint graph. In a fully connected ("complete") graph, $e = n(n-1)/2$ $(= \sum_{i:=1}^{n-1} i)$, and therefore, arc consistency is attainable in at most $O(n^2)$ wherein n denotes the number of variables (vertices in the binary constraint graph). In a sparse graph, $e = O(n)$; so, arc consistency has a linear time behaviour when the constraint graph has only a few edges. For instance, the constraint propagation algorithm of D. Waltz behaves linearly owing to the fact that his constraint graphs are planar, i.e., "sparse" in our sense. (Cf. [Mackworth/Freuder-85], pp. 66–69.)

1.1 Parallel processing

[Kasif-90] proved that binary constraint satisfaction is log-space complete for P. "However, this (worst-case) result does not preclude research in the direction of applying parallelism in a more controlled fashion. For instance,

---

[1]The variables of the CSP form the nodes in a constraint network whereas the (binary) constraints serve as arcs. The procedure "propagates" the admissible values (from the nodes) and the pairs of values (from the arcs) to the arcs and nodes directly connected to in order to check common consistency. This technique possibly yields to the detection of further restrictions; it performs a pre-processing task in order to prune the (subsequent) search space. (Note that local consistency does not guarantee that a globally consistent solution exists.) The termination criterion of the procedure to compute local ("arc") consistency is the test whether there is no further change in the constraint network.

we can easily obtain speedups when the constraint graph is very dense (the number of edges is large)." (See [Kasif-90], p. 285.)

The basis for a parallel approach is the fact that the solution of a CSP does not depend on the order of the propagation steps. Parallel propagation suggests to start at several points in the graph in order to propagate simultaneously the existing constraints. The aim is the fast computation of the locally consistent solution.

[Samal/Henderson-87] obtained a time complexity of $O(n)$ using $O(n^2)$ processors in order to compute binary ("local") consistency.[2]

2 Global consistency

The general CSP considers more than just binary constraints. So, generally more than only two variables are involved in a single constraint. Now, the higher-ary constraints are no longer representable as edges in a graph. Therefore, we have to change the representation in a way that also the constraints become nodes in a constraint hierarchy wherein the bottom level enumerates the unary constraints (potential values, "1-tuples") of the variables, the level above states the binary constraints between two variables (value pairs, "2-tuples"), the next higher level lists sets of triples ("3-tuples") concerning three variables, etc., and the highest level n corresponds to the n-ary constraint specification.

For ease of notation we assume the following:

Let $I := \{1, ..., n\}$ be an ("ordered"[3] non-empty) index set wherein n ($>$ 0) stands for the number of variables involved in the CSP.

In order to know which variables are involved in a particular constraint we provide each constraint expression with an index set where these variables are named. Let $K \subseteq I$; then, C_K shall list the $|K|$-tuples indicating (the combination of) the possible values of the variable(s) addressed by K.

The following figure symbolizes the network structure of a CSP with four variables:

---

[2]which is also obtainable in constant time using an exponential number of processors (cf. [Swain-88])

[3]here: "ordered" means that the indices appear in an ascending order indicating fixed positions in tuples (see the following text above)

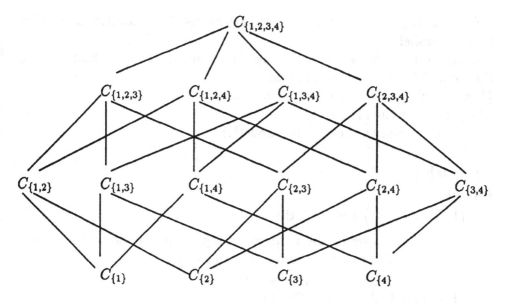

2.0 Sequential processing

Generally, at stage i one has to create $\binom{n}{i}$ sets of i-tuples. So, the total number of sets one has to "synthesize" in order to get the complete solution is $\sum_{i:=1}^{n} \binom{n}{i}$ which yields $2^n - 1$. (This result may illustrate the exponential complexity of global constraint satisfaction.) This bad (sequential) behaviour has been the motivation to try to tackle the problem by a parallel approach.

2.1 Parallel processing

In [Hower-90/91][4] is stated that it suffices to start the constraint propagation process at the bottom level (where the unary constraints are enumerated) and to proceed upwards until the top element ($C_{\{1,...,n\}}$) of the lattice structure (see the previous figure) has been reached. The following

---

[4]which—in the meantime—I have already revised, and which has both improved and extended [Hower-89]

algorithm[5] exploits this feature while performing global constraint satisfaction in parallel[6].

For ease of notation let the following ("loop invariant") specification hold throughout the propagation process:

$$\{\} \neq J \subset K \subseteq I := \{1, ..., n\}, \ |J| := j =: |K| - 1$$

The procedure then looks as follows:

(The "||" notation means "in parallel".)

$top := \textbf{false};\ j := 1$
repeat
    || **for all** $\binom{n}{j}$ nodes C_J **do**
            || propagate the j-tuples (of a particular node C_J)
              along its $n - j$ upward links to all
              corresponding nodes C_K;
    || **for all** $\binom{n}{|K|}$ nodes C_K **do**
        begin
            repeat ("wait") **until** all $|K|$ downward links (of a
                         certain node C_K) have come in;
                         (*)
            if $j < n - 1$ **then** $j := j + 1$ **else** $top := \textbf{true}$
        end
until top

Explanation w.r.t. "(*)":

    A node C_K is influenced by $|K|$ contributing nodes C_J (cf. the previous figure); the formation of the $|K|$-tuples may be performed via corresponding natural equi-joins (as in relational databases). (In the case that C_K is one of the constraints formerly specified as an explicit constraint, this original constraint specification (set of $|K|$-tuples) must then be intersected with the expression just computed. See also [Hower-90/91].)

---

[5] which correlates with the ascending phase of the procedure described in the paper just mentioned

[6] A preprint of the algorithm can be found in [Hower-91]. (A different approach is described in [Hölldobler/Hower-91] (where just binary constraints are considered).)

According to [Samal/Henderson-87] (p. 346), the "||" command is only completely performed after all the tasks mentioned by this command have finished. Generally, however, it is not necessary to wait until everything is computed at an entire level. As soon as one single node C_K has completely been computed it can already propagate its part to its $n - |K|$ nodes the level above (without waiting for the other nodes at the same level). (**)

2.1.0 Completeness and soundness

Claim:

Every C_Y on level y ($1 \leq y := |Y| \leq n$) contains all y-tuples allowed by any of the constraints on some path downward from C_Y in the hierarchy which are not excluded by C_Y itself; and only those tuples are included.

Proof:

Induction on the number of stages of the ascending phase:

a) Stage 1 (induction start):

Let C_Y ($|Y| = 1$) be any constraint on stage 1 (i.e., it represents the possibly restricted domain of a variable). Since there is no constraint on some path downward from C_Y in the hierarchy the claim is obvious for C_Y.

b) Induction hypothesis:

Let the claim be proven for stages $1, ..., i - 1$.

Stage i (induction step):

Let C_Y ($|Y| = i$) be any constraint at stage i (i.e., it refers to i variables). Let $w := (w_1, ..., w_i)$ be any instantiation tuple of the variables in C_Y.

(i) completeness ("deleting view"; in the "enumerating view": correctness)[7]:

Assume w contradicts any of the constraints below C_Y in the hierarchy, or assume w is excluded by C_Y itself; then the tuple either contradicts C_Y on level i or some C_{Y_1} on level $i-1$ (since all "lower"-ary constraints have already been propagated up to level $i - 1$ by the induction hypothesis). In the first case the tuple is eliminated by C_Y itself, in the

---

[7] "deleting view" means that we consider the algorithm as a technique which deletes impossible tuples; "enumerating view" means that we consider the algorithm as a technique which enumerates possible tuples

second case by the local ascending propagation step from level $i-1$ to level i.

(ii) correctness ("deleting view"; in the "enumerating view": completeness):

Assume w does not contradict any of the constraints below C_Y in the hierarchy, and assume w is not excluded by C_Y itself; then—since only contradictory tuples are eliminated—it remains in the set of possible instantiation tuples for C_Y.

Remark:

The proof already takes into account the note "(**)" stated above—thereby allowing the constraints to get propagated as soon as possible. Remember also that the algorithm terminates correctly since reaching C_I (the only *single* (constraint) node at a specific level) corresponds to the computation of the globally consistent solution.

2.1.1 Complexity considerations

(W.r.t. notation cf. [Samal/Henderson-87] (p. 348).)

a) The *inherent parallelism* (=: *IP*) of an algorithm may be defined as

$$\frac{serial\ complexity}{unbounded\ parallel\ complexity}.$$

Here, $IP = O(2^n)/O(n) = O(2^n/n) = O(2^{n-ldn})$.

b) The *maximum number of effective processors* (=: P_{max}) indicates that it won't yield any further speedup when more than P_{max} processors are provided.

Here, $P_{max} = \binom{n}{\lceil n/2 \rceil}$

(= maximal number of nodes which have to be stored at a single stage)[8].

$$ [8] = \binom{n}{\lfloor n/2 \rfloor} = \binom{n}{n - \lceil n/2 \rceil} = \binom{n}{n - \lfloor n/2 \rfloor} $$

3 Final remarks

Possibly, we always obtain a linear (parallel) time behaviour when the number of processors is about the number of constraints to be processed; frankly, this suggestion still needs further investigation.

In order to exploit already in a pre-processing phase some "constraining information"—as in [Hower-90/91]—it would be interesting to model the whole algorithm described therein by a parallel version. Furthermore, it seems to be worthwhile to compare our ideas with those presented in [Nishihara/Matsuo-91] which probably describes an interesting approach to parallel global constraint satisfaction, too.

Acknowledgement:

I would like to express my thanks to Peter Baumgartner for his general help and comments on the draft as well as to Uli Furbach for his support of my research activities.

4 References

Abbrev.:

AI-j :=
    Artificial Intelligence, Elsevier Science Publishers B.V., Amsterdam, The Netherlands,

Fb-I :=
    Fachberichte Informatik, Institut für Informatik, Universität Koblenz-Landau, Koblenz,

Ij-P :=
    International Journal of Parallel Programming, Plenum Press, New York/London,

[Hölldobler/Hower-91]
  Hölldobler, Steffen; Hower, Walter: Constraint Satisfaction in a Connectionist Inference System. Fb-I 2/91, April 1991; IV International Symposium on Artificial Intelligence, Cancún, Proceedings (eds.: Francisco J. Cantú-Ortiz, Hugo Terashima-Marín), Editorial Limusa, S.A. de C.V., México, pp. 215–221, November 13–15, 1991

[Hower-89]
  Hower, Walter: A Lattice-based Constraint Formalism. First Australian Knowledge Engineering Congress, Workshop on AI & Creativity, Melbourne, draft collection, Deakin University, Geelong, Victoria, Australia, March 14/15, 1989

[Hower-90/91]
  Hower, Walter: A novel algorithm for global constraint satisfaction. Fb-I Bericht 14/90, February 1991

[Hower-91]
  Hower, Walter: Parallel global constraint satisfaction. PPAI-91, Informal Proceedings of the IJCAI-91 Workshop on Parallel Processing for Artificial Intelligence, Darling Harbour, Sydney, New South Wales, Australia, pp. 80–85, August 24/25, 1991

[Kasif-90]
  Kasif, Simon: On the Parallel Complexity of Discrete Relaxation in Constraint Satisfaction Networks. AI-j 45 (3), pp. 275–286, 1990

[Mackworth/Freuder-85]
  Mackworth, Alan K.; Freuder, Eugene C.: The Complexity of Some Polynomial Network Consistency Algorithms for Constraint Satisfaction Problems. AI-j 25 (1), pp. 65–73/74, 1985

[Nishihara/Matsuo-91]
  Nishihara, Seiichi; Matsuo, Yoshikazu: On Parallelization of Merge Method for Consistent Labeling Problems. Probably in a Journal of the Japanese Society for Artificial Intelligence 6 (1), pp. 124–128, January 1991, 人工知能学会誌

[Samal/Henderson-87]
  Samal, Ashok; Henderson, Tom: Parallel Consistent Labeling Algorithms. Ij-P 16 (5), pp. 341–364, 1987

[Swain-88]
  Swain, Michael J.: Comments on Samal and Henderson: "Parallel Consistent Labeling Algorithms". Ij-P 17 (6), pp. 523–528, 1988

A Parallel Theorem Prover with Heuristic Work Distribution[1]

Christian B. Suttner

Forschungsgruppe für Künstliche Intelligenz
- Intellektik -
Technische Universität München
Augustenstr. 46 Rgb, D-8000 München 2
E-mail: suttner@informatik.tu-muenchen.de

Abstract

PARTHEO is an OR-parallel theorem prover for first order predicate logic. The underlying calculus, the computational model, and the system architecture of the prover will be described. An important aspect of the parallel system is the distribution of work among processors. Since improved performance can be expected if a heuristic work distribution is used instead of an uninformed one, two such schemes are proposed. They make use of an approach previously used to guide the search of the sequential theorem prover SETHEO.

1 Introduction

PARTHEO [SL90] is a theorem prover for first order logic which is based on OR-parallelism. The system is also intended to serve as a basis for extended logic programming, offering features that go beyond traditional PROLOG-style systems (e.g. non-Horn clauses, modularity, and global variables [LS88]) while still maintaining a clean declarative semantics and high efficiency.

PARTHEO consists of a uniform network of sequential theorem provers communicating via message passing. The underlying SEquential THEOremprover SETHEO ([LSBB90]) is implemented as an extension of Warren's abstract machine and is based on the model elimination calculus (an execution mechanism similar to PROLOGii's SLD-resolution). Different independent possibilities to continue the proof search represent different tasks. Since the number of tasks that can be generated this way usually by far outnumbers the number of available processors, the distribution of tasks between processors significantly influences the performance. We will propose how a method previously designed to guide the search of SETHEO ([SE90]) can be used to improve the task distribution in the parallel system.

In the following, we assume familiarity with the standard notions of automated theorem proving (for an introduction see [CL73]).

---

[1]This work was supported by the Deutsche Forschungsgemeinschaft within the Sonderforschungsbereich 342, Teilprojekt A5 (Parallelization of Inference Systems).

In section two the model elimination calculus and the computational model for exploiting OR-parallelism are presented. The system architecture of PARTHEO is described in section three. Then in section four the methodology of how to obtain and incorporate heuristics is explained. Finally, in section five two schemes are presented how such heuristics can be used to guide the distribution of tasks among processors.

2   Model Elimination and OR-parallelism

Model elimination is a sound and complete calculus for first order logic. Originally presented in [Lov68], it can be viewed as a tree-based refinement of the connection method ([Bib87]). For our purposes it is best viewed from its relation to tableaus (see [LSBB90] for details).

In short, a model elimination tableau for a formula F consists of a finite tree t where nodes represent literals and in which all nodes with the same immediate predecessor form an instance of a clause in F. A tableau is called closed if each path contains a pair of complementary literals, i.e. two unifiable literals with opposite signs. It holds that a given formula is invalid if and only if there is a closed tableau for the formula ([Bib87]).

Although model elimination is a refutation procedure, in the following we will use the term proof of a goal instead of refutation, since the refutation of the negated theorem which is searched for is equivalent to a proof for the original theorem, and thereby a better intuitive understanding is achieved.

In the model elimination calculus extension and reduction steps are used as rules of inference. Extension steps simply generalize an ordinary PROLOG-inference step in that any literal of a clause can serve as head. Reduction steps are additionally required to obtain completeness for non-Hornclause formulas. They allow to close an open node of the tableau if a complementary literal is found among its ancestors.

An example for a model elimination search tree is given in Figure 1.

Two types of nodes are encountered during the search. At AND-nodes, a proof for *each* of the immediate successors is required in order to prove the statement given by the node. At OR-nodes, it is sufficient to find a proof for *one* of the successors.

OR-Parallelism.   During the search for a proof there are usually several clauses which are candidates for expanding a given subgoal (i.e. literal). These choices represent independent possibilities to carry on the proof, and the literal to be expanded is said to create an OR-branchpoint. Therefore each OR-branchpoint allows to continue with a set of different tableaus. This can be conceptualized by a tree with a tableau at each node, which we will call OR-search tree. For a formula F consisting of n clauses such a model elimination OR-search tree is of the following form:

1. the root is labeled with the empty tableau, or
2. the root has n child nodes, where each node is labeled with a different tableau by taking each clause of F as a start clause once, and

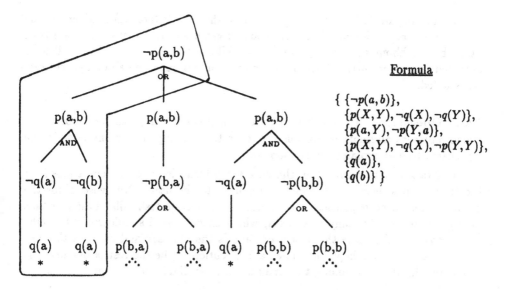

Figure 1: A partial model elimination tree for the formula given on the right. A '*' denotes a closed branch of the tree. The surrounded area marks a proof for the formula.

3. each internal node (labeled with an open tableau) has as children all those nodes labeled with all the tableaus that can be constructed from the open tableau by applying one step of inference.

Note that, while previously in the AND/OR search tree a proof was given by a subtree of the tree, a proof in the OR-search tree is self-contained within a node. In the following, we will call partial tableaus as they are represented by nodes in the OR-search tree *tasks*. Working on a task means to extend the partial tableau in search for a closed tableau. Since besides the anchestor relation there is no dependency between different nodes in the OR-search tree, processors working on different tasks (representing different nodes in the tree) do not need to communicate in order to fulfil their assignment.

3 PARTHEO

In the previous section, an abstract OR-parallel computational model has been described. In this section we want to describe how this is realized in the PARTHEO system ([Sch91]). Generally, the idea is to generate, distribute, and process proof-tasks. Since PARTHEO consists of a uniform network of processors with each processor running the same set of processes, the system is best understood by describing the individual processes and their interrelation.

In PARTHEO, on each processor three processes are running concurrently: the inference machine SETHEO, the stealer process for interprocessor communication, and a process for local task store maintenance (see Figure 2 also).

At the beginning, the initial proof task (the empty tableau) is given to one of the processors. This processor will start to generate proof tasks which are then taken by neighbour processors, and so on. After a while, all processors will have obtained tasks, and further communication will only occur when all of a processors' tasks failed.

Basic Operation. The work input for each processor is given by proof tasks, which represent alternative tableaus (i.e. each task corresponds to one node in the OR-search tree as explained in section two).

If a task can be solved (i.e. the encoded tableau is closed), then a proof for the theorem has been found, which is reported to the user. Otherwise, if for the encoded tableau no expansion is possible, the respective task fails. Lastly, a task may generate finitely many new tasks, which encode just its children in the OR-search tree. In that case the processor cancels the old task and encodes the new tasks. One of them is kept for immediate execution, while the rest is put into the processor's local task memory, thus making them available to other processors.

The Task Stealing Model. Parallelism is achieved by propagating tasks over the network. To keep the amount of communication low, a processor only sends tasks to his immediate neighbors (on request).

If a processor executes a task which fails, it tries to get a new one from its local task store. In case it is empty, the processor asks its direct neighbors for work. Incoming task requests lead to an inspection of the local task store, and therefore a processor having enough tasks will send some of them (e.g. half the number) to the idle processor.

The proof process is initialized by setting all processors into the state of requesting tasks, and by simply giving the root task, which encodes the empty tableau, to an arbitrarily chosen processor.

The search strategy of the prover can be influenced by choosing different orderings for storing, retrieving, and stealing tasks from the local task stores. As an example, the default of storing tasks in reverse order of generation and retrieving them in LIFO manner results in a depth-first left-to-right search.

Context Switching. On parallel computers based on message passing the amount and size of messages being exchanged are crucial in order to maintain a high system performance. Therefore, storing (and transmitting) complete tableaus is avoided by using a special coding scheme. Instead of a tableau itself, only the minimal information necessary to recompute the tableau is stored. Thus the representation consists of a sequence of numbers describing the choices made at OR-branchpoints. Together with a fixed selection function this allows its deterministic recalculation. The additional work introduced by this approach can be reduced by the concept of partial restart. If the (failed) task previously executed on a processor shares the beginning of its tableau with the task to be executed next (on that processor), this part of the tableau is kept and recomputation starts where the tableaus begin to differ.

Iterative Deepening. Currently iterative deepening is done by hand, i.e. various completeness bounds can be specified before the prover is started. If one of these bounds is reached during the proof process, the respective task fails. In case no proof at all can be found within the specified bounds, all processors will be idle after a finite amount of time. Since detecting this state is very expensive, at the moment this is done manually as well.

Implementation. Originally PARTHEO has been implemented in parallel C on a network of transputers ([SL90]). In order to increase portability and flexibility the concept has been adopted to the programming model of the MMK system using standard C and the MMK programming library ([Kar91]).

The MMK operating system ([BBB+91]) is part of the TOPSYS project[2] aiming at an integrated, hierarchical tool environment and programming library for parallel systems. It supplies a transparent multitasking process model with an object-oriented view. It offers a small set of objects such as processes (active objects) and mailboxes (communication objects), which can be manipulated only by predefined operations. The MMK kernel is available for several multiprocessor systems (e.g. INTEL iPSC/2 and iPSC/860) and is going to be ported to further architectures, and therefore a high portability of the parallel prover is achieved as well.

The basic structure of the MMK-based implementation of PARTHEO is shown in Figure 2. The three processes SETHEO, TASK STORE, and STEALER running on each processor are shown for two processors. Zooming in at one processor, the mail boxes used for the communication between processes can be seen. The SETHEO process either issues a request for a task (*gettask*) to the TASK STORE or sends a newly created task to the TASK STORE (*entertask*). In return, it receives either a task or is informed that the TASK STORE is empty (*notask*). The TASK STORE also sends the number of currently stored tasks to the STEALER (*task_nr*), which as soon as this value falls below some threshold in turn issues task requests to the TASK STORES of its neighbor processors (*treq*). In response to such a request the respective TASK STORE again will send either some tasks or a *notask* message to the STEALER, which either sends obtained tasks to the local TASK STORE or continues requesting tasks in case of *notask*.

4 Heuristics

In this section we will describe which heuristics are used, how they operate, and how they are obtained automatically. The exposition will be with respect to the

---

[2]The project started 1987 at the parallel processing group at the Institut für Informatik at the TU Munich and is now part of the SFB 342 activity.

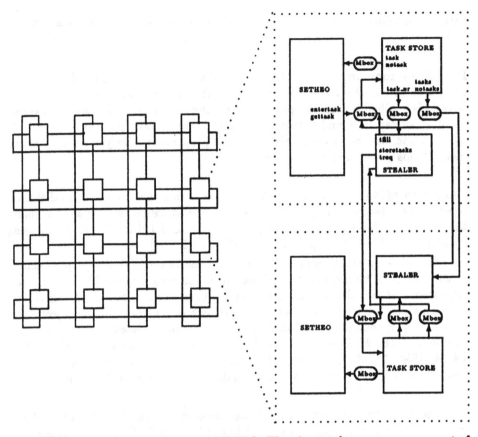

Figure 2: System Architecture of PARTHEO. The picture shows an arrangement of 16 processors in a hypercube topology. On the right, the processes of two processors and their interconnection are shown in more detail.

sequential case, while their application in the parallel prover will be described in the next section. A more detailed presentation of the heuristic approach for the sequential prover can be found in [SE90].

As mentioned earlier, OR-branchpoints represent very important decision points during the search for a proof. Since only one of the choices given at such a point will be used in a proof, the order in which the choices are tried has significant influence on the performance of the sequential prover. In short, the idea for learning heuristics is to use the empirical knowledge about such orderings as it is contained in previously derived proofs. The proofs are used to train evaluation functions which can rate a given choice according to their estimated usefulness for leading to a proof.

Representation. In order to utilize or even learn heuristics it is important to decide how to represent heuristics and on which information heuristic decision shall be based upon.

An important part of the information to be encoded is the syntactic structure of a formula (consisting of a set of clauses). In predicate logic, literals of a clause may contain many terms, and the terms may have arbitrary sizes. However, as input to evaluation functions and because of efficiency reasons fixed length representations are much more desirable. Therefore we use features (attributes) of the clauses to encode interesting aspects of clause occurrences in a simple and concise way.

A clause occurrence in a proof is a copy of the original clause together with additional information (e.g. instantiations or the current location in the search tree). A feature of a clause occurrence is a property of this occurrence which is assumed to contribute to the task of a heuristic in some way. Some typical syntactic features are the number of literals in a clause, the number of different variables in a clause, and the number of subgoals of a clause which are joined by some shared variables. Examples for features capturing run-time aspects of the proof process are the current depth in the search tree and features describing the consequences of variable instantiations. For details on the representation of information see [Sut90].

Learning. In order to obtain heuristics automatically, training data are required. For this purpose we use previously derived proofs. During the search for these proofs, the decision task which we want to resolve heuristically has been encountered as well, and a good choice for each decision has been made for the final proof (via backtracking it is possible to ensure that no superior solution exists).

In the basic approach, we used the feature-vectors of those choices which were contained in the final proof as positive training data and the feature-vectors for the other choices as negative training data. This setting defines a two-class pattern association task. In order to learn an evaluation function which gives a continuous estimate for a feature-vector regarding its class membership, we used connectionist networks with backpropagation learning ([SE91]).

While the results already showed that it is possible to reduce the search space by this method, several researchers of our group work on improvements to this scheme. For comparison reasons, experiments with a classical statistical approach using Bayesian decision theory were performed ([Wei91]). Besides variations in the learning method also work on improving the methodology is done. For example, if several proofs for a theorem exist and only one of the proofs is used for obtaining training data, some of the choices at OR-branchpoints will be used as negative training data even so they merely would have lead to a different proof. This obviously disturbs the idea of learning which clauses are good choices, and therefore different approaches to the selection of the training data can reduce the amount of contradictory information given to the learning system and thereby improve the heuristics ([Gol91]).

Application. Now, whenever an OR-branchpoint is encountered during the search for a proof in SETHEO, each choice is evaluated (the evaluation function is called for each clause occurrence with the respective feature-values as input), and a new ordering of the choices based on the evaluation is created.

5 Heuristic Task Distribution

In the parallel version of the prover the OR-branchpoints are used to generate sets of tasks. Our aim is to use heuristics as described in the previous section for distributing the tasks among processors. This is necessary since the number of tasks usually outnumbers the number of processors, and therefore one would like to distribute tasks such that those tasks assumed to be more likely to succeed will be executed earlier than others. Here we present two interesting methods how this can be done.

Local Branch Arrangement. An obvious idea is to keep the heuristics at their original place, that is, to use a heuristic for each sequential prover contained in PARTHEO. This means that the tasks generated by a processor are ordered with respect to their expected contribution to a proof. Thus the task that is kept for immediate execution is the task rated best among the current OR-branch choices. The remaining tasks are sent as an ordered set of tasks to the local task store. Since a processor uses it's local task store in a LIFO manner, this locally leads to the same behaviour as in SETHEO (i.e. the choices at an OR-branchpoint are tried in heuristic order). However, task requests from neighbors are usually handled FIFO (in order to reduce the overhead through context switches for local tasks by benefitting from partial restart). Since an arbitrary partitioning of the tasks usually destroys the heuristic orderings, the task transfer mechanism needs to be modified. Only groups of tasks representing complete sets of choices at OR-branchpoints should be transferred. This way it is possible to maintain the heuristic ordering obtained for the choices at OR-branchpoints.

The presented scheme also ensures that several of the choices originating from the same OR-branch are executed on the same processor, since tasks belonging to the same OR-branch are not separated by the task stealing. Together with the partial restart paradigm reduces the amount of work done for tableau recomputations.

Quasi-Best-first Search. A more elaborate method is to introduce priority values according to the heuristic evaluation. Each choice given at an OR-branchpoint is rated by the evaluation function. The result is assigned to the task as its priority value and is used to order the tasks in the local task store. This locally leads to an approximation of best-first search. It deviates from the usual best-first paradigm, since no global supervision is done to assure that the next task to be executed by an idle processor will be the task with the highest priority. Rather, the priorities make sure that out of the tasks contained in a local task store the most promising one will be selected. Furthermore, when a neighbor processor requests tasks, the priorities can be used to determine which tasks shall be transferred. For this purpose several schemes are possible, depending on the number of tasks to be stolen. As an example, let's assume that half the number of tasks shall be sent to the requesting processor.

Then, out of the ordering induced by priorities, starting with the highest priority task in the store, every other task should be sent to the requesting processor. This way the difference in the task priority distribution of both processors would be kept small.

References

[BBB+91] T. Bemmerl, A. Bode, P. Braun, O. Hansen, T. Treml, and R. Wismüller. The Design and Implementation of TOPSYS. Technical Report TUM-I9124 (SFB 342/16/91 A), Technische Universität München, 1991.

[Bib87] W. Bibel. *Automated Theorem Proving*. Vieweg Verlag, Braunschweig, 1987.

[CL73] C.-L. Chang and R. C.-T. Lee. *Symbolic Logic and Mechanical Theorem Proving*. Academic Press, 1973.

[Gol91] C. Goller. Domänenspezifische Heuristiken zur Suchraumreduktion im automatischen Theorembeweisen mit SETHEO. Diplomarbeit, Institut für Informatik, Technische Universität München, 1991.

[Kar91] T. Karasek. Implementierung eines parallelen Theorembeweisers auf einem INTEL iPSC-II Hypercube unter dem Betriebssystemkern MMK. Diplomarbeit, Institut für Informatik, Technische Universität München, 1991.

[Lov68] D.W. Loveland. Mechanical Theorem-Proving by Model Elimination. *Journal of the ACM*, 15(2), 1968.

[LS88] R. Letz and J. Schumann. Global Variables in Logic Programming. Technical Report FKI-96-b-88, Technische Universität München, 1988.

[LSBB90] R. Letz, J. Schumann, S. Bayerl, and W. Bibel. SETHEO: A High-Performance Theorem Prover. *To appear in the Journal of Automated Reasoning, 1992*. Technical Report TUM-I9008 (SFB 342/5/90 A), Technische Universität München, 1990.

[Sch91] J. Schumann. Efficient Theorem Provers based on an Abstract Machine. Dissertation, Institut für Informatik, Technische Universität München, 1991.

[SE90] C.B. Suttner and W. Ertel. Automatic Acquisition of Search Guiding Heuristics. In *Proceedings of the 10. International Conference on Automated Deduction (CADE)*, pages 470–484. LNAI 449, Springer-Verlag, 1990.

[SE91]   C.B. Suttner and W. Ertel. Using Back-propagation for Guiding the Search of a Theorem Prover. *Int. Journal of Neural Networks Research & Applications*, 2(1), 1991.

[SL90]   J. Schumann and R. Letz. PARTHEO: A High-Performance Parallel Theorem Prover. In *Proceedings of the 10th International Conference on Automated Deduction (CADE)*, pages 40–56. LNAI 449, Springer-Verlag, 1990.

[Sut90]   C.B. Suttner. Representing Heuristic-Relevant Information for an Automated Theorem Prover. In *Proceedings of the 6. IMYCS: Aspects and Prospects of Theoretical Computer Science*, pages 261–270. LNAI 464, Springer-Verlag, 1990.

[Wei91]   D. Weidlich. Lernen von Heuristiken für den Theorembeweiser SETHEO mit stochastischen Methoden. Diplomarbeit, Institut für Informatik, Technische Universität München, 1991.

Non-WAM Models of Logic Programming and their Support by Novel Parallel Hardware

Jiwei Wang[†], Andy Marsh and Simon Lavington

Department of Computer Science, University of Essex

Colchester CO4 3SQ U.K.

email: jiwei@uk.ac.sx, marsa@uk.ac.sx & lavington@uk.ac.sx

Abstract

Cost-effective parallel hardware for performing pattern directed (i.e. associative) search, transitive closure, etc., is becoming a reality. It is therefore appropriate to re-examine classical computational models for logic programming, to see whether the power offered by this new hardware can be exploited. We describe two computational models. One supports parallelism (AND-parallelism and OR-parallelism) by replacing a WAM stack-based configuration by associative memory; this is a direct consequence of using fixpoint computations instead of the traditional resolution rule principle. The other exploits the potential of parallelisms in logic programs (especially unification parallelism and the pipeline parallelism between inference and unification) with the idea of separating unification from inference, as proposed in the field of Theorem Proving. Both these approaches produce requirements for tasks which could be performed by special hardware. We comment on the prospects for implementing such hardware, based on our experience of a SIMD parallel associative memory which also offers a range of set and graph operations.

1 Introduction

The traditional computational models for logic programming have stemmed from SLD-resolution. The one-literal-at-a-time evaluation fashion is understandably linked with implementations on uniprocessor architectures, typified by the WAM. The need for greater computational power, identified in AI and Knowledge Base applications, has produced a requirement for high-performance logic programming machines. Due to the physical limitations of uniprocessor hardware, parallelism seems a natural alternative. However, the

---

†. Jiwei Wang is moving to the Department of Computer Science, University of Bristol, Bristol BS8 1TR

adaptation of WAM-like computational models for parallel processing has introduced a multitude of implementational overheads, such as management of binding environments and resolving binding conflicts. This suggests that a more radical review of parallel computational models is necessary. It also questions the effectiveness of using von Neumann architectures as the foundation to support parallel computational models.

In this paper, we present two novel approaches to parallel computational models of logic programming, namely the GENESIS and Wivenhoe schemes. GENESIS carefully examines the conventional types of parallelism, e.g. AND-parallelism and OR-parallelism, and provides a framework for their exploitation without incurring the overheads from the traditional model. The Wivenhoe model concerns itself with exploitation of new types of parallelism such as unification parallelism and the pipeline parallelism between inference and unification.

To begin with, however, we set the scene in Section 2 by considering how novel hardware may be used to speed up certain activities in conventional (WAM-based) Prolog implementations. This leads on to the GENESIS, described in Section 3, where we modify the WAM model so as to take more advantage of the novel hardware. The Wivenhoe models in Section 4 goes further, by departing radically from the WAM approach. Both the GENESIS and Wivenhoe model produce specifications for well-defined actions which, if implemented in fast (parallel) hardware, would speed up the respective logic programming implementations. In Section 5 we briefly describe novel parallel hardware which offers the functionality required by GENESIS and the Wivenhoe model.

2 Associative Memory Support for Conventional Prolog

When Prolog is applied to problems with realistic amounts of data as ground clauses, searching these ground clauses can take up much of the total run time. In these situations, a high percentage of calls to the unification procedure may produce a negative result. This implies that unification is being used as a selection mechanism to identify a small number of suitable ground clauses from amongst a large number of unsuitable clauses. In this respect, the usual technique of indexing by first argument is often much too coarse. Clearly, some form of pre-unification filter that eliminates the more obviously inappropriate clauses could significantly improve run times.

To be really effective, the pre-unification filter should act as a parallel-access associative (i.e. content-addressable) memory, holding sets of Prolog clauses (procedures) with given predicate-name and arity. The associative memory's interrogand may have wild cards in one or more argument positions during the parallel search process. The responders to a search command represent clauses of particular relevance to the original Prolog query.

To test the notion of pre-unification filtering, we employed a software simulation of the Intelligent File Store, IFS/1 [Lavington 88]. The IFS/1 contains a 4Mbyte semiconductor associative memory, implemented as 64 search engines working in SIMD parallel fashion. The IFS/1 simulator, written in C, was interfaced to KBMS1, the Prolog-based knowledge-base management system developed by Hewlett Packard (Bristol) Ltd. [Manley 90]. The KBMS1 meta-theory was used to place appropriate ground procedures in the IFS/1's associative memory. For a particular search, the speed gain offered by the IFS/1 clearly depends on the ratio:

(procedure cardinality / responder cardinality).

Instead of measuring raw speed, we measured reductions in the number of unification calls. Generally, the IFS/1 started to become effective for database sizes greater than about 1,000 clauses. At 5,000 clauses, the number of unification calls had been reduced by over two orders of magnitude. At 10,000 clauses, the reduction was typically 500 times.

There appears to be some scope for using an associative memory to support other aspects of conventional logic program execution - for example, storage of lemmas. The existing IFS/1 may not be suitable for these additional tasks because of its limited ability to store variables and the clumsy way in which predicates of different arities are handled. The functional requirements of an associative memory which is more suitable to general rule-based systems (both Prolog and Production Rule systems) would include the following features:

- ability to store both named and un-named variables;

- ability to store labels (i.e. tokens) which are short-hand references to other associative memory entries - (useful for handling structured data and function symbols);

- ability to store entries (tuples) of arbitrary arity and arbitrary length;

- ability to carry out one-way pattern-matching and two-way pattern-matching (i.e. unification of atoms), as well as straightforward CAM-type matching.

We will return in Section 5 to consider the implications of the above functional requirements for novel hardware design. It should be noted, however, that an associative memory satisfying these requirements is, of itself, unlikely to improve the efficiency of *ALL* Prolog programs because it only supports the clause-searching phase of the execution cycle.

Supposing that there exists the possibility of implementing cost-effective hardware such as novel associative memories, it is now appropriate to re-examine the Prolog approach to logic programming. In particular, can we devise new computational models that give greater scope for support by associative hardware techniques? The GENESIS model, described in the next

3 The GENESIS Model

Logic programming has predominantly employed SLD-resolution, a top-down goal driven deduction strategy, which may be drawn by recursive inference into an infinite (or at least too long) derivation process. Extensions of linear resolution that consist of storing encountered queries and proven answers aims to tame this problem, for example OLD-T refutation [Tamaki 86], QSQ and SLD-AL resolution [Vieille 86,89], RQA/FQI [Nejdl 87]. Another serious problem is the fast growth of the explored search space. An SLD-derivation may develop in many directions including ones neither relevant to the query nor supported by the actual data stored in the External Database (EDB).

Deductive databases on the other hand adopt a bottom-up generation processing strategy. A strong advantage of bottom-up generation techniques is their ability to guarantee finiteness of all inferences including recursive clauses. However a "brute force" generation of answers to a query would be very inefficient, deducing information useless to solving the query. Extensions to the bottom-up approach that consist of rewriting program clauses aim to minimize the generation of superfluous inference. See for example Magic sets [Bancilhon 86,Beeri 87], and the Alexander [Rohmer 86] methods. However, a major disadvantage of these techniques is their restricted Horn clause application domain (i.e. function-free, covered clauses).

A major goal of any technique is to restrict the flow of data while preserving soundness and completeness of the system. It therefore seems very natural to exploit both the actual data stored in the EDB and the problem specific information provided by a query, to guide the query evaluation procedure in a Horn clause application domain. This amount to the following common idea taken from the optimization of relational algebraic expressions. Selections and projections are applied as close as possible to the source of data since this obviously will cut down the amount of data exchanged in the system. For example, in the expression

$$\sigma_{T=c} (r(X,Y) \bowtie_{Y=Z} q(Z,T))$$

it would be better to apply selection directly to the second relation

$$r(X,Y) \bowtie_{Y=Z} \sigma_{T=c} q(Z,T)$$

The integration of logic programming and deductive databases has been a topic of much study. However a simplistic approach, for example interfacing Prolog to a relational database suffers from the problem of an impedance mismatch [Bancilhon 86] (a confliction of processing strategies; logic programming's tuple-at-a-time versus deductive databases' set-at-a-time). Fixpoint theory may provide a compromise. It has been argued that fixpoint theory can be applied to logic programming with a second fixpoint operator [Bry 89] rather than the bottom-up reasoning immediate consequence operator of van Emden and Kowalski [van Emden 76]. Although the so-called 'fixpoint semantics' is not procedural, it directly induces set-oriented query evaluation. Adopting a mixed processing strategy (depicted in figure 1), the GENESIS (GENEration of Simultaneously Inferenced Solutions) all-solutions Horn clause query evaluation procedure uses two-fixpoint computations: a top-down fixpoint (presented in section 3.1) deriving atoms of the EDB relevant to the query and a bottom-up fixpoint (see section 3.2) applying pre-selected clauses as generation rules. The concluding subsection (section 3.3) identifies the prospects for supporting hardware.

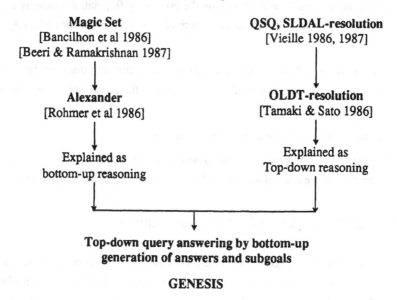

Figure 1: The antecedents of GENESIS, a dual-fixpoint query evaluation procedure

3.1 The Top-Down Fixpoint Computation

The top-down propagation of the problem specific information makes use of a 'dynamic sideways information passing strategy' to reorder subgoals to make full use of variable bindings. It can also be used to detect independent AND-parallelism. In summary:

1. Each goal is generalized before being recorded. The generalization concerns

truncating term structures that exceed a maximum term depth.

2. When a repeated descendent is encountered, only non-derivable atoms and lemmas are used as solutions. No additional inference is performed on this repeated descendant.

3. The solution of a repeated descendant is not complete until no additional solutions can be found to the goal of which it is a repeat. Therefore new answers to a goal are continuously plugged into all repeated descendants until quiescence occurs and no new answers appear.

3.2 The Bottom-Up Fixpoint Computation

The solutions to a goal are generated by the bottom-up fixpoint. A clause is applied to generate a lemma for the head atom, using non-derivable atoms/lemmas for each body atom as follows:

1. Find an instance of the clause using non-derivable atoms/lemmas for the body atoms by unifying each non-derivable atom/lemma with the corresponding atom in the body of the clause.

2. Generalize the clause instance, creating a lemma.

3. Compare the newly generated lemma with each previously generated lemmas. If no lemma is more general then it can be added to the collection of lemmas.

3.3 A GENESIS Perspective for Hardware Support

Apart from its advantageous theoretical implications (e.g. taming non-termination), memoisation (software caching) can be thought of as a simple form of learning, insofar as the program tends to speed up over time. The query evaluation procedure also allows for the notion of derived persistence whereby data can persist outside the scope of a query session. Subsequent queries can thus directly use any previously derived information without any recomputation as long as the original database remains monotonic.

The effects of adopting a dual-fixpoint computation also have radical consequences concerning supporting hardware. The emphasis has moved away from one-literal-at-a-time (stack-based) processing to a set-at-a-time (table look-up) form of computation. The excessive use of memory requires a vast near-CPU storage space that is accessible in a uniform time independent of its size. As Content Addressable Memory is superior to its counterparts with respect to these properties, the conventional WAM stacks may be replaced by CAM. Ideally, the CAM should be constructed with off-the-shelf technology to ensure it incorporates any future technical advances. Additionally, to be competitive with conventional Prolog-based systems, the CAM should be accessible at the same rate as on-board memory. It should also support the capability to handle variables and tuples of varying lengths

The use of any additional auxiliary control data structures can be avoided by using a structure copying closed binding environment representation [Kale 88]. Each goal is then self contained and therefore independent of all other goals. The independent goals can be processed simultaneously (OR-parallelism), thereby avoiding any interprocessor communication and memory locks to contain races between competing processes.

The application domains that provide for greatest improvement for GENESIS when compared with standard Prolog are 'many solutions search problems' [Ciepielewski 85], typically exhibiting an estimated order of magnitude speed-up. However, GENESIS requires more storage - for example seven times more storage for the four-queens problem. Of course, as with RAM on conventional computers GENESIS requires its CAM to be as 'large as possible'.

To summarize, the evolution of logic programming towards parallel machines has introduced unacceptable overhead's, some introduced due to the query evaluation model, some induced by the architectural model. GENESIS aims to minimize the former by separating the propagation of user information and the generation of solutions into two-fixpoint computations, allowing both to proceed simultaneously. The auxiliary control data structures are therefore simplified, thus providing a framework for future research to exploit massive parallelism efficiently.

4 The Wivenhoe Approach

GENESIS has introduced a framework to exploit massive parallelism whilst still using the basic underlying concepts attributed to conventional logic programming computational models. The abandonment of RAM for CAM has led to the concept of a potentially non-WAM architecture. Since it is our belief that a non-WAM model is possible, our research has continued to diverge away from the conventional logic programming approach, returning instead to the techniques developed in Theorem Proving. Having studied the approach of [Chang&Slagle 79], we have devised the Wivenhoe computational model with the basic idea of separating unification from inference.

4.1 The Wivenhoe Model

There are two essential aspects in a computational model for logic languages: one is unification, the other is the control of inference. Unification is the basic operation and commonly takes about 30% - 80% of the total execution time in executing a logic program. In many cases, the search space in executing a logic program is exponential in nature. The control of the search space, i.e. the control of inference, is crucial to the efficiency of a logic programming system.

In the traditional computational models, e.g. WAM, unification and inference have been mixed up in execution. We argue that this can be disadvantageous in two aspects. Firstly, the size of term for unification is limited to a relatively small grain, which is the reason that parallel unification has not yet been practical. Secondly, it is difficult to obtain a global view of inference, and thus the control of inference relies on clause ordering with blind backtracking or resorting to user's annotations. In the context of pure declarative programming where the execution details of logic programs is not of programmers' concern, it seems that unification failure messages are the only information which can be relied on for controlling the inference.

The Wivenhoe computational model aims at supporting pure declarative programming. It adopts the idea of separating unification from inference, widely proposed in Theorem Proving. On one hand, this can increase the granularity of terms in unification and hence gain the benefit of parallel unification. On the other hand, the separated inference can easily be controlled; unification failures can be identified precisely due to a global view of the unification; ordering among clauses and literals can be avoided.

The Wivenhoe model uses the rewriting rule approach of [Chang&Slagle 79] which allows us to extract the logical relations, specified by logical connectives, from a logic program and perform abstract inference. For details of how such extraction works, the reader is referred to [Wang&Lavington 90a]. Here, we only give an example for an intuitive illustration. For the program append and query :- append([1],[2,3],X):

> :- append([1],[2,3],X).
> append([],A,A).
> append([B|C],D,[B|E]):- append(C,D,E).

A connection graph is built and the connections (arcs) are given a unique label as shown in Figure 2.

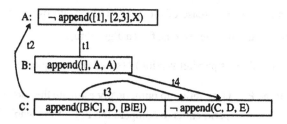

Figure 2: The connection graph of append program

Two rewriting rules for evaluating the query can be obtained, where S is called the start symbol which is the term to be rewritten in order to generate refutation plans, t_i is a connection (referred as a terminal), and $N(C1)$ stands for the first literal of clause C (referred as a non-terminal).

$$S ==> t2 \, N(C1) + t1$$
$$N(C1) ==> t3 \, N(C1) + t4$$

By rewriting the start symbol S with these two rewriting rules and collecting strings of t_i, abstract inference can be performed as obtaining a sequence of refutation plans. A refutation plan is a set of connections which indicates a set of unifications required for verifying the validity of the refutation plan. Such unifications can be viewed as one unification and done in one go.

It can be seen that the control of inference can be done by the rewriting strategy. Furthermore, the unification failure of certain refutation plans which are reflected by clashed connections can also be used to trim down doomed strings during rewriting. This is more familiarly known as the intelligent backtracking in the context of Prolog implementation. It has been shown that the search space of the Wivenhoe model cannot be bigger than other models, but in many cases it is much smaller than other models. The Wivenhoe model also has stronger termination powers than other models. For details, the reader is referred to [Wang&Lavington 90a].

4.2 The Gain of Parallel Unification

Intuitively, the Wivenhoe approach to implementing unification creates the opportunity for unification parallelism. To quantify the increase of parallelism, an empirical experiment has been done on measuring the potential parallel factor (PPF) for the common terms in practical logic programs. The *potential parallel factor (PPF)*, proposed in [Harland&Jaffar 87], defines the maximum possible speed increase of the parallel algorithm over the sequential one on a certain application domain. In other words, for an algorithm,

PPF = (speed of its parallel version) / (speed of its sequential version).

The main feature of the PPF is its ability to numerically estimate the somewhat vague quantity of "parallelisability". Our experiment is to compare the PPF of the whole refutation plan first as one unification and then as individual unifications in the refutation plan. The comparison thus indicates the difference of the "parallelisability" on performing unifications in refutation plans in the two different ways. The data is obtained by comparing a sequential algorithm of [Yasuura 84] [†] and its parallel counterpart.

Yasuura's algorithm is to construct a connected directed hypergraph from the dag representation of the terms to be unified. A vertex in the hyper-graph represents a combination of two nodes in the term dag, (so that a vertex is symbolised as f-g where f and g are nodes in the term dag). There is an edge between two vertices, say f-g and x-y, in the hyper-graph if there are arcs from f to x and from g to y. Hence, the unifiability of two terms, say with root nodes a and b, turns into the reachability from the vertex a-b to any vertex produced by different nodes in the term dags. The sequential algorithm is to search such a hypergraph sequentially, while the parallel version is to do the breath-first parallel search.

Program	No. of unifications in a refutation plan	Average PPF for individual unifications	PPF of the whole refutation plan
Append(100,1)	101	2.000	3.47
Naive reverse(65)	2211	1.971	114.88
Quick sort (50)	637	2.037	79.04
Intersection (40-40)	275	1.609	76.19
Fibonacci 13	1161	1.599	1253.80
Ancestor (of 100 generations)	198	1.500	173.25
8 Queen program 1	134	2.017	32.70
8 Queen program 2	39	1.863	26.00
8 Queen program 3	159	1.733	113.97
8 Queen program 4	146	2.138	145.12
8 Queen program 5	166	1.787	200.10
Hamilton	170	1.765	23.97
Color map	91	1.565	37.37
Farmer	42	1.531	299.29
Planner	2688	1.805	1326.70
FLL	1834	1.918	903.46

Table 1: Potential Parallel Factors for Yasuura's algorithm

The results indicate that for programs with recursive data types, e.g. append, naive reverse, the improvement is limited; whereas for programs with simple data structure, e.g. fib and ancestor, the PPF is linear with the number of unifications. For programs with complicated recursive structures, e.g. 8 Queens program, the result varies with different cases. However, generally, for large programs such as Planner (a planner with simple natural language front-end) and FLL (a functional logic programming interpreter) the improvement of PPF is quite significant.

4.3 The Wivenhoe Perspective for Hardware Support

Obviously, the rewriting process involves pattern directed search for rewriting rules. In the rewriting rules in the Wivenhoe model, there is no ordering in a string of terminals and non-terminals. We can take a set-theoretical view of the rewriting rules, where strings are taken as sets. The control of inference becomes a sequence of set-inclusion tests. Many parallel unification algorithms, e.g. [Bibel et al 87] and [Wang&Lavington 90a], invoke transitive closure on a dag representation of programs. This is another potential support that special purpose hardware can give.

Both GENESIS and the Wivenhoe model have identified the need for hardware support, for example, table look-ups, set operations, handling dags and transitive closure. These requirements have inspired the parallel architecture group at Essex to design a novel SIMD hardware unit which aims to satisfy these requirements.

5 Parallel Hardware Support

Combining all the functional requirements of Sections 2, 3 and 4 may not be the best way of designing a hardware unit to support general logic programming. However, it certainly presents an instructive architectural exercise and, on the positive side, ensures that any resulting hardware implementation is not specific to a single computational model. We assume that the design goal is to produce a novel unit which, when connected as a kind of co-processor to one or more conventional CPUs, is able to speed up the more time-consuming tasks in the computational models described in the previous Sections. It goes without saying that every opportunity should be sought to exploit parallelism - preferably in a way that is invisible to the source-level programmer.

From Sections 2 and 3 come the requirements for large amounts of associative memory. To prevent time-wasting transfers of data between this memory and a host CPU, it would be advantageous if the primitive operations such as transitive closure presented in Section 4 were to be performed on the data in situ. We thus arrive at the concept of **active memory**, justified in more detail in [Lavington&Davies 90]. The IFS/2, successor to the IFS/1 knowledge-base server described in [Lavington 88], is based on the active memory principle. The SIMD search engines of the IFS/2 are used both for associative memory and for a range of primitive operations on the super-type **relation**.

Briefly, each entry, or line, in the IFS/2's associative memory is known as a tuple. From these tuples other, more composed, objects are built. Each tuple may have many fields. A tuple has the format:

<system control word> <tuple descriptor> <field 1> ... <field n>.

The <system control word> includes a valid/empty marker. The <tuple descriptor> identifies the tuple format and the category of each field. Each of the n fields can be in one of three categories:

C   : ground - (i.e. known at the time of commencing a search);

W   : wild card. Wild cards can be named (NM) or un-named (UW). These
        may be used respectively for named or anonymous variables.

L   : label.

The C category may be used for numerical or lexical constants. When a field represents
a ground atom comprising an ASCII string of up to 120 characters, a fixed-length internal
identifier may be used to represent the lexeme - see [Wang&Lavington 90b]. The C category
can also be used to convey <type> information about an adjacent field, e.g. for union types.

During IFS/2 search commands, the interrogand format is similar to the above tuple
format. We plan to offer five kinds of comparison where the scope is tuple-wide, and five kinds
of comparison (=, >, <, =/, fuzzy) where the scope is field-wide. This gives a theoretical total
of 125 different kinds of search. In Table 2 we identify six common types of associative search
based on equality. The 'identical' entry in Table 2 corresponds to straightfoward bit-string to
bit-string comparison as in a conventional CAM chip. The 'negation' entry in Table 2 differs
from the 'simple' entry by inverting the comparator's result signal. Simple, one-way and two-
way searches are roughly comparable to parameter passing in procedural, functional, and logic
languages respectively. However, the 'two-way' entry in Table 2 corresponds to unification of
atoms whereas the 'unification' entry corresponds to full unification including structures.

The detailed action when matching a field in the interrogand with a stored field is
represented in Table 3, for the case of the first four entries in Table 2.

Type	Match scope
Simple	Field
One-way	Tuple (stored or interrogand)
Two-way	Tuple-pair (stored and interrogand)
Unification	Tuple-pair (stored and interrogand)
Negation	Field
Identical (i.e. meta-level)	Field

Table 2: Six common types of 'equality' search in the IFS/2

Interrogand field	Stored field	Action	Returned result
C1	C2	*compare*	Yes *if compare(C1, C2) succeeds* No *otherwise*
UW	C2	*skip*	Yes
NW1	C2	*retrieve*	C2
L1	C2	*skip*	No
C1	UW	*skip*	Yes
UW	UW	*skip*	Yes
NW1	UW	*skip*	Yes
L1	UW	*skip*	Yes
C1	NW2	*retrieve*	NW2
UW	NW2	*skip*	Yes
NW1	NW2	*retrieve*	NW2
L1	NW2	*retrieve*	NW2
C1	L2	*skip*	No
UW	L2	*skip*	Yes
NW1	L2	*retrieve*	L2
L1	L2	*compare*	Yes *if compare(L1, L2) succeeds* No (and returns L2) *otherwise*

Table 3: The detailed matching action for various combinations of interrogand field and stored field, for the first four entries of Table 2.

In addition to search, insert, and delete commands, the IFS/2 will offer a range of set and graph primitives as described in [Lavington et al 88] and [Robinson&Lavington 90]. As far as conventional logic programming is concerned, the initial aim is to support a useful range linear recursive rules - principally single-sided (single chain) and double-sided (n-chain). Research is in progress to extend the scope.

Based on our prototype relational algebraic hardware and OCCAM simulations of the IFS/2, we expect the following typical performance:

insert a tuple: 60 microseconds.

member operation: 40 microseconds (fixed time, independent of cardinality).

search with one wild card: 400 microseconds (independent of relation cardinality; varies with number of responders, but assumes these responders are kept within the IFS/2).

join operation: join of two 1000-tuple relations in about 5 milliseconds.

transitive closure: up to 600 microseconds for a 1000-node graph, depending on bushiness.

The prototype IFS/2 now being built will have 24 Mbytes of semiconductor associative cache backed by a single 700 Mbyte SCSI associatively-accessed disc. The SIMD configuration is modularly extensible. The above timing estimates assume access is confined to the 24 Mbyte semiconductor associative cache. The cache and disc are integrated into a one-level associative memory via a management scheme called Semantic Caching [Lavington et al. 87].

Note that although the CAM search speeds given above are two or three orders of magnitude slower that the access times of near-CPU RAM, at least the IFS/2's CAM is of large capacity, modularly extensible, and of a cost per bit only about twice that of RAM. Furthermore, the GENESIS computational model can take advantage of the IFS/2's set-based characteristics when manipulating large volumes of data. As for the Wivenhoe model, the IFS/2's ability to process large dags rapidly is an obvious advantage. Set operations, especially set-inclusion, are also very supportive of the Wivenhoe model.

6 Conclusions

These initial studies in both computational models and hardware support have determined the need for an add-on intelligent memory unit, which can support the massive parallelism revealed by the GENESIS and the Wivenhoe models.

More generally, the IFS/2 employs the **active memory** principle to exploit the inherent parallelism of operations on data structures based on the super-type **relation**. The GENESIS and Wivenhoe models can take advantage of this kind of natural data-parallelism.

7 Acknowledgments

The research described in this paper has been supported in part by SERC grants GR/F/06319 and GR/F/61028. It is a pleasure to acknowledge the many helpful discussions we have had with other members of the IFS Group at Essex.

8 References

[Bancilhon et al 86] F. Bancilhon, D. Maier, Y. Sagiv & J.D. Ullman, "Magic sets and other strange ways to implement logic programs", proceedings 5th ACM SIGMOD-SIGACT Symposium on Principles of Database Systems (PODS), pp. 1-15.

[Beeri&Ramakrishnan 87] C. Beeri & R. Ramakrishnan, "On the power of magic", proceedings 6th ACM SIGACT-SIGMOD-SIGART Symposium on Principles of Database Systems (PODS), San Diego, CA, March 1987, pp. 269-283.

[Bry 89] F. Bry, "Advanced fixpoint procedures for querying databases: A rule-based approach", Internal report No. IR-KB-61, ECRC, March 1989.

[Bibel et al 87] W. Bibel, F. Kurfess, K. Aspetsberger, P. Hintenaus & J. Schumann. "Parallel Inference Machines", Future Parallel Computers, Edited by P. Treleaven & M. Vanneschi, LNCS. No. 272, Springer-Verlag, 1987, pp. 185-226.

[Chang&Slagle 79] C.L. Chang & J.R. Slagle. "Using Rewriting Rules for Connection Graphs to Prove Theorems", Journal of AI 12 (1979), pp. 159-180.

[Ciepielewski et al 85] A. Ciepielewski, S. Haridi & B. Hausman. "Initial Evaluation of a Virtual Machine for OR-Parallel Execution of Logic Programs", IFIP TC-10 Working Conf. on Fifth Generation Computer Architecture, UMIST, Manchester, July 15-18 1985.

[Harland&Jaffar 87] J.H. Harland & J. Jaffar. "On Parallel Unification for Prolog", New Generation Computing, No. 5, 1987, pp. 259-279.

[Kale et al 88] L. Kale, B. Ramkumar & W. Shu, "A memory organization independent binding environment for AND and OR parallel execution of logic programs", proceedings 5th International Conference and Symposium on Logic Programming, R.Kowalski K.Bowen (ed), Seattle, August 1988, pp. 1223-1240.

[Lavington et al 87] S.H. Lavington, M. Standring, Y.J. Jiang, C.J. Wang & M.E. Waite. "Hardware Memory Management for Large Knowledge Bases", Proc. of PARLE, the Conference on Parallel Architectures and Languages Europe, Eindhoven, June 1987, pp. 226-241.

[Lavington 88] S.H. Lavington. "Technical Overview of the Intelligent File Store", J. Knowledge-Based Systems, vol.1, No 3. 1988, pp. 166-172.

[Lavington et al 88] S.H. Lavington, J. Robinson & F-Y. Mok. "A High-speed Relational Algebraic Processor for Large Knowledge Bases", Proc. of Intl. Workshop on VLSI for AI, Oxford, July, 1988. Also in VLSI for AI, (eds). Delgado-Frias and Moore, Kluwer Academic Press, 1989, pp. 133-143.

[Lavington&Davies 90] S.H. Lavington & R.A.J. Davies, "Active Memory for Managing Persistent Objects". Presented at the International Workshop on Computer Architectures to Support Security and Persistence, Bremen, FRG, May 1990. Proceedings published by Springer-Verlag, pages 137-154.

[Manley 90] J.C. Manley, "kbProlog: a Language for Knowledge Management". Proceedings of the UNICOM Seminar on Commercial Parallel Processing, London, June 1990, pages 164 - 173.

[Marsh 90] A.J.Marsh, "A query evaluation model supporting parallelism for logic programs", Thesis submitted for Ph.D., Dept. of Computer Science, Univ. of Essex, 1990.

[Nejdl 87] W. Nejdl, "Recursive strategies for answering recursive queries - The RQA/FQI strategy", proceedings 13th International Conference on Very Large Data Bases, Brighton, U.K. September 1987, pp. 43-50.

[Rohmer et al 86] R. Rohmer, R. Lescoeur & J.M. Kerisit, "The Alexander Method, a Technique for Processing of Recursive Axioms in Deductive Databases", New Generation Computing, Vol. 4 No. 3, 1986, pp. 273-285.

[Robinson&Lavington 90] J. Robinson & S.H. Lavington, "A Transitive Closure and Magic Functions Machine", Proc. of the Second International Symposium on Databases in Parallel and Distributed Systems, Dublin, July 1990, pp. 44-54.

[Tamaki&Sato 86] H. Tamaki & T. Sato, "OLD resolution with tabulation", proceedings of 3rd International Conference on Logic programming, London, U.K., 1986, pp. 84-98.

[Vieille 86] L. Vieille, "Recursive Axioms in Deductive Databases: The Query/Subquery Approach", proceedings First International Conference on Expert Database Systems, Charleston, 1986, pp. 179-194.

[Vieille 89] L. Vieille, "Recursive Query Processing: the Power of Logic", Journal of Theoretical Computer Science (Netherlands), vol 69, No. 1, December 1989, pp. 1-53.

[Wang 90] J. Wang. "A New Computational Model for Logic Languages and its Supporting Architecture", Forthcoming Ph.D. Thesis, Dept. of Computer Science, Univ. of Essex, 1990.

[Wang&Lavington 90a] J. Wang & S.H. Lavington, "The Wivenhoe Computational Model: in Search of More Parallelisms", Proc. of UK Association for Logic Programming 1990 Conference, Bristol, March, 1990.

[Wang&Lavington 90b] C.J. Wang & S.H. Lavington, "SIMD Parallelism for Symbol Mapping", International Workshop on VLSI for AI and Neural Networks, Oxford, Sept., 1990.

[Yasuura 84] H. Yasuura. "On Parallel Computational Complexity of Unification", Proc. of the fifth generation computer systems 1984, pp. 235-243.

The ADAM Abstract Dataflow Machine

Wolfgang Schreiner

Research Institute for Symbolic Computation (RISC-Linz)
Johannes Kepler University, Linz, Austria
Bitnet: K315640@AEARN

May 9, 1991

Abstract

This paper describes the design and implementation of the ADAM Abstract Dataflow Machine. This abstract machine has a hybrid distributed-memory architecture combining features from conventional register machines and from dataflow computers. The ADAM processor has a conventional two-address instruction set augmented by primitives for the creation and synchronization of parallel tasks that allow the simulation of dataflow behavior. Special memory units on each ADAM module are responsible for the management of non-strict data structures. The system will be programmed in the non-strict functional (dataflow) programming language EVE that will be compiled to ADAM machine code. A prototype implementation of the concept on a multi-transputer system shows promising speed-ups.

1 Introduction

In the last decade, there has been much international research on how to efficiently exploit the implicit parallelism inherent in all algorithms on machines with hundreds or even thousands of processors. Several non-von Neumann architectures have been proposed in order to effectively utilize this parallelism by hardware primitives that minimize the overhead for the creation and synchronization of large numbers of parallel tasks. Especially for functional and logic programming languages as well as for applications like automated theorem proving that provide a very large amount of implicit parallelism, such kinds of architectures are of great interest.

Dataflow architectures seem to be one of the most promising of these approaches. Since the early 1970s, several dataflow computers have been designed, simulated and partially also built in hardware. Some recent examples for such actually built machines are the *Manchester Dataflow Computer* [Gurd *et al.*, 1985], the *ETL SIGMA-1* at the Japanese Electrotechnical Laboratory [Hiraki *et al.*, 1984] and the *ETS Explicit Token Store "Monsoon"* at the MIT [Papadopoulos and Culler, 1990].

In spite of these efforts, commercially available dataflow systems have not yet come into existence. One of the main reasons for this disappointing fact is the enormous amount of knowledge that has been gathered on the design and use of conventional processors, as well from the hardware engineer's as from the software engineer's point of view. Moreover, the dataflow paradigm of program execution requires substantially more complex hardware support than the conventional von-Neumann princple. Therefore, several attempts have been made to combine the benefits of both worlds, of data-driven and of control-driven architectures [Iannucci, 1988].

In this paper, the main results of the author's diploma thesis [Schreiner, 1990] are presented. This thesis dealt with the design and the implementation of a dataflow simulator on conventional parallel hardware. For this purpose, we designed a hybrid two-level concept combining the advantages of von-Neumann processors with those of the dataflow model. The result of this work is the ADAM Abstract Dataflow Machine that achieves dataflow-like behaviour by basically control-driven program execution. This abstract machine has been successfully implemented by a simulator that interpretes the ADAM machine code on a multi-transputer system. A compiler for the high-level functional programming language EVE is currently under implementation.

However, in spite of this dataflow research we want to emphasize that we are actually not interested in hardware design *per se*. Actually, our work is motivated by the fact that the dataflow style of programming has essential benefits that have no competitive counterpart in parallel programming based on conventional (imperative) languages. We want to show how both worlds, i.e. data-driven and control-driven execution, are related and how the former can also be built on top of the later one.

The following sections describe in a top-down fashion the different levels of the ADAM design and operation principles and also give a short introduction of how to compile a declarative language into ADAM machine code. A substantially shorter description of the ADAM has also been published in [Schreiner, 1991a].

2 Basic Idea

The basic idea of our approach is as follows. We take a mathematical expression, e.g.

$$(a + b) * (-y) \text{ where}$$
$$a = -x$$
$$b = x/y$$

This expression should be viewed as the body of a function $f(x, y)$ with formal parameters x and y. In the dataflow model, this body is translated into a directed acyclic graph (the *dataflow graph*) as depicted in Figure 1.

In dataflow machines, this dataflow graph is represented by a program like the following one where each instruction consists of an operation code and the address of its successor instruction:

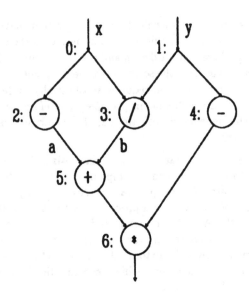

Figure 1: A Dataflow Graph

```
0:   copy 2 3.1
1:   copy 3.r 4
2:   neg 5.1
3:   div 5.r
4:   neg 6
5:   add 6
6:   mul 7
```

Each node of the graph is translated into one instruction of the program where the arcs of the graph are represented by the instructions' successor addresses. Branches are usually translated into explicit copy instructions that duplicate their input values. If the successor is a binary instruction, the predecessor must also specify which of the "input ports" of the successor (the left or the right one) is actually referenced.

The execution of a dataflow program proceeds as follows: between different instructions, values are transmitted by pieces of information called *tokens*. These tokens flow along the arcs of the dataflow graph and trigger the execution of the instructions on their way *(data-driven execution)*. If some token passes a binary instruction, i.e. an instruction with two input arcs, a special synchronization mechanisms has to ensure a *rendezvouz* with the partner token: the instruction may only execute and *fire* (i.e. produce a result token) if both input tokens have arrived (the so called *firing rule*).

In the ADAM model, the interpretation of a dataflow graph is substantially different. The arcs of the graph denote registers and the nodes represent two-address instructions operating on these registers:

```
0:    copy   x_1, x_2, 2
1:    copy   y_1, y_2, 4
2:    split  3, 6
3:    neg    x_1, x_1, 8
4:    split  5, 6
5:    neg    y_2, y_2, 10
6:    wait   e_0, 7
7:    div    x_2, y_1, 8
8:    wait   e_1, 9
9:    add    x_1, x_2, 10
10:   wait   e_2, 11
11:   div    x_1, y_2, 12
```

Each instruction operates on two registers where the first one receives the result value. After an instruction has been executed, control flow is routed by the address field to its successor, i.e. each instruction performs a jump to its successor. Since the above program has two input arguments that may asynchronously arrive, two threads of control enter the code block at addresses 0 and 1, respectively. split instructions are used to fork a thread of control into two parallel threads starting at the specified successor instructions. The execution of each thread may be unhinderedly continued as long as no wait instruction is encountered.

Each wait guards a binary *event* encoded in the first field of this instruction. Each event may have one of the values "occurred" or "not occurred", initially no event has occurred. If execution reaches a wait whose event has not yet occurred, the actual thread of control is interrupted and the referred event is set to "occurred". The next time, this event is tested, the actual thread may unhinderedly pass the wait.

split and wait control the generation of parallel processes and the synchronization between them, they are basically the only instructions related to parallelism. However, together with the function call mechanism (discussed in section 6), they suffice to control the program execution in such a way that dataflow semantics is simulated.

We want to emphasize the essential difference between the pure dataflow model and our approach: In dataflow architectures, all data physically "flow" between instructions and, by this, control the computation. In the ADAM processor, threads of instructions are executed *without* any data flowing between them. Communication between different instructions is done via shared registers, synchronization between parallel threads are explicitly handled by wait statements.

This approach has two essential advantages:

1. In dataflow machines, all data referenced by more than one instruction have to be **explicitly duplicated** and sent to the required instructions, even if they belong to the same activation of a function and reside on the same processor.

   In our model, parallel program paths may **share data** held in common registers, an explicit duplication can be avoided in most cases. The compiler may optimize register allocation in such a way' that the overall number of required registers is reduced to a minimum.

2. In dataflow architectures, the synchronization model is fixed in hardware. Parallel program paths have to be generated and finally synchronized even if parallelism is not really utilized. This is especially the case if only whole function activations are placed on new processors i.e. parallel paths within an activation are always executed on the same processor.

In our approach, a compiler is able to detect in which cases parallel paths may be safely (i.e. without changes to the dataflow semantics) executed in sequential and **serialize the code** by the use of **wait** statements[1].

Using both optimizations, register sharing and serialization, we may rewrite the above program as follows:

```
0:   wait   e_0, 1
1:   copy   x_2, x_1, 2
2:   div    x_2, y_1, 3
3:   neg    x_1, x_1, 4
4:   add    x_1, x_2, 5
5:   neg    y_1, y_1, 6
6:   mult   x_1, y_1, 7
```

Assuming that there are two parallel input threads delivering their arguments in registers x_1 and y_1, there is only one **wait** instruction required to synchronizes these tasks. All other instructions may be sequentially executed requiring only one additional register x_2. Hence, the efficiency of the function body drastically increases, while the overall dataflow-like behaviour of a program consisting of a set of such functions remains unchanged.

After this introduction to the basic principles of our approach, the following sections present the ADAM architecture in more detail.

3   Global Architecture

The ADAM is a parallel machine with distributed memory. It consists of several equally constructed worker modules that are connected by a network of unbuffered uni-directional channels. These channels represent the only communication medium of the ADAM; there is nothing like some global memory that all modules might have access to. One special module, the *master*, is connected to the peripheral devices for input and ouput. The master handles all interactions with the outside world, in particular it is responsible for loading and distributing the program to be executed, for triggering the execution of the program and for delivering the result values of the computation. On the other hand, the worker modules perform the actual computational tasks.

---

[1]Sequentialization is not allowed in the case of non-strict functions, i.e. functions that may return values even if not all arguments have yet arrived. In general, a process called *strictness analysis* [Peyton Jones, 1987] has to detect to which extent function bodies may be safely serialized.

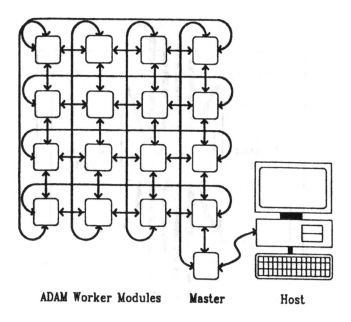

ADAM Worker Modules   **Master**   Host

Figure 2: The ADAM Network

Figure 2 shows a sample network of ADAM modules (each double-arrow represents two channels for communication in both directions).

Each ADAM worker consists of three components as illustrated in Figure 3:

- **The Arbiter** is the only unit with an interface to the neighbour modules. When the ADAM is booted, the arbiter is responsible to distribute the program to be executed over the network. During program execution, it receives messages from the other local units and from the neighbour modules and routes them to their correct places of destination.

- **The Processor Unit** executes the given program and, thereby, performs the actual computation. It receives messages (basically arguments for the local function activations) from and sends messages (basically results of local function activations) to other processors in the network. Moreover, it communicates with its memory unit and those on other modules by request and result messages.

- **The Memory Unit** contains a heap-organized store holding tuples, i.e. data structures of variable size. Tuples may be allocated and referenced by a (local or distinct) processor via messages to the memory unit. Result values (either atomic values or references to other tuples) are sent as messages back to the callers.

Each worker module has only a restricted view of the network. It knows about the addresses and certain state parameters of its neighbours but has in general no global information about the network. The only exception is the arbiter that holds a network

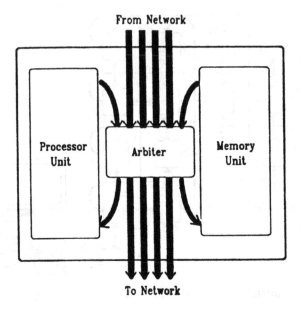

Figure 3: An ADAM Worker Module

routing table in order to forward incoming messages to their correct destination (either to the local processor or memory unit or to some neighbour module).

4 The Processor Unit

4.1 Construction

The ADAM processor is basically a conventional control-driven processor with several extensions that allow the efficient simulation of dataflow behaviour. The ADAM therefore represents a hybrid two-level design combining features from conventional register architectures and from true dataflow computers.

The processor consists of the following components (depicted in Figure 4):

- **The Execution Unit** is the heart of the processor performing the arithmetical/logical computations. Program execution is basically control-driven but constrained by special *synchronization instructions* that are used to express the data dependences within a program.

- **The Program Store** holds a sequence of *code blocks* each of which corresponds to one user-defined function. Every processor holds the whole program code and may therefore execute any function of the program.

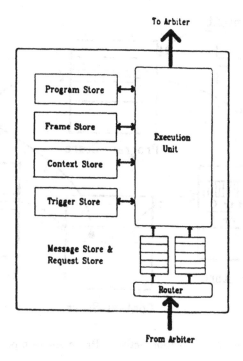

Figure 4: The ADAM Processor

- **The Frame Store** is a heap-organized store holding a set of *activation frames* each of which corresponds to one particular function activation. Each frame represents the actual state of its activation by describing the contents of the registers and the state of the events.

- **The Context Store** is a table of activation descriptors called *contexts*. Each context uniquely describes one function activation on the processor by the base addresses of the activation's code block and of its register frame.

- **The Trigger Store** contains a set of *instruction triggers*, each of which is the description of a thread that may be started but has not yet been. When a split instruction is executed, the processor continues execution with one thread while it puts a trigger for the other thread into this store

- **The Message Store** and the **Request Store** buffer all messages received. The message store holds arguments for local function activations and result values of parallel activations. The second store holds requests to activate new function instances.

The interaction between these components is described in the following subsection.

4.2 Execution

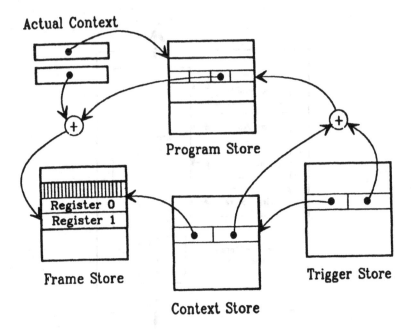

Figure 5: Interaction between Processor Components

(tasks) that may be distributed among processors *(function-level parallelism)*. Each activation has therefore its own address space, communication between different activations is only possible via messages. However, also within an activation several instruction sequences may be concurrently executed. These sequences represent light-weight processes *(threads)* that share the same address space and may directly communicate via memory locations *(instruction-level parallelism)*.

The execution the processor now proceeds as follows (see Figure 5): each time the execution of a new function activation is started, the description items of this activation (i.e. the base addresses of the code block and of the register frame) are stored into two *context registers*. Any register number encoded in an instruction is therefore actually an offset to the base address of the frame and every function activation has therefore its private set of registers. All event numbers referenced by `wait` instructions are actually *negative* offsets to the frame base address. Hence, every activation has also its private sets of events each of which is represented by a bit in the frame.

Instruction execution proceeds in a control-driven fashion, i.e. if an activation is started, there is one thread of control executing one instruction after the other. The sequence of instructions is denoted by the extra address field of each instruction. Each instruction operates on the local set of registers in the usual way.

If a `split` instruction is executed, the actual thread of control is split up into two parallel threads. The start address of one of the branches is pushed on the trigger store while the other branch is continued by the current thread. If the thread will be eventually interrupted (e.g. by a `wait` instruction as explained below), then one of the triggers will be popped from the store and used to restart execution at the desired position.

This mechanism therefore manages some kind of *multi-tasking* of parallel threads within function activations.

If a wait instruction is executed and fails, the actual thread is terminated. Then, as explained above, a trigger is popped from the trigger store and a new thread is started within the current activation (i.e. the context registers remain unchanged). Only if the trigger store is empty, a context switch has to be made, i.e. a new activation is started and the context registers have to be redefined. The start of a new activation may be triggered by one of two events:

1. **A message** is received from the message store. In this case, a new thread is started beginning with the instruction that represents the destination of the message. The context in which this thread shall execute is also encoded in the message as a pointer to the context store (delivering the base addresses of the context's activation frame and code block). The message value itself may be either an input argument for the function activation or the result value delivered by some other function activation or it may also hold the result of a memory request (see the next section).

2. **An activation request** is received from the request store. In this case, some neighbour processor has sent a request to activate a new instance of some particular function. When the processor decides to fulfill this request, a new activation frame has to be allocated. Then a free descriptor in the context store is initialized with the base addresses of the activation frame and of the function's code block. Finally, a reference to this context descriptor is sent back to the caller.

The decision between these two possibilities depends on the actual load of the processor. If it is heavily loaded, argument messages will be preferred, if the load is low, more activation requests will be fulfilled. This alternative is (besides the decision to which processor to send activation requests to) the basic tool for load balancing.

As described above, the ADAM processor represents a hybrid concept combining features of register architectures and of dataflow machines:

- Within a function activation, sequential threads are executing in a **control-driven** fashion: each thread executes one instruction after the other each of which performs some register operation. Concurrent threads within the same activation are synchronized by the application of wait statements.

- Between function activations, execution is controlled by messages in a **data-driven** way: each message transmits a value from one activation to another and starts a new thread of control in the target activation. Special request messages are used to create new function activations, possibly on different processors.

The ADAM concept therefore corresponds to a dataflow model where the nodes of the dataflow graph are whole user-defined functions. Inside the nodes, execution proceeds as on conventional von-Neumann architectures.

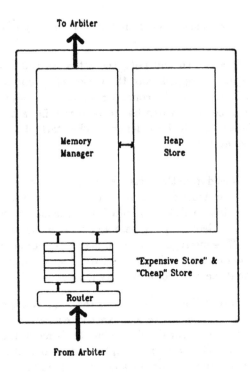

Figure 6: The ADAM Memory Unit

5 The Memory Unit

5.1 General

Since processor units are only able to handle atomic (integer) data, the management of compound data structures has been shifted to separate memory units. Each worker module contains one memory unit that is constructed as follows (see Figure 6):

- **The Heap** holds a set of tuples, i.e. data structures of arbitrary but fixed size. Each field of a tuple is either empty or holds an integer atom or a tuple reference. All heaps on all network modules represent a global store, i.e. all references denote unique tuples within the network.

- **The Memory Manager** handles incoming requests to allocate a new tuple (alloc), to write a value into some tuple field (write) or to return the contents of some tuple field (read). Furthermore, it is responsible for garbage collection i.e. for reclaiming the heap space that is occupied by tuples that are nowhere referenced any more.

- **The "Expensive" Store and the "Cheap" Store** hold all incoming requests classified into two categories: the request may require the allocation of additional heap memory ("expensive") or not ("cheap"). This distinction helps to manage the heap store more efficiently.

5.2 Memory Access

All tuples are *non-strict* i.e. tuple references may be exchanged between parallel processes even if (some or all of) the tuple fields do not yet contain valid data. As a consequence, one process may allocate a tuple and send the tuple reference to another process *before* it has written any value into the fields of the tuple! The one process (the *producer*) may therefore fill the tuple fields with values while the other process (the *consumer*) simultaneously reads these fields and processes their values. This form of producer-consumer **parallelism** is one of the main sources of parallelism in declarative programs ([Arvind *et al.*, 1987]).

However, in order to preserve determinism of program execution (i.e. to avoid that the consumer process reads some undefined tuple slot and thus receives a random value), special synchronization tools have been introduced: Each field of a tuple has associated a **full/empty flag** indicating if a value has yet been written into this field or not. These flags are maintained by the heap manager in the following fashion:

- **Allocation Requests:** If a request arrives to allocate space for a new tuple, all fields of this tuple are marked as empty and a reference to this tuple is returned to the sender of the request.

- **Read Requests:** If a read request arrives for a field that already contains some value, the value of this field is returned to the sender of the request. However, if the field that has not yet been defined, the request is put into a waiting queue and a reference to this queue is stored in the field.

- **Write Requests:** If a write request for some tuple field arrives, all waiting read requests queued into that field are released: the value delivered by the write message is returned to the senders of the deferred read requests and is then written into the field (setting the flag to full). However, if an attempt is made to overwrite an already defined tuple field, an error is reported: all tuples have to obey the *single-assignment rule* which is essential for receiving deterministic result values in parallel systems.

Access to the services provided by the memory unit is entirely handled via the use of these messages. However, an ADAM program has a more abstract view of the memory access which is described in the next subsection.

5.3 Memory Instructions

Corresponding to these tree types of memory requests, there exist three instructions alloc, read and write in the ADAM instruction set. From the point of view of program execution, all three instructions are non-blocking: alloc and write immediately return their results, i.e. a reference to a new tuple and the contents of some tuple field, respectively; write immediately writes the desired value and then continues execution.

However, alloc and read are actually **split-phase operations**: Having submitted the memory requests into the network, the processor immediately interrupts the execution of the actual thread and starts another one. The interrupted thread is only continued at the arrival of the desired value. In case of the **write** instruction, execution is continued immediately after the write request has been submitted (i.e. *before* the actual write operation has actually been performed).

This behavior of the memory access instructions has a crucial consequence on the overall performance of the system: since the actual process does *not* wait for the result of a memory operation, the architecture is able to **tolerate extremely long memory latencies.** It does not matter how long the message and the delivered result is on its way, as long as there are other processes still to be executed. This is especially important in a distributed memory architecture, since any pointer may reference a tuple that is sited on another (even non-neighbour!) module of the network.

5.4 Garbage Collection

The ADAM architecture uses for garbage collection an improved version of the **weighted reference counting** algorithm [Bevan, 1987]. This garbage collection method has (compared to all other garbage collecting schemes) the advantage of being very simple and easily adaptable for distributed memory architectures: garbage collection is done *during the normal computation*, all unreferenced cells are immediately reclaimed and no separate collection phase (eventually involving the whole network) is necessary. Morover, it is also rather memory efficient only requiring an overhead of a few bits per reference.

The basic idea of this method is to associate to each reference a *weight* and to each tuple a *reference count*. The algorithm then always maintains the invariant

> **The reference count of a tuple is equal to the sum of the weights of all references to it.**

This ensures that, if a tuple is not referenced any more, its reference count drops to zero which signals that the tuple space may be reclaimed.

In detail, this algorithm works as follows (see Figure 7):

- **Allocating Tuples:** If a new tuple is allocated, the tuple is given some reference count that is a power of two. The binary logarithm of this count is stored as the weight in the new reference that is returned as the result of the allocation request.

- **Deleting References:** If a reference is not used any more, it is deleted by sending a *decrement message* to the memory unit that holds the referenced tuple. The reference count of the tuple is then decreased by the weight of the deleted reference (taken to the power of two). If the count drops to zero, the tuple may be reclaimed.

- **Duplicating References:** If a reference is duplicated, both of the copies get half of the weight of the original reference. Since weights are stored as their binary logarithms, this means to decrease the weight field by one.

  However, if the weight would drop to zero, the reference must not immediately be copied: first, an *increment request* has to be sent to the memory unit that contains

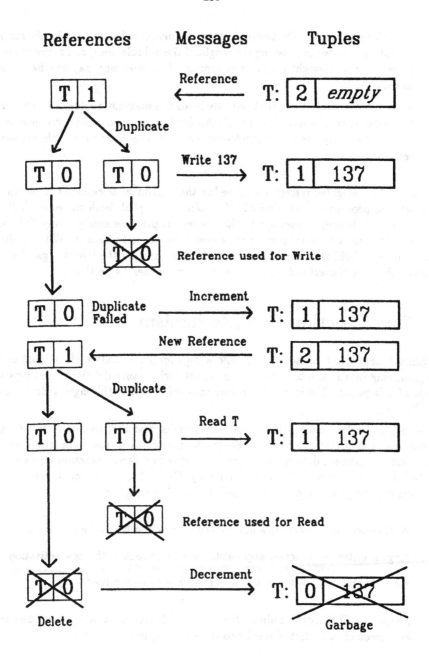

Figure 7: The Garbage Collection Mechanism

the referenced tuple. The reference count of this tuple is increased by the maximum weight minus one (considering the weight of the old reference) and a new reference is returned with a weight set to its maximum. This reference may now be duplicated as usual.

If the reference count of a tuple already holds the maximum value to be represented, this value is considered as "infinity". All further increment and decrement requests will not have any effect on the reference count any more and the tuple will never be reclaimed.

The use of this weighted reference scheme has the additional advantage that communication between processors is minimized: If a pointer is copied, both copies get half of the original weight, hence, no message to the involved tuple is necessary. Only if the weight decreases to zero, a memory request for a new reference is to be sent. With an eight bit reference count field and a two bit reference weight (storing the binary logarithm of the weight), the overall overhead for garbage collection is then neglectible.

6 The Function Call Mechanism

A general description of how to compile a high-level declarative (functional or logic) programming language into code for the ADAM architecture definitely goes beyond the scope of this paper. The interested reader may refer to the still ongoing diploma thesis [Loidl, 1991].

However, for understanding the operation principles and the benefits of the ADAM architecture, it is important to know about the function call mechanism that serves as the interface betweeen data-driven execution (between different function activations) and control-driven execution (within an activation). Generally, the compilation of a function call requires the generation of ADAM code for the following tasks:

1. **Activation:** a request for a new function activaton has to be submitted;

2. **Arguments:** the function arguments have to be sent to the new activation;

3. **Result:** the result value of the activation has to be received.

For example, a call $f(a, b)$ of a binary function f with arguments a and b will be compiled into some piece of code that is similar to the following one:

```
i:        call    f
i + 1:    recv    r, m
i + 2:    recv    s, i + 3
i + 3:    split   j, k

j:        wait    e₀, j + 1
j + 1:    send    a, r₃, 0
j + 2:    jump    k + 2

k:        wait    e₁, k + 1
k + 1:    send    b, r₃, 1
k + 2:    wait    e₂, n
```

There are **three concurrent threads of control** that enter the code at addresses i, j and k, respectively:

- **The 'f' thread:** The first thread enters at address i as soon as it becomes certain that the result of f is required and hence a new function activation has to be created. By executing the call instruction at address i, a request message is submitted to some processor in the network that will eventually start a new activation of f. However, the actual thread is interrupted immediately after having submitted the request.

- **The 'a' thread:** The next thread enters at address j as soon as the value of the first argument of f has become available in register a. However, the thread immediately encounters a wait e_0 statement and is therefore blocked.

- **The 'b' thread:** Similarly, the last thread enters at address k as soon as the value of the second argument of f has been computed into register b. The synchronization statement wait e_1 will block this thread, too.

The request message sent by the first thread will cause some processor in the network to create a new activation of f and start a thread in this activation (see the explanation below). However, the processor will immediately return the descriptor of this new f activation to the caller. The caller receives this descriptor by the recv statement at address $i + 2$ into register s and starts a new thread there.

This thread is split at address $i + 3$ into two parallel threads starting at addresses j and k. At these points, the threads are synchronized by wait instructions with the corresponding threads that have computed the argument values a and b, respectively. Each argument value is independently sent by a send instruction to the new f activation. Finally, both threads synchronize themselves by the wait at address $k + 2$.

Eventually, f will compute its result value and return it to the caller. The caller receives the value by the recv instruction at address $i + 1$ and continues execution by a new thread starting at address m.

The whole code block above is exited by **two concurrent threads of control:**

- **The result thread:** This thread starting at address m signals that the result of the function call has been delivered into register r. Any successor instruction in this thread can rely on this.

- **The argument thread:** The second thread at address n signals that both argument values a and b have been submitted. This thread is necessary, because it is possible that a function returns a proper result even if not all arguments have yet been submitted to that function (see the explanation below).

While the first exit thread delivers the result of the function activation, the second one is necessary in order to detect when all outstanding arguments have been received and all instructions have properly executed. Only then the actual function activation may be terminated.

The reader may wonder, why in this function call mechanism separate concurrent threads are used to activate a function and to submit its arguments. The reason for this is the **non-strict semantics** of the language that we have in mind for programming the ADAM architecture. Consider e.g. the function definition

$$f(a, b) = \quad 0, \text{ if } a > 0$$
$$b, \text{ else}$$

On a function call $f(1, b)$, we need not know the value of b in order to determine the result of f, i.e. f is *non-strict* in its second argument. Operationally spoken, the execution of f may start and perform some sensible operations (namely the test $a > 0$) while the value of b is still under computation. Generally, during the evaluation of expressions of the form $f(g(x))$, the execution of f may go on *in parallel* with the execution of g.

This form of *vertical parallelism* (i.e. the parallel execution of nested function calls) is complementary to the better known *horizontal parallelism* (i.e. the parallel evaluation of function arguments) but can be only exploited in languages with non-strict semantics: in such languages, the execution of a function must *not* wait for the values of its arguments but proceed in an independent fashion.

The above piece of code just implements the non-strict semantics of a function call with the activation of a function being handled by a separate thread that runs in parallel with the threads that are in charge of the parallel argument evaluation. However, optimizations may detect cases in which this general form of function call is superfluous and then synchronize the function thread with the argument threads *before* the function body starts to execute.

7 Implementation

Our work on the ADAM architecture is part of the project "ADAM & EVE" dealing with the prototype implementation of the non-strict functional programming language EVE

Program	Input	1T / 2W Ring	2T / 2W Ring	4T / 4W Full	8T / 8W Chordal Ring	16T / 16W Torus
FIBO	20	54(1.0)	28(1.9)	16(3.3)	10(5.4)	7(7.7)
PRIMES0	2000	302(1.0)	163(1.8)	93(3.2)	59(5.1)	41(7.4)
PRIMES1	10000	237(1.0)	127(1.9)	88(2.7)	65(3.7)	51(4.6)

Figure 8: Several ADAM Benchmarks

[Schreiner, 1990] on conventional parallel hardware using principles of dataflow architectures. While the EVE compiler is still under implementation, the implementation of the ADAM concept has already been finished:

The target hardware consists of a distributed memory multiprocessor containing 16 INMOS T800 transputers that may be dynamically configured to the desired topology. On this system, a simulator for the ADAM concept has been implemented in the OCCAM2 language. This simulator is organized in such a way that each transputer simulates one ADAM module where the components of the module (arbiter, processor, memory unit and their subcomponents) are implemented as processes concurrently executing on the same physical processor.

For debugging and testing purposes, a PC-based ADAM assembler has been implemented generating ADAM machine programs from manually written ADAM assembly programs. In the final system, the compiler will generate this assembly code from programs written in the EVE language.

Using the assembler, several test programs have been hand-coded and show rather promising speedups. Some of the results are listed in Figure 8. Each column of the table represents one particular processor configuration with the number of transputers (T) used, the number of worker modules (W) simulated and the topology of the transputer network listed above. Each item in the table denotes the elapsed time in seconds, the values in parentheses denote the relative speedups achieved.

The performance of the implementation has been tested with the benchmark programs FIBO (a doubly recursive fibonacci number generator), PRIMES0 (a prime number generator using lots of intermediate lists) and PRIMES1 (a prime number generator making use of the concept of difference lists). The efficiency (speedup/processor ratio) ranges in both of the first test programs from more than 90 % to about 45 %. From these results, we are not yet able to estimate the influence of the processor topology on the results. The third test program shows significantly lower speedups, which is propbably a consequence of the load balancing which is not yet satisfactory.

8 Future Work

Our future work on this project will concentrate on three aspects:

1. **The EVE Compiler** is currently under implementation and will be finished until the summer of 1991. When the first prototype is available, we will be able to write bigger programs and learn more about the dynamical behaviour of the ADAM architecture.

2. **Symbolic Algorithms:** One of the main goals of our work is to detect the suitability of the dataflow concept for purposes of symbolic computation (computer algebra, automated theorem proving, computational geometry, ...). We will therefore implement some symbolic algorithms in use at our institute in the EVE language and learn about the behaviour of this class of applications on our system.

3. **Optimizations:** From the results of these experiments, we will probably be able to optimize and maybe partially redesign the ADAM concept in order to avoid several possible bottlenecks. Moreover, we will experiment with different code generation strategies in the compiler to detect the actual sources of parallelism in declarative programs.

Moreover, the author currently investigates a possible topic for his Ph.D. thesis to which the findings of the ADAM concept might lead [Schreiner, 1991b]: The idea is to restrict the extensive ADAM runtime system that supports the main features of dataflow architectures and interpretes an abstract machine code to a minimal set of high-level functions that can be added to any sequential language (e.g. C). A compiler could then translate a declarative language to this explicitly parallel imperative form.

The result would be a highly portable system consisting of a compiler generating standard C code and a few machine-dependent functions that have to be rewritten for each parallel back-end. In this sense, the dataflow style of programming could be also efficiently supported on conventional parallel architectures which would certainly help to make its features and advantages more widely known and used.

References

[Arvind et al., 1987] Arvind, Rishiyur S. Nikhil, and Keshav K. Pingali. I-Structures: Data Structures for Parallel Computing. Computation Structures Group Memo 269, Laboratory for Computer Science, Massachusetts Institute of Technology, Cambridge, MA, February 1987. Also in: Proceedings of the Workshop on Graph Reduction, Los Alamos, New Mexico, September 28 – October 1, 1986.

[Bevan, 1987] D.I. Bevan. Distributed Garbage Collection Using Reference Counting. In *Proceedings of PARLE, Parallel Architectures and Languages Europe, Volume 2: Parallel Languages*, pages 176–187, Eindhoven, The Netherlands, June 15–19, 1987. Volume 259 of Lecture Notes in Computer Science, Springer, Berlin.

[Gurd et al., 1985] J. R. Gurd, C. C. Kirkham, and I. Watson. The Manchester Prototype Dataflow Computer. *Communications of the ACM*, 28(1):34–52, January 1985.

[Hiraki et al., 1984] Kei Hiraki, Toshio Shimada, and Kenji Nishida. A Hardware Design of the SIGMA-1, a Data Flow Computer for Scientific Computations. In *Proceedings of the 1984 International Conference on Parallel Processing*, pages 524–531. IEEE Computer Society, August 1984.

[Iannucci, 1988] Robert Alan Iannucci. A Dataflow / von Neumann Hybrid Architecture. Technical Report MIT/LCS/TR-418, Laboratory for Computer Science, Massachusetts Institute of Technology, Cambridge, MA, May 1988.

[Loidl, 1991] Hans Wolfgang Loidl. A Compiler for the Programming Language EVE. Master's thesis, RISC-Linz, Johannes Kepler University, Linz, Austria, 1991. To appear.

[Papadopoulos and Culler, 1990] Gregory M. Papadopoulos and David E. Culler. Monsoon: An Explicit Token-Store Architecture. In *The 17th International Symposium on Computer Architecture*, pages 82–91, Seattle, Washington, May 28–31, 1990. IEEE. Volume 18, Number 2 of ACM SIGARCH Computer Architecture News, June 1990.

[Peyton Jones, 1987] Simon L. Peyton Jones. *The Implementation of Functional Programming Languages*. Prentice-Hall, New York, 1987.

[Schreiner, 1990] Wolfgang Schreiner. ADAM & EVE — An Abstract Dataflow Machine and Its Programming Language. Master's thesis, Johannes Kepler University, Linz, Austria, October 1990. Also: Technical Report 90-42.0, RISC-Linz, Johannes Kepler University, Linz, Austria, 1990. Also: Technical Report 91-1, Austrian Center for Parallel Computation, January 1991.

[Schreiner, 1991a] Wolfgang Schreiner. ADAM — An Abstract Dataflow Machine and Its Transputer Implementation. In *Distributed Memory Computing, 2nd European Conference, EDMCC2*, pages 392–401, Munich, Germany, April 22–24, 1991. Volume 487 of Lecture Notes in Computer Science, Springer, Berlin. Also: Technical Report 90-53, RISC-Linz, Johannes Kepler University, Linz, Austria, November 1990. Also: Technical Report 91-3, Austrian Center for Parallel Computation, January 1991.

[Schreiner, 1991b] Wolfgang Schreiner. Macro-Dataflow in C. In *2. Scientific Meeting of the Austrian Center for Parallel Computation (ACPC)*, Wilhelminenberg Castle, Vienna, Austra, March 8–9, 1991.

PARALLEL COMPUTATION MODEL FOR PARALLEL PROLOG

Roman Blasko
Institute of Technical Cybernetics, SAS
Dubravska cesta 9, CS 842 37 Bratislava
Czecho-Slovakia
tel.(+427)374703, telex:093355,
fax:(+427)376045 or 281361

ABSTRACT

A new parallel computation model for logic programs is
described. A parallel logic programming language Parallel
Prolog has been considered as a high level language. A
data-flow model is a theoretical background of our
computation model. Owing to this the model is asynchronous
and utilizes innate kinds of parallelism for a highly
parallel all solution strategy in logic programs. We have
designed new basic operators for Parallel Prolog supporting
OR and AND-stream parallelism. We have designed an abstract
parallel machine with distributed structure memory, which is
based on data-flow principles. Basic formats of a data-flow
instruction, operand and structure memory cell are
introduced. A special operator for head unification, calling
the first and other body literals, for completion of the
clause body, for processing of the facts, built-in predicates
and output of results have been designed. A stream, an
asynchronous data structure, is used as a communication
channel between body literals. A data structure called a
template is used for selection of the goal terms for calling
of each body literal. A parallel logic program in the form
of the data-flow program graph generated by the compiler is
introduced as a simple example of the complete program. The
designed model will be implemented by its introduced abstract
machine. Owing to larger operator granularity this new model
has much lower requirements for a communication overhead in
comparison with our previous fine grain version.

1 INTRODUCTION

The programming language Prolog [6] is the main representative of logic programming languages. The main sources of parallelism in Prolog based programming languages are the following. OR parallelism is used if the given goal is unifiable with several heads of the clauses simultaneously. AND parallelism is used by parallel processing of the body literals. Unification or term parallelism is utilized by parallel unification of all terms in the goal and head of the clause. AND-stream parallelism is implemented when clauses or body literals are processed in a pipeline way.

Several Prolog-based parallel logic programming languages have been designed so far, which can be divided to two main classes. The first class is based on "committed choice" designed for control of parallelism. The main representatives are GHC (Guarded Horn Clauses) [12], Concurrent Prolog [10] and Parlog [5]. The second class is based on "pure parallelism", which is utilized as an innate property of Prolog. This class is closer to the standard Prolog [1,3,9]. Also Parallel Prolog considered in our project is a representative of this class. The language Parallel Prolog uses an all solutions strategy and does not use a cut operator and backtracking. The OR parallelism is utilized implicitly. Clauses can be processed in AND sequential or AND parallel way. This is determined by special operators (, - sequential, // - parallel) between body literals specified by a programmer. The AND-stream parallelism is a matter of implementation and due to this fact it will be mentioned by a description of the designed computation model.

We have developed a computation model for Parallel Prolog and an experimental parallel inference machine DAFIM (DAta-Flow Inference Machine) [4]. This model was a fine grain version exploiting all sources of parallelism in logic programs. The model was based on a data-flow computation model [11] and ideas from [8]. An architecture of the DAFIM machine is based on Transputers [7]. After thorough evaluation of the mentioned machine we have developed a new model, which could be characterized as a large-grain version in comparison with the previous one. Diminishing of communication overhead was the main stimulation for development of the following new computation model.

The basic features of an abstract machine designed for this computation model are introduced in chap.2. Data paths in logic program are described in chap.3. New basic operators or primitives, which we have developed for Parallel Prolog are defined in chap.4. A logic program on an operator level of the abstract machine is described in chap.5. Future steps of our project are mentioned in concluding remarks.

2 ABSTRACT MACHINE

Our abstract machine is based on the data-flow (DF) computation model [11]. The basic features of the DF model are functionality and asynchrony. Basic functions or primitives developed for an intended high level language are called data-flow operators (instructions). A data-flow program graph (DF graph) is a useful graphical representation of the DF programs in which nodes represent the DF operators and directed arcs represent data dependencies between them. We have used principles of an unfolded interpreter [2] for multiple calls of the same operators and procedures.

The basic instruction format for our abstract machine is in Fig.1. An activity name (AN) is designed for dynamic data-flow interpreter and an operation code (OC) identifies the DF primitive implemented as a machine instruction. An operand fields (OP1, OP2) are for allocation of the operand values directly or pointers for data structures. A destination fields (D1, D2) are for specification of the next operators. The number of operands is one or two and the number of destinations is from zero to two in our case. The operand field (see Fig.2) is divided into a tag and value part. The tag consists of an attribute field and a type field. The attribute field and type field identify a type of the predicate term and a data type (integer, string, etc.) respectively. The attribute field distinguishes a nonground term, shared variable and structured data.

A structure memory of the machine is a functional block responsible for storing and management the structured data. A common address space of the structure memory is distributed into several physical modules working independently and asynchronously. The garbage collection mechanism is based on a reference counter method. The basic considered data structure is a list. The basic structure of the Lisp cell has been added by synchronizing bits R - Ready, P - Pending and RC - Reference Counter for the garbage collector. The basic format of the structure cell is in Fig.3. The stream (see Fig.4) is a dynamic asynchronous data structure used as a communication channel between the body literals or parent and descendant processes. A head item of the stream is a stream descriptor (SD) embodied by one mentioned structure cell (see Fig.3). The stream descriptor is fixed during whole life of the stream and is identified by a value ASD - Address of Stream Descriptor. It is composed of three basic fields. In this context the initial value of the RC - reference counter indicates a number of awaited solutions to be placed to the stream. The first and second value fields of the stream descriptor are called WDP - Waiting Data Pointer and STP - Stream Tail Pointer respectively. The RC counter is decremented by one after writing of each solution to the stream. The STP pointer is changing for indication the new attached solution as the last new cell in the stream. The WDP pointer includes a structure with a process identifier (IP), destination address to the next body operator (DEST) under a pointer P and a data output (Par and E) under a pointer PPar created by a clause body operator (see operator CALF and CALK in chap.4). A stream element (SEi) has two values (see Fig.4). The first value (PS'i) is a pointer to a compound solution and the second one (SEi+1) is the pointer to the next stream element or the end of the stream (fail). The compound solution has two parts. The first part (PSi) is a pointer to a pure solution (Si - list of solution) and the second part (PPar) is the mentioned waiting data output from the CALF or CALK operator.

3 DATA PATHS THROUGHOUT A CLAUSE

Now we consider only sequential data passing throughout a clause body. Let us have a simple example (see Fig.5). Data dependencies between the terms of the body literals are illustrated in a simple way in Fig.5a. A set of the literal terms can be considered as a list of the items e.g. [F,E,C,M] for the predicate ca(). It means that a list of the specified terms is "going in" the literal and the (same) list of the terms is "going out" the literal after

processing. It is supposed that proper instances of the
input variables have been found during processing of the
literal. After processing of the k-th body literal it is
necessary to prepare a set of the literal terms for the next
(k+1)th body literal. In general, after processing of the
k-th literal we have a list of the terms from the k-th
literal and a list of the terms from previous literal (-s)
which have not been processed in the k-th one. It means that
we have a list of the terms composed of two parts i.e. the
terms from the k-th literal and the list of the terms
bypassing the k-th literal (e.g. for predicate po() those
are [F,E] and [C,M], see Fig.5b). It is necessary to select
required terms for preparation of the literal terms for the
next (k+1)th literal. This preparation of the required terms
between each pair of the consecutive body literals and the
clause head is done by a selection procedure specified by a
term template (T - template) of each literal. A simple
example of the templates is in Fig.5b. The template is a
list of order numbers or new terms in the body sequence. The
number of template items is the same as the number of the
literal terms for the next literal. The order number in the
template indicates, which term should be selected for the
term list of the next literal. A place in the output term
list is determined by a position of the order number in the
template. Unselected terms from the input list will be
placed in the same order into the second output list of the
select procedure which will bypass the next (k+1)th literal
(e.g. for predicate po() those are [F,E,M] and [C], see
Fig.5b). A whole example of the input and output term lists
and term templates for each selection procedure in a clause
are introduced in Fig.5b. The last template in the clause
should return the terms in the same order as they are in the
clause head. The templates in the program are generated by a
compiler.

4 OPERATORS FOR PARALLEL PROLOG

Our approach to parallelization is based on a new
operator set developed particularly for this computation
model, likewise as in [8,9]. We have defined seven operators
for interpretation of Parallel Prolog programs. There is a
special operator for unification, two operators for calling
the body literals, an operator for the fact and built-in
predicate and a special operator used for an output of the

found solutions. The designed operators cover program constructs for OR and AND-stream parallel execution. The pure AND parallelism has not been considered yet.

UNIF operator (UNIFication) with two inputs and one output (see Fig.6a) is for the unification of the goal terms and the head terms of the clause. The goal terms (A) are received on the first input together with an address of the stream descriptor (ASD) created for collection of all solutions to be found for the clause. The head terms of the clause are placed as a constant on the second input of the operator (B). A list of the unified terms or their instances together with the binding environment for shared variables (C) and the mentioned value ASD are generated as an output of the operator. The binding environment (E) for each shared variable is a twotuple [shared variable, instance]. Other possible values of the environment are "nil" if there is no shared variable and "fail" for an unsuccessful unification. The input and output tokens have the following values: in1=ASD+A, in2=B, out=ASD+C.

CALF operator (CAL1 First) with two inputs and one output (Fig.6b) is for calling of the first body literal. The first input is a list composed of two basic items [template, initial value of the reference counter (RCo)]. The second input is a list composed of two items [ASD, unified head terms with the binding environment]. Two lists of the necessary (B) and unnecessary (D) terms with environment are selected by the template from the input token. A new stream for the solutions is created by generating the stream descriptor and its address ASD'. The address ASD' together with the list of the necessary terms (B) create the output from the operator. The list of the unnecessary terms and the environment (D), together with the activity name of the process (IP) and an address of the next operator (DEST) in the body are stored in the stream under the WDP pointer (see Fig.4). The input and output tokens have the following values: in1=T+RCo, in2=ASD+A, out=ASD'+B.

CALK operator (CAL1 K-th) with two inputs and one output (Fig.6c) is for calling any body literal besides the first one. The first input is the same as in the CALF operator. The second input has two parts [coming solution, WDP. pointer]. If the coming solution (A) is successful, then a check consistency procedure is carried out on the binding environment of the coming solution and the binding environment from the previous parts (under the WDP) and the proper reference counters are modified. Other functions of the operator are the same as in the CALF operator. The output token includes the address ASD' and a list of the terms for the called predicate definition (C). The operator also prepares the waiting structure (E) under the WDP pointer. An additional function of the CALK operator is a recursive call of the same body literal but for the next coming solution. The input and output tokens have the following values: in1=T+RCo, in2=A+B, out=ASD+C.

ASOL operator (Append SOLution) with two inputs (Fig.6d) is used in the end of the clause body. Its function is to write an obtained solution from the clause body into the stream of the solutions (an indirect output). The first input is a template (T) derived from the clause head. The second input has the same structure as in the CALK operator. The first part of the internal functions of this operator is the same as in the CALK operator. After the successful check consistency, the selection procedure is carried out with the template from the first input. Then the obtained solution is written to the stream for collection of all solutions from the clause and its RC counter is decremented by one. The input tokens have the following values: in1=T, in2=A+B. The operator is without an (explicit) output but its "hidden" output is generated to the stream of the solutions.

FACT operator with two inputs (see Fig.6e) is for total processing of the fact in the predicate definition. The inputs are the same as in the case of the UNIF operator (see above). The internal functions of this operator are composed of the UNIF operator functions and the last functions of the ASOL operator, i.e. writing a solution to the stream. Also this operator has the "hidden" output as the ASOL operator.

BIP operator (Built-In Predicate) with two inputs (see Fig.6f) is for total processing of the built-in predicate. The first input is the same as in the FACT or UNIF operator. The second input is a name of the built-in predicate. It comprises special procedures embodying the innate function of the given built-in predicate and functions common with UNIF and ASOL operator.

OUTS operator (OUTput of Solutions) with one input (see Fig.6g) is for sending the final solutions from the program to the output.

5 LOGIC PROGRAMS ON OPERATOR LEVEL

An operator level of the logic program corresponds to the data-flow program graph to be generated by the compiler. The DF graph for the logic program transformed from Parallel Prolog is composed of the defined DF operators (see chap.4). We will introduce a construction of the logic programs on this level by description of the simple example.

The Parallel Prolog program from Fig.7 is translated to the DF graph in Fig.8. The beginning and the end is created by the graph representing the query. A single literal query is composed of only one body literal. The DF graph of the query is composed of the CALF operator and OUTS operator. There is no template in the first CALF operator because of all terms of the query are received on the second input (A) of the operator. The initial activation name (inicol) of the program is received instead of the ASD on the second input too. The query terms are sent to the called predicate definition (A) and the obtained solutions (C) are transmitted to the OUTS operator for generation the final solutions (B).

The predicate "car" is defined by one clause with three body literals. The DF graph of the clause is composed of the following operators. The head unification procedure is represented by the UNIF operator with the first input (A) embodying an coming goal and the second input specifying the head terms (B1). An output (C1) calls the CALF operator for invocation the processing of the first body literal. The output (B2) of the CALF operator is directed to the predicate definition of the given first literal. The called predicate definition is composed of the two facts. The solutions found in the predicate definition are sent through the stream, used as an asynchronous communication channel, back to the clause (C2). Those are connected together with the waiting data (WDP) i.e. (D2). This compound token is sent to the next CALK operator for an invocation the next body literal. Every other body literal is invoked by the CALK operator. The second input of the CALK operator represents the coming solution from the previous literal (A3) and needed waiting data (B3). The output (ASD+C3) of the operator is sent to the predicate definition of the k-th literal. The found solutions (D3) are coming through the stream and are connected with additional waiting data (E3) under the WDP. This compound token is sent to the next operator. The CALK operator is called recursively for each coming operand (A3+B3). The CALK operator representing the invocation of the last body literal sends its result to the ASOL operator. The ASOL operator puts the solution to the stream of the clause and is called recursively for each coming solution from the clause body. Every obtained solution from the body literal calls the next body literal before receiving other solutions to be found. This mechanism allows the AND-stream parallelism. The definitions of the predicates "power", "type" and "paint" are specified by the similar DF graphs composed of the FACT operators. The goal (query) ":-car(F,E,red,M)" will generate three different solutions.

6 CONCLUSIONS

We have introduced the new parallel computation model for Parallel Prolog. The mechanism supports the OR and AND-stream parallelism. The OR parallelism is implicit. The AND-stream parallelism is an inherent property of the designed model. It utilizes asynchronous principles of the data-flow computation model and also should not be specified by an user. A pure AND parallelism was not considered yet. The granularity of the operators have been changed in such a way, that the number of independent operators is diminished about ten times for the same program in comparison with the previous version by rough estimation. A thorough evaluation will be carried out by simulation and real implementation.

C

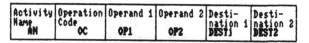

Fig.1 Basic instruction format

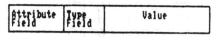

Fig.2 Operand format

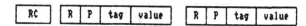

Fig.3 Structure cell format

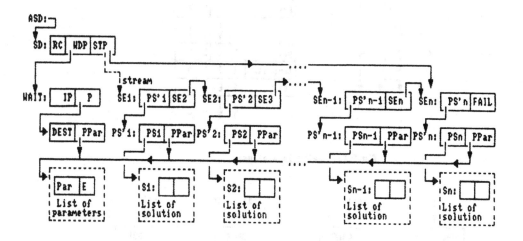

Fig.4 Structure of the stream

ca(F,E,C,M) :- po (F,E), ty (F,E,M), pa (F,C).

(query)

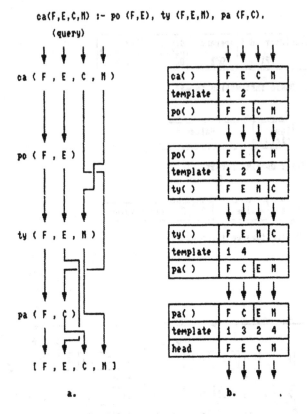

a.   b.

Fig.5 Data paths in a clause

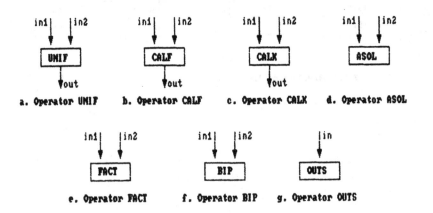

a. Operator UNIF   b. Operator CALF   c. Operator CALX   d. Operator ASOL

e. Operator FACT   f. Operator BIP   g. Operator OUTS

Fig.6 Data-flow operators for Parallel Prolog

```
          :- car(F,E,red,M)

car(Firm,Engine,Colour,Model):- power(Firm,Engine),
                                 type(Firm,Engine,Model),
                                 paint(Firm,Colour).

type(renault,1900,chamade).
type(renault,1900,fuego).
type(fiat,2000,tempra).

power(renault,1900).
power(fiat,2000).

paint(renault,red).         solutions:
paint(renault,blue).        [renault,1900,red,chamade]
paint(fiat,red).            [renault,1900,red,fuego]
paint(fiat,green).          [fiat,2000,red,tempra]
```

Fig.7   Parallel Prolog program

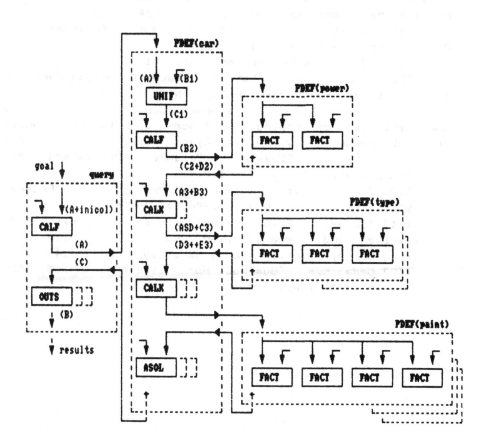

Fig.8 Complete data-flow graph

REFERENCES

[1] Ali K.A.M.: "OR-Parallel Execution of Prolog on BC-Machine", Proc. of the 5th Int. Conf. and Symposium on Logic Programming", 1988, pp. 1531-1545.

[2] Arvind, Gostelow K.P.: "The U-Interpreter", IEEE Computer, February 1982, pp. 42-49.

[3] Baron U. et al.: "The Parallel ECRC Prolog System PEPSys: An Overview and Evaluation Results", Proc. of the Int. Conference on Fifth Generation Computer Systems 1988, ICOT, 1988, pp. 841-850.

[4] Blasko R.: "Highly-parallel Computation Model and Machine for Logic Programming", Parallel Computing '89, D.J. Evans, G.R. Joubert, F.J. Peters (eds.), Elsevier Science Publishers B.V. (North-Holland), 1990, pp. 541-546.

[5] Clark K., Gregory S.: "PARLOG: Parallel Programming in Logic", RR DOC 84/4, Imperial College of Science and Technology, London, April 1984, 54 p.

[6] Clocksin W.F., Mellish C.S.: "Programming in Prolog", Springer-Verlag, 1984, 279 p.

[7] INMOS: The Transputer Family, 1986, 130p.

[8] Ito N. et al: "Data-flow Based Execution Mechanism of Parallel and Concurrent Prolog", NGC, 3 (1985), p. 15-41.

[9] Omara F.A., Jesshope C.R.: "A Parallel Implementation of Prolog for Process or Data Concurrency", Parallel Computing '89, D.J. Evans, G.R. Joubert, F.J. Peters (eds.), Elsevier Science Publishers B.V. (North-Holland), 1990, pp.411-418.

[10] Shapiro E.: "Concurrent Prolog: A Progress Report", IEEE Computer, August 1986, pp.44-58.

[11] Treleaven Ph.C., Brownbridge D.R., Hopkins R.P.: "Data-Driven and Demand-Driven Computer Architecture", Computing Surveys, Vol.14, No.1, March 1982, pp.93-143.

[12] Ueda K.: "Guarded Horn Clauses", TR-103, ICOT, Tokyo, July 1985, 12p.

APPLICATION OF CONNECTIONIST MODELS
TO FUZZY INFERENCE SYSTEMS

C. TOUZET & N. GIAMBIASI

LERI
(Laboratoire d'Etude et Recherche en Informatique)
Parc Scientifique Georges Besse
30000 Nîmes, FRANCE
Tel. : (+33) 66.38.70.29, Email : leri@frmop11.bitnet

Abstract

In this paper, we will try to shed light on the usefulness of neural networks by describing an application which combines connectionism and ruled-based systems. In the present fuzzy ruled production systems, propagation of uncertainty coefficients is carried out by means of computational formulae stemming from mathematical models of fuzzy reasoning. But the use of a formula provided by a general abstact model, and not intimately related to the application, can lead us to a fuzzy procedure not reflecting the fuzzy reasoning of the human expert. The connectionist approach proposed here solves this problem of fuzzy inference. An uncertainty propagation rule specific to the application domain is determined by learning from examples of fuzzy inferences.

Key words

Expert system - Production rule - Fuzzy inference - Connectionism - Backpropagation.

Introduction

Today, some people consider artificial neural networks as the panacea to all unresolved problems in artificial intelligence. Contrary to this, others describe a phenomenon of fashion without a future. The great majority do not take sides in the discussion, and are waiting for an answer to the principal question : What is the use of artificial neural networks? There are clearly other additional questions reflecting the curiosity of everyone: What are neural networks? How do they work? What are their applications? What are the practical problems of their use?

Since our goal is to answer these questions as well as possible, we will propose an illustrative utilisation of neural networks to resolve the problem of fuzzy inference. We have deliberately chosen to couple connectionism and artificial intelligence, fields often considered as competing, so as to prove that they are not exclusive of one another. The experiment is a typical example of a hybrid system [1] making the best use of the advantages of both fields. The objective is to provide more specific expert systems of the application domain which will then be more performant.

The first part will serve as a reminder of artificial neural networks. In particular, the mechanisms involved in the selection of a potential application will be specified. The connectionist construction will be illustrated in detail concerning the problem of fuzzy inference as expressed by expert systems. We will describe the results obtained for two well-known fuzzy inference rules, those of Lee and MYCIN.

1 Artificial neural networks

Connectionism is a fairly new discipline which proposes numerous models and definitions. Those interested in an extensive overview of the field may refer to [10], [8] and [3].

Definition :

It is useful to recall the scientific context at the origin of connectionnism. The central nervous system demonstrates the ability to process information which is far out of the reach of present-day computing techniques. The commonly admitted hypothesis is that brain-processing is linked to its structure. With the goal being to increase the abilities of computing systems, brain-like or brain-inspired computers have been under development for several decades now [12] [6]. Such models, inspired by the architecture and the processing of the central nervous system, are called artificial neural networks.

"Artificial neural networks are massively parallel interconnected networks of simple processing elements and their hierarchical organizations. These processing elements modelize a simple behaviour of the biological neuron."

Artificial neural networks have already achieved their goal in part by ehibiting properties such as learning by example, tolerance to faults in the network and to noise on the inputs and the possibility of parallel processing.

Subsequently, from among the one hundred of different connectionist models currently proposed [7], we will focus to supervised learning models.

Description :

Each simple processing element of the neural network exchanges information with the other connected elements by sending its activation level. The activation value of a cell is computed by a transfer function from the weighted sum of its inputs. The behaviour of the network is determined by the transfer functions of its elements, the topology and the connection weights. A neural model can also be completely described by the specifications of the following three elements:

- the processing element,
- the topology of the network,
- the learning algorithm.

The processing element is called alternately : elementary processor, cell, neuron or unit. Each cell computes its state using an activation function based on the information received. In the case of the model used here, the cell state is computed from the weighted sum of the inputs using a continuous function of the sigmoïdal type.

The topology of the network is described by the interconnection scheme of the processing elements. In this presentation, the network has a multi-layer architecture. Cells activated by at least one input are part of the input layer. Cells whose values are accessible constitute what is called the ouput layer. Since all the other cells have no connection to the outside, they are called hidden cells. All connection weights are variable.

The learning algorithm allows us to adapt the network behaviour to the application. With this end in mind, the network weights are adjusted so as to gear the network response to that desired for the learning examples. An example of this is an input pattern associated with an output pattern. The input pattern is coded as an activation vector on the input cells. The coding is the affectation operation beginning with the input pattern to the activation vector. According to custom, the input pattern is improperly confused with the activation vector of the input cells and, likewise, the output pattern with the activation vector of the ouput cells. The most widely used learning algorithm for multi-layer networks is the so-called gradient back-propagation technique.

The simulation of a neural model on a sequential computer imposes the selection of a mode for updating the cell states (synchronous or asynchronous, for example). The adopted simulation process is a priori independent of the network model. Nevertheless, it usually interacts with the observed performances and thus is most often implicitly associated with the model.

2 Application domains

Application domains are: pattern recognition, signal processing, diagnosis, etc. In fact, an application is considered potential if it can be represented as a mapping between two spaces and if there is a sufficient number of representative examples of the mapping.

It should be pointed out that until the gradient back-propagation algorithm became widely used (in 1985), realizable functions were restricted to linear functions [13]. This learning algorithm for multilayer networks allows us to consider non-linear problems, the most representative of which is the exclusive or. The Darpa [2] lists a certain number of demonstrative applications based on this paradigm.

The term "application" should however be used with care. As a matter of fact, one must distinguish between "candidate applications" which can, in principle, be solved by the connectionist technique , "developping applications" whose feasability has been demonstrated on a toy problem and "proven applications" which are not numerous.

Determining a potential application

Neural networks can be viewed as systems with learning abilities in mapping whatever the field may be. For example, le Cun [11] proposed the use of connectionist techniques to solve problems in medical diagnosis of emergency cases. In this experiment, the network mapped the input space of the symptoms with the output space of the diagnosis. The network learned the mapping function from a set of real cases (fig.1).

Determining a potential application is equivalent to trying to express a problem as a mapping function between two spaces and establishing a representative examples data base of the mapping behaviour. However it is not simply a question of selecting a potential application, one must also specify the network model best suited and most likely to solve the problem and its numerous parameters (number of neurons, number of layers, etc.).

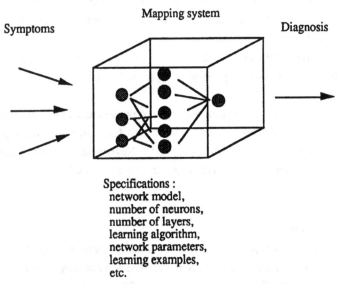

Specifications :
network model,
number of neurons,
number of layers,
learning algorithm,
network parameters,
learning examples,
etc.

Figure 1. Application for a problem in medical diagnosis

Approximation of a mathematical function or mapping by neural networks

Theorem [7] :

"Given any $\varepsilon > 0$ and any L_2 function $f : [0, 1]^n \to R^m$, there exists a three-layer back-propagation neural network that can approximate f to within ε mean squared error accuracy."

The space L_2 includes every function that could ever arise in a practical problem (continuous or discontinuous). It is important to realize that this theorem does not comment on the number of units in the hidden layer. On the other hand, if one hidden layer is a minimum, then, in practice, two or three layers are often used. Finally, although this theorem guarantees the ability of a multilayer network with the correct weights to accurately implement an arbitrary L_2 function, it does not give any idea regarding the learning law needed to compute these weights.

Nature of the developed applications

We have not yet described in precise terms the developed applications. For the great majority, these applications are purely connectionist. There are several reasons for this with the least justifiable being that the developer may not possess enough competency in the other domains to plan a coupling with more conventional techniques. Secondly, a purely connectionist development emphasizes the neural possibilities more advantageously. Last but not least, to couple classic and connectionist techniques is a difficult problem. However really interesting applications are to be found in this direction. Neural networks are have not been around long enough to be able to propose a complete solution. On the contrary, artificial intelligence exhibits real-world applications resulting from years of research and development. It seems opportune to try to involve neural networks in these systems, so as to generate hybrid systems. Our study falls into this framework. From among a certain number of unresolved problems in artificial intelligence, one has been selected for which we propose a connectionist solution.

3 One unresolved problem in artificial intelligence

In a rule-based system, the knowledge base is divided into two parts: the rule base and the fact base. The rule base contains knowledge expressed in the following form: If <condition> Then <action>. The inference engine is charged with executing the rules and facts. In simpler terms, its work consists in selecting and then applying rules whose left part agrees with the established facts. Generally in this kind of system, rules act as logic implications between propositions or predicates. Thus, reasoning is reduced to a succession of logic deductions. In certain applications, it is necessary to process unreliable, imprecise or incomplete knowledge. In such a case, we speak of fuzzy reasoning or, in more precise terms, non-exact reasoning.

Representation and processing of fuzzy knowledge

In the case of expert systems, the notion of fuzziness is generally modelized by introducing uncertainty coefficients taken in the real interval [0,1]. 0 means certainly fault, 1 means certainly true and intermediary values mean more or less true/false. These uncertainty coefficients are associated together with the established facts and the rules. We have at our disposition a weighting of the facts and of the deduction itself.

Fuzzy inference

Manipulation of fuzzy rules and facts results in several practical problems [4]. The propagation of uncertainty coefficients, also called fuzzy inference, may be summarized in the following question:

How can the uncertainty coefficients of a rule and its premise be combined in order to determine the uncertainty coefficient of its conclusion?

In order to combine uncertainty coefficients, current expert systems refer to computational formulae derived from mathematical models of fuzzy reasoning. In these formulae, the basic idea consists in using the following conventional equations:

$$UV \, (P \, \& \, Q) = \min [\, UV \, (P) , UV \, (Q) \,]$$
$$UV \, (P \vee Q) = \max [\, UV \, (P) , UV \, (Q) \,]$$
$$UV \, (\neg P) = 1 - UV \, (P)$$

where P, Q   indicate facts,
       UV   indicates the uncertainty measure (uncertainty value),
       &,v,¬ indicate the logic connectors AND, OR, NOT.

The problem regarding the propagation of the uncertainty coefficients (fuzzy inference) goes back to determining a function g such as:

$$UV \, (Q) = g \, (\, UV \, (P), UV \, (P \to Q))$$ for each rule P->Q of the system,

with:

UV (P->Q) = uncertainty coefficient of the rule P->Q,
UV (P) = uncertainty coefficient with which the condition P is established,
UV (Q) = uncertainty coefficient of the conclusion Q, to be determined.

In present expert systems, the function g is computed using a mathematical model of the fuzzy inference (for example, Lee's fuzzy inference) or built by the knowledge engineer (for example, as in the case of MYCIN). However, it is difficult to insure that the mechanism used reflects the expert's reasoning. In fact, we know of no mathematical models that we perfecly express fuzzy reasoning by humans. Moreover, a general mathematical model is a priori independent of both the application and the domain of expertise. This is not the case in the real world. An analysis of the formulae used clearly shows that they are, in large part, arbitrary. This remark is still valid when dealing with formulae designed by the knowledge engineer (cf. for example, the formula used in MYCIN).

Fuzzy inference is a mapping function between the uncertainty coefficients (UCs) of the premises and that of the rule with the uncertainty coefficient of the conclusion. When the uncertainty coefficients are numerical values of the real interval [0, 1], the fuzzy inference is a function $g : [0,1]^{n+1} \rightarrow [0,1]$ (n is the maximum number of premises).

4 Connectionist fuzzy inference

We propose using a neural network to approximate the fuzzy inference by learning from examples of fuzzy inference. If g is the function establishing the mapping between the uncertainty coefficients (UCs) of the premises and that of the rule with the UC of the conclusion, the learning examples given to the network will be vectors: (v1,v2...vn,vn+1,v0) with v0 = g (v1,v2...vn,vn+1). The values (v1,v2...vn) are those of the UCs of the premises.
The value vn+1 is that of the UC of the rule and v0 is the value of the UC of the conclusion. The learning law modifies the behaviour of the network f so it follows the behaviour described by the learning examples. We consider that the network has learned when the function f is equivalent to the function g.

Figure 2 shows schematically how to operate the learning on the network.

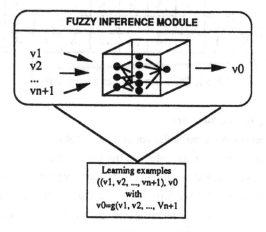

Figure 2. Learning of the fuzzy inference

5 Lee's fuzzy inference

Lee's fuzzy inference [9] is an example of a mathematical model of fuzzy inference. It is expressed by the following calculation:

$$UV(Q) = \begin{cases} [0, UV(P\text{->}Q)] & \text{if } UV(P\text{->}Q) = 1 - UV(P) \\ UV(P\text{->}Q) & \text{if } UV(P\text{->}Q) > 1 - UV(P) \\ \emptyset & \text{if } UV(P\text{->}Q) < 1 - UV(P) \end{cases}$$

For practical reasons, we have reduced the size of the problem by limiting to one the number of premises for the rules (n = 1) and by allowing only ten discrete values for the uncertainty value (p = 0.1).

Table 1 shows the UC of the conclusion UV (Q) computed from the UCs of the condition UV (P) and of the rule UV (P->Q) (to simplify the coding, we have replaced the interval [0, UV (P->Q)] by the single value UV (P->Q)).

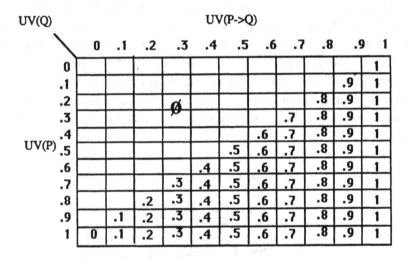

UV(Q) / UV(P)	UV(P->Q) 0	.1	.2	.3	.4	.5	.6	.7	.8	.9	1
0											1
.1										.9	1
.2				Ø					.8	.9	1
.3								.7	.8	.9	1
.4							.6	.7	.8	.9	1
.5						.5	.6	.7	.8	.9	1
.6					.4	.5	.6	.7	.8	.9	1
.7				.3	.4	.5	.6	.7	.8	.9	1
.8			.2	.3	.4	.5	.6	.7	.8	.9	1
.9		.1	.2	.3	.4	.5	.6	.7	.8	.9	1
1	0	.1	.2	.3	.4	.5	.6	.7	.8	.9	1

Table 1. Table showing Lee's fuzzy inference

Heuristic building of the network

Using a neural network for a particular application is not as easy as one might think. Indeed, today there neither rules nor formulae which allow the best possible selection of the numerous parameters of a network: input and ouput coding, network structure in terms of the number of units and number of layers, type of model, selection of the learning and test examples, etc. Everyone must make the most of the experience gained through developing previous applications, use his intuition and proced cautiously through trial and error.

Coding of the uncertainty coefficients

The input layer codes the UCs of both the n premises and of the rule. The output pattern represents the UC of the conclusion. The UCs are located in the intervalle [0,1]. With the aim to simplify, all uncertainty coefficient values are choose discrete. The UCs belong to the following set $\{0, 0.1, 0.2, ..., 1\}$. The fuzzy inference then becomes a function f: $\{0, 0.1, 0.2, ..., 1\}^{n+1} \rightarrow \{0, 0.1, 0.2, ..., 1\}$.

There are numerous coding possibilities for the UCs on the input layer [5]. The one we have selected is a thermometer coding for all values between [0, 1] and a special code for Ø (distant in the sense of the Hamming distance). It should be noted that this coding minimizes the Hamming distance between two neighbouring values. For instance, codes for 0.2 et 0.3 differ by only one unit value (the third from the left). On the contrary, distant values such as 0.2 et 0.9 differ by a larger number of cells (7). This coding is shown in table 2.

UV	Codage
0	1 1 1 1 1 1 1 1 1 1 1
.1	1 1 1 1 1 1 1 1 1 1 -1
.2	1 1 1 1 1 1 1 1 1 -1 -1
.3	1 1 1 1 1 1 1 1 -1 -1 -1
.4	1 1 1 1 1 1 1 -1 -1 -1 -1
...	
.9	1 1 1 -1 -1 -1 -1 -1 -1 -1 -1
1	1 1 -1 -1 -1 -1 -1 -1 -1 -1 -1
Ø	-1 1 1 1 1 1 1 1 1 1 1

Table 2. Uncertainty coefficient coding

Structure

A priori, the number of hidden layers is not specified. Theoretical results impose one hidden layer, however it is sometimes easier to obtain a solution using two or more hidden layer networks. On the other hand, if the number of units in the input and ouput layers is defined by the coding, it is not the case for the hidden layers. Due to our previous experience in that domain, we have obtained a satisfactory solution after a certain number of attempts. Resulting from this more or less intuitive process, the selected model is a 66-neuron, 1080-synapses, three-layer network. There are 24 cells in the input layer, 12 in the output layer and 30 cells in the hidden layer.

Learning examples

The network is trained using a set of examples which are presented repeatedly. A learning example is a pair, the uncertainty coefficients (UC) of the premises and the rule and the associated UC of the conclusion. Learning examples are randomly selected from all possible values. There are 121 examples that we distribute arbitrarily between the learning set and the test set. It is extremely important that the learning example represent the problem and, for this, be selected at random with a fixed probability density.

Table 3 shows a learning set and its associated test set.

UV(P) \ UV(Q)	0	.1	.2	.3	.4	.5	.6	.7	.8	.9	1
0											1
.1										.9	1
.2									.8	.9	
.3			∅					.7	.8	.9	1
.4							.6	.7	.8	.9	
.5						.5	.6	.7	.8	.9	1
.6					.4	.5	.6	.7	.8	.9	
.7				.3	.4	.5	.6	.7	.8	.9	1
.8			.2	.3	.4	.5	.6	.7	.8	.9	
.9		.1	.2	.3	.4	.5	.6	.7	.8	.9	1
1	0	.1	.2	.3	.4	.5	.6	.7	.8	.9	1

▓▓▓ : Learning examples (52), ☐ : Test examples (69)

Table 3. Learning and testing example bases

Learning

Before learning, network weights are set at random in the interval [-.3, .3]. The network response to an input vector (v1,v2) is of no importance. The gradient backpropagation algorithm modifies the connection weights iteratively so as to establish the mapping between the input vector and the desired output. For each presentation of an input vector, the network computes by propagation its ouput cell values. An error representing the difference between the obtained and the desired value is measured. This error is backpropagated and allows the algorithm to modify the weights in order to reduce the error.

Generalization : After the learning phase, we test the ability of the neural network to generalize, i. e. to give the correct answer for an unknown input vector by referring to the learning examples.

Results

The network has been implemented using the software SACREN [16]. It is a general event-driven neural network simulator for SUN or Apollo workstations. This simulator is written in C and Pascal and allows the description of all neural models. Procedures have been written to facilitate the learning process and the statistical analysis of performance. The network response is thresholded: all positive or zero values of an output cell are considered equal to 1 and all negative values are -1.

A learning trial is the presentation of all the learning examples to the network and the modification of all the weights by the learning algorithm. After 25 learning trials, a minimum has been obtained for the error value: all learning examples produce the desired output.

After the learning phase, the 81 unknown examples of the test base are presented to the network so as to measure the generalization performance. Figure 3 shows this performance in relation to the number of learning examples.

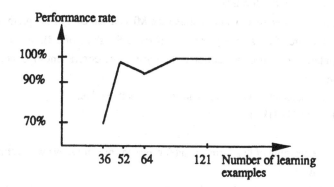

Figure 3. Impact of the number of learning examples on test performance

Generalization performance is deemed 72% effective when using 40 learning examples if the network response is considered true when equal to the correct value. If we accept an error value of 0.1 on the network response, then the generalization performance is 100%.

6 Fuzzy inference used in MYCIN

A second example which illustrates the capabilities of the connectionist approach concerns using examples to find the formula used in the well-known MYCIN system [15] for the propagation of UCs. This fuzzy inference is described by:

Let $R = F1 \& F2 \ldots \& Fn \rightarrow F$ be a coefficient rule UV (R); the coefficient associated to F is then defined by:

$$UV (F) = UV (R) \times v$$

with :

$$v = \begin{cases} w + UVp(F) - w \times UVp(F) & \text{if } w \geq 0 \text{ and } UVp(F) \geq 0 \\ w + UVp(F) + w \times UVp(F) & \text{if } w \leq 0 \text{ and } UVp(F) \leq 0 \\ (w + UVp(F))/1 - MIN(w, UVp(F)) & \text{if } -1 < w \times UVp(F) < 0 \\ 1 & \text{otherwise} \end{cases}$$

$$w = \begin{cases} MAX(UV (F1), \ldots UV (Fn)) & \text{if } UV (Fi) \leq -0.2 \text{ " i} \\ MIN(UV (F1), \ldots UV (Fn)) & \text{if } UV (Fi) \geq +0.2 \text{ " i} \\ 0 & \text{otherwise} \end{cases}$$

$$UVp(F) = \begin{cases} \text{Previous coefficient of F} & \text{if F is already deduced} \\ 0 & \text{otherwise} \end{cases}$$

It should be noted that in this formula:

- The computation of w attempts to establish the MIN of the UCs of the premises in absolute values (if the values are of the same sign and superior to a threshold of 0.2).

- The computation of v tries to reinforce the uncertainty coefficient of a fact if this fact is involved in several rules.

- The coefficient associated with the conclusion is something like:

$$UV (R) \times MIN (UV (Fi)).$$

With regards to the learning of this formula and for reasons of clarity, we will restrict the problem to the following case:

- Rules do not allow more than 2 premises: $n \leq 2$.

- Conclusions are inferred for the first time: $UVp(F) = 0$.

With these restrictions in place, the formula becomes:

$$UV (F) = UV (R) \times v$$

$$v = w = \begin{cases} MAX(UV (F1), UV (F2)) & \text{if } UV (F1) \leq -0.2 \text{ and } UV (F2) \leq -0.2 \\ MIN(UV (F1), UV (F2)) & \text{if } UV (F1) \geq +0.2 \text{ and } UV (F2) \geq +0.2 \\ 0 & \text{otherwise} \end{cases}$$

Network structure

The selected network is a 69-neuron, 1100-synapses, three-layer network. There are 33 cells in the input layer, 11 in the output layer and 25 cells in the hidden layer.

Example base

The uncertainty coefficients belong to the set {-1, -.6, -.3, -.2, -.1, 0, .1, .2, .3, .6, 1}, so there are 1331 possible behavioural examples of the fuzzy inference rule. Learning examples are chosen at random.

Results

Figure 4 shows performance in relation to the number of learning examples.

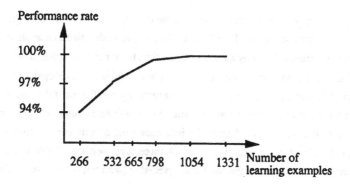

Figure 4. Impact of the number of learning examples
on the performance of the MYCIN fuzzy inference

665 learning examples are sufficient to allow a 100% performance rate when a deviation of 0.1 from the exact value of the output is tolerated.

7 Discussion

Performances have been presented in terms of the number of learning examples, with the goal being to illustrate the generalization capabilities of a neural network. We are seeking the minimum density of learning examples which allow a good performance in generalization. It is clear that this value is strongly connected to the nature of the function described by the examples (in our case, fuzzy inferences: Lee or MYCIN).

Only the case of rules with one or two premises has been processed here. Practical problems alone limit the application to multi-premis rules:

1) The number of input neurons increases in relation to the number of premises.

2) The size of the learning base grows in relation to the number of premises n and the selected precision p of a factor equal to n/p.

3) Increasing the precision is also expressed by an increase in the number of neurons, more or less linearly.

As a matter of fact, the practical implementation of our connectionist module of incertainty propagation in a real system comes up against the problem which is posed by the variable number of premises. Even if we fix a priori an upper limit to the number of premises, how tshould rules having a variable number of premises be handled? An expensive solution, in terms of the neuron number, consists in building a network for each case.

8 Conclusion

We hope that we have provided some answers to the questions put forth in the introduction of this paper. Concerning the usefulness of neural networks, we have described an application which allows fuzzy expert systems to learn by experience and thus to be better adapted to the application domain. A method based on connectionist networks and gradient backpropagation has been proposed to set up the computational formula for the uncertainty coefficient of the conclusion from the uncertainty coefficients of the premise and the rule. Starting from examples of fuzzy inferences, the network learns to behave as according to the inference rule, despite the fact that no rule has been explicitly programmed in the neural network. A three-layer network is able to learn how to compute the uncertainty coefficient of the conclusion precisely (with respect to level of discreteness adopted) for learned examples. In the case of unknown examples, this network is able to generalize correctly.

The proposed solution can be envisaged in two cases:
- If the knowledge engineer (+ possibly the expert) is able to find by trial and error the uncertainty propagation formula (as we suppose was the case for the MYCIN system), we can then foresee determining a formula by learning which is reasonably close in nature and free the knowledge engineer from this problem.
- If the knowledge engineer (+ possibly the expert) is not able to find such a formula, we can try to find it by learning from examples formulated by the expert.

With the same aim of evaluating the usefulness of neural networks, we can cite the coupling between a connectionist model and a classical theorem demonstrator that makes it all the more pertinent [14], in this work.

9 References

[1]   B. Amy, A. Giacometti & A. Gut, "Modèles connexionnistes de l'expertise," Neuro-Nimes 90, Nimes, France, EC2 Eds., pp 99-119, November 1990.
[2]   "DARPA Neural network Study," AFCEA International Press, 1988.

[3] J. Dayhoff, "Neural Networks Architectures," Van Nostrand Reinhold, 1990.

[4] N. Giambiasi, R. Lbath & C. Touzet, "Une approche connexionniste pour calculer l'implication floue dans les systèmes à base de règles", Neuro-Nîmes 89, Nîmes, France, EC2 Eds, November 1989.

[5] P. Handcock, "Data representation in neural nets: an empirical study," Proc. of the 1988 Connectionist Models Summer School, D. Touretzky & al. Eds, Morgan Kaufmann Publishers, 1988.

[6] D. O. Hebb, The Organization of Behaviour," New-York : Wiley, 1949.

[7] R. Hecht-Nielsen, "Neurocomputing," Addison-Wesley, pp. 132, 1989.

[8] K. Karna and D. Breen, "An artificial neural networks tutorial: part 1-Basics," The International Journal of Neural Networks Research and Applications, Vol. 1, No. 1, pp 4-23, January 1989.

[9] A. Kaufmann, "Nouvelles logiques pour l'Intelligence Artificielle", Ed. Hermès, 1987.

[10] T. Kohonen, "An introduction to neural computing", Neural Networks, Vol. 1, No. 1, pp 3-16, 1988.

[11] Y. Le Cun, "Modèles connexionnistes de l'apprentissage," Thèse de Doctorat, Université Paris 6, July 1987.

[12] W. S. McCulloch & W. Pitts, "A logical calculus of the ideas immanent in nervous activity," Bulletin of Mathematical Biophysics 5, pp 115-133, 1943.

[13] M. L. Minsky & S.A. Papert, "Perceptrons," Expanded Edition, MIT Press, 1988.

[14] C. Suttner & W. Ertel, "Using back-propagation for guiding the search of a theorem prover," The International Journal of Neural Networks Research and Applications, Vol. 2, No. 1, pp 3-16, March 1991.

[15] E. Shortliffe, "Computer-Based Medical Consultations : MYCIN", American Elsevier, N.Y., 1976.

[16] C. Touzet, SACREN : Système d'Aide au Choix d'un Réseau de Neurones, Rapport final du contrat ANVAR n° A8801006, juillet 1989.

CHCL - A Connectionist Inference System

Steffen Hölldobler

FG Intellektik, FB Informatik
TH Darmstadt
Alexanderstraße 10
D-6100 Darmstadt
Germany
steffen@intellektik.informatik.th-darmstadt.de

Franz Kurfeß

International Computer Science Institute
1947 Center Street
Suite 600
Berkeley, CA 94704
USA
kurfess@icsi.Berkeley.edu

Abstract

CHCL is a Connectionist inference system for Horn logic which is based on the Connection method and uses Limited resources. This paper gives an overview of the system and its implementation.

1 Introduction

No matter which definition of intelligent behavior one favors, the ability to draw conclusions from well-established facts certainly plays an important role. The formalization of this reasoning process has been the major goal in mathematical logic, leading to the development of various languages and calculi to express and formally compute the truth of statements. Automated inference systems based on predicate logic or derivatives and extensions thereof allow the computation of the truth of statements once these statements have been formulated. In this paper we present an inference system CHCL based on the connection method, a framework of calculi for the evaluation of predicate logic formulae. The execution of CHCL relies on connectionist techniques, giving rise to the exploitation of massive parallelism on one hand while opening the door towards the treatment of uncertain, incomplete and inconsistent information on the other hand.

The application of connectionist techniques to higher-level cognitive tasks such as reasoning has been suffering from a certain inadequacy in the representations used. The ease and elegance with which symbolic manipulation techniques are applied to dynamically changing data structures in conventional processing paradigms has not yet been matched with connectionist means (see [Güsgen and Hölldobler, 1991] in this book). One particular problem with respect to logic is the treatment of variable bindings; although some proposals to solve this problem have been made (see eg. [Ballard, 1986; Touretzky and Hinton, 1988; Shastri and Ajjanagadde, 1990b]), their integration into a logical framework is not fully satisfying. The approach proposed within CHCL relies on a full-fledged, distributed unification algorithm which computes the most general unifier for a set of terms [Hölldobler, 1990b]. The time required is linear to the size of the terms in the worst case, and constant (two steps) for important special cases like the word or the matching problem. The drawback of the algorithm is that it requires a number of nodes quadratic to the size of the terms in the worst case. The overall strategy pursued by CHCL is to identify so-called spanning matings in the formula under investigation, which represent potential alternative solutions. In order to really constitute a solution, the terms in these candidate matings have to be unifiable.

This article gives an overview of CHCL and its implementation. It is not concerned with technical details. They can be found in [Hölldobler, 1990a] and [Kurfeß, 1991b]. CHCL is based on Bibel's [1987] connection method and determines whether a set of Horn clauses is unsatisfiable. Therefore, we introduce the connection method for sets of Horn clauses in the following section 2. To avoid possible confusion between the connection method and a connectionist realization of the connection method, we will be very precise about the use of the word *connection*. A *connection* consists of a positive literal $P(t_1, \ldots, t_n)$ and a negative literal $\neg P(s_1, \ldots, s_n)$ with the same predicate symbol. In a figure literals defining a connection are connected by a curve. If in a connectionist network a unit directly excites or inhibits another unit, then there is a *link* between these units. Hence, *connection* always refers to the connection method and *link* refers to a connectionist network.

Section 3 gives an overview of the structure of CHCL and brief description of how a formula is represented and how queries are answered. A central part of each deductive system is the unification computation. In CHCL there is no restriction on the syntactic form of Horn clauses. Hence, the structured connectionist unification algorithm built into CHCL must be able to unify arbitrary first-order terms. This algorithm is presented in section 4. To prove the unsatisfiability of a given formula, we have to identify an appropriate set of connections (eg. [Stickel, 1987]). Bibel [1987] calls such sets of connections *spanning matings*. A spanning mating defines a proof iff all connected literals are simultaneously unifiable. In CHCL the spanning matings are computed one at a time and this process is described in section 5. As soon as a mating is selected all unification problems are solved in parallel. Section 6 presents the reduction techniques built into CHCL. These include the evaluation of isolated connections [Bibel, 1988] as well as the removal of nonunifiable or useless connections. In section 7 we modify CHCL such that binary constraint satisfaction problems can be solved efficiently. CHCL is currently been implemented at the International Computer Science Institute in Berkeley. Section 8 gives an account of this implementation. Finally, we conclude by outlining future work in section 9.

2 The Connection Method

The connection method is a formalism to compute the relations between different statements in a first-order language [Bibel, 1987]. It employs the propositional structure of a formula, which is defined by the various connections of the formula. A *connection* consists of a positive and a negative literal having the same predicate symbol. The central concept is a *spanning mating*, which is a set of connections such that the connections define a proof for the propositional structure of the formula. A proof for the first-order formula is obtained from a spanning mating if all connected atoms are simultaneously unifiable, in which case the mating is said to be *complementary*.

We have chosen the connection method since it allows for a global treatment of the whole search space, which – as we believe – is one of the main requirements for the development of massively parallel inference systems and intelligent global strategies. The method also separates the structure of a proof from the computation of the corresponding unifiers, which not only leads to a massively parallel computation of those unifiers but also allows the process of finding a proof to concentrate on the essential features of the given formula.

To illustrate the connection method (and its connectionist realization in the following sections) we consider a (simplified) program segment taken from the L_0 project at the International Computer Science Institute [Weber and Stolcke, 1990]. This project constitutes a recent effort in Cognitive Science to build a natural language aquisition system for a limited visual domain. The segment considered herein deals with spatial reasoning, namely the question of whether there is a circle X above a dark object Y.

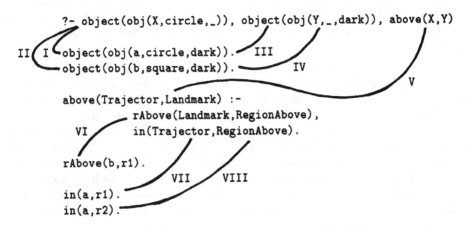

In the visual scene shown in figure 1 we find a dark circle a and a dark square b. We know that a trajector is above a landmark if the trajector is in the region which is above the landmark. To keep the example small we simply assume that r_1 is the region above the object b and that object a is in the striped region r_1 as well as in the dotted region r_2, whereas the simulation in [Weber and Stolcke, 1990] provides further rules for the predicates rAbove and in to describe these regions. The structure of the formula is given by the connections I to VIII. There are the eight spanning matings

```
{ I,       III,       V, VI, VII         },
{ I,       III,       V, VI,      VIII },
{ I,             IV, V, VI, VII         },
{ I,             IV, V, VI,      VIII },
{     II, III,       V, VI, VII         },
{     II, III,       V, VI,      VIII },
{     II,         IV, V, VI, VII         },
{     II,         IV, V, VI,      VIII }
```

defined by the various alternatives to solve subgoals which are engaged in more than one connection. But only the third mating $\{I, IV, V, VI, VII\}$ is complementary and yields the bindings $\{X \mapsto a, \ Y \mapsto b\}$ for the variables occurring in the initial query.

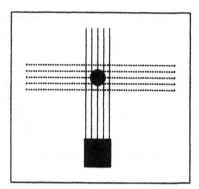

Figure 1: A dark circle a is above a dark square b and is in the striped and dotted regions.

3 An Overview of CHCL

CHCL uses Bibel's connection method. It generates systematically the spanning matings of a given formula one by one and unifies all connected atoms simultaneously. But CHCL is also a purely structured connectionist system in the sense of Feldman and Ballard [1982]. There is no central control or memory. The computing elements are simple neuron-like units which perform thresholding operations. They are interconnected through a network of weighted links, whose structure is determined by the given formula. The network is activated by clamping on certain inputs units. The activation is spread through the network until certain output units are activated indicating whether a proof of the formula has been found or not.

Figure 2 gives an overview of CHCL. The terms of the formula are represented in the term layer and the connections of the formula are represented in the connection layer. The computation starts by externally activating the ?-unit. This will cause the spanning set layer to output the next spanning mating. Consequently, activation from the spanning set layer will spread through the connection layer and into the unification layer, where the connected atoms (viz. the corresponding terms) are simultaneously unified. More precisely, they are unified over the domain of rational trees [Colmerauer, 1982]. If the user wants to unify the terms over the domain of finite trees, then she or he has to activate the occur check request unit OCR, which will cause an occur check to be performed in the occur check layer. Depending on the outcome of the unification either the Yes or No unit will be activated. Repeated activations of the ?-unit will cause the system to generate and test new spanning matings until an active AG unit indicates that all spanning sets were generated.

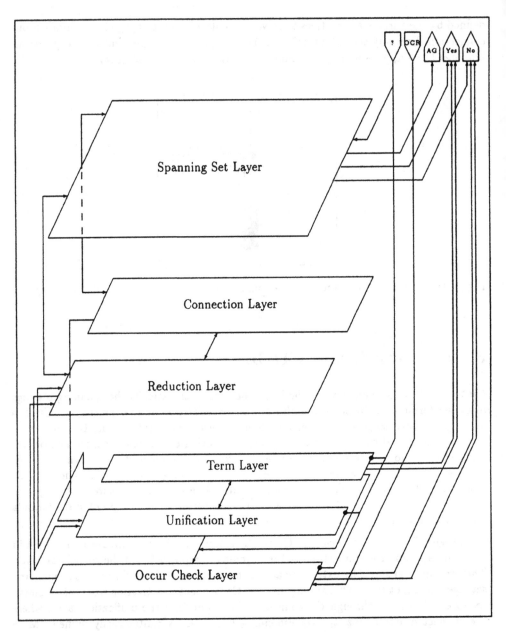

Figure 2: An overview of CHCL. An arrow from layer A to layer B indicates that units in A excite units in layer B. Similarily, a line with a bullet from A to B indicates that units in A inhibit units in B.

The above mentioned process describes the general procedure for the operation of the network. But before this general procedure is activated the formula will be reduced. By inspecting the possible spanning matings of our running example we find that each mating contains connections V and VI. In fact, these connections are *isolated* as the connected atoms are not engaged in any other connection ([Bibel, 1988]; see also subsection 6.3). In our example, the connections V and VI can be evaluated in parallel, the affected clauses can be replaced by their resolvents, and we obtain the following reduced formula.

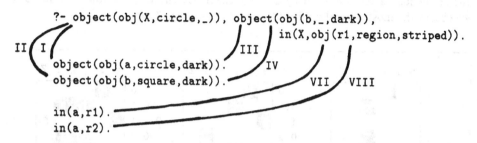

```
?- object(obj(X,circle,_)), object(obj(b,_,dark)),
                                in(X,obj(r1,region,striped)).

   object(obj(a,circle,dark)).
   object(obj(b,square,dark)).

   in(a,r1).
   in(a,r2).
```

But this is not the only reduction mechanism built into CHCL. Note that the atoms connected by II are not unifiable since the constants `circle` and `square` occupy the same position in these atoms. For similar reasons the atoms connected by III and VIII are also non-unifiable. All these non-unifiable atoms will simultaneously be detected in the reduction layer and, consequently, the connections II, III, and VIII will be eliminated. This leaves the connections I, IV, and VII. Since each of them is now isolated, they will be evaluated in parallel and the formula collapses to the empty clause. In other words, a proof for the formula was found by reduction techniques only and these techniques were applied in parallel.

In the subsequent sections we will describe in more detail how the various parts of the connectionist inference system are designed and how they work together.

4 A Connectionist Unification Algorithm

At the heart of the inference system is a connectionist unification algorithm. The algorithm computes the most general unifier of two first-order terms as defined by Robinson [1965]. Terms and substitutions are represented by a set of position-label pairs. This representation is very similar to the role-filler representation used by Smolensky [1987]. For each position π and for each symbol s occurring in a term the term layer contains a unit $\langle \pi, s \rangle$. A term like `obj(X,circle,dark)` can now be represented by externally activating the units $\langle 0, obj \rangle$, $\langle 0.1, X \rangle$, $\langle 0.2, circle \rangle$, and $\langle 0.3, dark \rangle$.

From [Paterson and Wegman, 1978] we know that the most general unifier of two terms can be obtained by computing a finest valid congruence relation on the representation of the terms. As shown in [Hölldobler, 1990b] this congruence relation is the closure of the operations

SINGULARITY   if $\langle \pi_1, X \rangle$, $\langle \pi_2, X \rangle$, and $\langle \pi_1, s \rangle$ are active then activate $\langle \pi_2, s \rangle$ and
DECOMPOSITION if $\langle \pi_1, X \rangle$, $\langle \pi_2, X \rangle$, and $\langle \pi_1.\pi, s \rangle$ are active then activate $\langle \pi_2.\pi, s \rangle$,

where π, π_1, and π_2 denote positions, X denotes a variable and s denotes a symbol. Informally, operation SINGULARITY ensures that multiple occurrences of a variable are bound to the same term and operation DECOMPOSITION decomposes terms of the form $f(t_1, \ldots, t_n)$ and $f(s_1, \ldots, s_n)$ and forces the unification of the corresponding arguments t_i and s_i, $1 \leq i \leq n$. It is quite straightforward to encode these operations in a structured connectionist network. This network is the unification layer in figure 2. Figure 3 shows as a simple example the representation of the terms $f(X, X, X)$ and $f(g(a), Y, g(Z))$ as well as the activation pattern obtained by unifying them. By checking the rows 0.1 and 0.1.1 we obtain the most general unifier $\{X \mapsto g(a),\ Y \mapsto g(a),\ Z \mapsto a\}$.

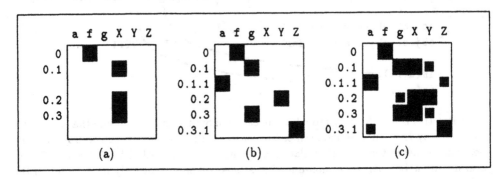

Figure 3: The representation of (a) $f(X, X, X)$ and (b) $f(g(a), Y, g(Z))$ in the term layer. Note that the matrix in (a) does not have a row for 0.1.1 and 0.3.1. The two representations are merged in (c) and the closure of the operations SINGULARITY and DECOMPOSITION is computed, which leads in one step to the activation of the units shown as small black boxes.

Not all unification problems admit a most general unifier. If during the unification computation two different function symbols occupy the same position, then the initial terms are not unifiable. The unification layer will detect such a case and the NO unit shown in figure 2 will be activated. The other reason where the unification computation may fail is in the presence of an occur check problem. This problem occurs if a variable X is to be bound to a term t which contains an occurrence of X. The unification algorithm within CHCL ignores this problem unless the user has activated the OCR unit shown in figure 2. In this case the occur check layer will eventually detect the problem and activate the NO unit.

[Hölldobler, 1990b] contains a formal definition of the term, unification, and occur check layer as well as a proof that the network computes the finest valid congruence relation for a unification problem if such a relation exists. The complete network for solving the unification problem requires $O(N^2)$ units and takes $O(N)$ time in the worst case to settle down, where N is the number of positions in the unification problem. This behavior is not surprising since unification is known to be logspace-complete [Dwork et al., 1984]. However, for important special cases such as the word or the matching problem, the network computes the solution in two steps and this behaviour is independent of the size of the unification problem.

The unification algorithm in CHCL does not unify one pair of terms at a time. Rather it simultaneously unifies all corresponding terms with respect to the connections in a selected spanning mating. Note that if all connections in a spanning mating define matching problems, then the unifiability of all connected atoms in the spanning mating is determined in two steps. This situation occurs – for example – whenever constraint satisfaction problems are solved within CHCL (see section 7).

5 The Selection of Spanning Matings

As described above the unification computation is triggered by the selected spanning mating. More precisely, for each connection in the given formula there is a unit called **spanning** in the connection layer. If a connection is in the currently selected spanning mating then its **spanning** unit will be activated. The **spanning** unit transmits the activation to the unification layer, where the connected atoms are unified.

But how is a spanning mating selected? The spanning layer shown in figure 2 can be regarded as a kind of structured Jordan [1986] or Elman [1989] network. It has an internal state q on which the two functions **next** and **output** operate. Whenever the user activates the ?-unit, the function **output** generates the current spanning mating and **next** updates the state, ie.

$$\text{spanning}_t = \text{output}(q_t, \text{connected}_t, ?)$$

and

$$q_{t+1} = \text{next}(q_t, \text{connected}_t, ?),$$

where **spanning** denotes the generated spanning mating, **connected** denotes the active connections of the formula, and t denotes time. This process continues until all spanning matings are generated and tested, in which case **output** activates the AG-unit. The active connections are determined by the connection layer. Initially, each connection in the formula is active, which is indicated by an active **connected** unit in the connection layer. But some of the connections may not be a member of any spanning mating and, thus, should not be selected by the **output** function. One reason might be that the connected atoms are not unifiable. Reduction techniques built into CHCL and presented in section 6 will find those connections. They are thereafter removed by inhibiting their **connected** units in the connection layer.

Bibel's connection method generally requires to take copies of the clauses into consideration. Consequently, the set of spanning matings may be infinite. However, for various reasons discussed in section 9 the resources of CHCL are limited in that it can use only a fixed number of copies. In fact, for the purpose of this paper CHCL can handle only the original clause, where we assume that all clauses are standardized apart (ie. do not share common variables). Techniques for handling a fixed number of copies can be found in [Shastri and Ajjanagadde, 1990a]. Since there are now only finitely many different spanning matings, the logic is decidable.

The alert reader may have observed that finding a spanning mating now corresponds to deciding the satisfiability of the propositional structure of the given formula. Since all clauses are Horn, a sequential algorithm may find a spanning mating in time linear to the number C of connections in the formula [Dowling and Gallier, 1984][1]. In the spanning layer the connections of a formula are encoded as an AND-OR-tree, where the AND-branches correspond to the various conditions of a rule and the OR-branches correspond to the various alternatives to solve a condition. An activated ?-unit excites the root of the tree, from where the activation spreads through the tree such that

- at each encountered OR-node one and only one alternative is selected and

- at each encountered AND-node all branches are selected.

The encountered leaves of the tree constitute the selected spanning mating (viz. the result of the function output). The function next decides which OR-branch is selected such that each time a different spanning mating is selected. Consequently, in the worst case it takes time linear to the depth of the AND-OR-tree to select a spanning mating. If the tree is balanced a spanning mating will be generated in time $O(log(C))$. On the other hand, the depth of the AND-OR-tree may be linear to C, in which case the tree is a chain. One might expect that this defines a worst case situation for the computation of the spanning mating. However, if the AND-OR-tree degenerates to a chain, then all connections are isolated [Bibel, 1988] and the respective reduction techniques presented in the following subsection 6.3 will generate the corresponding spanning mating in one step. For more details the reader is referred to [Hölldobler, 1990a], where all units together with their thresholds and weighted links in the spanning layer are defined.

6 Reduction Techniques

As the name indicates reduction techniques are used to reduce the search space. They can typically be applied in parallel and in time linear to the size (viz. the number of connections) of the formula. Several of these techniques are built into CHCL and they are presented in this section. However, we can give only an informal account of the various techniques and their realization in CHCL. All details can be found in [Hölldobler, 1990a].

6.1 Removal of Non-unifiable Connections

A connection cannot participate in any proof if the connected atoms are not unifiable. Hence, the obvious technique would be to test all connections in advance. Unfortunately, since the representation of each term is such that for each position in the term there is precisely one row in the term layer and since unifiers are computed on this representation, we cannot perform this test in parallel. It would be a test of whether all connected atoms in the formula are simultaneously unifiable. Usually, this would lead to cross-talk if a variable occurs in an atom which is engaged in more than one connection and is bound to different terms in the various connections. There are cases where such a cross-talk cannot occur and these are treated in subsection 6.3.

---

[1]See also [Scutella, 1990] for a correction of a bug in Dowling's and Gallier's algorithm.

However, it is easy to detect cases where atoms are not unifiable because different function symbols occur at the same position in these atoms. As an example consider the atoms

$$object(obj(X, circle, \_))$$

and

$$object(obj(b, square, dark)),$$

which are connected by connection II in our running example. Since the constants circle and square occur both at position 0.1.2, these atoms can never be unified. CHCL determines this non-unifiability with the help of the reduction layer and, consequently, the connected unit for II in the connection layer is inhibited. As described in section 5 this essentially removes connection II from the formula. This simplified test for the unifiability of connected atoms takes four steps and is performed for all connected atoms in parallel.

6.2 Removal of Useless Connections

The technique to remove useless connections is based on the close correspondence between propositional Horn formulas and context-free grammars (cf. [Dowling and Gallier, 1984]). In context-free grammars a non-terminal symbol is said to be useless if it does not occur in a sentenial form or cannot generate a terminal string (cf. [Aho and Ullman, 1972]). Correspondingly, we will call the head of a clause (viz. each connection of the head) *useless* if it does not occur in an SLD-resolvent of the initial clause or if the conditions of the clause cannot be solved. The important property of useless non-terminal symbols and connections is that they can be determined statically by analyzing the set of productions and clauses, respectively. Algorithms for context-free grammars can be found in [Aho and Ullman, 1972].

Informally, these algorithms are encoded in the following rules, where we assume that the initial formula does not contain any useless connections.

- If the head of a clause is not engaged in any connection (ie. if all connected units for connections with the head are deactivated), then inhibit all connected units for the connections with conditions of the clause.

- If a condition in a clause is not engaged in any connection (ie. if all connected units for connections with the condition are deactivated), then inhibit all connected units for the connections with the head of the clause.

These rules can easily be realized in a structured connectionist setting.

6.3 Evaluation of Isolated Connections

As mentioned in subsection 6.1 we can generally not test in parallel whether connected atoms are unifiable. However, besides the simple test in subsection 6.1 there is another exception which is due to [Bibel, 1988]. A connection is said to be *isolated*

- if the connected atoms are not engaged in any other connection, or

- if the connected atoms are ground (ie. do not contain variables), or

- if one of the connected atoms is ground and the other atom is not engaged in any other connection.

The rationale behind this definition is that atoms engaged in isolated connections can be unified in parallel without causing any cross-talk or backtracking. There is no alternative to the bindings generated by unifying isolated connections.

From our chosen representation of terms in the term layer and connections in the connection layer it is straightforward to encode these rules in a structured connectionist network such that all isolated connections are evaluated simultaneously. If a connection is found to be isolated, then the respective parts of the unification layer are activated forcing the unification of corresponding terms. If the unification fails, then the connection will be useless and its connected unit in the connection layer will be inhibited.

Our running example has initially the isolated connections V and VII. As shown in section 3 both connections (viz. connected atoms) unify simultaneously and the formula was reduced by replacing the clauses by their resolvents. The latter process will be described in more detail in the following subsection.

6.4   Removal of Solved Connections

Under certain conditions isolated connections can be removed by replacing the connected clauses by their resolvents. This is the case if the connections are solved. The motivation for this technique stems from the observation that a condition A in a clause can be eliminated if there is a unique minimal substitution σ such that σA is a logical consequence of the given program and if the minimal substitution is applied to the remainder of the clause.

More formally, a connection between subgoal A' and head A of clause C is said to be *solved* if

- the connection is isolated,

- the atoms A' and A are unifiable, and

- each subgoal occurring in C is solved.

Obviously, a solved connection may participate in any spanning mating. As before, these rules can easily be encoded in a structured connectionist system.

In our running example we find that initially only connection VI is solved, whereas connection V is isolated and unifiable, but the above-clause contains unsolved connections engaged with its conditions. Fortunately, as soon as connection VI is unified, the variable RegionAbove is bound to the region obj(r1, region, striped). Consequently, connection VIII is found to be non-unifiable by the technique described in subsection 6.1 and will be eliminated. Thus, connection VII becomes isolated as well as solved and, now, connection

V is also solved. At the same time a similar process leads to the discovery that connections I and IV are also solved. In other words, the complete formula was solved by reduction techniques only and it was found that the circle a is above the square b in the scene of figure 1.

7 Constraint Satisfaction in CHCL

As finite constraint satisfaction problems can be stated as satisfiabilty problems in propositional Horn logic[2], CHCL can easily handle them. However, CHCL is not especially adapted for constraint satisfaction problems and will not handle them efficiently. In particular, CHCL does not perform a check for arc consistency. In [Hölldobler and Hower, 1991] it was shown how a slight modification of CHCL achieves arc consistency. This section contains a brief account of this modification.

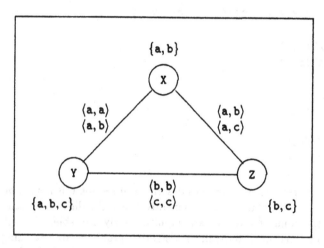

Figure 4: The constraint graph for a simple constraint satisfaction problem. The sets denote the domains (viz. unary constraints) of the variables and the tuples denote the binary constraints between corresponding variables.

As an example consider the simple constraint satisfaction problem shown in figure 4 as a constraint graph. The goal is to find bindings for the variables X, Y, and Z such that all unary and binary constraints are simultaneously fulfilled. This problem can be expressed by the following formula, where the D-clauses express the domain facts and the C-clauses express the binary constraints.

```
?- CXY(X,Y), CXZ(X,Z), CYZ(Y,Z)

CXY(a,a) :- DX(a), DY(a)
```

---

[2]See [Mackworth, 1987] for an introduction to constraint satisfaction.

```
CXY(a,b) :- DX(a), DY(b)

CXZ(a,b) :- DX(a), DZ(b)
CXZ(a,c) :- DX(a), DZ(c)

CYZ(b,b) :- DY(b), DZ(b)
CYZ(c,c) :- DY(c), DZ(c)

DX(a)  DX(b)  DY(a)  DY(b)  DY(c)  DZ(b)  DZ(c)
```

All connections between domain facts and the conditions of the constraint rules are isolated and will be evaluated simultaneously using the technique described in subsection 6.3. In fact, the connections are either non-unifiable or solved and the formula reduces to the following set of clauses.

```
?- CXY(X,Y), CXZ(X,Z), CYZ(Y,Z)

CXY(a,a)
CXY(a,b)

CXZ(a,b)
CXZ(a,c)

CYZ(b,b)
CYZ(c,c)
```

Since none of the reduction techniques described in section 6 is now applicable anymore, CHCL – as specified so far – has to generate the eight different spanning sets and to test whether the connected atoms are simultaneously unifiable. Though all unification problems encountered in a constraint satisfaction problems are matching problems and, hence, the unification is performed in two steps, this behavior is far from being optimal since the example can be solved by local constraint propagation techniques without any search.

The technique needed for solving our example is the test for arc consistency. *Arc consistency* states that a variable X may have value a if for each other variable Y there is a value b such that (a, b) is a valid binary constraint between X and Y (viz. CXY(a,b) is true). The arc consistency condition allows to remove any value from the domain of X which is unsupported.

In our example, we find that the value b in the domain of X as well as the value a in the domain of Y is unsupported. Hence, these values should be removed. In analogy to subsection 6.2 this can be done in CHCL by inhibiting all connected units for connections engaged with DX(b) and DY(a). As a consequence, the formula may now contain useless connections. The interested reader is encouraged to apply the various reduction techniques presented in section 6 to the example. He or she will find that the formula eventually collapses to the empty clause generating the substitution $\{X \mapsto a, Y \mapsto b, Z \mapsto b\}$.

To implement the arc consistency condition we need an additional OR-of-AND unit in the sense of [Feldman and Ballard, 1982] for each domain fact. Such a unit will be activated if there is a variable which does not support the value anymore. This solution is very similar to the encoding described by Cooper and Swain [1988] and used by Güsgen [1990]. But whereas Cooper's and Swain's system is restricted to local satisfaction problems, our system can handle global constraint satisfaction problems as well. Güsgen's system may also handle global constraint satisfaction problems. But his units transmit Gödel numbers and compute greatest lower bounds and least common multiples. These messages and operations are fairly complex and usually not allowed in truly connectionist systems (cf. [Feldman and Ballard, 1982]). An alternative encoding of the Gödel numbers as bit vectors, however, increases the number of units in the system considerably.

8 Implementation

8.1 ICSIM

The implementation of CHCL currently pursued at the International Computer Science Institute is based on a connectionist simulator called ICSIM, developed at the same institution by H.-W. Schmidt [1990]. ICSIM provides a set of basic building blocks for connectionist networks as a collection of library classes. It is implemented in EIFFEL [Meyer, 1988], an object-oriented language and development environment. The use of an objet-oriented methodology allows for both flexibility and reuse of basic classes and enables the user to get an easy start by mainly relying on the classes provided through the library as well as modifying some of the classes and their routines for efficient customized implementations. ICSIM currently is being ported to SATHER, an offspring of EIFFEL aimed at simplification and more efficient execution [Omohundro, 1991]. The modular construction of ICSIM also allows an easy portation to dedicated hardware, eg. the neural network coprocessor RAP [Morgan, 1990].

8.2 Unification

The first step in the implementation of CHCL was a realization of the unification algorithm [Kurfeß, 1991a]. The structure and behavior of the unification network are derived in a straightforward way from the algorithm described in Section 4, or in more detail in [Hölldobler, 1990a].

Structure of the Network The unification network is modeled according to the representation of terms as position-label pairs. These pairs are arranged as a matrix, with positions as rows and symbols as columns. Each entry of the matrix consists of one *term unit* and as many *unification units* as there are positions in the unification problem to be evaluated. The term unit indicates if a symbol occurs at a certain position, or, during the unification process, if it has the same value as another symbol at the same position. The unification units are used to indicate that the corresponding term unit has to be activated during the unification process.[3] Both term and unification units are simple boolean units with a threshold activation function; the output is 0 if the weighted sum of the inputs is lower than the threshold, and 1 if the sum is equal to or greater than the threshold. There are two types of *links* in the network: *weak links* with a weight $w = 1$, and *strong links*, with a weight w equal to the sum of possible weak connections for any unit in the network, which is $w = \frac{1}{2} \times n \times m \times (m - 1)$, where n is the number of symbols and m is the number of positions in a unification problem.

A term unit has $2 \times (m - 1)$ strong inputs: from each of its own unification units except for the one pointing to its own position, and from the unification unit corresponding to its own position of the other occurrences of the same symbol.[4] The threshold of a term unit $t_t = \frac{1}{2} \times n \times m \times (m - 1)$ is the same as the weight of a strong connection, so that the term unit is activated as soon as one of its unification units raises its output. The threshold of a unification unit $t_u = t_t + 1$ is slightly higher than that of a term unit, and, hence, the unification unit is only activated if at least one strong link plus one weak link is active on its inputs. A symbol s at the first position, for example, receives inputs form all its own unification units except for the first one, and from all the first unification units of the occurrences of the same symbol at other positions. Within one position, there are weak links between unification units corresponding to the same position; in ICSIM terminology, these units are bus-connected. Here we have to distinguish between two types of symbols: variables on one hand, and function symbols and constants on the other. The weak links between the unification units within a position go from each variable to all other symbols; this mirrors the effect of shared variables, namely the occurrence of the same variable symbol at different positions. The links described so far are used to achieve SINGULARITY; all instances of a symbol at different positions must have the same value, and all symbols occurring at the same position must also have the same value. Figure 5 gives an overview of these singularity links in the network. The links between term units and unification units of other positions are shown for one symbol only on the right side of the picture.

Additional links are required to achieve the other operation in the unification algorithm, DECOMPOSITION. This operation performs the unification of the corresponding arguments s_i and t_i, $1 \leq i \leq n$, of two subterms $f(s_1, \ldots, s_n)$ and $f(t_1, \ldots, t_n)$. Decomposition is relevant if two subterms are forced to assume the same value due to shared variables, which in our example is the case for $g(a)$ and $g(Y)$ because of the occurrence of the variable X at both of these positions in the other term. As a consequence, the corresponding arguments must assume the same value, in our case a and Y. The propagation of decomposition from two parent symbols to their respective children requires weak links from the unification unit of the one parent position which connects it to its partner parent position to the respective unification units of all symbols at the particular child positions. Figure 6 shows the decomposition links required in our example. The variable X occurs at positions 1 and 3, and weak links must be established from the fifth unification

---

[3]In the current implementation, the network is compiled from scratch for each new unification problem; a generic version which adapts a precompiled network to the particular problem is under construction. The current implementation also uses twice as many unification units as necessary, which made the implementation a little easier and does not do any harm.

[4]One set of unification units actually would be sufficient.

333

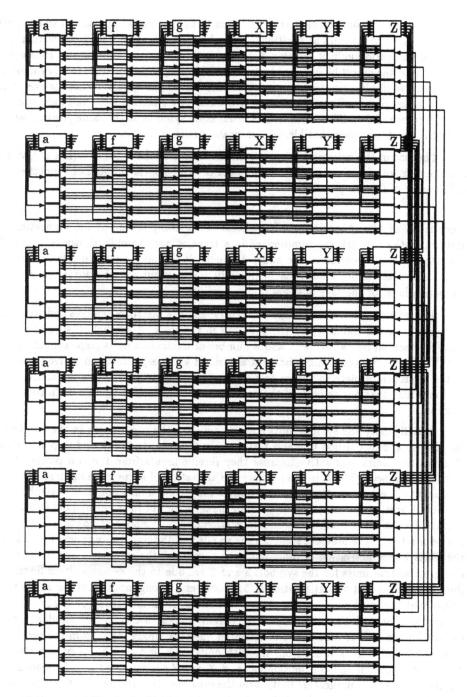

Figure 5: Unification network with singularity links.

unit of position 1 (which represents the relation to the partner at position 3) to the sixth unification unit of its child at position 1.1, and from unification unit 2 of position 3 to the third unification unit of position 3.1. These decomposition links are established at compile time; they must be installed from all variables of parent positions to all symbols at the respective children positions since shared variables might appear during the execution of the unification algorithm. Decomposition links only emanate from variables because the occurrence of two different constants or function symbols at the same position would make the two terms incompatible, and unification fails.

The size of the network in this implementation is of the order of $\mathcal{O}(m \times n^2)$, where n is the number of positions and m the number of symbols; the number of connections is of the order of $\mathcal{O}(m^2 \times p^2)$.

Execution of the Algorithm The effects of the computation of the unification algorithm in the network are summerized in a trace of our example, shown in Figure 7. One step in the execution is one sweep through all the units in the network; whereas ICSIM allows for various kinds of asynchronicity in the execution[5] we assume synchronous evaluation here for the sake of easier understanding.

The information within a single step is arranged as a matrix of symbols and positions, the symbols in the columns and the positions in the rows. A symbol consists of a term unit (represented by "=" or "#"), and a number of unification units (represented by "-" or "|"). The occurence of a symbol s at a position π corresponds to an active term unit at the appropriate place in the matrix and is shown as "#"; an active unification unit "|") indicates that one or both of the partner symbols identified by this unification unit is active.

Initially, only the symbol units corresponding to the occurrences in the two terms are active, eg. f at position 0, g and X at position 0.1, etc. In the second step, a number of unification units gets active because they receive inputs from the two partner term units they connect. The third step shows the activation of some more unification units, this time via weak links. Consider for example the second unification unit of symbol g at position 0.2; it receives a strong input from the term unit of the same symbol at position 0.1 and a weak input from the second unification unit of symbol X at position 0.2, which has been active in the previous step. This is an effect of the singularity connections, which also leads to the activation of more unification units for the symbols g and Y. The two active unification units for the symbols a and Z are due to the decomposition links: the third unification unit of a at position 0.3.1 receives a strong input from the active term unit of a at the third position, 0.1.1, and weak input from the second unification unit of the symbol X at position 0.3, which is the parent postion of 0.3.1. In a similar way the last unification unit of Z at 0.1.1 is activated due to a strong input from the term unit Z at 0.3.1 and a weak input from the fifth unification unit of X at its parent position 0.1. In step 4, term units of the symbols a, g, Y, and Z are activated as a consequence of the activation of the unification units form the previous step. In the last step, some more unification units become active, but without further consequences, and the network has reached a fixpoint.

---

[5]Eg. not all units are evaluated in one sweep.

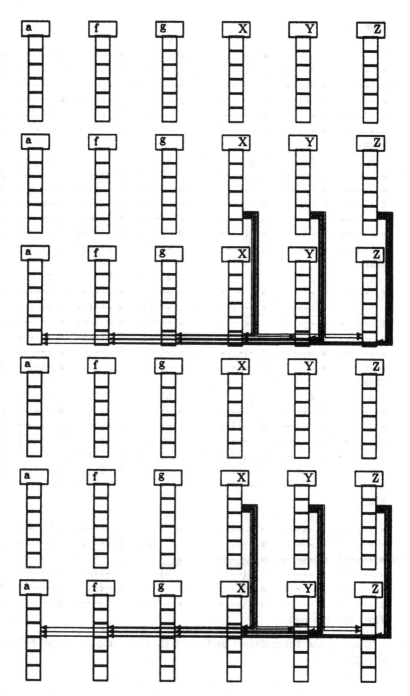

Figure 6: Unification network with decomposition links.

```
STEP: 1
    a          f          g          X          Y          Z
= ------   # ------   = ------    = ------   = ------   = ------   0
= ------   = ------   # ------    # ------   = ------   = ------   0.1
# ------   = ------   = ------    = ------   = ------   = ------   0.1.1
= ------   = ------   = ------    # ------   # ------   = ------   0.2
= ------   = ------   # ------    # ------   = ------   = ------   0.3
= ------   = ------   = ------    = ------   = ------   # ------   0.3.1
STEP: 2
    a          f          g          X          Y          Z
= ------   # ------   = ------    = ------   = ------   = ------   0
= ------   = ------   # ----|-    # ---||-   = ------   = ------   0.1
# ------   = ------   = ------    = ------   = ------   = ------   0.1.1
= ------   = ------   = ------    # -|--|-   # ------   = ------   0.2
= ------   = ------   # -|----    # -|-|--   = ------   = ------   0.3
= ------   = ------   = ------    = ------   = ------   # ------   0.3.1
STEP: 3
    a          f          g          X          Y          Z
= ------   # ------   = ------    = ------   = ------   = ------   0
= ------   = ------   # ---||-    # ---||-   = ---|--   = ------   0.1
# ------   = ------   = ------    = ------   = ------   = -----|   0.1.1
= ------   = ------   = -|--|-    # -|--|-   # -|--|-   = ------   0.2
= ------   = ------   # -|-|--    # -|-|--   = ---|--   = ------   0.3
= --|---   = ------   = ------    = ------   = ------   # ------   0.3.1
STEP: 4
    a          f          g          X          Y          Z
= ------   # ------   = ------    = ------   = ------   = ------   0
= ------   = ------   # ---||-    # ---||-   # ---||-   = ------   0.1
# ------   = ------   = ------    = ------   = ------   # -----|   0.1.1
= ------   = ------   # -|--|-    # -|--|-   # -|--|-   = ------   0.2
= ------   = ------   # -|-|--    # -|-|--   # -|-|--   = ------   0.3
# --|---   = ------   = ------    = ------   = ------   # ------   0.3.1
STEP: 5
    a          f          g          X          Y          Z
= ------   # ------   = ------    = ------   = ------   = ------   0
= ------   = ------   # ---||-    # ---||-   # ---||-   = ------   0.1
# -----|   = ------   = ------    = ------   = ------   # -----|   0.1.1
= ------   = ------   # -|--|-    # -|--|-   # -|--|-   = ------   0.2
= ------   = ------   # -|-|--    # -|-|--   # -|-|--   = ------   0.3
# --|---   = ------   = ------    = ------   = ------   # --|---   0.3.1
Fixpoint reached...
```

Figure 7: Trace of the computation performed in an attempt to unify f(X,X,X) and f(g(a),Y,g(Z)).

8.3 CHCL

In the last subsection we have given a detailed description of the implementation of the term and unification layer and of the operations performed on these layers. The remaining layers can easily be implemented in very much the same way. The units and links are precisely specified in [Hölldobler, 1990a].

9 Future Work

The current status of CHCL shows the correctness of the approach through its formal description as well as its feasibility through its implementation. There is no doubt, however, that in order to be useful for a wider range of applications CHCL must be enhanced and improved with respect to a number of issues. One of the main points is to enhance the functionality by allowing copies of clauses, and providing means to deal with cycles and recursion. Another is the selection of *promising* spanning matings, eg. through strategies based on learning from previous examples. The implementation needs an increase in efficiency, which may be achieved by mechanisms to restrict the execution to those units which are actually needed for the current program. These issues are described in more detail below.

9.1 Functionality

In its current version, CHCL is restricted by the requirement that only one instance of a clause may be used, and there are no copies. Hence, the logic is decidable and a large and important class of formulae cannot be handled. This is an instance of a more general problem encountered in almost all connectionist systems developed so far. It is the problem of how to recruit new units if the units used so far are incapable of representing additional knowledge. Techniques like recruitment learning [Feldman, 1982; Diederich, 1988] are promising, but the structures recruited so far using this technique are much simpler than the structures used in CHCL.

Copies An extension to handling a finite number of clause copies can be based on the use of different phases in the execution for the different copies as described in [Shastri and Ajjanagadde, 1990a]. It is not clear, however, if this approach can handle an arbitrary number of clauses at runtime, which would be necessary in the case of recursive formulae. In addition, one may argue that this is a clever implementation maneuver, but not really a fundamental solution to the problem how to represent multiple instances of a clause. Another possibility is the use of an recursive auto-associative memory [Pollack, 1988; Pollack, 1990], which provides a way to store variable-sized recursive data structures in patterns of a fixed width.

Cycles Cycles in a logical formula can be handled in two ways: the first is to explicitly resolve them by creating as many new copies of the affected clauses as necessary; the other is to analyze the structure of the formula, detect cycles, and apply transformations to the formula to eliminate or simplify the cycles. The latter basically is an analysis of the graph given by the logical connections of the formula, and to some degree can be applied statically at compile time [Bibel et al., 1991]. An approach to improve the first one can be based on observing the execution of the formula: if certain actions, eg. the creation of clause copies, are repeated over and over, it might be possible to identify the changes for each iteration, and modify the execution scheme accordingly.

Spanning Matings   The treatment of spanning matings currently is sequential: one is investigated after the other. The other extreme would be to create a copy of the network for each spanning set and examine the unifiability in parallel.

9.2   Learning

Strategies   The selection of the next spanning set is currently based on syntactic criteria. This can be enhanced by learning semantic strategies based on experience gathered from the solution process of previously solved formulae [Suttner, 1989; Schumann et al., 1989; Ultsch et al., 1990]. Learning can be useful in different stages of the execution, and on different levels in the network. It can be applied during the detection and elimination or transformation of cycles, for the selection of promising spanning sets, and for the creation of clause copies. It is questionable, however, if general strategies can be derived from the structure of the formula alone; more likely is the development of strategies for certain domains, or classes of applications.

9.3   Implementation

The completion of the current implementation is expected for the summer of 1991. This implementation certainly will not rival logic programming systems or theorem provers with respect to speed and functionality; it is meant to demonstrate the feasibility of the approach, and for experimentation. Mid-term goals are the portation to dedicated connectionist architectures like ICSI's RAP [Morgan, 1990], or to massively parallel systems like the connection machine [Thi, 1987].

Representation   An important goal for future implementations will be to overcome the quadratic number of units. In most cases, only a small fraction of the units are actually used for a particular problem; thus the recruitment of units from an overall pool of units and the dynamical establishment of the necessary links is a promising way to substantially reduce the space requirements. Another problem concerns the representation of clause copies: Currently only one copy of a clause is allowed, which certainly is an intolerable restriction in the long run. As mentioned before, possible solutions for this problem are the use of phases, indices or signatures or the use of a recursive auto-associative memory. Promising first experiments using a recursive auto-associative memory to learn a restricted version of the unification problem have been performed by [Stolcke and Wu, 1991].

Execution As a result of the enormous number of units and connections, execution times at the moment are rather slow even on relatively fast workstations. In addition to the use of dedicated or massively parallel machinery, optimizations are pursued in the implementation of ICSIM . Virtual units or working memory can be used to achieve a lazy evaluation scheme, only evaluating units whose inputs have changed. In the CHCL implementation, garbage collection could eliminate rows and columns in the term layer which become identical during evaluation. Another possiblity is the pre-compilation of the body of a logic program (without the query), adding the necessary units for a particular query upon request; this approach, however, mainly decreases compilation, not execution time. Although unification is pursued in a parallel way, it still may consume a considerable part of the execution time. Here weak unification may be useful to eliminate spanning sets before full unification is applied, or which are not unifiable for any query.

9.4 Applications

The ultimate goal of CHCL is not only its implementation, but also the usage for *real* applications. One currently pursued is spatial reasoning in the context of the L_0 project at the International Computer Science Institute [Feldman *et al.*, 1990]. The intention of this project is to associate sentences describing spatial relations between objects and the corresponding scenes. CHCL is particularly suited for such a task: sentences can be represented as logical formulae, whereas the representation of scenes can be based on a connectionist representation.

Acknowledgement Most of work on CHCL has been done while both authors were at the International Computer Science Institute. We are therefore indebted to Jerry Feldman for providing such an exciting and stimulating environment which made this research possible. We also like to thank Andreas Stolcke, Susan Hollbach-Weber, Heinz W. Schmidt, Lokendra Shastri, Joachim Diederich, Hans-Werner Güsgen, and Walter Hower for their constructive criticism and their help in many ways.

References

[Aho and Ullman, 1972] A. V. Aho and J. D. Ullman. *The Theory of Parsing, Translation, and Compiling*, volume I: Parsing. Prentice-Hall, Englewood Cliffs, N. J., 1972.

[Ballard, 1986] D. H. Ballard. Parallel logic inference and energy minimization. In *Proceedings of the AAAI National Conference on Artificial Intelligence*, pages 203 – 208, 1986.

[Bibel *et al.*, 1991] W. Bibel, S. Hölldobler, and J. Würtz. Cycle unification. Technical Report AIDA-91-15, FG Intellektik, FB Informatik, TH Darmstadt, 1991.

[Bibel, 1987] W. Bibel. *Automated Theorem Proving*. Vieweg Verlag, Braunschweig, second edition, 1987.

[Bibel, 1988] W. Bibel. Advanced topics in automated deduction. In Nossum, editor, *Fundamentals of Artificial Intelligence II.* Springer, 1988.

[Colmerauer, 1982] A. Colmerauer. Prolog and infinite trees. In Clark and Tarnlund, editors, *Logic Programming*, pages 231–251. Academic Press, 1982.

[Cooper and Swain, 1988] P. R. Cooper and M. J. Swain. Parallelism and domain dependence in constraint satisfaction. Technical Report 255, Computer Science Department, Univ. of Rochester, 1988.

[Diederich, 1988] J. Diederich. Connectionist recruitment learning. In *Proceedings of the European Conference on Artificial Intelligence*, pages 351–356, 1988.

[Dowling and Gallier, 1984] W. F. Dowling and J. H. Gallier. Linear-time algorithms for testing the satisfiability of propositional Horn formulae. *Journal of Logic Programming*, 1984.

[Dwork et al., 1984] C. Dwork, P. C. Kannelakis, and J. C. Mitchell. On the sequential nature of unification. *Journal of Logic Programming*, 1:35–50, 1984.

[Elman, 1989] J. L. Elman. Structured representations and connectionist models. In *Proceedings of the Annual Conference of the Cognitive Science Society*, pages 17–25, 1989.

[Feldman and Ballard, 1982] J. A. Feldman and D. H. Ballard. Connectionist models and their properties. *Cognitive Science*, 6(3):205–254, 1982.

[Feldman et al., 1990] J. A. Feldman, G. Lakoff, A. Stolcke, and S. H. Weber. Miniature language acquisition: A touchstone for cognitive science. In *Proceedings of the Annual Conference of the Cognitive Science Society*, pages 686–693, 1990.

[Feldman, 1982] J. A. Feldman. Dynamic connections in neural networks. *Biological Cybernetics*, 46:27–39, 1982.

[Güsgen and Hölldobler, 1991] H.-W. Güsgen and S. Hölldobler. Connectionist inference systems. In B. Fronhöfer and G. Wrightson, editors, *Parallelization in Inference Systems.* Springer, 1991.

[Güsgen, 1990] H. W. Güsgen. A connectionist approach to symbolic constraint satisfaction. Technical Report TR-90-018, International Computer Science Institute, Berkeley, CA, 1990.

[Hölldobler and Hower, 1991] S. Hölldobler and W. Hower. Constraint satisfaction in a connectionist inference system. In *Proceedings of the 4th International Symposium on Artificial Intelligence*, pages 215–221, 1991.

[Hölldobler, 1990a] S. Hölldobler. CHCL - A connectionist inference system for a limited class of Horn clauses based on the connection method. Technical Report TR-90-042, International Computer Science Institute, Berkeley, CA, 1990.

[Hölldobler, 1990b] S. Hölldobler. A structured connectionist unification algorithm. In *Proceedings of the AAAI National Conference on Artificial Intelligence*, pages 587–593, 1990. A long version appeared as Technical Report TR-90-012, International Computer Science Institute, Berkeley, California.

[Jordan, 1986] M. I. Jordan. Attractor dynamics and parallelism in a connectionist sequential machine. In *Proceedings of the Annual Conference of the Cognitive Science Society*, 1986.

[Kurfeß, 1991a] F. Kurfeß. Unification on a connectionist simulator. In *Proceedings of the International Conference on Artificial Neural Networks*, 1991. ICSI.

[Kurfeß, 1991b] F. Kurfeß. Unification with ICSIM. Technical report, International Computer Science Institute, Berkeley, CA, 1991.

[Mackworth, 1987] A. Mackworth. Constraint satisfaction. In Shapiro, editor, *Encyclopedia of Artificial Intelligence*, pages 205–211. John Wiley & Sons, 1987.

[Meyer, 1988] B. Meyer. *Object-Oriented Software Construction*. Prentice Hall, 1988.

[Morgan, 1990] N. Morgan. The ring array processor (RAP): Algorithms and architecture. Technical Report TR-90-47, International Computer Science Institute, Berkeley, CA, 1990.

[Omohundro, 1991] S. Omohundro. Differences between Sather and Eiffel. *Eiffel Outlook*, 1991.

[Paterson and Wegman, 1978] M. S. Paterson and M. N. Wegman. Linear unification. *Journal of Computer and System Sciences*, 16:158–167, 1978.

[Pollack, 1988] J. B. Pollack. Recursive auto-associative memory: Devising compositional distributed representations. In *Proceedings of the Annual Conference of the Cognitive Science Society*, 1988.

[Pollack, 1990] J. B. Pollack. Recursive distributed representations. *Artificial Intelligence*, 46:77–105, 1990.

[Robinson, 1965] J. A. Robinson. A machine-oriented logic based on the resolution principle. *Journal of the ACM*, 12:23–41, 1965.

[Schmidt, 1990] H. W. Schmidt. ICSIM: Initial design of an object-oriented net simulator. Technical Report TR-90-055, International Computer Science Institute, Berkeley, CA, 1990.

[Schumann et al., 1989] J. Schumann, W. Ertel, and C. Suttner. Learning heuristics for a theorem prover using back propagation. In *Österreichische AI Tagung*, 1989.

[Scutella, 1990] M. G. Scutella. A note on Dowling and Gallier's top-down algorithm for propositional Horn satisfiability. *Journal of Logic Programming*, 8(265-273), 1990.

[Shastri and Ajjanagadde, 1990a] L. Shastri and V. Ajjanagadde. From associations to systematic reasoning: A connectionist representation of rules, variables and dynamic bindings. Technical Report MS-CIS-90-05, Department of Computer and Information Science, University of Pennsylvania, Philadelphia, School of Engineering and Applied Science, PA 19104-6389, 1990.

[Shastri and Ajjanagadde, 1990b] L. Shastri and V. Ajjanagadde. An optimally efficient limited inference system. In *Proceedings of the AAAI National Conference on Artificial Intelligence*, pages 563–570, 1990.

[Smolensky, 1987] P. Smolensky. On variable binding and the representation of symbolic structures in connectionist systems. Technical Report CU-CS-355-87, Department of Computer Science & Institute of Cognitive Science, University of Colorado, Boulder, CO 80309-0430, 1987.

[Stickel, 1987] M. E. Stickel. An introduction to automated deduction. In W. Bibel and P. Jorrand, editors, *Fundamentals of Artificial Intelligence*, pages 75 – 132. Springer, 1987.

[Stolcke and Wu, 1991] A. Stolcke and D. Wu. Tree matching with recursive distributed representations. International Computer Science Institute, Berkeley, CA, 1991. submitted to NIPS 91.

[Suttner, 1989] C. Suttner. Learning heuristics for automated theorem proving. Master's thesis, Institut für Informatik, Technische Universität München, 1989.

[Thi, 1987] Thinking Machines Corporation. Connection Machine Model CM-2 Technical Summary. Technical Report HA87-4, 1987.

[Touretzky and Hinton, 1988] D. S. Touretzky and G. E. Hinton. A distributed connectionist production system. *Cognitive Science*, 12:423 – 466, 1988.

[Ultsch et al., 1990] A. Ultsch, R. Hannuschka, U. Hartmann, and V. Weber. Learning of control knowledge for symbolic proofs with backpropagation networks. In R. Eckmiller, G. Hartmann, and G. Hauske, editors, *Parallel Processing in Neural Systems and Computers*, pages 499–502. Elsevier, 1990.

[Weber and Stolcke, 1990] S. H. Weber and A. Stolcke. L_0: A testbed for miniature language aquisition. Technical Report TR-90-010, International Computer Science Institute, Berkeley, CA, 1990.

PART III

PROJECT SUMMARIES

Parallel Unification Machine Design and Simulation

Contact Person: Professor Fadi N. Sibai

Dept. of Electrical Engineering
University of Akron
Akron, OH 44325-3904
U.S.A.
mail: rlfns@vax1.cc.uakron.edu

Keywords
Parallel Unification, Term Matching, Consistency Check, Shared and Distributed
Memory Organizations

Summary
A parallel machine architecture for first-order unification was designed by F. N. Sibai.
This machine can be used as a hardware unifier by itself, or can be used as a co-processor
to a host PROLOG computer. The machine takes two terms to be unified for input, and
outputs the most general unifier in case of unification success, or FAIL in case of failure.
The machine is composed of an array of match processors (MPs) in charge of matching the
arguments of the two terms in parallel and can therefore detect early failures at the match
level. If no match failure exists, the MPs send the generated bindings to a consistency
check processor (CCP) in charge of checking the consistency of the bindings. The CCP
is a powerful unification processor which maintains the bindings in a content-addressable
memory for fast search and retrieval. Thus the operations of the array of MPs and the
CCP are pipelined in the machine. The performance evaluation of two versions of PUM
has been conducted with simulation. The first version is based on a shared-memory organization whereas the second uses a distributed memory organization.

Reference
Sibai, Fadi N.,"A Parallel Machine for the Unification Algorithm: Design, Simulation,
and Performance Evaluation," Ph.D. Dissertation, Dept. of Electrical Engineering, Texas
A&M University, College Station, Texas 77843, U.S.A., December 1989.
Sibai, F.N., Watson, K. L., and Lu, Mi, "A Parallel Unification Machine," IEEE MICRO,
Vol. 10, No. 4, August 1990, pp. 21-33.

Parallel Rule-Firing Production Systems

Contact Person: Daniel Neiman

Computer Science Dept.
University of Massachusetts
Amherst, MA 01003
mail: dann@cs.umass.edu

Keywords
Parallel Rule-Based Systems, Parallel OPS5

Summary
At the University of Massachusetts, we have developed a parallel rule-firing production systems based on OPS5. We are using this system to investigate the control and correctness issues involved in firing rules in parallel. In particular, we have developed an asynchronous rule-firing policy and are studying its implications upon the design and performance of parallel heuristic programs.

Parallel Closure-Based Automated Reasoning

Contact Persons: Ewing Lusk and William McCune*

John Slaney**

*Mathematics and Computer
Science Division, Argonne National Laboratory, Argonne
Illinois 60439, USA

**Automated Reasoning Project, Australian
National University, Canberra ACT, Australia

Keywords
Parallel Theorem Proving, OTTER, ROO

Summary
This project's goal is to exploit high-performance parallel machines for classical automated theorem proving. We have adapted OTTER, a fast sequential theorem prover developed at Argonne National laboratory, to a class of parallel machines via a parallel closure algorithm. The result is ROO, a parallel theorem prover completely compatible with OTTER that runs on shared-memory multiprocessors such a the Sequent Symmetry. It obtains near-linear speedups on many problems, but performs less well on others. Research is continuing on ways to increase levels of parallelism on such problems, and on algorithms for closure-based distributed-memory algorithms.

Parallel Completion

Contact Person: Prof. Katherine Yelick

505 Evans Hall
Computer Science Division
University of California
Berkeley, CA 94720
internet: yelick@cs.berkeley.edu

Keywords
Term Rewriting, Knuth-Bendix Procedure, Completion, Proof Orderings

Summary
We have designed and implemented a parallel completion procedure for term rewriting systems, a problem for which the Knuth-Bendix procedure is a well-known sequential solution. Straightforward parallelization of the Knuth-Bendix procedure did not perform well in our experiments, because the outermost loop contains unnecessary serialization. Instead, our parallel procedure is a refinement of inference rules given by Bachmair, Dershowitz and Hsiang. The challenging part of this refinement was the definition of a bookkeeping mechanism that: 1) guaranteed the required liveness property, 2) kept the rewriting system small and inter-normalized, and 3) had low computational overhead and no synchronization bottlenecks. The current implementation runs on the Firefly shared-memory multiprocessor and exhibits nearly linear speedup on some inputs, including problems in group theory. We are currently investigating ports to machines with more processors and physically distributed memory.

Parallel Logic Programs on Transputers

Contact Person: Roman Blasko, PhD.

Institute of Computer Systems
Dubravska cesta 9
842 37 Bratislava
Czechoslovakia

Keywords
Logic Programming, Parallel Implementation, Transputer Network

Summary
It is a project at the Institute of Computer Systems. The project is planned for 2-3 years. Within the scope of the project the parallel implementation of the logic programming language FCP(:,7) (Flat Concurrent Prolog) is realized. As a first step, we work out a sequential computational model for this language. We implement this model on a transputer. This sequential implementation we want to utilize for the analysis of the needed run-time support for systems. In the next period of work, we want to work out a parallel computational model of FCP(:,7) for distributed memory multiprocessors, i.e. transputer network. This model will utilize OR-parallelism and AND-parallelism among predicates, when the predicates have not any shared variables. We work out the compilation and optimization rules for this model. The last step of this project will be the implementation and performance analysis of the system on a multitransputer network.

Parallel Distributed Belief Networks

Contact Person: Wilson X. Wen

AI Systems
Telecom Research Labs.
770 Blackburn Rd.
Clayton, Vic 3168
Australia
mail: w.wen@trl.oz.au
Tel: (61-3) 541-6273
Fax: (61-3) 541-6173

Keywords
Belief Networks, Information Theory, Minimum Cross Entropy, Markov Fields,
Boltzmann-Jeffrey Machine Networks, Jeffrey's Rule, Encore Computer

Summary
A parallel distributed computational model, Boltzmann-Jeffrey Machine Network (BJM-Net), for Minimum Cross Entropy (MCE) reasoning is proposed based on information theory and the theory of Markov fields. Each autonomous component in BJMNet is a hypercube of parallel processors called Boltzmann- Jeffrey Machine (BJM). Each BJM in a BJMNet has its own prior distribution and updates its distribution according to Jeffrey's rule, which is a special case of MCE principle, if the distributions in its intersections with other BJMs are changed. The belief change is propagated throughout the whole BJMNet until an equilibrium is finally reached.

A BJMNet simulator has been implemented for Encore Computer to do parallel reasoning and to simulate the corresponding hardware architecture.

The IFS Parallel Architectures Group
University of Essex

Contact Person: Simon Lavington

University of Essex
Department of Computer Science
Colchester CO4 3SQ
mail: lavington@uk.ac.essex
phone:(+44)206 872 677
fax: (+44)206 872 788

Keywords
Novel Hardware for Symbolic Computation, Associative Memory, Non-WAM Computational Models

Summary
Our main line of research is to investigate ways in which novel parallel hardware can support non-numeric (eg symbolic) computer applications. The overall aim is to speed up run times and reduce software complexity. The principal applications areas are smart information systems, eg knowledge bases, which may draw on a range of techniques from relational DBMS, logic programming, AI paradigms, etc. Our research interests cover a variety of topics from theory to technology, as described below.

The IFS group currently consists fo six academic staff, three senior research officers, two technicians, and two Ph.D. students. Sources of suport include SERC, DTI, and ICL. The group has been continually funded since October 1983.

A tangible result of our research has been the design and implementation of a knowledge-base server, the IFS/1, which was first delivered to an external site in December 1987. The IFS/1 won a British Computer Society Silver Medal for Technical Achievement. We are now working on the successor, the IFS/2. This is a kind of *structure store*, or add-on *active memory* unit, which both stores and manipulates objects such as sets and graphs. The IFS/2 carries out whole-structure operations.

Current research interests include:

1. Knowledge representation formalisms, for example extended semantic networks, with the aim of providing expressive power and the potential for parallel implementation;

2. Non-WAM computational models for logic programming, for example those based on the matrix or connection methods of Prawitz and Bibel, with the aim of providing an alternative basis for exploiting parallelism;

3. Novel representations of production rule systems, for example based on associative tables, with the aim of speeding up the matching phase;

4. Extensions to relational algebra, for example transitive closure and other graph primitives, with the aim of handling linear recursive queries in deductive databases;

5. New strategies for Constraint Satisfaction Systems, with the aim of reducing computational effort;

6. Connectionist models of learning, for example those making use of parallel nearness-matching algorithms, with the aim of reducing run times;

7. SIMD techniques for organising value-comparisons in set and graph operations, with the aim of exploiting natural data parallelism;

8. Memory management in large associative (ie content-addressable) storage hierarchies, for example by semantic caching, with the aim of providing easy protection and manipulation of variable-granularity objects;

9. Use of transputers for distributed control of SIMD data-manipulation, with the aim of providing flexible, modularly-extensible, exploitation of the natural parallelism in AI-related data types.

A recent outgrowth of the IFS Group is PACE: Parallel Associative Combinator Evaluation. PACE is a new computational model for SK combinators, which offers effective modular parallelism for functional languages. The intention is to integrate structure stores such as the IFS/2 into the PACE graph reduction framework.

METEORs:
High Performance Theorem Provers
Using Model Elimination

Contact Person: Owen Astrachan

Duke University
Dept. of Computer Science
Durham, NC 27706 USA
mail: ola@cs.duke.edu
phone: (919)-660-6522

Keywords
Parallel/Distributed Inference, Caching, Model Elimination

Summary
Our Model Elimination theorem prover compiles clauses into a data structure that is interpreted at run time by either a sequential machine (currently any UNIX machine with a C compiler; we have tested the machine on Suns, Decstations, and HP workstations), a parallel machine (currently a Butterfly GP1000 or TC2000), or a network of sequential machines (currently sun workstations).

We have investigated methods for reducing redundancy using caching techniques and applied these methods to yield performance gains for a significant class of problems.

ESCAPE: Expert System Compilation and Parallelization Environment

Contact Persons: Robert Chun, Brad Perry, Steve Birminghan

Hughes Aircraft Company
P.O. Box 3310
Fullerton, CA 92634
mail: rchun%atr-2s.hac.com@hac2arpa.hac.com

Keywords
Ada, Compilation, Expert System, Parallel Processing, Real Time

Summary
ESCAPE represents a synergistic approach utilizing compilation, compaction, and parallelization to achieve real-time computing throughput from rule-based expert systems. The methodology involves synthesizing a set of concurrently executable Ada tasks from a knowledge base of rules. Compaction of code size is accomplished by eliminating the overhead associated with inference engine control constructs not utilized by a particular knowledge base. Heuristics are used to customize the generated Ada code for optimum performance gains given the characteristics of the source knowledge base and target processor. The effectiveness of this approach depends on both the characteristics of the knowledge base and the efficiency of the Ada compiler's task invocation mechanism. A prototype compilation system based on this multifaceted approach has demonstrated speedups in excess of 100X for certain knowledge bases, as well as, additional benefits in terms of increased embeddability and maintainability of the knowledge base.

Data Parallelism in Logic Programming

Contact Person: Giancarlo Succi

DIST, Universita' di Genova
Via Opera Pia 11a
I-16145 Genova, Italia
Tel: +39 10 353 2747 / +39 10 353 2750
Fax: +39 10 353 2948
E-mail: charmi@dist.unige.it

Keywords

Data Parallel Implementation of Logic Languages, Set-Oriented Abstract Machine, Abstract Analysis - Object-Size Analysis, Persistency Analysis -

Keywords

This project is focussed on the parallel implementation of a set-based logic language (SEL = Subset Equational Language). A data-parallel "approach" (targeted to the CM) is taken, nevertheless a competitive and conservative process parallel implementation is also under design (for a transputer implementation), in order to have, as a long term goal, an integrated framework. SAM (Subset Abstract Machine), the abstract machine under development, belongs to the WAM family, and it is augmented with several abstract analyzers placed at different levels of the "compilation flow". Being SEL a set-based logic language, we think that our data parallel SEL implementation will be a very efficient way of implementing inference systems.

People involved in the project:
Diego Co', Giancarlo Colla, Joy Marino, Sergio Novella, Amedeo Pata, Alex Regoli, Giancarlo Succi, Luca Vigano'.

Distributed Logic Programming

Contact Person: Nissim Francez

Technion
CS department
Haifa 32000
Israel
e-mail: francez@cs.technion.ac.il

Keywords
Prolog, Logic Programming, Distributed System, SDP

Summary
We develop a notion of sequential and distributed execution of Prolog programs. The setup is a network of nodes interconnected on a broadcast network. Each node has a certain collection of Horn-clauses, and nodes cooperate to answer queries (arriving at ANY node, possibly in overlapped manner) in the same way that a central Prolog interpreter would answer.

The main idea is to use local (finite) failure as a synchronization primitive. NOT allowed to communicate rules/facts, only subqueries. The implementation was on an Ethernet with SUN2s, and is planned to be moved to SUN4s.

Reference
Amir Rahat, Nissim Francez, Oded Shmueli: "SDP: Sequential, Distributed Logic Programming", in: Declarative systems (G. David, R.T. Boute, and B.D. Shriver, eds.), North-Holland, 1990 (An IFIP conference).

Programming Methods for Neural Computing (NEULOG)

Contact Persons: Henry Tirri (project manager), Petri Myllymki, Pekka Orponen, Patrik Floreen

University of Helsinki
Department of Computer Science
Teollisuuskatu 23
SF-00510 Helsinki, Finland
mail: tirri@cs.Helsinki.FI
Fax: + 358 - 0 - 708 4441
phone: +358-0-7084226

Keywords
Hybrid Systems, Bayesian Reasoning, Connectionism

Summary
NEULOG was a 3-year project, which started in 1988 as part of the FINSOFT-program organized by the Finnish Technology Development Centre (TEKES). The purpose of this project was to develop new, truly high level programming methods for neural computing, particularly in view of applications in symbolic computation (expert systems, probabilistic reasoning). The concrete result of the project is a hybrid neural-symbolic programming environment, consisting of a high-level NEULA-language and a compiler that is capable of realizing the symbolic syntax as a neural net. The system is provided with a novel computational mechanism, which efficiently approximates Bayesian reasoning.

The MUSE Parallel Prolog System

Contact Persons: Khayri A.M. Ali and Roland Karlsson

Swedish Institute of
Computer Science, SICS
Box 1263
S - 164 28 Kista, Sweden
mail: khayri@sics.se and roland@sics.se

Keywords
Full Prolog, Or-Parallelism, Multiprocessors

Summary

Today, multiprocessor machines are commercially available. However, writing programs that effectively utilize processing power of such machines is not an easy task. Ideally, programming of multiprocessors should not be harder than sequential ones. The programmer should consider the machine as a black-box and parallelism in a program should be detected and exploited by the system. Additionally, running a program on multiprocessors should not be slower than on uniprocessor machine. Although this seems to be a difficult task, in the field of symbolic computing and knowledge based applications, we are reaching that goal for Prolog programs. At SICS we have developed a system called MUSE that largely achieves that goal.

MUSE is an Or-parallel implementation of the full Prolog language. It is currently run on a number of shared memory multiprocessor machines, e.g., TP881V from Tadpole Technology, Sequent Symmetry, and the BBN Butterfly I and II. The sequential SICStus Prolog, a fast, portable system, has been adapted to Or-parallel implementation. The extra overhead associated with this adaptation is very low, around 3 - 5%. The speedup factor is very close to the number of processors for a large class of problems.

Parallel, Concurrent Theorem Proving

Contact Person: Robert Johnson

Computer Science Department
Queen Mary and Westfield college
University of London
Mile End Road
London E1 4NS
mail: robj@dcs.qmw.ac.uk
tel: 071-975-5259
fax: 081-980-6533

Keywords
Parallel, Concurrency, Tableaux, Connection Method, Theorem-Proving

Summary
My research principally involves the parallelisation of the tableaux approach to theorem proving, and the development and evaluation of parallel, concurrent systems. I am currently using Strand over a distributed Sun/Sparc network but aim to utilise other hardware paradigms as Strand is ported to them. I have a concurrent propositional tableaux system completed, and a concurrent connection method system for comparison. Future work will involve the development of parallel, concurrent systems for modal logics.

ROBIN: Massively Parallel Inferencing and Disambiguation in Structured Connectionist Networks

Contact Person: Trent E. Lange

Artificial Intelligence Laboratory
Computer Science Department
University of California, Los Angeles
Los Angeles, CA 90024
e-mail: lange@cs.ucla.edu

Keywords

Structured Connectionist Networks, Spreading-Activation Networks, Inferencing, Disambiguation, Natural Language Understanding, ROBIN

Summary

Structured connectionist (or spreading-activation) networks offer substantial promise for the problems of reasoning and natural language understanding because of their inherent parallelism and constraint satisfaction abilities. Unfortunately, like most types of connectionist models, they have been limited because of the difficulty they have had in representing variable bindings and performing rule-based reasoning. ROBIN (ROle Binding and Inferencing Network) is an ongoing research project to solve some of these problems. By using uniquely-identifying patterns of activation called "signatures" to represent variable bindings (Lange & Dyer, 1989) and propagating them across the network to perform dynamic inferencing, ROBIN has shown how structured connectionist networks can utilize simple general knowledge rules to infer a plan/goal analysis of the input for short natural language texts. Most importantly, because ROBIN's networks retain the normal constraint satisfaction abilities of spreading-activation networks, they are able to disambiguate between multiple inference paths instantiated in parallel to select the best interpretation in a given context for ambiguous texts that are difficult for traditional symbolic systems (Lange, in press). Research in ROBIN continues to find ways allow its networks to handle more complex rules and hold more dynamic knowledge so that it can reason with and understand longer stories while retaining its massively-parallel inferencing and disambiguation abilities.

Reference

Lange, T. & Dyer, M. G. (1989). High-Level Inferencing in a Connectionist Network. Connection Science, 1 (2): 181-217, 1989.

Lange, T. (in press). Lexical and Pragmatic Disambiguation and Reinterpretation in Connectionist Networks. To appear in the International Journal of Man-Machine Studies.

Parallel Production Systems

Contact Person: James G. Schmolze

Dept. of Computer Science
Tufts University
Medford, MA 02155 USA
Phone: 617/381-3681
mail: schmolze@cs.tufts.edu

Keywords

Parallel Production Systems, Multiple Rule Firing Systems, Parallel Forward Chaining Systems, Asynchronous Parallel Rule Firing

Summary

To speed up production systems, researchers have studied how to execute many rules simultaneously. Unfortunately, such systems can yield results that are impossible for a serial system to produce, leading to erroneous behaviors. We have devised a formal solution to the problem of guaranteeing serializable behavior in parallel production systems that execute many rules simultaneously, and we have a variety of algorithms that implement this solution. Some algorithms are targeted primarily for synchronous execution on a shared-memory multiprocessor, and we have an initial implementation of these algorithms that runs on the Sequent or Encore multiprocessors in Top Level Common Lisp. Another algorithm is targeted for asynchronous execution on a distributed-memory, message-passing machine, and an implementation is under construction for the NCube hypercube.

ElipSys

Contact Persons: Michel Dorochevsky, Kees Schuerman, André Véron, Jiyang Xu

European Computer-Industry Research Centre
Parallel and Distributed Systems Group
Arabellastr. 17
D-8000 München 81
mail: elipsys@ecrc.de
mail: michel@ecrc.de
Tel. + (49) 89-92699-107
Fax. + (49) 89-92699-170

Keywords
Logic Programming, Parallelism, Constraints Satisfaction, Database,
Shared/Distributed Memory

Summary
ElipSys is a logic programming system being developed at ECRC. It combines the three
major technologies required to build large decision support systems: constraint satisfaction, tight database coupling and parallel evaluation.

The project addresses issues at all levels; from language design to implementation. Of
particular note is the work to improve the expressiveness and declarativeness of logic
programming, and the design of an execution model that is appropriate to a range of
hardware platforms, from shared to distributed memory.

A prototype version of ElipSys is running on a 12 processor Sequent Symmetry and a
network of SUNs running the MACH operating system. Prototypes of a number of commercial applications have been implemented on ElipSys.

Project PARIS: Parallelisation of Inference Systems

Contact Persons: Wolfgang Ertel and Christian Suttner

Institut für Informatik
Technische Universität München
Augustenstraße 46 Rgb.
D-8000 München 2
Tel.: +49-89/521097
email: <name>@informatik.tu-muenchen.de

Keywords
High Performance Parallel Theorem Proving, Or-Parallelism,
Massive Parallelism

Summary

The potential for parallelism in automated theorem proving as well as in logic programming is very high. Exploiting this potential efficiently is the main goal of this project.
The starting point for our work was SETHEO, a high performance model elimination theorem prover for first order logic (a free copy of the SETHEO-sources (C,Unix) is available from the contact persons). Based upon SETHEO we developed the parallel theorem prover PARTHEO which runs on transputers as well as on the Intel iPSC/II machine with very good efficiency.
Currently we are aiming at an automated reasoning system with at least four orders of magnitude shorter run-times compared with existing systems. With better proof calculi and heuristic search methods we will achieve drastic search space reductions. Together with scalable parallel implementations on massively parallel architectures this will allow us to solve realistic reasoning problems. We are working on a very flexible easily portable parallel execution mechanism which allows the efficient parallelisation of large classes of arbitrary inference systems with very little effort. This will enable us to exploit the large computational power of heterogeneous networks of powerful computers.

Experiments with Parallel Software Architectures for Information Filtering: Trellis and FGP

Contact Persons: Scott Fertig and David Gelernter

Yale University
Department of Computer Science
New Haven, Connecticut 06520-2158
US mail: Yale University Department of Computer Science
P.O. Box 2158 Yale Station
New Haven, CT 06520-2158
email: Fertig-Scott@cs.yale.edu

Keywords

Information Filtering, Realtime Control, Intelligent Databases,
Software Architecture, Learning, Linda, Medical Informatics

Summary

"Information Filtering" is an area of decisive importance for the future of computer science. The proliferation of electronic data-gathering and data-recording devices has created two related, enormous problem-opportunities. First, data that might be relevant to the realtime control of machinery or organizations, or the "management of situations" in general, emerge too rapidly for humans to respond. Second, data that might contain valuable information in the aggregate collect in pools too gigantic to be manageable. Advances in information-filtering technology are required in both cases. Accordingly, the information filtering problem encompasses in our view (at least) two different but related problems. (1) How to squeeze knowledge out of a collection of realtime data streams—potentially a large and diverse collection of fast-moving streams; (2) how to squeeze knowledge out of a potentially enormous database. "Knowledge" refers to integrated, high-level, problem-specific information—"big-picture" information as opposed to low-level, undigested data. Our group at Yale has developed and implemented two experimental software architectures, one for each of these two sub-problems. Both systems take aim at "high performance" in the same way: by using asynchronous parallelism to run complex, compute-intensive algorithms fast. Both use the Linda[1] coordination language, which is a portable high-level system for expressing asynchronous parallelism; systems built using Linda will run on any platform on which Linda is supported—generally speaking, on any shared- or distributed-memory asynchronous parallel machine, and on local area networks.

---

[1] a registered trademark of Scientific Computing Associates.

Parallel Linear & UR-Deduction

Contact Person: Geoff Sutcliffe

Department of Computer Science
The University of Western Australia
Stirling Highway
Perth, Western Australia, 6009
Phone : (09) 380 2305
mail: geoff@cs.uwa.oz.au

Keywords
Parallel Theorem Proving

Summary
The deduction system developed in this project, called GLD–UR, has two deduction components. One component runs a chain format linear deduction system and the other a UR-deduction system. Lemmas created in each of the deduction components are passed to the other component. An extended version of GLD–UR, in which the lemmas created are distributed via a separate 'lemma control' component has also been developed. The speed-ups obtained in GLD–UR are largely due to cross-fertilisation between the deduction components. There is definite potential for superlinear speed-ups. GLD–UR is implemented in Prolog-Linda. Prolog-Linda provides the appropriate data transfer and synchronisation facilities for implementing parallel deduction systems. The implementation of GLD–UR is highly modular, and new deduction or other components can easily be added to the system. A hyperresolution deduction component will be the next component added.

An Optimally Efficient, Limited Inference, Connectionist Rule-Based Reasoning System with an Included Type Hierarchy

Contact Persons: Lokendra Shastri, Venkat Ajjanagadde and D. R. Mani

Department of Computer & Information Science
University of Pennsylvania
Philadelphia, PA 19104, USA

Keywords
Connectionism, Knowledge Representation, Reasoning, Type Hierarchy

Summary
Humans draw a variety of inferences spontaneously and with remarkable efficiency as though they are a reflex response of their cognitive apparatus. This work is a step toward a computational account of this remarkable 'reflexive' reasoning ability. We develop a connectionist knowledge representation and reasoning system that performs a limited but interesting class of inferences over a restricted class of first-order sentences with optimal efficiency. The proposed system can answer queries in time proportional to the length of the shortest derivation of the query and is independent of the size of the knowledge base. Further, the space complexity of the system is just linear in the size of the knowledge base.

Reasoning requires the dynamic representation and propagation of variable bindings. The system does so by propagating rhythmic patterns of activity wherein bindings are represented as synchronous firing of appropriate nodes in a connectionist network. Rules are encoded by interconnection patterns that propagate and transform these rhythmic patterns of activity while facts act as pattern matchers.

Rule-based reasoning has been combined with reasoning about inheritance and classification by introducing a connectionist Type Hierarchy in the reasoning system. This enables the system to use generic facts ('Cats prey on birds') and qualified rules ('if an animate agent walks into a solid object then the agent gets hurt'), thereby extending the class of rules and facts the reasoning system can handle.

Work in progress concerns extending the system to model abductive reasoning where the plausibility of rules, the feasibility of making certain assumptions and the computational cost are all considered in generating the 'best' explanation for a given set of observed facts.

The project lays emphasis on the use of the connectionist paradigm, which in addition to modeling reflexive reasoning, attempts to explain how such a system may be realized using a network of neuron-like elements operating without a central controller. Neurophysiological evidence suggests that similar mechanisms, which depend on the synchronous firing of appropriate nodes, may in fact be used by the brain to represent and process sensorimotor information.

Compile-Time Analysis of Concurrent Logic Programs for Multi-processors

Contact Persons: Andy King and Paul Soper

Dept. of Electronics and Computer Science
The University of Southampton
Highfield, Southampton, S09 5NH, UK
Phone: +22 (0)703 5930553
FAX: +44 703 593045
JANET: amk@uk.ac.soton.ecs
Bitnet: amk@ecs.soton.ac.uk
uucp: amk@sot-ecs.uucp

Keywords
Program Analysis, Concurrent Logic Language, Granularity Analysis, Schedule Analysis, Abstract Interpretation

Summary
A concurrent logic program naturally divides into processes which are, in principle, well-suited to distribution on a multi-processor. Performance can be impaired, however, if processes are either too fine-grained or too coarse-grained. An analysis of grain-size enables compile-time decisions to be made as to whether to distribute or coalesce processes, however, incurring unnecessary overheads. An analysis of the data-dependencies between coalesced processes reveals how processes can be scheduled at compile-time. This permits the removal of complex binding operations, a reduction in the enqueuing and dequeuing of processes, and can cut down the generation of garbage.

qwertz

Contact Persons: Joachim Hertzberg, Hans Werner Güsgen

GMD, AI Research Division
Schloss Birlinghoven
D - 5205 St. Augustin

Keywords
Massively Parallel Constraint Satisfaction, Connectionist Networks, Boltzmann Machines

Summary

The goal of the qwertz project is to evaluate classical methods and techniques for AI planning. A subgoal in the project includes the development of massively parallel constraint satisfaction algorithms, which may be viewed as a special form of algorithms for limited inferences. Currently, two approaches are considered:

- A connectionist network (Feldman-Ballard network) which spreads activation in order to find a solution of a given constraint satisfaction problem.

- Boltzmann machines which view constraint satisfaction as optimization problems, finding "almost" solutions for possibly inconsistent problems.

Parallel Implementation of Guarded Horn Clauses

Contact Person: Handong Wu

Department of Telecommunication and Computer Systems
The Royal Institute of Technology
S-100 44 Stockholm
Sweden
mail: wu@tds.kth.se

Keywords
Guarded Horn Clauses, Dataflow, Language Implementation

Summary
An execution model for Guarded Horn Clauses (GHC) has been developed based on the principles of Extended Dataflow Architecture (EDA). The execution model is able to explore both Shallow-Or-parallelism and Stream-And-parallelism inherent in GHC programs, which are encoded in the form of EDA graphs. The problem of a nested guard computation can be handled efficiently by the hierarchic structure of control frames at runtime. An EDA graph is of large-grained dataflow graph, and two mechanisms for communication and sychronization are provided: token passing and variable access. The variable operations are classified by local variables or global variables. A local variable belongs to a particular node and cannot be accessed from other nodes; while a global variable can be shared between nodes, and operations on it are restricted. The execution model has been simulated in SICStus Prolog and some preliminary results have been obtained.

Reference
Handong Wu (1990): "Extension of Dataflow Principles for Multiprocessing", TRITA-TCS-9004, The Royal Institute of Technology, S-100 44 Stockholm, Sweden, April 1990. (Ph.D thesis)

A System for Distributed Simplification-Based Theorem Proving

Contact Persons: Maria Paola Bonacina and Jieh Hsiang

Department of Computer Science
SUNY at Stony Brook
Stony Brook, NY 11794-4400
email: bonacina,hsiang@sbcs.sunysb.edu

Keywords

Parallel Automated Deduction, Simplification-Based Strategies, Unfailing Knuth-Bendix Completion

Summary

Our project consists in the design and implementation of *simplification-based* strategies [?] for parallel automated deduction, on a multi-processor with *distributed memory*. For equational logic the basic inference mechanism is an enhanced version of Unfailing Knuth-Bendix completion. Ordered resolution, ordered paramodulation and several contraction inference rules will be featured for first order logic with equality. We plan to develop a first prototype of our system, for equational logic, on an Intel hypercube. The extension to first order logic with equality will follow.

The basic idea in our approach is to have all processors, or *nodes, searching in parallel* for a proof of the input theorem. The processors have a high degree of *independence*: they are all peers, working asynchronously and cooperating by exchanging messages. In addition to the basic components of a theorem proving strategy, i.e. the *inference mechanism* and the *search plan*, our strategy features a *distributed allocation algorithm* and several policies for the *routing/broadcasting* of messages. The distributed allocation algorithm distributes among the nodes first the input equations and then those generated during the execution. Thus, at any stage of the derivation, each processor has its own, local data base of equations. The union of these data bases forms the global data base. The processors communicate by sending messages, either *data-messages*, containing equations, or *control-messages*. Each node is responsible for performing inferences by using the equations in its own data base and those received in form of messages. Data-messages are further classified depending on the status of the carried equation: for instance, newly generated equations are treated differently from normalized equations. Different message-handling policies are defined for the different types of messages.

We expect the highly distributed nature of this approach to help significantly in attacking the huge search spaces usually generated by theorem proving problems.

References

[1] M.P.Bonacina and J.Hsiang, Towards a Foundation of Completion procedures as Semidecision procedures, Technical Report, Dept. of Computer Science, SUNY at Stony Brook, available through ftp.

Research supported in part by grant CCR-8901322, funded by the National Science Foundation. The first author is also supported by a scholarship of Università degli Studi di Milano, Italy.

Parallel Reform Computations

Contact Persons: Sten-Ake Tarnlund, Hakan Millroth

Computing Science Department
Uppsala University
Box 520
S-75120 Uppsala, Sweden
mail: hakanm@csd.uu.se
Fax: +46 - 18 - 521270

Keywords
Logic Programming, Large-Scale Parallelism, Reform

Summary

The Reform machine, a parallel abstract machine for logic programming based on the inference system Reform, is designed and implemented in this project. The machine is primarily designed for running the logic programming language Prolog. The basic idea is to retain the sequential left-to-right depth-first backtracking scheme of Prolog with one exception: the recursion levels of a recursive program, including the head unifications at each level, are computed in parallel. The Reform machine is currently being implemented on parallel hardware based on the Inmos Transputer.

Integrating Rules and Connectionism for Robust Reasoning

Contact Person: Ron Sun

Brandeis University
Waltham, MA 02254, USA
rsun@cs.brandeis.edu

Keywords
Connectionism, Combining Symbolic and Subsymbolic Reasoning

Summary
This work tackles the problem of the problem of modeling commonsense reasoning and alleviating the brittleness of traditional symbolic rule-based models by combining rules with connectionism in an integrated framework. This idea leads to the development of a connectionist architecture with dual representation that combines symbolic and subsymbolic (feature-based) processing for evidential robust reasoning: CONSYDERR.

Psychological protocols are analyzed based on the notions of rules and similarity, and are modeled by the architecture which carries out rule application and similarity matching in a massively parallel fashion throught the interaction of the two levels. In order to understand rule encoding in the architecture, a formal analysis of the model is performed, which shows that it handles a superset of (propositional) Horn Clause logic and Shoham's logic. To further improve the rule-based reasoning capability of the architecture, a solution to the variable binding problem is proposed. This work also explores the notion of causality and shows that commonsense causal knowledge can be well represented by CONSYDERR.

An important aspect of this research is that the architecture utilizes the synergy resulting from the interaction of the two different types of representation and processing, and is thus capable of handling a large number of difficult issues in commonsense reasoning.

The results so far suggest that connectionism coupled with rule-based symbolic processing capabilities can be effective and efficient models of reasoning for both theoretical and practical purposes.

Lecture Notes in Artificial Intelligence (LNAI)

Vol. 345: R.T. Nossum (Ed.), Advanced Topics in Artificial Intelligence. VII, 233 pages. 1988.

Vol. 346: M. Reinfrank, J. de Kleer, M. L. Ginsberg, E. Sandewall (Eds.), Non-Monotonic Reasoning. Proceedings, 1988. XIV, 237 pages. 1989.

Vol. 347: K. Morik (Ed.), Knowledge Representation and Organization in Machine Learning. XV, 319 pages. 1989.

Vol. 353: S. Hölldobler, Foundations of Equational Logic Programming. X, 250 pages. 1989.

Vol. 383: K. Furukawa, H. Tanaka, T. Fujisaki (Eds.), Logic Programming '88. Proceedings, 1988. IX, 251 pages. 1989.

Vol. 390: J.P. Martins, E.M. Morgado (Eds.), EPIA 89. Proceedings. 1989. XII, 400 pages. 1989.

Vol. 395: M. Schmidt-Schauß, Computational Aspects of an Order-Sorted Logic with Term Declarations. VIII, 171 pages. 1989.

Vol. 397: K.P. Jantke (Ed.), Analogical and Inductive Inference. Proceedings, 1989. IX, 338 pages. 1989.

Vol. 406: C.J. Barter, M.J. Brooks (Eds.), AI '88. Proceedings, 1988. VIII, 463 pages. 1990.

Vol. 418: K.H. Bläsius, U. Hedtstück, C.-R. Rollinger (Eds.), Sorts and Types in Artificial Intelligence. Proceedings, 1989. VIII, 307 pages. 1990.

Vol. 419: K. Weichselberger, S. Pöhlmann, A Methodology for Uncertainty in Knowledge-Based Systems. VIII, 132 pages. 1990.

Vol. 422: B. Nebel, Reasoning and Revision in Hybrid Representation Systems. XII, 270 pages. 1990.

Vol. 437: D. Kumar (Ed.), Current Trends in SNePS – Semantic Network Processing System. Proceedings, 1989. VII, 162 pages. 1990.

Vol. 444: S. Ramani, R. Chandrasekar, K.S.R. Anjaneyulu (Eds.), Knowledge Based Computer Systems. Proceedings, 1989. X, 546 pages. 1990.

Vol. 446: L. Plümer, Termination Proofs for Logic Programs. VIII, 142 pages. 1990.

Vol. 449: M.E. Stickel (Ed.), 10th International Conference on Automated Deduction. Proceedings, 1990. XVI, 688 pages. 1990.

Vol. 451: V. Marík, O. Stepánková, Z. Zdráhal (Eds.), Artificial Intelligence in Higher Education. Proceedings, 1989. IX, 247 pages. 1990.

Vol. 459: R. Studer (Ed.), Natural Language and Logic. Proceedings, 1989. VII, 252 pages. 1990.

Vol. 462: G. Gottlob, W. Nejdl (Eds.), Expert Systems in Engineering. Proceedings, 1990. IX, 260 pages. 1990.

Vol. 465: A. Fuhrmann, M. Morreau (Eds.), The Logic of Theory Change. Proceedings, 1989. X, 334 pages. 1991.

Vol. 475: P. Schroeder-Heister (Ed.), Extensions of Logic Programming. Proceedings, 1989. VIII, 364 pages. 1991.

Vol. 476: M. Filgueiras, L. Damas, N. Moreira, A.P. Tomás (Eds.), Natural Language Processing. Proceedings, 1990. VII, 253 pages. 1991.

Vol. 478: J. van Eijck (Ed.), Logics in AI. Proceedings. 1990. IX, 562 pages. 1991.

Vol. 481: E. Lang, K.-U. Carstensen, G. Simmons, Modelling Spatial Knowledge on a Linguistic Basis. IX, 138 pages. 1991.

Vol. 482: Y. Kodratoff (Ed.), Machine Learning – EWSL-91. Proceedings, 1991. XI, 537 pages. 1991.

Vol. 513: N. M. Mattos, An Approach to Knowledge Base Management. IX, 247 pages. 1991.

Vol. 515: J. P. Martins, M. Reinfrank (Eds.), Truth Maintenance Systems. Proceedings, 1990. VII, 177 pages. 1991.

Vol. 517: K. Nökel, Temporally Distributed Symptoms in Technical Diagnosis. IX, 164 pages. 1991.

Vol. 518: J. G. Williams, Instantiation Theory. VIII, 133 pages. 1991.

Vol. 522: J. Hertzberg (Ed.), European Workshop on Planning. Proceedings, 1991. VII, 121 pages. 1991.

Vol. 535: P. Jorrand, J. Kelemen (Eds.), Fundamentals of Artificial Intelligence Research. Proceedings, 1991. VIII, 255 pages. 1991.

Vol. 541: P. Barahona, L. Moniz Pereira, A. Porto (Eds.), EPIA '91. Proceedings, 1991. VIII, 292 pages. 1991.

Vol. 542: Z. W. Ras, M. Zemankova (Eds.), Methodologies for Intelligent Systems. Proceedings, 1991. X, 644 pages. 1991.

Vol. 543: J. Dix, K. P. Jantke, P. H. Schmitt (Eds.), Non-monotonic and Inductive Logic. Proceedings, 1990. X, 243 pages. 1991.

Vol. 546: O. Herzog, C.-R. Rollinger (Eds.), Text Understanding in LILOG. XI, 738 pages. 1991.

Vol. 549: E. Ardizzone, S. Gaglio, F. Sorbello (Eds.), Trends in Artificial Intelligence. Proceedings, 1991. XIV, 479 pages. 1991.

Vol. 565: J. D. Becker, I. Eisele, F. W. Mündemann (Eds.), Parallelism, Learning, Evolution. Proceedings, 1989. VIII, 525 pages. 1991.

Vol. 567: H. Boley, M. M. Richter (Eds.), Processing Declarative Kowledge. Proceedings, 1991. XII, 427 pages. 1991.

Vol. 568: H.-J. Bürckert, A Resolution Principle for a Logic with Restricted Quantifiers. X, 116 pages. 1991.

Vol. 587: R. Dale, E. Hovy, D. Rösner, O. Stock (Eds.), Aspects of Automated Natural Language Generation. Proceedings, 1992. VIII, 311 pages. 1992.

Vol. 590: B. Fronhöfer, G. Wrightson (Eds.), Parallelization in Inference Systems. Proceedings, 1990. VIII, 372 pages. 1992.

Lecture Notes in Computer Science